THE ROCK

ALSO BY BARRY HILL

Non-fiction
The Schools
Sitting-In

Fiction
A Rim of Blue
Near the Refinery
Headlocks
The Best Picture

Poetry
Raft
Ghosting William Buckley

The Rock

Travelling to Uluru

BARRY HILL

A Rathdowne Book

ALLEN & UNWIN

First published in 1994

A Rathdowne Book
Allen & Unwin Pty Ltd
9 Atchison Street
St Leonards, NSW 2065, Australia

National Library of Australia
cataloguing-in-publication data

   Hill, Barry, 1943−
      The Rock: travelling to Uluru.

      ISBN 1 86373 778 2.
      ISBN 1 86373 712 X (pbk.).

      1. Ayers Rock (N.T.)—Description and
      travel. I. Title.

      919.4291

Designed by Guy Mirabella
Typeset by Solo Typesetting
Printed in Australia by Southwood

10 9 8 7 6 5 4 3 2 1

CONTENTS

For Anangu and Dick Kimber
CUSTODIANS OF STORIES

ACKNOWLEDGEMENTS

I AM MOST GRATEFUL to a host of people who have helped me in the two years of travelling to the Centre. The book would not exist without the welcome, as well as the political achievements of Anangu, especially the people at the Mutitjulu community. I am especially in debt to the following individuals who gave their time: Tony Tjamiwa, Barbara Nipper, Maureen Natjuna, Yami Lester, Leroy Lester. Jon Willis, their Community Liaison Officer, helped me when he could. So did Bob Seaborne, Director of Australian Nature Conservation Agency at the Rock, as well as his staff, especially Park Rangers Julian Barry and David Carter. I also want to thank Tracker Tilmouth and David Avery at the Central Land Council; David Hugo and staff at the Strehlow Research Centre; Steve Morton at the CSIRO; Lynn Baker; Peter Latz and Ken Johnson at the NT Conservation Commission; Susie Bryce and Greg Snowden of Desert Tracks; Jenny Tonkin, of the Rare Books and Named Collections, State Library of South Australia; Philip Jones, from the Museum of South Australia. For hospitality and help in Alice Springs: Neil and Fay Bell; and Dion Weston. For assistance with accommodation or travel: the Felix Myer Scholarship from the University of Melbourne; and (for my last visit to the Rock) Wayne Kirkpatrick at the Ayers Rock Resort and the NT Tourism Commission. Throughout the project my freedom as a writer was, as is often the case, enabled by the Literature Board of the Australia Council, whose funding was there at the right time.

Indispensable people commented on parts of the book in draft: Susan Woenne-Green, Jon Willis, Steve Morton, Peter Latz, Tim Rowse, John Bryson, Ross Howie, Garry Stoll. And Dick Kimber—generous, industrious scholar to the hilt—Dick read everything, much of it more than once, the poor bloke. He commented widely, argued and praised, and the book's merits, such as they are, owe much to him.

Finally one turns to one's travelling companions: to my children, Joe and Vanessa, who were able to come to the Rock and have the privilege of meeting its traditional owners; and to my wife Ramona, who shares my love affair with the Centre, of which this book is merely a transitional expression.

*With this charming extract from Byron for breakfast I saddled my
horse, having nothing more to detain me here . . .*
ERNEST GILES 1873
Australia Twice Traversed

*For the benighted the illusions of the world
For the enlightened the knowledge that all is vanity
In the beginning there was no east and no west
Where then is there a north and south?*
OLIVER STATLET
Japanese Pilgrimage

*Straight in the heads and straight in the hearts, that's how they learnt
their Law. No pens, no typewriters. And some parts of the Law they
would never put in a typewriter.*
TONY TJAMIWA
Traditional owner, Uluru

PROLOGUE

ONE DAY SOUTH of the Rock, in the beautiful Mann Ranges, I went on a kangaroo hunt. It took me further than I expected. The driver was a Pitjantjatjara elder, Ilyatjari, and the co-driver was Greg Snowden, his employee, a white man sitting up like Cocky with a .22 Browning Magnum. Snowden worked for 'Desert Tracks', the Anangu-owned outfit we were with.

The afternoon was quietly lying down between the trees as Ilyatjari trundled us across country in the Toyota. His favourite grandson, a naked three-year-old, was on his knees. Soon enough we spotted malu, the lovely red kangaroo of the region. Snowden took aim and shot it straight out of the passenger window.

As if to the sound of the rifle, the splendid animal leapt and twisted in the air: the spirit of life flies out of it, but it takes a chase and another shot before it is down. Before it can hit the ground, the six black boys are out of the vehicle, running towards it. Us white fellas (three of us on a Community Aid Abroad study tour, all eyes and ears for Aboriginal teachings) tumble out too, jogging along behind the boys who go like bloodhounds through the bush.

I get to the animal after them. It is writhing on the ground, trying to hobble up on one leg and they are beating it down with sticks. The muzzle of the animal has stiffened with terror. The black kids are jostling to get behind its head; they are raining blows on the flat of its neck, but in the excitement some blows go wrong and the animal is hit on the head and eyes.

Young Des, one of the white kids, is in on the act. He has a stick—a stupidly light stick, actually, and he is not using it. Instead he is charging at the animal from the front, trying to kick it in the mouth.

All the language going up in the air is Pitjantjatjara.

—*Palya. Palya.*

—Good. Good.

Ilyatjari has arrived in the Toyota and his favourite little grandson is dancing around the kangaroo. The wild legs lash out and the baby black boy is dancing in their weave.

—*Palya. Palya.*

—Get a bloody stick, you idiot. You don't kick it, you hit it. This was shouted in English—thrown out, I discovered, by me.

—*Palya*, said Ilyatjari, as the boys' blows on the neck of the animal gained in accuracy. *Palya*, as the animal subsided, and quivered and lay still. Done.

All of a sudden the baby boy seemed to be holding the prize. In his hand was a pink writhing thing. He leapt about, immensely proud of his tiny foetus.

The dead ma̱lu is picked up by the forelegs and tail and slung into the back of the vehicle.

—What's going to happen to the baby, Greg? What's going to happen to the baby? Adam asked as we were getting back in. Adam is our other white boy. Des lives rough with his mixed race bush family: Adam is all white from Alice.

Now, where were those other ma̱lu? Ilyatjari knew and we were heading off already, the warmth of the animal rising from the floor of the Toyota, the round belly and hind legs of the mother pressing against our legs, flesh against flesh. The black baby with us in the back, on his brother's knee, showing off his prize. It was all jaw and its eyes were closed and its legs extended as its belly was squeezed. It did the rounds of the black boys; each had a squeeze and was rewarded with a squirm of life. Adam was mesmerized.

When we ran up to the second wounded kangaroo it seemed the kids had smaller sticks than before, and that the whole killing business, the men's business could be done with greater despatch. I yelled at Greg who was leaning against the door.

—Shoot the bloody thing. Put a bullet in its head, will ya?

He yelled back.—This is their way. They are learning things by doing it this way. At last the animal lay still.

This time the foetus was a big one. All legs and eyes, it seemed, for the triumphant boys.

Ilyatjari, who has seen the white man's consternation and tendency to interfere—hardly new—was kneeling over the animal, about to knick the belly. As he cut into the intestine to see how fat it was for the eating, he growled in his own language.

—You may not like it but this is the way we do things here.

—Greg, said Adam, what's going to happen to the babies?

—I dunno, Adam, I dunno, the white man finally said, and swung back up into the truck.

And we were off again. Three white men, two warm kangaroos (another one soon to come), five kids, a baby and two foetuses. Whenever the larger one was allowed to rest in a lap it twisted and turned in search of the nipple. The black boys were pleased and picked it up and passed the rubbery figure on again. It was when one of the boys held a foetus in either hand and bumped their faces together that I could not stand the slow death any longer.

—No, I said. No.

—What? the looks from the black kids said. What? Who are you?

I'm a human being who cares for animals, I said to myself. I have my culture too. It says you don't torture animals. For whatever this was for the black boys, this was torture to me.

The big foetus had come to Des, who pressed against me in the squash of the car.

—Kill it, I said to him. Put it out of its misery.

He slewed me a look.

—There's a difference, I hissed, between killing and cruelty. You know that?

It was hard to tell what he knew as he passed the foetus to me.

—Hey, hey, said the black boys in their language, with furious looks.

No, my face said back, and I held the foetus. Pink and cold and still writhing, as if any minute its eyes would open wide to its own death that I had now resolved to speed up. However preposterously, I now realised I had embarked on some kind of ambassadorship. I had taken it upon myself to end a misery. I put my thumb and forefinger on either side of the animal's neck and began to squeeze.

The boys watched the animal do a super squirm and stretch its legs out straight. The legs continued to kick.

Sitting opposite me was a chaplain from Melbourne University. He seemed to be paying me the respect of not looking at my hands. He asked my eyes: how's it going, any success?

None, mine said, incredulous.

I changed my grip.

I bent the head back. It was like rubber, unsnappable.

I returned to the steady pressure under the ear, resolved to keep it on all the way home if need be. The other foetus, the tiny one in the black baby's lap, was almost dead. Why wouldn't mine die? Had the black boys pointed a bone at my sweating hand?

—No? inquired the chaplain, as we pulled into camp.

—No, I said, miserable and embarrassed and yet somehow by then stuck in resolve. In conscience I could not now give it back to the boys. Not before putting it out of its misery. Out of the vehicle I got, determined to find final amnesty for the baby kangaroo.

—Welcome, welcome, cried the women, as we pulled up: how was the hunt, how was the men's business? The white women had been back at the camp learning about bush tucker. Malu were dragged out, someone had already started digging the hole for the fire, and in a few minutes the creatures would be beautifully gutted by Ilyatjari.

—Fine, fine, we white men said, and how was the women's business? While we were away the black women elders, under the guidance of another admirable elder Nganyintja (Ilyatjari's wife), had taken the white women into the fold and told them things. What things? Ah, but that was the women's business. It could not be said except perhaps to say it was about women's bodies and giving birth. Yes, it was about the creation of life.

The black boys had seen me move away from the bus. I could hear their cries go up, and reports begin about my theft. I got to our camp table and put the foetus on the chopping board, but I couldn't find the knife, couldn't find the blasted knife anywhere. I was rummaging by then, rattling around in some kind of white madness. Snowden strode past and looked at me as if I was certifiable, but he did not interfere with my interference.

The boys were making their way towards me as I inspected the foetus on the board. At last—yes—it was limp. It was not quite dead, but it was limp, very close to death.

—Here, I said, here.

They glared and took it and ran off with it.

They would—I was given to understand—play with it some more. Then they might cook it. They might eat it.

Later I looked into the big fire that was cooking ma_lu, which had become a communal gathering as night fell. I wondered if the boys had put the foetus in there, if I could see it if I looked in and around the coals, my feeble end to the men's business. Much later during the feast (which I couldn't eat, I couldn't come at the dripping rawness of ma_lu), much later on that sleepless night, as I lay in my swag under the full moon with the morning star coming up as thick as a witchetty grub, I realised that I wouldn't have behaved like that if it were not for the presence of the white boys. I felt culturally responsible for their view of the hunt. The other complication was the Toyota, and the white man with the gun. What was Aboriginal or natural about that? Why shouldn't I butt in?

It took a few days for another point of view to settle in me. While the women were back in camp reflecting on life, the men were off contending with death-in-life. The boys' 'cruelty' with the foetus was their way of laying hands on the mortally unborn, a harsh reality which I had trouble facing. It was possible that a larger scheme of things held existence in balance. Did I owe the black boys an apology? I wondered.

An anthropologist who knows these people and their language well, wrote to me.

No, she said, you do not owe the black boys an apology!

I got sucked into your story with a Bosch-inspired zoological garden of baby animals mewing and limping into my memories, twanging strands of personal guilt, revulsion and cowardice: kangaroo and wallaby foetuses, pyjama-clad baby emus, newly born rabbits, billycans full of struggling newly hatched parakeets and the times of hoping against common sense that the shooter of the kangaroo will get a head shot with a .22 and kill the animal straight away.

It would not have explained everything but it would have helped if someone had told you that one cannot give the *coup de grâce* (by gun or knife) to a downed kangaroo. One cannot unnecessarily cause it to lose blood. You do what is necessary to down it, and then it has to be bludgeoned; you cannot pierce its skin . . . they forgot to warn you that, despite the trappings of Toyota and .22, the Malu hunt is sound tight with the Law, for the kangaroo is one of the primary sources of the Tjukurpa. In Pitjantjatjara the term Tjukurpa is glossed as 'the Dreaming' but is also the 'Law'. In English the former has softer overtones than the latter.

The writer was Susan Woenne-Green, a linguist and anthropologist who has spent twelve years in Central Australia. Susan was there in the hard years leading up to Handback; she played an important part in the Uluru Land Claim and was the first Community Liaison Officer at the Mutitjulu community. She is a key author of the walk guide to the Rock, the publication that most clearly expresses what Aboriginal people want to present to tourists. That perspective, and what goes into our culture's understanding of it, is one key to our pilgrimage. We are going there to gather in as much of the country as we can on the way, the better to arrive, perhaps, at a point of reconciliation, where no-one owes anyone an apology.

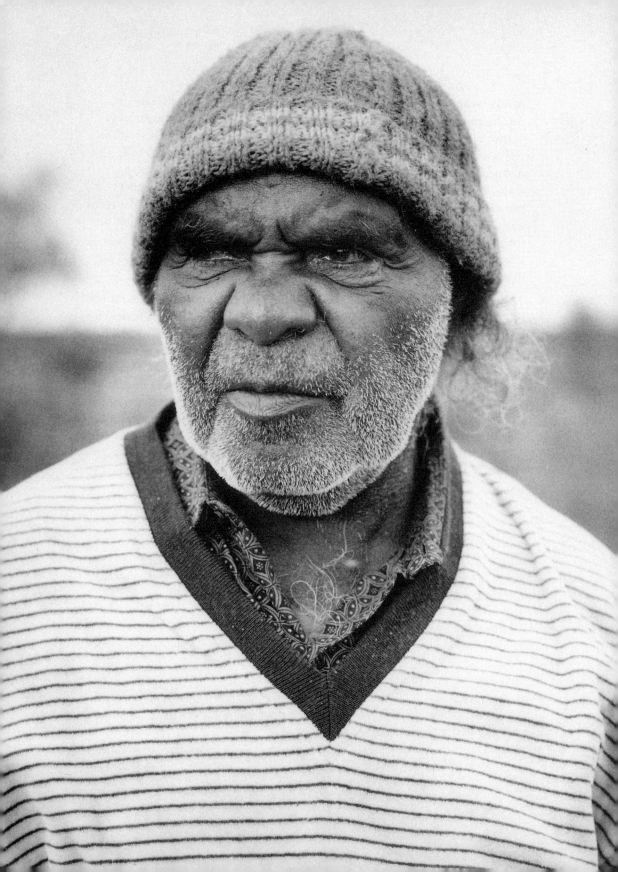

INTRODUCTION

TONY TJAMIWA, one of the traditional owners of Uluru, or Ayers Rock as it was called before it was handed back to the Aborigines in 1985, sparked the idea for this book. He told me that Bill Harney got it all wrong.

—Bill Harney didn't know anything, Tjamiwa said.

—I told him—you're not from around here. You're a fish! You're a crocodile!

I was sitting with Tjamiwa out at the Rock. We were in a kitchen at the Mutitjulu community, which owns the place. Through the window I could see the hump of Uluru rising out of the mulga scrub that protects the community from tourists. That morning I had seen a pale lilac sky rise over the southern flanks of the Rock; and then, all of its northern side warm the way beach cliffs do when the sun floods a bay with heat. Now it was hot, the Rock heavy, sullen.

Tjamiwa wasn't looking at me, but I had seen his eyes. They had the liquid light of morning and he gave off the strength of the Rock.

The man Tjamiwa was speaking about was the first Ranger at the Rock, back in the days when tourists started coming. Bill Harney (1895–1962), a celebrated bushman and friend of the Aborigines who married an Aboriginal woman, Linda (and had two children with her), camped there in the holiday seasons between 1957–9, when Ayers Rock and the Olgas were taken out of the Aboriginal Reserve and made a National Park. Harney's travelogue and guide book, *To Ayers Rock and Beyond* (1964), was the first to be written about the Rock, and has long been considered a reliable account of the Aboriginal beliefs about the place. It is still as popular a guide to the Rock and the Centre as it was about thirty years ago.

Tjamiwa's accusation of 'The fish, the crocodile' was his inimitably vivid way of saying Harney had spent most of his life in Northern Australia—which was true—and that he did not know the desert, the desert people, or Uluru. Instinctively, Tjamiwa was saying something else: Harney said what he wanted to say about the Rock. Now it's time for Anangu to say what they want to say.

Tony Tjamiwa, traditional owner. 'He gives off all the strength of the Rock.'

1

Anangu is Pitjantjatjara for 'We people', the term Central Desert people use to refer to themselves. Its common use reflects the relative political success Aboriginal people have had in the Northern Territory over the last twenty-five years.

In 1970 the Aboriginal people usually lived on government reserves, mission stations, pastoral properties or the fringe settlements of a town. They owned no land. Today 33 per cent of land in the Northern Territory is in Aboriginal hands. The larger part of that is the drier, more remote country of the former reserves, but the rest has either been won by legal claim under the Northern Territory Land Rights Act (1976), or purchased on the open market. Some of the purchases have been of pastoral holdings such as 'Elsie', where that novel of frontier myth-making, *We of the Never Never*, was set.

Ayers Rock, so long regarded as central to the romance of pilgrimage to the Centre too had changed hands in so far as a land claim was fought, and won, for much of the area around it in 1980. In 1985 the National Park was leased to the traditional owners for ninety-nine years, on the understanding that the Park be jointly managed by Anangu and Park authorities. With his profound grip on political reality, Tjamiwa was saying, 'We have the power now to speak for ourselves, to tell our stories in our own way.'

Such politics can't help but frame any journey to the Rock today. It's a new kind of journey that requires new ways of telling (and vice versa). Everything is more complicated than before. We require a certain cognizance of what has already been said about the Rock, and the journey to it. Travelling here today, one is obliged to move through the previous literature of the Centre, including the records of men like Giles and Gosse, the first white explorers of the country who had to encounter the 'natives' for the first time, records which today invite us to read between their lines, the better to intuit what the traditional owners might have thought of them. There is, in the Centre, a vast account of interpretation and re-interpretation to be traversed before arriving at the present period that begins, in essence, with Harney. Having said that, it pays to be aware of his two contemporaries, without whom the modern story cannot be told either. Both have had as much influence on recent travellers as Harney.

C. P. Mountford (1890–1976) published his book, *Ayers Rock*, in the same year as Harney. As it happened, Tjamiwa did not sound off against Mountford, but his indictments are similar. Anangu consider Mountford's work offensive and out of bounds. Yet in his day Mountford, a gentle man who considered himself a beloved friend of the Aborigines, was considered a renowned authority on the Rock, its legends and its artwork. As an anthropologist he was an amateur, but there was no amateurism about his photography, which often splendidly captured the luminous

Bill Harney, 1965. First Ranger and 'crocodile'.

landscape of the Centre, as well as its native inhabitants that the daily press called the 'Stone Age'. At the same time, Tjamiwa's contemporaries were in their mission school at Ernabella. Mountford did most of his work in the 1940s and 1950s, years before Harney got to the Rock, but first visited the place in 1935 for dark reasons that are part of our story. He camped only for two nights and then had to go. He wrote in his diary:

> We left at midday, with the camel-string leading us back to humdrum civili-sation and monotony. I following on unwilling feet, for the lure of the great rock was upon me, calling me back to wander round its base, to look up at its mighty walls, to explore its numberless caves, and to hear the strange creation legends from its Aboriginal owners.

'Lure' is a good word—it expresses the pull of the Rock, the logic of compulsive pilgrimage. If something casts its spell you don't need reasons to move in a certain direction. The force is simply there. 'I am in Central Australia, I must to go down to the Rock.' Or 'I have to go to the Centre, to see the Rock.' This is certainly the shape of the experience as it is expressed by those who have travelled a long way to get here, as the great majority of us have. But it also applies to those who have grown up in Central Australia.

With Mountford at the Rock in 1935 was T. G. H. Strehlow (1908–75), who had spent the first fourteen years of his life at the Hermannsburg Mission. There he had grown up with Aranda children; their tongue was his third language (his first was German, his second English, though his erudite father, Pastor Carl Strehlow, also educated his son in Latin and Greek). In the confines of that Mission on the grand Finke River, he knew the splendours of the MacDonnell Ranges. But this did not check his wonder. On 11 June he wrote in his diary:

> The Rock was reached at last, the goal of my boyhood dreams—the shadow of a great rock in a weary land, and how welcome it was.
>
> All is hushed tonight; only the moon is shining down upon the great black walls of rock—and one feels that the land of God is indeed near. It is like the great silence of eternity. And near by lies the body of a dead man; and that body has brought us hither to this vast pile that shall endure long after our own bodies will be only dim, scattered dust, known to no man, forgotten by all save God alone who moulded them first even as He fashioned this great Rock, that sleeps tonight in a still moon-dream.

C. P. Mountford's self-portrait, 1935.

The dead man was a relative of Paddy Uluru, one of the traditional owners of the Rock. He had been shot at the Rock by the policeman travelling with young Mountford and Strehlow. Their journey, on that visit, involved a certain quest for white man's justice, but from the point of view of Anangu, the whole episode and the events leading up to it was yet another brutal encroachment upon their sacred understandings. At the time neither Mountford nor Strehlow made claims to special knowledge of the Rock, they were content to let its power work on them. In years to come it would be a different matter.

Pilgrimages invariably involve claims to knowledge. Whatever the manner of the pilgrim's travel—be it earthy sauntering down to Canterbury or the zealous, straight road to Mecca—the knowledge to come is always a dimension of the destination. The worship at the end of pilgrimage is self-confirming, and yet, if the journey has been conducted in daylight, with the wakefulness that befits a quest, there is a new edge to one's experience, perhaps even an enlightenment. At the Rock today, the knowledge visitors share with Aborigines, and what they may share with us about Nature is a live issue in the enterprise of sharing the Park. Tjamiwa told a recent conference of National Park administrators that a Park is no good if it only has 'one leg':

—Aboriginal land that is just a national park is just like a table with one leg or like a bird. It's not very stable. Shove it and it will fall over. Just one leg is not enough for Aboriginal land. It has to have the other legs there: the leg that Aboriginal Law and ownership provides.

So we are going down to the Rock to see how the Park is going on two legs, and what that means for the ecology of the place. Bear in mind the hard-won nature of scientific understanding of the Centre, which started with the Horn Expedition of 1894, the first full-scale scientific excursion into the mysterious and savage interior of the country. Our principal voyager then was not a bushman nor amateur anthropologist nor scholarly, if mission-bent, linguist: rather he was the eminent Darwinian biologist Baldwin Spencer. His trip a century ago is a reminder that to go to the Rock today is again to be in quest of a certain kind of knowledge of Nature. As a man of his age, Spencer was inclined to devalue indigenous knowledge in the larger scheme of things. Today, due to complex developments in Western culture, we are inclined to do the opposite. Speaking for myself, I know that I have wanted to go to the Rock and keep going through the literature of the Rock, for at least two reasons: in the hope of encountering the Aboriginal presence in some kind of instructional way (recapturing some kind of first encounter all over again, an impossible dream, of course); and in order to acquaint myself with what it is they know about their place, what under-

T. G. H. Strehlow and 'informant' at Henby Station, 1935.

7

standings they have about their habitat that might or might not compare to our Science.

Thus, as cultural baggage goes, we are going down to the Rock in all manner of travellers, and the richness of difference between them is instructive, a way of elucidating our journey. What I should say to Tjamiwa the next time I see him is: I have come on my pilgrimage to the Rock as much because of all these others as you. This whole place, this Centre, is a congregation of pilgrims' tales. If, somehow, one was able to grasp them, then one would have something approaching the song of the Centre. Remember the grand beginning of Peter Brook's version of the Indian epic, the *Mahabharata*? Ganesh the elephant, harbinger of memory, offers himself as a scribe for the 'poetic history of mankind'. 'If you listen carefully, at the end you'll be someone else.'

Ideally, that poetical history would have to contain an ocean of voices. Even by the turn of the century a historian spoke of *waves of intruders* who would make some kind of impression (to put it mildly) on the Aboriginal population. There were those who came in the wake of the telegraph line such as labourers and bullock drivers; and another wave who came in the ruby boom of 1888—prospectors, navvies, runaway sailors, pedlars, Afghan camel men. All this was before the gold boom at Altunga, and then, the dingo scalp hunters, scientists, government officials, anthropologists, each entering the idiom of the Australian Outback.

What could possibly unite them in the Outback—lust, exile, greed, yearnings for encounter? Beautiful lies, Mark Twain once said, when he tried to put his finger on the Australian ethos. Story-telling, moved by the need to disguise, deflect or exaggerate or discover one's identity in the great Australian loneliness. Harney was the quintessential man of the Outback, the great yarner, the almost non-stoppable story-teller. An early book (*North of 23*) was favourably compared to that classic of the Australian tradition, *Such is Life* by Joseph Furphy, alias Tom Collins. The narrator in *Such is Life* sets the tone: 'The fact is that the *Order of Things*—rightly understood—is not susceptible to any coercion whatever, and must be humoured in every possible way. In the race of life, you must run *cunning*, reserving your spirit for the *tactical* moment.'

On any trip to Central Australia you have to run a bit cunning. Poetical history needs a bullshit detector to encompass the bullshit . . .

—Did you know Baden Bloomfield?

—Know him! Me and him used to tell lies to one another. We were mates!

Nowhere is the bullshit detector more necesary than when reading the present political scene of the Northern Territory. Today, it is still a colonial society in transition where politics counts for a great deal. The big money has always been in mining, cattle and defence. These days it is also in tourism, which exploits the image of the Outback through shifting, ambiguous images of Aboriginal life and culture. The Northern

Territory strongly encourages tourism, knowing that there are tourist dollars from Aboriginal culture, which it pays to present favourably. When it comes to debating the present complexities of Aboriginal life, however, the political climate of the Territory is degenerate. The print media, for example, still operates with racist stereotypes and massive condescension. Not suprisingly, the Aboriginal response can mirror white intolerance and distrust, so that between the lines of any 'liberal' dialogue, especially if you follow the talk into the bar, there is the bristling of historical antagonisms. After all, slaughter is still part of living memory in the Territory, the last massacre (there is no other word) was at Coniston in 1928.

In 'the bad old days', which historian Dick Kimber brackets as the years between 1871 and 1891 (when the Overseas Telegraph (OT) line linked Adelaide to Darwin and hence the colony of Australia to Imperial Britain, and the rail head to Oodnadatta opened the interior to pastoralists), some 500 and quite possibly upwards of 1000 Aborigines were shot in Central Australia. And when they were not shot—to take our culture's crudest measure of 'control' of a dispossessed people—they were ruined by disease brought by whiteman: small pox, measles, influenza and venereal disease. 'Gin shepherding' was a frontier sport that spread the pox like wild fire; by 1911, nine out of ten Aborigines in Oodnadatta were diseased. Ironically, this was thought at that time to be an improvement in Aboriginal health.

Very little can be said about Central Australia without looking at the map. A comprehensive history of the Centre, which has yet to be written (partly because so much of it is being rapidly lived by two cultures in transition), would be grounded in geography. It was from Oodnadatta that the railway was extended to Alice Springs in 1929. This was the third strengthening of the main artery to the Centre; the first was the initial 'discovery' of the north–south route in 1862, when John McDouall Stuart soldiered from one end of the continent to another. The second was the OT line, which helped put a little place called Stuart on the map, a rudimentary settlement until it was renamed Alice Springs to mark the arrival of the railway. It was the railway that opened the Centre in a new way. Before that there were only two other white centres of settlement: the Hermannsburg Mission out in the MacDonnell Ranges where Lutherans established themselves in a biblical wilderness as early 1877—barely four years after Giles and Gosse explored the country near the Rock; and the gold town of Altunga, where a rush began in 1887 and petered out in 1905.

The railway was a new rail head for pastoral expansion, even though the cruel drought of the time would have delayed that. In due course cattle grazing had reached its limit of expansion to the east of that line. Aborigines would continue to inhabit the land east of the railway line even if they had no legal right to it. The rule of law— official policies in general—was bound up with the places to which Aborigines had retreated or been relegated, or those which had become, as the European grip on the

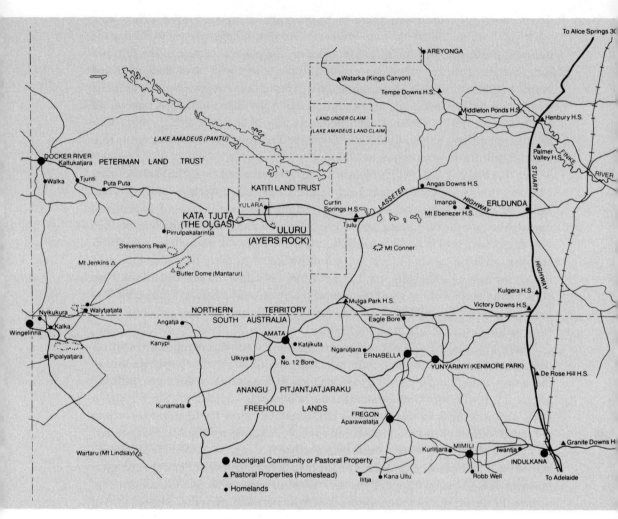

Aboriginal communities and their proximity to Uluru.

country tightened, a problematic attraction. For the ruination of the tribes, as they were then called, was clear: witness the wretched creatures who had chosen to live in states of various disease along the railway line. Witness also those in need in the township of Alice Springs, where they were an eyesore and an irritation. Until 1940, Aborigines were welcomed into the Australian army, but were still kept out of Alice Springs. Places such as the Western Reserve, gazetted for the desert people in 1920 were meant to keep the worst away from the railway line. As for the rest of the

Aboriginal population, white authorities hoped they would remain content to live on—away from the Centre.

Many did. The black stockman is part of Northern Territory lore. Today, on the Aboriginal-owned cattle stations, the skills acquired in pastoral industry are still valued. Aboriginal elders think cattle work gives the modern young man a sense of purpose. The story of Aborigines on the cattle stations has yet to be written, though the oral history is alive and well. Tjamiwa, in his early days, worked on a sheep station south of the Rock in the Mann Ranges. On some stations, things seemed to work well enough for both sides. In return for cheap black labour the white pastoralist fed his worker and allowed the worker's family to camp on 'his' land, when in fact the land might be the employee's land, replete with sites of religious significance. For the Aborigine it was a particularly good deal if the rhythms of stock work allowed for ceremonial walkabouts, which sensible pastoralists permitted. On less harmonious properties all manner of things could go wrong. The pastoralist might, as white frontiersmen were prone to, take too many liberties with Aboriginal women ('gin shepherding', as the roughhouse, racist bushmen called it). He might take the government subsidy for providing Aboriginal rations, but cut the rations short. The Aborigine, the intolerant frontiersman would say, lived up to that reputation he surely deserved as a cunning, lazy, exploitative fellow, shiftless to a fault: he might go walk-about too often. Despite all the efforts to 'help' him, he could be too black for his own bloody good.

If you were an Aborigine in the Territory in 1964, this is how one historian describes your position:

> you are declared a ward and are one of 15,000. If your skin is not too dark,
> and your lifestyle closely resembles that of some whites, you can appeal against
> being a ward. Superintendents of missions or settlements and police officers are
> powerful in your life. The Director of Social Welfare can tell you where to live
> and take charge of your property (both powers subject to approval by a court
> of summary jurisdiction). He can make your boss pay part of your wages, which
> are set below that of non-wards, into a trust fund which the director controls.
> If you are on social service benefits and live in an institution, only a portion of
> that money goes into your own pocket. If you live on a cattle station, the boss
> gets your child endowment. It is only two years since you could not marry
> without the director's permission. He still controls aspects of your relationship
> with your children. He can punish you and white people for mixing socially.
> You cannot buy a drink until later this year.

This state of affairs was very largely the result of government assimilation policies which lasted until the Federal referendum of 1969 gave Aborigines the right to vote.

For the first time in Australian history, Aborigines were counted in the census as Australian citizens. The *theory* of assimilation was that Aborigines be helped to join white society through the right schooling and all other needs — health, housing, welfare and so on. In practice, the policy demeaned Aboriginal culture and perpetuated a counter-productive social dependence.

The basis for the policy was the establishment of permanent Aboriginal 'communities', which resolved to locate the Aborigines. By 1969 there were nine government settlements, three dating from the 1940s, but their methodology of settlement was the same. For people who no longer *seemed* to have any real place of their own, or where they did (out on the reserves, for instance), to have lost their interest in, or ability (especially in drought) to hunt and forage in their old ways, a bond was made with the new place. The key to that bond was food. Rations. In the bad old days of the frontier ration depots had been set up in times of drought and had saved lives. In the bad old days also, the mission stations hinged their operations on the supply of food. Aborigines who sought refuge at the mission were fed on the condition that they reward God's gift of food by attending Church, or learning to work in the European way. (Not surprisingly, a black belly full of white flour did not necessarily put an end to black belief. A pastor might thunder at heathen ways, while heathen ways thrived out bush, out of sight of chapel. It took the Hermannsburg Mission a century to broach the evidence of their failure, even though a select few Aborigines from each generation were baptised, and went on to become evangelical preachers.) This exchange was imposed on the 'settled' communities in the absence of any consideration of whether the schools were worth going to or the work worth doing.

The assimilation policy consisted of unashamed paternalism. *Welfare* paternalism, in that it was philanthropic. But paternalism itself is the authority of false love, which is to say love that pretends to cultivate independence and self-respect while engineering the opposite. Government policy of trying to transform the parental authority of Aboriginal culture was therefore doomed from the start, especially when you consider the details of life at the settlements. There was, for instance, the barracks' philosophy of feeding. In place of the small, clan-based campfire where food had been distributed convivially and ritualistically for hundreds of generations, there was the communal canteen. In defiance of laws against mingling with the mother-in-law and forbidden kin, people were herded in to eat food they had not sought and helpings they did not handle. The result was chaos and shame, as senior men held back, or ate with dogs on the floor. So dislocated, in every sense of the term, could Aboriginal life become that mothers could cease to care for their babies, and feed their dogs instead. Ted Egan (the popular singer/story-teller now living in Alice Springs and a member of Prime Minister Keating's Committee for Reconciliation) was Superintendent at Yuendumu in the 1950s. So distressed was he in the year when no new baby survived that he ordered 50 dogs shot.

One baby, 50 dogs. It is a hellish equation. Of course the settlements varied. Out of the social morass at Papunya, for instance, grew the flower of dot painting, that enduring expression of cultural strength which sprouts all over the Centre today. But it was dark earth from which it sprang, as James Bardon so unforgettably describes in his novel, *Revolution by Night* (1992), one of the few books that create, to my mind, the kind of *poetic unities* about the Centre that have the full ring of truth. For the truth is much more than the bones of social history I have been summarising so far, though all that needs tabling for a factual human map of the Centre.

Bardon weaves a story where the *imagined* journals of explorer Sturt, on his journey to the Centre in search of the inland sea, runs in and out of the minds of living Aboriginals still grounded in their own culture at the settlement. Bardon weaves his story in such a way that to the literary imagination, the individual lives in both cultures intermingle, and are implicated in each other in finite and metaphysical ways. In effect, Bardon's book is a definitive reminder that the heart of darkness does not belong to Africa. Dark journeys into the interior are here, in the arid heart of the continent.

Out of the botch-up of welfare paternalism came much nightmare. But out of the resistance to it, and quirks in time across the unique space of Central Australia, grew the strength of political achievement. Former nightmares, both real and imagined, are here to be visited. But I have very largely chosen to affirm a *daylight* journey to the Rock.

The important point for our journey is that in many ways the settlements failed and the aggression of European culture produced a resistance, especially in the senior Pitjantjatjara men (other language groups had been more weakened by white contact earlier on). While official policies did manage to hold Aborigines back from the cash economy, they did not succeed in keeping people in their new place. Instead, most wandered when and where they saw fit across the country, from one settlement to another — sometimes for their own reasons such as ceremony and initiations, but also because they knew there to be more water at one place than another, or more leeway with camping, and eating and drinking arrangements. Again, this was especially true of the Pitjantjatjara people, who could, when they wanted to really avoid white settlement, go far west into their traditional lands west of the Rock, into the Petermann Ranges. The incongruity of the situation was further highlighted when the Docker River settlement was established in 1968: the Aboriginal people wanted that settlement because it was in the heart of their traditional homelands, where pastoralists had never trod.

This fortunate historical accident is inseparable from what the Rock is today: an exemplar of Aboriginal cultural confidence. Maybe confidence is too weak a word — assertiveness — that is certainly there. Philip Toyne, the first white lawyer to work for the Pitjantjatjara council, described the good fortune of his friends in this way.

Reflecting on his years spent at Haasts Bluff, where he tried to work as a teacher, he said:

> They had a really fierce attachment to country and culture and language, and the Pitjantjatjara in particular had what you would describe as a cultural *arrogance*, I think, about their place in the world; an enormous sense of confidence about themselves and refused absolutely to accept that Aboriginal people descended from people coming through from Asia or India . . . just thought that was a lot of nonsense. Also, they refused to accept that the intactness of their culture and their language was largely a demographic, fortuitous accident in the sense that nobody decided to build a town like Alice Springs on their lands, and nobody found gold there, and nobody thought the land was suitable for cattle stations, which had happened to over run so many other people's lands. They believed that they were where they were because of an inherent strength of their own, and of course it has given them an enormous presence, I think, in Aboriginal affairs. (My italics)

When the Australian Governor-General, Sir Ninian Stephens, presided over the Handback ceremony in 1985, he spoke of the Rock as part of the spiritual heart of Australia. There is some truth in it. Sir Ninian seemed to overlook the perspective of Anangu, though they were all around him. On the platform were some of the key men of the land rights campaign that led up to the Handback, local men like Tjamiwa, as well as Yami Lester, then leader of the Pitjantjatjara Council. When Lester made the return speech that ratified the joint management of the Rock in the National Park, he made a famous joke. 'We own it for these few minutes', he said, 'some people think we gunna make it disappear, but we're not.' As he spoke a helicopter flew over the Rock, trailing a sign that said 'The Rock belongs to All Australians', as if to say that Aboriginal repossession might exclude others. The sign expressed the redneck opposition to the Handback, including those by the Northern Territory government and the tourist industry who were worried for their purse, and about the kind of authority Anangu would exercise over the Park. Of central *political* concern it all was, which was not to say, however, that the Rock for Anangu was a cultural centre in the way white tourism had made it. The place is one of many important 'centres' in the Centre. As Strehlow pointed out well before Handback, it was one of a hundred or more totemic sites in Central Australia.

The Rock was more important than some sites for two reasons: first, it could be a better water place than others. Second, it was where several Tjukurpa stories intersected, and as such, had considerable religious significance. Tjukurpa is the Western Desert term for the ancient Law, which roughly translates as the Dreaming. Tjukurpa refers to the traditional teachings, stories and codes that explain how things have been for all time. Beyond this—the Rock is nothing. Stories came to the Rock from afar and then made their way well beyond the Rock, just as we do, especially if we are coming to the Rock with Anangu in mind. Even if the Centre turns out to have nothing in it, to be an emptiness, or a place that is there just to pass through, it has to be part of poetical history as well.

In any case, I have come to think of Tjamiwa and people like him as poets. The Tjukurpa makes them so. Might we then come to the Rock in quest of an ancient Law, the ground of all things? Do we come to the Rock in quest of origins? It could well be, assuming we can get out of ourselves sufficiently to . . . what? Acquire Aboriginal knowledge? No—too possessive. This is not a prospecting trip. We come to stake no claims. To be acquainted with, perhaps? To meet, to encounter to the best of our ability—the Rock as the place of rendezvous of two cultures.

There are any number of attempts to define the Dreaming in the literature we are travelling through in order to get to the Rock. Many are confusing to me, and, I imagine, to you. The one I like best is by the anthropologist Deborah Bird Rose. For Rose, Dreaming refers to:

—the creative beings who were born of earth and who walked first, creating geographic features, different species, and the Laws of existence
   —the creative acts of these beings
   —the period in which these things happen
   —many of the relationships between humans and other species.
Dreaming is both a model for, and a celebration of, life as it is lived in the present. As a model, Dreaming can be understood as a particular kind of map. Stanner's proposition that the Dreaming constitutes a 'kind of logos or principle of order' best expresses the abstract and enduring qualities of Dreaming as a map. As a source of celebration, Dreaming maps are used with reference to past, present, and future. Stanner's definition of Dreaming as *a poetic key to Reality*' hints at the dynamism of Dreaming in the present. Models and practices all emanate from this life. Neither map nor inspiration to action, Dreaming is the source which makes possible all maps and celebrations—life in its variety, particularity, and fecundity. (My italics)

In this model, and in our language, Dreaming is the poem. It is commonly said that white culture has no Dreaming, a premise I think is unduly self-deprecating. We have our poets: those who fully use the language with its archaeology of meanings, and who, in their song, seek coded unities of past, present and future—they offer us a 'poetic key to Reality'.

To the Rock then, as a place of the poem. Harney or no Harney.

Besides, by the time I met Tjamiwa, I was already in love with Central Australia and wanted to come back anyway. I would return to find the place in the Centre where it seemed right to marry my wife, Ramona. Hitherto I had been smitten by the Centre twice. The first was in 1985, when I was invited by the ABC to come to Alice Springs for the opening of the first Aboriginal radio station. Based in Alice, it was going to broadcast in several Aboriginal languages, far out into the desert. The idea itself was inspiring enough: that a traditional oral culture be able to use the technology of white culture to spread their voices and provide their songs with a vehicle for trans-continental transmission. I was to write about this for the *Age* newspaper, where I was the radio columnist.

It was a big bash. Hundreds of Aboriginal people had come into town for the occasion, converging on the Central Australian Media Association's studios just near the Gap, at the foot of the MacDonnell Ranges. Few whites had been invited, and the gathering of black people was one of the largest seen anywhere—a couple of rodeos' worth—men, women and children, all around the station, stomping in the red earth to the band up on the stage, the live concert broadcast in all directions from Alice. Dust, not earth came up like smoke, and many in the crowd swirled too. A wild black man wandered past with a flagon. A wilder woman followed with a stick. When fights broke out, the organisers used the microphone to make an appeal. The sun was going down. Great rays came out of the west and struck the anvil of the Ranges. Dancers stomped, the sky flared, and subsided to bruised purple that suddenly cleared. It was night but a furnace held the whole country wide open around us. Up there somewhere was the satellite, and beside it, brighter by the minute, was the ancient evening star. Hope gleamed in the world. I began to weep. I would come back.

The second visit was a few years later. As a guest of Community Aid Abroad, I went to one of the outstations a few hours south of the Rock, in the Mann Ranges. The outstations, smaller settlements on the homelands were the Anangu's creative response to the barracks mentality of welfare settlements. Scores of them sprang up in the 1970s as the political campaign for land rights grew. They were yet another example of Anangu's survival skills and creative powers—they had defied the now-ancient pessimistic prognosis that they were a dying race. This one was run by two impressive elders, a woman called Nganyintja and her husband Ilyatjari, Pitjantjatjara people who had grown up at the Ernabella mission. On that trip, sleeping in swags, learning the emu dance, going to Tjukurpa sites, I had an 'initiation experience' that shook me greatly. I was shocked by the *difference* of Aboriginal culture, and to make sense of it I had to come back. The Centre is a different place. *Difference* is the pull: we want to know, in love affairs, what difference it will make to us.

Finally another wonder. I had been travelling here before arriving, thanks to one of the great books. For some years I'd been working on a long poem about the life of William Buckley, the 'Wild White Man', who had lived with the Aborigines for thirty-two years in southern Australia. This is the story of a white man 'lost' in the wilderness until he was taken in by the clans. Naked, exposed to the elements of Nature until then, but thereafter wrapped around by the new culture. But what was that culture like? What songs did the white man learn to sing? In quest of Aboriginal forms of ceremony I turned to the monumental work on Aboriginal poetry, Strehlow's *Songs of Central Australia* (1971). There were the songs all right; days and nights of songs, weeks of them written down by a great linguist in Aranda and a man who had come to love the way Aborigines connected with the country; a Christian alive to the way the land itself could be sacrament—flesh—to the whole spirit of Aboriginal culture. Despite Strehlow's personal complexities, his book is a kind of *Song of Songs* of Australia . . .

To the Rock we go then, looking out on the country, travelling in it and some of its history, in Harney's tracks for some of the way, broadening out, backtracking, yarning, singing, lying, stopping and then moving on, the Rock always ahead of us. Until we get there to find that it is blood red, it is purple, it is of the earth, it was made by water, it has the weight of the world, it is *sandstone* changing and unchanging, like those who live there, like the poem we might make.

PART 1 On the way

Number one myth

SPRING, AND WE ARE ON the way to the Rock. It is a beautiful day and the desert is in bloom. But we have been told to pull the curtains on the splendid expanse of Central Australia. Yes, folks, says the driver of our double-decker luxury coach, it's video time. What our uniformed driver says goes.

The film is *The Cattle King*, about Sir Sidney Kidman, once the biggest land owner in Australia. In the 1920s Kidman's empire stretched from the Gulf of Carpentaria in the far north to the Murray River in South Australia—a swath of properties interlocking across the legendary 'Outback' of Australia. At one stage Kidman owned 325 thousand square kilometres of land, an area as large as Spain.

Kidman on screen is all youthfulness and vitality. He has sharp features, with a trim goatee. There is a touch of the conquistador about him, and as the voiceover sings praises of his hardy adventurism, his pioneering spirit and lust for riches, Kidman's story becomes even more reminiscent of the ruthless Spanish conquest of the New World—our model these days of ignorance and greed in the face of the integrity of indigenous culture. But here, in this home movie, there is also an acutely Australian story, a very local fable.

Thrifty he was, says the narrator, and thrifty he was known to be. Why, Sir Sidney was the kind of man who would rebuke a fella for using a match to light his smoke instead of a twig from the camp fire. Sir Sidney would spend half a day straightening out bent nails with his bare hands rather than waste materials. Once when he saw his men taking a longish smoko in the shade of a veranda—the veranda of their own sleeping sheds—he decided to remove the verandas so they could not rest there again.

Sid. The bastard. Aussies in the gloom of the bus grin wryly at the characterisation. We're good at making vices sound like virtues because irony is sometimes all we have. But what are the other travellers—from America, Germany, England, Japan—thinking about our local hero? It's impossible to tell.

The bus slows. A steer is crossing the road.—Look, the driver says through his microphone, there is the rest of the herd.

We pull the curtain on the glare of the actual country, and see the animals strangely all over the place. There are no fences in this part of the country; so vast are the pastoral estates that stock roam free. A day's mustering away is Owen Springs, the first of Sir Sidney's acquisitions, and one of the earliest stations in the Centre. The cattle crossing the road probably belong to Orange Creek Station, one of the eight properties we pass through on the way to the Rock. Our driver is the full bottle on these matters, and talks as most drivers do, without prompting, as if only his ear bashing will make it a satisfying journey for us. He also seems to think that the more we know about the pastoral industry, the more we will know about Central Australia.

The cattle have dropped their heads to clip across the bitumen. Disconsolate Herefords, crushing the paper daisies and the pin-cushion daisies on the roadside and then lumbering around a flare of violet grevilleas before scattering in the mulga scrub.

Back on screen, Sir Sidney is in trouble. The 1926 drought has arrived—the drought that will undo him, as indeed it will undo much of the pastoral country physically, as well as profoundly affect the Aboriginal people who lived on the estates right through to the Rock, and beyond. Before that ruination, however, there is more glorification of the conquering white man. We see Sir Sidney at his desk in Adelaide, alert, his instincts aroused. He can smell the drought coming! His response? He declares war on the drought. 'He decides to meet it head on.' The picture then cuts to the great herds, his mobs of cattle marshalled up north. They bellow and stomp in the dust *en masse*; this is an army deployed to defeat cruel Nature.

We get the story of the drought, a story because if there is one that interweaves with all of the stories of Central Australia it is that of drought, a tale that can be told, like most stories, in different ways. Sir Sidney's saga is told as you might expect the story to be that of the jungle that defeats the missionary, or the ice that defeats the polar explorer, or the mountain that wins over the seeker of Shangri-la. The drought—relentless, far-reaching—defeats Sir Sidney's greatest schemes because it is unpredictable Nature at its most fickle; it is Nature that cannot be defeated 'head on' by one man, not even a hero like Kidman.

22

The Cattle King is beaten. We see him sitting on a log, head in hands. The nationalist in you wonders what the other tourists must make of such a dejected figure. Must Australians always make heroes of ourselves in defeat? There is, however, another edge to the story, now spoken by Sir Sidney.

'You know what', says the Cattle King, 'the blacks had the right idea. They work with the country . . .'

The story winds to a close with the great celebrations of Sir Sidney when he retired in Adelaide in 1932, soon after the drought. National honours and international fame crown the man's career, and the London *Times* remarks that his story is one of true romance.

So there you have a myth story with two levels of meaning. On one level the film glorifies ruthless ambition and acquisitiveness, a man who set out to conquer and to possess the country. At the same time, it presents a warning: you have to work with the country. The message here seems to be: *you can own everything and know practically nothing.* Or, put another way, *the white man can make the country work only if he respects the black man's knowledge.* What we have seen manages to honour the pastoralist while indicting him for his lack of understanding, his ignorance of the wisdom that belongs with the indigenous people of the country.

We've hardly seen an Aborigine during the course of the film, but they have become a presence of sorts even though the bus driver will barely mention them all the way to the Rock. Our driver is speaking even as the credits come up (the film was made by Dick Smith, the famous inventor/explorer/businessman much given to the promotion of the white man's cult of individual competitiveness). It's a relief to open the curtains again. There is no sign of an Aborigine out there, either.

All at sea

OPEN THE CURTAIN and there is the country again. The cattle have gone, apparently vanished into it. In its place you have sky, earth, glare. The glare can make it hard to look at individual things, and so you are conscious, if not of the emptiness of Central Australia, then of its space. Space all the way down to the horizon, and beyond the horizon to wherever the space must go.

The desert, to the mind's eye, has nothing in it. It is space. Will this space be part of your journey as you pass through a place that is empty, one aspect of the Self, in order to come to a place that is solid, the Rock of the Self?

To journey like this is like being at sea. Out there, even as we sail on the quiet winds of the double-decker coach, is a maritime landscape. A sea of red sand in an ocean sky of blue. Shores of spinifex and islands of mulga. An endless beach of flowers along an infinite lake of salt.

You can sense as much even before hearing Western truths about rocks and earth—the Geology story—or the Explorer's story, which is of an inland sea. Even before finding that fossil of seashell in the Rock of the oldest riverbed in the world, the Finke, which we'll cross any minute now, the sea sense is there—in the monotony (some say) of the space all around, in the undulations of the dunes, in the sandhills shaped like waves.

This is ancient recognition, as old as desert travelling itself, and as comforting to one's mind as the sound of the sea echoing in a shell held to the ear. The explorer Gregory put the matter poetically in as early as 1909 when he spoke of travelling over 'shore-like tracts of sand, and past its sheets of brine to the welcome havens in its oases, scattered like islands in the waste'.

'The desert', he says later (having confessed a boyish yearning for lands rather than seas), 'not only projects our imagination into the future—not only is it true, as an Oriental proverb says, that "the desert is the garden of Allah"—but at the same time it recalls instincts and recollections from the past.'

Gregory mainly travelled around Lake Eyre and was very conscious that arid parts of Australia could be productive. Today Lake Eyre is a day's bus ride south-west of here. Then it would have been weeks by camel, or months by foot. To think of desert travel as sea voyaging might make it easier: an imaginative conversion of toil into plain sailing. It was also perhaps a way of saying to oneself: I am adrift here on a sea of monotony, where all is nameless because there is nothing to name. It was as if the vast space inhibited the task of putting words to separate things, of identifying what was new.

Our driver is talking again, putting his names to things as we sail past.—That, he says, is another corkwood tree, that a bloodwood.

And that fleshy green plant by the side of the road, the one with the purple flower, is parakeelya, which the cattle love. The cattle so love the parakeelya that they wander far in search of it, so far from their waterholes that they cannot return and often perish out there in the desert, or where the real desert begins.

As we sail along we look out of the window for more of the parakeelya, the plant the white man's beasts love so much they will die for it. For the plant was, we are told, not a native of the country. Its seeds fell out of Afghan saddlebags a century ago, when the first camels swayed across the desert, admirably toiling for the pioneers, those men and women who conquered the country, who came to it by possession. There is that theme again: how the white man came into the country and arrived, by some right of work, at an ownership of it.

Clearly, our driver's job is to put us at ease, as if a uniform and a repetitive grip on the rules and regulations of bus conduct will meet the security needs of people projected onto a 'wilderness space'. And so our timetable, which is made by clockwork, is repeated like clockwork. In the driver's mind all travel must be a straight line through time. Along the span of his garrulousness, the patter of naming, of sedation by titbits about local history, Nature, the local economy. Hence his interest in cattle. The pastoral industry is a way of introducing travellers into several themes at once, none of it too unfamiliar to arouse anxiety, most of it shaped to fit the official white accounts of the place, a recounting still much dominated by white pastoralists.

That scrubby-looking country out there, for example, where the red earth has loosened to sand because of the overstocking (as well as the rabbits), our driver is not going to say much about that. He won't tell us that Sir Sidney did so much damage to his first property Owen Springs that it is yet to recover; or that only three of the eight pastoral properties we pass through on the way to the Rock are well managed in the eyes of government scientists. Nor would there be mention that the notion of white men helping make the land a desert was registered in local lore as early as 1936, by Kidman's hagiographic biographer. Even as Sir Sidney was honoured, he was placed in the line-up of those who disturbed the balance of Nature.

On the fuller complex stories about Nature, the white man and the knowledge of the indigenous people, our driver's narrative repertoire is meagre.

Nature.

The vastness of the term. The ocean of considerations that surface in the mind as soon as we say it. Yet as one travels towards the Rock all that it means and might mean becomes the natural object of consideration.

Look look – nothing

AS WE DROVE out of Alice Springs we saw some Aborigines. The dew had hardly left the leaves of the old red gums along the Todd River, where the people were waking up. Fires had been lit on the dry riverbed. A man had rolled out of his blanket and sat up to have a smoke. A woman bent over a dish, and called out to kids who were running off towards another camp site. The shelters are lean-tos of wood, cardboard, and the cheaper plastics whites use for tents, but which here serve merely as wind breaks. Traditional 'building' methods die hard, as does the habit of nomadism, which displays a certain attitude towards non-possession.

These people were in the middle distance as the bus left the Sheraton (now the Melia; how times change!). So it is possible—it seems to me—to have a good look without being rude. Any closer, as you are if you walk along the riverbed in daylight (one would not walk at night for fear of stepping on someone in their bed, or breaking into a family group), and our own basic politeness demands that you look away, place these settlers on the periphery of your vision. These family groups become what they are around the town, or on the lawns outside the public library in the centre of town: humanity on the periphery of one's vision, figures incidentally recorded and remarked upon.

Our driver's silence, it is possible to speculate, might come from politeness. Then again, it might speak of the world of difference between his life and theirs, the vast social distance that separates him from the indigenous people in his own town, a distance akin to the one still separating us from the Rock, which is, surely by some cultural aberration, owned by them. Do our visitors place these apparently derelict nomads with the street people of Calcutta, who nowadays are the picturesque subjects of sumptuous coffee-table books? Are they the poor Indians once seen on the American reservations? Are they our untouchables, which the Japanese like to conceal?

National statistics answer many questions about these river people. In aspects of health, education, housing and income, they are at the bottom of our social order. The deaths in custody are an intimate, complex reflection of that. Australian Aborigines very largely belong with the peoples of the Third World; in so far as they are part of our larger society, they are our Fourth World. How do you talk about that while glorifying the old pastoral industry?

Appearances are, however, deceptive. The river people are a small minority of the Aboriginal people in town who constitute 25 per cent of the overall population. A great majority of the Aboriginal people in town, a quarter of the citizens—which makes Alice Springs the most Aboriginal town in the country after Darwin—live in housing settlements that tourist buses avoid. In those communities, which were once humpy towns, a complicated cultural life is lived, administered largely by the Aboriginal people themselves, and materially assisted by government funds and their own entrepreneurial activities. In Alice Springs there are something like thirty Aboriginal organisations which administer health, education, housing, jobs and cultural matters (including radio and television outlets). You cannot really begin to understand the politics of Central Australia unless you appreciate that in a regional economy worth about $550 million, some $284 million would not be there without the contribution of Aborigines and their organisations.

To know this much is perhaps to cast a different eye along the riverbed. Some of the people would be sleeping out by choice, in town on a brief visit. The weather is splendid, the sand soft and dry, the stars overhead emanations of the ancestor spirits that brought them here to conduct their manifold clan business. Yet it is when you see these camps in winter that the picture changes. People huddle at dawn, they shiver by fires, walk in rain without pullovers or coats. In the wet weather bandages stand out: bandaged legs and heads, as if the war-wounded refugees are bivouacking along the river. Such images still mock the self-respect, and what has been achieved under the Land Rights Act of 1976.

As we went through Heavitree Gap, the dramatic break in the MacDonnell Ranges, I thought of old Bill Harney, who used to speak of his 'raggle taggle' friends. It's not such a bad expression for its time. Less complicated than 'spinifex fairies', his term for the young and no doubt desirable Aboriginal girls. Outside town, there are Aborigines along the river—people walking due south, as if they have a long way to go, but there is no hope, from the bus, of asking them where they might be heading or what they have in mind for the day. The big bus has sealed us off; the Rock, as the big destination, leaves us no time to ruminate on what should be within human reach. How different things are to Harney's time, when you could drive out of Alice with a mind to the human significance of what you were passing, what was past and what was still in the present.

'Legend is everywhere in this area', he says. 'This Heavitree Gap, named by the explorers after Charles Heavytree Todd, was originally called "Andareppa" by the Aranda Aborigines, a small cave to the right, as we go through the opening. It is a sacred and secret place, a repository of the ceremonial objects of their ritual. But man in his desire for progress broke down the cave as he made a cut into the cliff face for stone to build the railway line. Now all that was has gone with the roar of trains as they go north, or south, the thumping of motors along the bitumen, and the laughter of children as they pass through the gateway of the Centre on their way to the schools of Alice Springs.'

Through the Gap then, and down towards the Rock, having violated a sacred Aboriginal place in order to make the passage. Harney is matter-of-fact, perhaps too easily resigned, about the trespass. More than any other popular writer of his time, he honoured the 'legends'. I do like the way Bill Harney presents his approach to the Rock. He took it slowly, in the old Australian way, the one born of necessity in the days before the motor car, when you had to stop off overnight with friends or in the bush and therefore, at steady stages, take stock of your journey. No matter that there is a bit of stopping and starting, or some detouring in the story-telling. What you are doing is getting used to the country, meeting the people who know stories about it, and preparing yourself for the arrival, when it comes. A white man's sense of ceremony, which is regularly supplemented by Harney's sense of Aboriginal significance, runs throughout his journey to the Rock; and when he arrives, he holds off some more, the better to respect the cultural reality of the place.

As Harney tells us when he got there: 'After a day of resting—and getting adjusted to their country once more—my two mates and I [Harney's Aboriginal informants] were around the Rock, me to listen, they to tell me the full story of its mythology. I drew a blank the first day for all they did was to just walk to "look look nothing", a term which meant they were trying to get the "feel" of the mountain.'

—Now, our driver is saying, piping up out of the blue, when you encounter

27

Aboriginal people, as you will when you stop for morning tea, photographs are not allowed. They are not permitted.

His tone of voice is still geared to putting us at ease. He goes on: —There are reasons for this, which I'll perhaps go into later. But you don't do it. When people have done it in the past, what has happened is a broken camera, or a broken nose or a broken window of the bus.

As it happens he doesn't go into the reason at all. The simple human fact that most of us don't like our photographs taken by strangers is not mooted. But later he says that we can take photographs of Aborigines if we go on a particular tour—The Dreamtime Tour—which has its offices back in town, and is one of the many shopfronts that advertise some kind of material interest in promoting Aboriginal culture.

It may be a good tour, I don't know. All I know—as I continue to wonder about the evolving complexities of Aboriginal culture—is that the office of Dreamtime Tours put me off completely. I had walked in one lunch time, after lunch on the grass as the Aboriginal families strolled about or sat under the trees nearby. Behind the front desk were two shop-window models—straight out of David Jones—naked and painted black, with shields and spears and body paint, all gestures towards some idea of Aboriginality.

A white woman was behind the desk. I could not resist exclaiming:

—You call these Aboriginal?

Her mouth stiffened.

—What would you call them?

—Oh, come on, I said. You know they are nothing like Aborigines.

—Well, she said, what's an Aborigine? You tell me—what's an Aborigine?

She had flared. I backed away because I would not and could not answer such questions under such circumstances.

—Now, our driver is saying, here is our morning tea and we will be here for thirty minutes. I ask you to be punctual on your return to the bus, and to refrain from bringing food or alcohol inside the bus, and suggest to you once again that you leave the camera where it is. That way there won't be any unpleasant incidents.

Simple maps

WE HAVE BEEN travelling down the Stuart Highway, the north–south artery of the country that nourishes the Centre. Stuart was the dour, tenacious, Scottish explorer who traversed the continent from south to north. Not one given to meditation on the meaning of travel, Stuart knew how to mark an occasion. On 23 April 1860, on his fourth expedition to the interior, he was able to say, after consulting the instruments that were still in working order, that he had come to the Centre of Australia. He built a large cone of stones, and placed in its centre a pole with the British flag nailed to it.

'Near the tip of the cone I placed a small bottle, in which there is a slip of paper, with our signatures to it, stating by whom it was raised. We then gave three hearty cheers for the flag, the emblem of civil and religious liberty, and it may be a sign to the natives that the dawn of liberty, civilisation and Christianity is about to break upon them.'

Precisely what the natives thought about the dawn that was about to break over them is unclear. Up until then they were a vaporous presence to Stuart: it was by the smoke of their distant fires that he knew they were there; it was by remote, but ever-present signals that his anxiety about them was to be sustained. In the end it was the natives' hostility (among other things) that turned the party back. One encounter succeeded another in mystery and risk.

One day a few weeks after taking possession of the Centre for the King, Stuart and his party were resting their horses in the afternoon sun when they were visited by two natives, who presented them with four possums and a number of small birds and parrots.

'They were much frightened at first', Stuart tells us, 'but after a short time became very bold, and coming into our camp, wanted to steal everything they could lay their fingers on. I caught one concealing the rasp that is used in shoeing the horses under the netting he had round his waist, and was obliged to take it from him by force. The canteens they seemed determined to have, and it was with difficulty we could get them from them. They wished to pry into everything, until I lost all patience and ordered them off.

'About half an hour later two men came back. Ben gave them water which they appreciated. Then at dusk one of the first men came again, bringing three others with him—two of whom were young, tall, powerful, well made and good looking, as fine as specimens of the natives as I have yet seen,' Stuart says. On their heads they had magnificent ornaments made of feathers and wood, Stuart calls them 'helmets' before turning to the old man, who seemed to be the father of the fine young men.

'He was very talkative, but I could make nothing of him. I have endeavoured, by signs, to get information from him as to where the next water is, but we cannot understand each other. After some time, and having conferred with his two sons, he turned around, and surprised me by giving me one of the Masonic signs. I looked at him steadily: he repeated it, and so did his two sons. I then returned it, which seemed to please them much, the old man patting me on the shoulder and stroking down my beard. They then took their departure, making friendly signs until they were out of sight.'

Stuart was suffering frightfully with scurvy, though this does not excuse him for his ethnocentric love of Masonic signs. His hands were a mass of sores he could not wash, and his mouth and gums were so bad that he could only eat flour and boiled water. Some days he could not sit in the saddle, and at night he lay awake wreaked with pain. Stuart had prayed to the Almighty but that did not seem to help as much as native cucumbers, which he had begun to eat a few days before meeting the black Masons. After eating the native cucumbers he began to mend, though there is suggestion here that it was the natives who had the knowledge that made it possible to so physically flourish in the country. Like Burke and Wills, the recipe for disaster was set in Stuart's insulation from indigenous knowledge.

The Centre Stuart claimed is just north of Alice Springs. This classic episode of incomprehension happened at Kekwich Ponds, just south of Tennant Creek that Stuart named after his companion, James Kekwich, whose uncomplaining loyalty Stuart admired. Ben was the only other member. No other name was given for him when the explorer's journals were published. So named, we might assume Ben to be black (Stuart started out with a native on a previous expedition but the boy had absconded) but he was not. He was the first in a league of relatively anonymous young men, desperadoes of all sorts, who were to pursue their fortunes in the Northern Territory.

Abasements

EBENEZER IS OUR pitstop, the roadhouse on the Lasseter Highway, about forty-five minutes west of the Stuart Highway. It's about 250 kilometres back to Alice and 240 to the Rock. The roadhouse is owned by an Aboriginal community, and if the cattle station goes up for sale it will probably be bought by them as well. Incidents, what did the driver mean by incidents, when all he can talk about when we pull up is scones. This is the home of giant scones, we are told, supplied to us 'free' by the bus company, along with a limited spread of jam and cream, making of the place a permanent location in the gastronomic memory. We pile out.

But before we can get to our tucker, we have to walk past some Aboriginal people. They are outside the log-cabin building, sitting in the dirt by the horse rails. You have to tower over them and step around them to get inside, and there is no way, if one of these dusty people chose to look up, that you can avoid their gaze. They are selling paintings and carvings, some of which they are working on right there, the masonite board in their lap, or the mulga wood pointed to the ground as they whittle.

A four-year-old sits by his grandmother, his nose full of snot. His father—is that his father?—looks on, sitting on the rail in the shade, ready, it seems, to monitor a transaction.

The compulsion is to squat, to come down to the earth and engage with the crafts person rather than tower over them when contemplating the possibility of exchange. But the odd thing is that no-one is looking up anyway: they are going on with their work almost—well, almost *impassively*. Do they want to sell their work or not? If so, how much does it cost, what are 'they' going to charge?

Still, the driver has already told you that Aboriginal people own this roadhouse which has in recent years become a financial success (under white management). He has also said that the art and craft available is made by the people here and is cheaper than in town, which seems to me to be saying that you should expect to pay the starting price of a work, rather than barter for it.

An ugly story of bartering comes to mind. It was well told by Bill Harney when he stopped at Ebenezer about thirty years ago.

'People who have paid sums of money to visit the Centre are just interested in the things about them,' he wrote. '"We have paid" is their motto, and having paid they are out to get their money's worth . . . To the tourists the Aborigines were terrible. To the Aborigines the tourists were karnaba (crows) because of their combined cry, two bob, two bob, as they moved towards a group of Aborigines who were peddling their wares.'

Harney watched one of the travellers, a woman given to complaining about the treatment of the blacks, brandishing a well-made boomerang over her head and haggling with an elderly Aboriginal woman about the price.

'The black mother had a small girl sitting straddle across her shoulders and was endeavouring to get a word into the argument. Apparently she has said something that has made the white bargainers' hackles rise, for I heard her voice rise to a bleat as she exclaimed, what rot, ten bob for this.'

'Five karnaba . . . that right . . . we save,' said a bush-whiskered old man who happened to be passing and wished to air his knowledge.

'If ever there was such a thing as bargain basement here it was at its worst,' Harney says. 'The bargainer knew it was a good boomerang by the obvious way she clutched it in her hand, and attempted to push some money into the black mother's hand. How long the show would have gone on I do not know; the only things that decided the matter was the little girl weeping bitterly as she spoke in her mother's ear. In a flash the mother snatched the money from the tourist's hand and only afterwards did Bessie [a black friend of Harney's] tell me that the tourist won because the little girl wanted some lollies and fruit that the money would buy, and under the law of tribal kinship the child was always the master and must not be denied.'

It is a nice story and seems to end there. But in true bush tradition, where stories are often deceptions, exaggerations or lies, or a mixture of each, it is not over.

'The tourist waved her prize above her head in an elated manner, but I noticed that the ends of the boomerang were—unknown to her—inverted as a sign of defeat.

31

With no more objects to sell, the mother and child moved out of the bargaining battle. As she did I noticed a smile spread over her rugged face when one of the elderly woman tourists thrust something into her hand then hurried away as though she was afraid of being seen. I did not see the amount she gave, but her actions somehow redeemed the meanness of the other, and it made me happy to think that many white seers were not of the bargain *abasement* mob.' (My italics)

Abasement indeed. The paintings against the rail are not too good: a slack application of the dot method, but the goanna emerging from its wood is different. The burnt red of the mulga, its dustiness that is like the dustiness of the woman's knee, the crease in the goanna's neck that is like her own as she bows over it, these make the work automatically of this place.

Why, if the woman looked up from her work and offered it for sale you would buy it, automatically. Thereafter you have something other than culinary memory to mark your bus stop. But such is her concentration or preoccupation or indifference or evasiveness that she does not look up, so you finally pass inside, to the scone feast.

Gluttony is international. The Japanese might be poor doers with sweet things, but the French, Scandinavians and Americans are not. For once the Germans removed their cameras from their necks, grunting in their own language as they scoffed. A buxom Londoner, a woman encrusted in gold jewellery who had got on at the Sheraton was at my table. With cream on her upper lip she spoke of dingos. She said, between gobfuls, that if she did not see a dingo at the Rock she would be convinced that Chamberlain woman had killed her baby.

As we got back on the bus, a voice behind me said: —Excuse me please.

—Yes, I said to a Japanese tourist. He was in his mid-twenties, wearing jeans and a tartan vest over a spotless white shirt. He had huge black eyes and black hair which he had tied in a plait. And black leather shoes, shiny pumps.

—We were, he said, eating dampers?

—Oh no, I said. They were scones, but most of us ate so many of them they feel as heavy in the belly as damper.

—What then is damper?

Here I reached for my Bill Harney again. This is the kind of book that would tell you.

—I have never made a damper, I said.

—No worries, he smiled.

—How did you like Ebenezer? I asked, as we found our seats.

—I am very sad, he said, that these people are selling their culture. If your culture is strong you do not sell it.

—Are you talking about the carvings?

—No, the whole thing, he said.

He meant the art and craft shop inside the roadhouse. Around the floor, carefully set up and propped are snakes and lizards among rocks. Canvas and boards lean against the wall; some are hung. But the warehouse effect is the big table, on which a battery of small and large work tends to be lumped, along with metal key rings, ashtrays, postcards, spoons and native animals of synthetic fur manufactured in Taiwan. The Aboriginal artefacts, a word that demeans most things to which it points, are the collective offerings of work done by indigenous people over a vast area out from the Rock. The art centre we are coming to at the Rock is Maruku, its headquarters.

What we trade in an exchange is sometimes visible, sometimes not. As the bus moved onto the Lasseter Highway, so named after the man whose gold lust takes the traveller way beyond the Rock into the materialistic dreaming endemic to our culture, I wondered what impressions of cultural exchange, or lack of it, my Japanese friend would gain by the end of his pilgrimage. Two hundred and fifty kilometres to the Rock, all of them in the direction of the setting sun.

Why these flowers?

OUR BUS IS FLYING along the Lasseter Highway now: an aeronautical rush. Slowly, slowly, my mind says, look look, nothing. But the body is hurtled through space, the foreground is a blur, and each scene beyond is distanced through tinted glass. Everything is *out there*. The more you look the less you know. Modern travel: a concertina of time, the encapsulation of ignorance.

—We see a kangaroo? says my Japanese friend, leaning over to my seat.

His name was Endo. He said he was a student at Kyoto University, specialising in American politics and history.

—Maybe, I said hopefully.

The country was flat and sandy; it had spinifex and mulga, but I did not really know whether it was kangaroo country. The vista the bus gave me was as waterless to my imagination as it was to Stuart's.

—In Pitjantjatjara, I told Endo, the grand red kangaroo of the region is malu. In the distance you would hardly see them at all, the red kangaroo would merge into the colour of the sand. You'd probably spot them in the middle distance, when their ginger pelts would not be quite so lost against the grey-green sea of mulga.

—My dream, Endo said, has always been to see one of the noble creatures close up and at ease.

—Is that right? I said, I know what you mean.

—Unthreatened, in its natural habitat, Endo mused. —Standing still, head up,

33

quivering, its muzzle as moist and tender as a foal's, its virile haunches, and as D. H. Lawrence said in his wonderful poem, 'that great muscular python stretch of tail',

> *Her sensitive long pure red face.*
> *Her full antipodal eyes, so dark*
> *So big and quiet and remote, having watched so many empty dawns in silent*
> *Australia.*

—You are a poet, I said.

—It's all I know, he said. I learnt it for this trip.

—Too hot for poetry today, I said.

It was a relief, I had to admit, to draw the curtain a little on the glare out there.

How long, I wondered, does it take to be fully at home with our native creatures? What kind of knowledge do you need to travel well in a place like this?

In a fast air-conditioned bus the gap between what you might know and what you experience is profound. Heat, you think, but it does not look that hot out there. You have to step down out of the bus for the throb of it to be felt: it is then that the country pulsates with its ferocious light, and the ground you stand on is as warm as something baked dry and drawn from the oven.

The hardness of the country—*killingly so*—to use the brave Stuart's words. A country that calls up stoicism almost as its vast spaces dull the mind and numb a full sense of what it is that one needs to know. Stuart's project was essentially practical: to cover the distance of the country rather than to understand it. A rudimentary naming was his limit. The natural order of the place—plant, animal, Rock—confused him. Of the air around him he wrote: 'At sundown there was a beautiful rain for an hour. It is very strange, the clouds came from the north-west, and the wind from the south-east. The rain seems to be coming against the wind.'

Root quandaries haunted the early explorers, even those who came into the country with what might be called a scientific brief. Ernest Giles, who cut a swath overland west of Alice Springs and south-west to the Rock (the second white man to be there) was forever collecting plants for his friend and patron, Baron von Mueller, the botanist who would contribute so much to the classification of Australian flora. The list of specimens would comprise twenty pages of plants to be sent to London, the better to supplement taxonomies based on the work of Linneas. But Giles himself was less the naturalist than a diligent collector. When he came upon a number of the most beautiful flowers in an otherwise desolate glen in the MacDonnell Ranges, he was confounded. 'Why Nature should scatter such floral gems in such a stony sterile region is difficult to understand, but such a variety of lovely flowers of every colour and perfume I have never met with previously.'

Making sense of the water courses was the problem for travellers. They might follow a creek bed for hours and find none. They would dig a metre down and find some water but not enough for the horses. When water was there it did not make local sense, as the gully and the rocks were as dry as the 'desert all around'. The rain explained nothing: 'We had scarcely gone two miles when the thunderstorm returned, and the rain fell rather heavily. The country, however, was so sandy and porous that none remained upon the surface. I had no alternative but to travel on, hoping to find a spot where it might lodge. The rain continued to fall heavier and heavier; still we could not stop for not a drop of water was to be had, the ground sucking it up as fast as it fell.'

Any wonder then, if a man could not track or comprehend the water supply, his spirits fell. 'The whole horizon was dark and gloomy,' Giles writes as he travels between ranges. A dreadful region. Eventually he will come to on oasis, a perfect paradise, but only after stumbling around untold miles of scrub and going in all directions up the channel of a wretched dry creek. Days before the blissful arrival, he writes of things in a state of bewilderment:

A few quandong trees exist among these gullies; also a tree known by the name of corkwood. The wood certainly is soft and light, but it is by no means a handsome tree. Those I saw were nearly all dead; they grow in the little water channels. The ants here, as in nearly all tropical Australia, build their nests from four to five feet high, to escape I suppose from the torrents of rain that at times fall in those regions; it also protects their stores and eggs from the fires the natives continually keep going. This fact probably accounts for the absence of insects and reptiles so conspicuously here. One night however I actually saw some glow worms. The native poplar is also found in the scrubs and water channels of this part of the country. The climate of this region appears very peculiar; scarcely a week passes without thunderstorms and rain; but the latter falls in such small quantities that it appears useless.

And so on. Giles is puzzled and disgruntled; the country is not as it might be. It seems to be an unlucky, unfriendly place. Yet at the same time there is much effort applied towards comprehension, and the quoted passage suggests a glimmer of ecological insight: it is in the natural order that things are interconnected. Would Giles have deepened this insight if he had befriended the natives he mentions above, those people inexplicably setting fire to the country, and rating a mention incidentally, after the observations of ants?

It is doubtful, as Giles' attitude towards them was hardly conducive to mutual instruction. His record of first encounters with the natives of the Centre reveal most of what he had to say about them, which was very little of a favourable nature. Only six days into their first expedition Giles tells us: 'Soon after we had unpacked and let go our horses, we were accosted by a cooee from a native on the opposite side of the creek, our little dog became furious, and two natives then made their appearance. We made an attempt at a long conversation, but signally failed, as neither of us understood one word the other was saying; so I shot a hawk for them and they departed.' Three days later, he sights the natives again, 'Some twenty or thirty scudding away over the rocks and hills to our right. One gentleman most vehemently apostrophised us from the summit of a rocky hill, and most probably ordered us away out of his country. We paid, as may be supposed, but little attention to his yells; as his words to us were only wind, we passed on, leaving him and his camp mere incidents in a day's march.'

Stuart at least ascribed some meaning to the native signs—those Masonic gestures. Giles plays with the language of communication, the man 'apostrophising' from the hill, only to declare their words wind. He passes on into native country, while executing his paternalism with the authority of arms. To his credit he did not shoot a native on either expedition, sometimes bravely putting himself at risk rather than doing so (which is more than can be said for many earlier pastoralists and policemen). But with regard to the natives he used the language of imperial scorn throughout: fiends, demons, persistent persecutors. Of their art, which he saw in caves along the way, he found 'rude representations of creeping things, among which the serpent class dominated: there were also other hideous shapes of things, such as can exist only in their imaginations, and they are but the weak endeavours of these benighted beings, to give form and semblance to the symbolisms of the dread superstitions, that haunting and vacant chambers of their darkened minds, pass among them in the place of either philosophy or religion'.

This is pejorative language applied to a mythic underworld. Does it hint of Giles' dread of what was then considered, by all educated men, the primitive, the savage? Perhaps, Giles does not give his fears away; an aspect of his charm is his command of irony in the face of great hardship. But there was no irony when he drew himself up for the inexorable logic that could issue from the racist Christian reasoning of the day. He might refer to natives as sons of the soil, but they would not remain so. It was when Giles came to the finest country ('the most charming and romantic spot I shall ever behold', he said of a watered place in the Western Musgraves which he christened Fairies Glen) that he proclaimed: 'No creatures of the human race could view these scenes with apathy or dislike, nor would any sentient beings part with such a patrimony at any price but that of their blood. But the Great Designer of the Universe, in the long past periods of creation, permitted a fiat to be recorded, that the beings, whom it was His pleasure in the first place to plant amidst these lovely scenes, must eventually be swept from the face of the earth by others more intellectual, more dearly beloved and gifted than they.'

Giles travelled without the assistance of these 'less gifted' people. Admittedly, he once had it in mind to include an Aboriginal in his party. A young man set off with him on his first expedition in 1872. His 'name' was Dick. He came from Queensland and had attended school in Kew in Victoria. He was described by those who valued his unpaid labours as a small, very handsome, light complexioned, very intelligent but childish boy, a splendid rider and tracker who was also a great wit. Dick had enough wit to know that the country he was going through was not his own, and would become even less so the further they travelled into Central Australia. He abandoned Giles before they left Chambers Pillar.

In any event, if we take our bearing from the Rock, Giles was not the most successful of the explorers. On his expedition in 1872 he failed to cross the mysterious and treacherous lake of salt — Lake Amadeus, which he named after the King of Spain, a patron of science admired by von Mueller. The bogs stopped his progress south to the alluring peak of Mount Olga. On his second trip in 1874, he came towards Mount Olga (and incidentally, the Rock) from the south, only to discover that another explorer, William Christie Gosse, had passed through the country ahead of him, including the possibly rich pastoral land to the south-west, down through the Mann Ranges. It was Gosse who named the Rock after Sir Henry Ayers, Governor of South Australia. Gosse had camels and horses, travelled with an Aboriginal as well as Afghan camel men, and moved through the country more efficiently, naming many more places than Giles, including, as we shall see, places of Aboriginal import.

Mixed blood

JUST OVER THERE is Angas Downs Station, one of the places Harney stopped at on his way to the Rock. You can't see it from the Lasseter Highway, it's slightly off the road to the north, but it was a regular stopping place for the early tourist buses. It was at Angas Downs that Harney watched all that bargain abasement going on.

The owner was Arthur Little and his wife Bessie, who welcomed them in.

'Arthur', Harney tells us, 'was the son of a well-known pioneer settler called Billy Little who took to this country in 1927, and it was he who gave it its present name. Billy was a sheep man so the indigent Aborigines who hunted over the country became his shepherds and shepherdesses responsible for his flocks.'

Shepherds and shepherdesses, hey.

The terms suggest an Arcadian picture, but the country was too hard for sheep. Besides, Harney's warmth towards the Little family was probably connected to something else other than the idyll of sheep-farming. The Littles were part-Aboriginal, and Harney, as a man who had married an Aboriginal, seemed to have had a special affection for them. Their hospitality must have contrasted to Harney's white 'mates' who could not put him up when, in the old days, he turned up with Linda and their two children. Arthur's mother was a woman called Mary from the Aranda tribe. Arthur was born in 1919, the fourth of their children. Later on his father had four other children to as many Aboriginal women. Alfie was born to Owuchurra in 1928, but Teddy's mother, who died young, is not known. A daughter June was born to Yangewaru in 1932, and Tommy to Imbidi in 1940.

When Harney passed by in 1962, Angas Downs was a clannish settlement of some fifty or eighty people, depending on the season.

'The people don't like the Europeans' names', an anthropologist who stayed there observed, 'especially giving them to young babies. Call a girl Edith for child endowment purposes, that might be OK. But a father might never use it, and not hear it said when it passed the lips of others. A bad name—bad magic. The same with photographs. Black magic all round. Or else—thinking of names and photographs as records, it could mean a half-caste baby would be taken away.'

The tourists would have seen these people as they pulled in, though Harney does not mention what an eyesore it was to the European gaze. To the left of the road were about forty humpies, some no more than a sheet of galvanised iron leaning up against the wind, others a mix of iron and timber and blankets, with grass roofs strong enough to stack bags of flour out of the reach of camp dogs. Outside some humpies the men played cards. At others women and children sat around the campfires. These people in rags, these *hovels* (hovels as the converse to any pastoral idyll) on the bare earth in the middle of 'nowhere' must have jolted bartering tourists, until they perhaps realised that people lived there by choice, more or less. At which point, also, they'd have liked to know the Pitjantjatjara for simple shelters, *wiltja*. That these *wiltja*s were built not entirely of the local delible materials but rather the tougher durables of the white man's culture signify a mark of Aboriginal adaptability, and is worthy of sympathetic interest. In any case, alternative white settlement was one of the mission stations—with the Lutherans at Hermannsburg, which was Aranda country, or way down south at Ernabella, the Presbyterian mission on their homelands, or it was at a government reserve, where the rations and the chance for some employment as well as the freedom to travel were not so good.

'Never much singing to be heard in the camps, though house girls would deliver their Christian hymns in Aranda', so noted the anthropologist who won some trust by either not taking their photographs without permission, or by paying for those he did take. He looked after the petrol bowser when Arthur Little went bush, and to his shed came the people with the money they wanted him to count, their sacred objects to sell, and their litany of ailments, some of them minor, some not.

'I was over in the camp to see how no. 55 was', he wrote in his diary (having given individuals numbers in order to resolve the problem of naming), 'she had not collected her rations on Monday which was very unusual and Arthur had asked me to see what was wrong with her. I looked in her wiltja (the more permanent type of residence) and found her covered by a blanket but as soon as I made my presence known she raised herself up on her knees but seemed to be unable to open her eyes. I went back to my shed to get her some Vitamin-B tablets and at the same time put a smear of Borsable on the inside of a lid of an empty tobacco tin which she should rub on her eyes. I met her husband, no. 54, as I walked back—he was going to draw some water at the tank— and I gave him the tin and the Vitamin-B tablets with instructions. None of her re- lations other than no. 54 seem to take much notice of her and Arthur was quite worried. He never goes into the camp and Bess only very rarely, when there is sickness.'

The anthropologist was Frederick Rose, a mate of Harney's. Rose, a Marxist who had returned to Australia from East Berlin, failed to gain government permission to study polygamy on government reserves, and had, at Harney's suggestion, come to the people at Angas Downs. 'A great study place for contact,' Harney told him. 'These people have been pestered with tourists and they cut crude weapons for sale, which are a good subject of artefact deterioration.'

One prize artefact had been the long spear used for hunting kangaroo. It was too long to put in tourist buses so a shorter spear was made for commercial purposes. Rose could see the real weapons leaning against the humpies, or stacked in the roofs, which were still used to kill kangaroo, though Rose never actually saw that happen. He watched men go out with dogs, spears and .22 rifles and bring back malu, the staple meat for the community. It was their main source of protein. Carbohydrates came mainly from white man's white flour, and sugar, which the store issued already mixed with tea. With the flour, the women made the damper. He met no woman who still gathered seeds; in general women's traditional work had gone by the wayside, as had the old vibrancy of native health.

Rose took a splendid photograph of a hunter carrying the dead malu on his head, legs tucked up, head under the heels, ears flat. The intestines the hunter carries in his hand. He sat with the men when they cut up the malu.

The animal was sectioned like beef is at the butchers'—this part of malu for that man, this one for the other, and so on, until the ten main sections are parcelled out. 'The liver went to no. 11. The intestines went to no. 118.'

Rose was of the opinion, as was Harney (in most of his books), that the Aborigines were doomed, a perspective that already had a long history, as we shall see. He cites a demographic survey that estimated 7352 'nomads' in the territory in 1938 just before the war, which had declined to 400 by 1960. 'Yesterday evening', he wrote in his diary, 'Arthur was telling me that when he first came to Angas Downs (1928) the Aborigines all went naked . . . they always carried a spear with them. During the cold

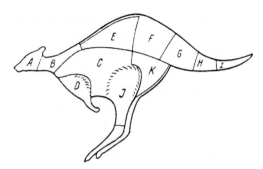

Frederick Rose's kangaroo cuts, Angas Downs, 1962.

weather they carried a firestick to keep them warm. Not only the men, but also the women went naked and those working in the house left their clothes on a tree 150 to 200 yards away when they went to the camp.

'Now the people were in rags, cast-off clothes that they shared, and sometimes washed. The women', Rose judged, 'washed their clothes more than the men.'

Rose was mainly interested in the profane world of these people. The sacred domain he thought inevitably ill-fated since the 'superstructure of belief' (to use his Marxist term) is determined by the 'material base' of a society. When one is damaged, as the whites have done to nomadic society, the other is bound to suffer as well. That was Rose's theory. The reality was different and Rose had to admit to a time lag between theory and practice. Sacred beliefs were obviously in better shape than the old hunting and gathering activities. The men put on a corroboree for him, as part of an increase ceremony for malu. It was performed only 100 yards from the road, and he was to be charged £3 for it. Even as he records it objectively, the power of the sacred comes through.

'That night the singing began at about 2100 hours and went on continuously until about 2300 hours, when five men broke away from the circle and retired to another fire . . . These Aborigines stripped naked and went around plucking leaves and twigs . . . About twenty minutes after the younger Aborigines had retired to their own fire, one came back to the circle and asked if anyone had a pocket knife. I lent him mine. At the end of the proceedings it was returned to me, the blade blunted and bloodstained. It was clear that the knife had been used to scrape bark off mulga branches and the blood was from cutting the penis of the individual Aborigines.'

At times he was warned—asked—not to look.

'However', he wrote, weakly excusing his profane transgression, 'it was inevitable that in moving my position which at times became most uncomfortable I would glance behind me.'

All that he saw he put in his journal, which was published as part of the genre called 'anthropology'. To reproduce the details again would probably be, in the light of today's cultural politics, offensive and distressing to Anangu. Suffice to say that Rose seems to have been, almost despite himself, stirred by the re-enactments.

He saw two more fires lit: burning dead trees, two flaming torches as 'stage' illumination. Shavings and twigs were in a man's hair to make it resemble the kangaroo's. Mulga twigs drooped like paws. The nose twitched, the body shivered. Five young Aborigines leapt out, decorated in the same way: red-ochred all over, blood congealed on their backs, their shoulders, their chests; black-and-white markings on their chest and upper arms, the blood and the black and white lit by the burning trees. Rose was transfixed by the vivid, fecund re-enactments where, in the continuous presence of the Tjukurpa, man becomes creature, spirit enters place, and place is in vital touch with Law. He saw:

the doe kangaroo feeding . . .
Buck and doe grazing . . .
Buck and doe mating . . .
A miming of doe and joey.

Quick, short acts, none of them more than two minutes long, the young men on 'stage', the older men singing, chanting and recharging their chants of malu through-out. Rose's blood running as he looked, as he watched a play already wet with blood, a later quickening as he wrote it all down, as I quicken (as well as censor!) his descriptions here.

'And then', he was at last able to write, 'it was sleep time, and we each turned in by the fire. The younger men slept in their clothes without any covering. I woke up during the night quite cold but scraped the fire together and went to sleep again.'

Multiple shrines

−So this is not a desert, Endo said.

He had slipped into the seat beside me. Our driver had been rattling off rainfall statistics . . . in Alice Springs . . . at Curtin Springs, which we were approaching . . . at the Rock.

—No, it is not. A semi-desert, perhaps. Depending on the run of seasons.

This holiday, he explained, he could not afford to visit the USA. When he went there he would need more time. Besides, his understanding was that there was an affinity between the two countries. He had, however, failed to see the joint defence installation as we left Alice Springs.

41

—You mean Pine Gap?

—Right.

—You see it best flying in, it's tucked away in a valley in the ranges.

—Is it important to the town?

—It is, but the town does not talk about it much. The Americans at the base live in their own community, and when they mix in social activities in the town they know how to blend in.

—The Americans own the town?

—No, they do not own the town, but there is a deep understanding between governments and the Americans. The visitors can do what they like at their base. They are left alone to do this, rather as if Central Australia has not really entered the twentieth century. When local politics are discussed they are still presented as if it's a nineteenth-century frontier.

He smiled: —We are out here, on your Oregon trail?

—I suppose, though I don't know much about that, I said.

—I know a lot, he said, and also about the American Indians, their present state of affairs. All over the States they are recovering their land. They own resort hotels, supermarkets, golf courses. Did you know they have a large chunk of Palm Springs?

I did not.

—That is semi-desert also, said Endo.

—So you are making your pilgrimage to the Rock. The Centre, I said.

—Do you see it as a centre?

—In many ways, yes.

—What is it the centre of?

—Of the continent, physically speaking.

—And spiritually.

—Depends on your religious perspective, I think. Is Mount Fuji a centre?

—No, but it is a shrine. People scramble up it for hours through the debris of Coke cans to get to the top. It has its own power. You only have to see it, even from a distance, to know that. And if you are sufficiently sympathetic to the animistic tradition, there is more, much more.

—So it must be climbed.

—Not necessarily. There is a more famous Japanese pilgrimage where climbing is not the be all and end all.

—Where is that?

—Around the island of Shikoku. Pilgrims follow the path of the ninth-century Buddhist saint, Kobe Dashi. Admittedly, they start at a temple which is on a mountain top, and from time to time, the pilgrim will climb other mountains to other shrines, since there is nothing quite like a high cloudy peak from which to commune with

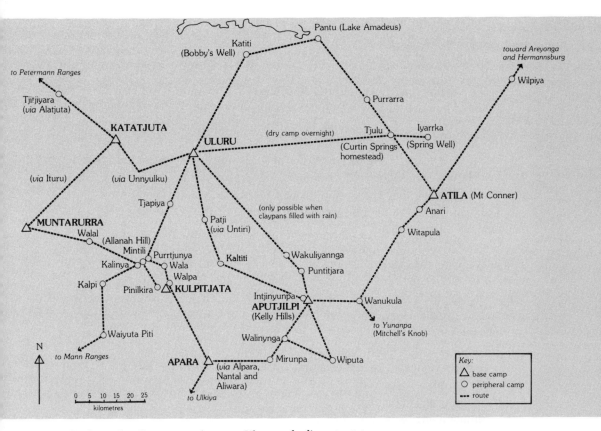

Traditional walking routes between Uluru and adjacent estates.

ancient deities. As the pilgrim proceeds the point is not so much to keep climbing, but to circumnavigate the island, to journey slowly on foot from one place to another, until the life course of the saint has been completed.

—I like that, I said. —You can't know a place unless you do some walking in it. You have to travel light. You have to leave your possessions behind. What could be lighter than the remark by the travelling poet, Basho:

> *My house burnt down*
> *Now I have a clear view*
> *of the Autumn moon.*

—Perhaps, Endo said, you are a hopelessly romantic character. I like planes and fast cars. This bus is wonderful. It keeps us cool and enables us to talk without, I believe, flies getting into our mouths.

43

—You're not wrong, I said, I suppose all I'm saying is that I'd like to have the time, the resources and whatever it takes to walk the whole songline of malu, from where it starts to when it runs into the sea, if it goes that far.

—But what is your pilgrimage here? You can't pretend to be an Aboriginal.

—Oh, I realise that, I said, secretly crestfallen. —Look at this.

I showed him the walking map in Robert Layton's book, *Uluru: An Aboriginal History of Ayers Rock*. Layton's book was written in 1986, nine years after the Uluru Land Rights case. Layton was the anthropologist who presented the claim on behalf of the traditional owners. His book comes out of the political struggles of the 1980s, in the way Harney and Mountford's belong to the era of welfare paternalism, when governments thought they knew what was best for blacks.

The map shows the hunting and foraging range of the people who lived on a one-hundred-kilometre radius from Uluru, and then, further west, out from Kikingkura (near Docker River) in the Petermann Ranges, that lay beyond the Rock. We should look at this map and think of the region as a set of runs (if you like the cattle man's term) or of interrelated camps, or *ngura*, as they are called in Pitjantjatjara. The base camp is *ngura pulka*, the smaller one, *ngura tjukutjuku*. These camps, taken overall, indicate the people's foraging range. When *ngura* is simply used for 'country' it indicates the people's estate, a term first used by the anthropologist W. H. Stanner to indicate the country for which Anangu felt responsible and to that extent 'owned'. The unity of estates is created by the ancestral tracks of the Tjukurpa, and along these tracks are the places that require care and attention as people pass through the country, hunting and gathering.

—Shrines along the way, said Endo.

—I suppose so, yes. *Ngura inmanguru*. Country from the *inma*. Country from the ceremony.

—So what is out there now? What ancestor tracks are we near? Endo asked me.

—We are in the country of the Ice Men, I know that much.

The bus driver's voice cut across ours.

—Ladies and gentlemen, if you care to look out of the bus on our left-hand side, you may see what you have been waiting to see for some time now.

We looked. Even those of us who had been before looked again, such is the power of command from bus drivers.

You could see across the mulga and sand dune. Over the rise of red waves, in the far distance, in a sea of blue that was brightening as we travelled west, was a red mountain. No—a red top of a mountain. The flat top, glowing in the sun.

—Ah? cried the novitiates.

—Ayers Rock! Yes!

—Wow.

The driver let us float before breaking the bubble of illusion.

—That is Mount Conner, he said, it will be another twenty minutes or so before you get your first view of the Rock.

Everyone subsides. Bemusement and resentment.

—A mesa, said Endo, now we *are* in cowboy country.

We were pulling into the roadhouse at Curtin Springs.

The life ahead

ANANGU TRAVELLED for food and ceremonial purposes and these reasons were as interconnected as heat and light. The arts of survival were theirs, which is not to say that in hard times, in the cycles of drought, they did not suffer. They did. Newborn were killed; old people forsaken in the desert. The white man, new to the place, had to learn basic understandings about the country, but he, too, had to be tough to survive. The Centre has demanded stoicism of both cultures, creating a common ground for myth-making.

Two images come to my mind when I think of endurance tests. There is the miner commemorated in the museum out at the gold-mining ghost town of Altunga. He remains nameless, but he was the man who *walked*, with all of his possessions in a wheelbarrow, from Oodnadatta to Alice Springs. The load, as a character out of Joseph Furphy's *Such is Life* might say, is always ahead of ya.

The other image is one Giles gives of himself when he struggled back from the Gibson Desert. Giles writes with the self-deprecating irony of the naturally courageous, and we value his courage all the more because his vanity is masked by irony. His account is unforgettable, but it is too long to use here (the best literature of the Centre is also a trek!). Here is a latter-day traveller recounting the classic feat of survival, playing the tune of Giles' own account.

His companion was Gibson, a young man who joined the expedition at Mt Peake Station. On appointing him, Giles had asked: 'Can you shoot? Can you ride? Can you starve? Can you go without water? And how would you like to be speared by the blacks outside? He said he could do everything that I had mentioned, and he wasn't afraid of blacks. He specially asked to be taken on the last dash, and as he had more than his share of remaining in camp, Giles reluctantly took him in place of Tietkins (Giles' second-in-command). These two men and four horses started out from Fort Mackellar to go west. At twenty miles west they left Circus Water, and on the second day out from it, they cached most of the water they were carrying, two five-gallon kegs, turned two

45

of the horses back on the tracks to make their way to Circus Water, gave their two mounts most of the water in the large waterbags, and kept the remaining few pints in a small bag for themselves. After a rest they made another twenty miles west by night of the same day, in spinifex and sandhill desert. When they camped one of the horses took the water bag in her teeth and squirted out almost all the contents, leaving them only a pint or two. After eighteen miles next morning, at ninety-eight miles from Circus Water, Gibson's horse knocked up. They had come upon some stony ground, with a range of some twenty-five miles farther on, country which looked possible for water, but they could not reach it. Much disappointed, Giles turned; but in a few miles from Circus Water, Giles saw that they could never get back at the rate they were making; there was only a pint of water left, and both were already suffering from thirst. The position was desperate. He halted, and when they had drunk the last of the water, Giles directed Gibson to ride on, taking Giles' Fair Maid of Perth, his own special horse on which the safety of their retreat now depended, the horse on which he had hoped to make his triumphant entry into Perth at the journey's end. Gibson was to give the horse a good drink at The Kegs, leave some water for Giles, and then hasten on over the remaining eighty miles to the camp and bring back help. He had only to follow the tracks due east, with the Rawlingson Range soon rising up ahead. At the last moment he asked Giles for his compass, which Giles was at first unwilling to give him, as he knew he did not understand it, but he finally consented. The compass was probably Gibson's undoing. On 23 April 1874, they parted; and Giles began his 110-mile walk back to the camp. By the afternoon of the next day he had made the thirty miles to The Kegs without food or water. Here he found a keg containing two gallons of water, and also one pound of dried horse meat. Gibson had not left any waterbag, and there was no small vessel, so he had to carry the keg, weighing fifteen pounds, with two gallons of water, a very awkward burden, under which he staggered on. A whole week passed, during which he lost count of the days, and walked in semi-consciousness, or lay down, at one time for perhaps forty-eight hours. At fifteen miles from The Kegs he saw where the tracks of the two loose horses had turned back and left the main track in an east–south-east direction. To his horror he saw that the tracks of the Fair Maid of Perth had followed them. Giles followed the tracks for a mile, but returned to the main track, watching anxiously for the return tracks of Gibson or the loose horses; but they never came. The man and three horses had been swallowed up by the remorseless desert, never to be seen again. The pound of meat was soon gone; the two gallons of water lasted five days, till 29 April, when he was twenty miles from the Circus Water. Only an iron will could have enabled him to conserve his water so long. At dawn next day, 30 April, he reached the Circus Water, and drank. Gibson had not been there. A startled wallaby had discarded its young, and he heard the creature's cry. He found it; it only weighed a few ounces. He ate it living, raw, fur, skin, bones, skull, and all. 'The delicious taste of that creature', he says, 'I shall never forget.'

The writer is C. T. Madigan, an Oxford-educated geologist whose splendid book, *Central Australia* (1936), was researched when men who knew Giles were still alive. It is dedicated to 'The Old Timers'. By placing Giles at the centre of concept-shaping, what is conveyed? Perhaps that courage, endurance and single-mindedness are noble things, as is the drive to cross the country efficiently; if travelling is there and back in a straight line, so that men might better return with profits in hand, all the better. There is an ideological equation at work here: the white man's pioneering powers of endurance entitle him to possess the land. Giles, if you recall, thought that the 'Great Designer of the Universe' intended that Aborigines would 'eventually be swept from the face of the earth'. Madigan, whose language is less apocalyptic, and who spoke hopefully of the day when the sexual relations between the races might be civilised, also took a dim view of Aboriginal future. *Their* frontier life, he thought, once the white man had arrived, was ruined by their inordinate desire for European goods; *their* only hope was complete isolation, reserves that could protect Aborigines from themselves. But how could you do that without putting a useless fence around the reserves? 'Even as Kipling's dogs were drawn into man's camps by the smell of the cooking meat, so the black man must creep in to watch and steal from the white. So thought a colonially conscious Englishman in that part of Australia which still remains to be decolonised.'

Stranger

HERE WE ARE at Curtin Springs, the last of the wild-west stops before the National Park, frontier of the pastoral estate. Bowser, toilets, motel block and the sandstone bar, which has a sign at its door:

> SEX.
> Now that we've got your attention,
> No Shirts, No Service.

Our bus unloads and we slouch through the heat to the bar. Who can the sign be meant for? I've never seen white stockmen without shirts, or black stockmen for that matter. Along the bar sit three white men in sleeveless shirts and cowboy hats. Further along, two Aborigines have their beer cans sitting up in front of them. Bloodshot eyes all along.

Posters galore, lurid maps of the Centre, a chart of Dangerous Snakes, of mining at Coober Pedy. A news clipping says, 'There is life in the Dead Centre'.

Through the side door limps a young man with a gammy leg. Black singlet, freshly showered, and looking as sweet as only labourers can when they have washed up after a long hot job.

—If you can't fix it fuck it, he says, as he steps in.

—No worries, someone replies.

Every travelling salesman in the Territory seems to have pinned his card on the wall. All local drinkers have at some time or other had their picture taken for the wall. They adopt swilling or vomiting or lewd poses. Girlfriends have ridden horses into the bar. The piebald looks drunk.

Another sign says: Love is like manure. It's best to share it around.

Above it all, presiding in a nice frame, is a fine black-and-white photograph of Bill Harney. Further along, high over the bar, is a more recent one of Bill Harney's old mate, Peter Severin, who still owns the place, as he has since 1956, when he bought the property once called Mount Conner Station.

Severin's presence in this self-mythologising bar is paramount as soon as you know anything of the local history. To the pastoralists who have no sympathy for Aboriginal landrights, he is a figure of strength and resistance; to those who do he is the *bête noire*—racist, reactionary, bootlegging enemy of the Aboriginal people. Severin has been accused of callously exacerbating the drink problem by selling to Aborigines who come to him from their self-declared dry communities like Mutitjulu.

Something of Severin's presence can be gathered if you take a trip around that mesa. Mount Conner is on his property, which stretches north–south along the eastern border of the Uluru National Park for about a hundred kilometres. You cannot get to Mount Conner without the pastoralist's permission, a privilege recently negotiated by the tour company 'Uluru Experience'. They have done a deal with Severin to get the key to his gate, take tourists out and about the ancient mountain and then back to his country kitchen, where, with its laminex tables, hot ovens and plain fare, they eat as might a worker in the pastoral industry. It's a tour that appeals to people feeling confined by the Rock and its environs. They get the wide open spaces, dirt tracks and close quarters with suspicious cattle—a touch of the real thing compared to manicured tours through a National Park. You might also see kangaroo, which has been shot out near the Rock, principally by the Aborigines themselves!

So says the guide. He slips the comment in as we turn around the east side of the slopes, moving through the light woodland that is malu country. The implication seems to be that white man looks after the kangaroo better than the black man, even though the black man says malu is of religious significance. I let it pass. The guide seems to be ambiguous about matters Aboriginal. He has shown me Beefwood Dam, which Severin has built. He has spoken well of the work involved in that, and of the owners' anticipation of being able to put a boat on it in the good season, if it gets all of the runoff from Mount Conner. What is valued here is the dignity of the white man's labour and his outback hopefulness, both ancient virtues. The guide has also shown me another old thing. The Toyota has veered up towards the ice-age mesa and stopped at an outcrop of stromatolite, one of the oldest fossils on earth. Stromatolite once grew as marine life and can only be seen living today on the shores of Western Australia. Here is evidence of inland sea. Then we were back on the track, trundling the long way round through scrub that gives way to more open country.

—Keep your eyes peeled, says the guide, with a proprietorial air. — You might see some kangaroo.

Malu, I say to myself and ask, —Are there songlines for the kangaroo through here?

—I don't know about that, it's more snake, says the guide. —There's a woman from Sydney University doing some work on it, that's all I know.

Then he goes quiet.

Soon we are around the 'back' of Mount Conner. The shock is the staged set. Up front it is the grand mesa, from the back, it is a horseshoe that falls away towards the vast plain. The Toyota gets us up a spur, we get out and there, on a rocky outcrop where the wallabies live, and without any pioneering exertion, we have an astonishing view of Central Australia.

To the south, you can see the Musgrave and Mann Ranges. To the west, the tops of Uluru and Katatjuta behind them; and further west the suggestion of other mountains, and beyond them the desert where Gibson perished. To the east more plains, beyond which is the Simpson Desert. The other natural boundary is the MacDonnell Ranges, which are out of sight behind you to the north. But here, spreading in all other directions is the basin that was once the sea. The Amadeus Basin, as geologists have come to call it. An undulating, blue-green-pink expanse of country. Plains that compose, between one range and the other, *the* centre of the continent. There is no other word for it.

—Wonderful, I said to the guide.

—Certainly is, says the guide, as if it were his own. He tells you he has a name for this region which perhaps the Northern Territory government might consider. *Kurkapi*. The desert oak.

We are looking out over the old maritime floor upon which the desert oak is flourishing, a verdure of green greys as softly undulating to the eye as the sea itself.

The west side of Mount Conner is the human aspect. Along a sandy ridge are the ruins of an old homestead. Two ruins: the first where the quarters were partly underground; the second, the rubble of the building, which progress and the arrival of the wife at the station, had brought to construction in glowing ginger sandstone. You look down on a green pan of fresh saltbush that makes a natural coral, and up at the west face of Mount Conner as it catches the late afternoon sun. The light shifts on the saltbush, making it luminous as the rockface flares. The scene is picturesque in the grand manner, the kind of thing that pioneer Scotsmen (the men who named the Angas cattle) would have framed majestically for their drawing rooms.

Any minute, I thought, as I stood there, this mountain will burst into flames.

I said to the guide, —This *must* have been a ceremonial site.

The guide shrugs, —We don't talk about that much.

—What do you mean?

—We don't talk about the Aboriginal side of things here, because it would be offensive to Mr Severin. It is his view that Aborigines did not live here, or if they did, they only passed through, infrequently. Would you like a champagne?

—No thanks, I said, I'll have a beer back at the ranch.

What would we toast out here, I wondered. The callousness of such tour-guide reasoning? The pastoral possession of the 'true story'? It is hard to think of a better example of a golden rule in Northern Territory society: if you own the place you own the narrative. Occupying the telling is more than half the law.

Peter Severin is a fluent, assertive talker. As soon as we met he mentioned that what he was going to say would not please the Pitjantjatjara Land Council. He said this at the first mention of landrights. But we were also there to speak of older times, when he was a mate of Bill Harney's.

—To me he was a wonderful bloke, says Severin.

Severin built the house that Harney lived in at the Rock. He camped out there with Harney, when Harney had just started as a Ranger. Harney used to come back after his day's work with the tourist parties, which came out to camp twice a week, and they would lay their swags out together. Bully beef and tea, the peace of the campfire at night, especially when the tourists were not there. For six months the season lasted, between March and September, and then Harney was fed up with the talking, though it took a lot to tire him of talking. At the campfire he told Severin about his life at the Top End. He recited poems, he sang.

I had an audio tape of Harney made by the ABC not long before his death in 1962. Harney recited with gusto a piece a friend had written: 'A masterpiece', Harney said, 'of native philosophy'.

I like to love the Asian girl, the lass from Manila makes eyes,
The lubra grins in her nakedness, the half-caste laughs and lies,
The Javanese are not bad sorts, the Jap and the Chinese maid,
Zulu and Kaffir and Hottentot, they're all of an A1 grade.

Chorus:
The bushman's gin, a very fine thing,
A very fine thing to have.
Twinkling eyes and gleaming teeth, eyes to shock an Irish priest:
Ways that are always knave,
Rollicking, rolling, rollicking, rolling, real Australian maid.

The Australian nigger's a lazy beggar, he sits in the shade all day.
Won't hunt tucker, his wife is clever, you'll give your tucker away.
He sits in the shade his lubra made, far better than the white feller man,
You may think you're clever, but by hell you'll never get the better of her
benjiman.

Chorus:
The bushman's gin, a very fine thing, etc.

As Harney recited Severin leaned forward and mouthed the words. We were sitting in the lounge room of his modest fibro-cement home, modest when you think of the thirty years' work Severin has put into his place. On the bookshelves there are encyclopaedias, Australiana and wooden carvings of deer and elephants his American wife had brought back from safari in Africa. Harney went on about how the natives had several names for him. 'Rockhead' was one. 'Wireless' was another. He was called 'Wireless' by his black friends because whenever he came back from camp he had all the news. People used to sit down with him and tune in.

—The legends of the Rock. What did Harney give to the tourists? I asked.

—To give them a talk about Ayers Rock, Severin told me, Bill got a fella called Sneewie, Big Foot Sneewie. His name was Snowy but he couldn't say Snowy so he used to call himself Sneewie, or Newie. So anyway, he got Newie out, and said, Newie, tell me the story about Ayers Rock. And Newie, coming from Areyonga said, I don't know the story. And Bill said, why don't you know the story, you're an Aboriginal? He said, I'm a Luritja, I come from Areyonga, and Luritja, is stranger. And he got another old fella out too, and he was a Luritja man too, he was a stranger. So Bill said, tell me the story. Blackfellas always like to do the right thing, so they told him a story.

—So Bill wrote it down. He brought out a little book, about ten pages. And we used to sell it here for five shillings. Bill used to sign all the books and the money he got back from them he gave to an Aboriginal society in Alice Springs. We used to sell hundreds of them. Then the Reserve Board said, Oh, we'll correct Bill's errors, and they brought out a *glossy* book, which cost a little bit more. And now the ANPWS (Australian National Parks and Wildlife Service) have picked up on that. They say we have been talking to the people. Now, the people don't come from there. They come from everywhere else but there. So we Caucasians have *made* the history and the story of Ayers Rock.

Severin paused, as if to underline the profound implication, as if he had just said, Yep, that's what I'm saying. Bill Harney's stories about the Rock are bullshit.

He went on: —Commercially, we're selling Ayers Rock. We're building up a big mythology about Ayers Rock because we want money.

Severin said this with great force.

I wondered then whether to tell Severin how exciting I found it that the people at the Rock were now getting their stories written down, accurately for the first time, perhaps. But I refrained because I did not wish, just then, to contend with his opposition about landrights.

—Actually, I said, the first debunking of Harney was done by another anthropologist, Ted Strehlow. Did you meet Ted Strehlow?

—No, I never did meet Strehlow, said Severin with a positive glow. —But that's right, Strehlow did that.

We were both thinking of a long article Strehlow wrote for the short-lived magazine *Inland Review* in 1968. The magazine was edited by Paddy Ethel, whose pen name was Peter B. English, the author of *Storm Over Uluru*, a ferocious polemic against Handback. Severin said that Ethel was a mate of his, had been since he came to his help when he was 'in deep trouble, dragged into' the Uluru landrights case. Severin put money into the magazine.

It was in response to Ethel's inquiries that Strehlow wrote about Harney:

Bill Harney did not know any of the Centralian languages. He had come to Central Australia only halfway through World War II and his best Aboriginal contacts were with the Top End folk. Wisely, Bill did not put any 'song translations' into his book, *To Ayers Rock and Beyond*. His preoccupation with the motifs of the Earth Mother and the phallic serpent [his version of the Rainbow Serpent of the Northern Australian cults] is also responsible for his distortions of the Ayers Rock traditions, even though there may be some—at present very slender—connections between the Central Australian myths of the huge water serpent that were believed to live in the great waterholes of The Centre and the Rainbow Serpent tradition of the North.

—Tell me a bit about the Uluru land claim.

—Oh, you're going back a long way now, Severin said.

—There was some dispute about a well.

—Purrarra Well, he said, that's right. And I'll tell you a story about that!

The story Severin told was about the Court's visit to the well. The issue was whether Aborigines had regularly visited his property for ceremonial purposes. If the answer was positive, then their claim to rightful ownership was, under the new Land Rights Act of the Northern Territory (1976), well on the way. If not, it would be hard to make a claim based on current possession, and the case would have to be argued differently, perhaps in terms of kinship, conception sites or custodianship over stories that were attached to particular places.

—Twice, Severin said sneeringly, twice the Court came out and could not find the well. First time I asked if they wanted me to take them to it.

—Oh no, they said, we have people here whose well it is blah blah. So off they went, fifteen of them, and got bogged in the salt lake. The Commissioner had to fly back without seeing the place. Second time, they all went out again and overshot the mark and ended up at Lake Amadeus. So much then for the importance of the sacred site. No bastard could find it!

Severin told a similar story about Bobby Well. He seemed to be saying that Aborigines had never had any serious beliefs about the country that he owned.

—To come back to Harney, I said, did you learn much about Aboriginal culture from Bill Harney?

—Well, he didn't know much of it down here, said Severin. —He knew about it up there.

Severin was talking about the Centre as distinct from the Top End.

—He's a Luritja man too, said Severin. —He comes down here. He's a stranger. So he's got to ask. He used to ask me, but I lived in a different world to Bill. Though I lived among them I was a stockman. And the idea in those days was that there was a group of Aboriginals there and if you wanted to work them, you'd pick up four or five blackfellas and work them for three or four weeks and if they wanted to leave you put them off, and pick another four or five, and if they wanted to leave . . . it was a pool of labour. No, they didn't want to work like we do, for twelve months. If you kept them on, they'd find an excuse to leave. So we knew how to work them. Now, my greatest regret was that I didn't learn their language. I was only fifteen, sixteen. And I could have learnt it easily, living among them, but in those days the world spoke English. But today, it's turned around—black is beautiful—and everyone wants to learn black.

—Harney didn't speak Pitjantjatjara, I confirmed.

—That's right, said Severin, but because of the way he lived with Aborigines, he had their respect.

Earlier, Severin had made it clear that while he employed Aborigines, he did not mix with them as Harney did.

—After his wife Linda died, did Harney continue to fraternise with Aboriginal women?

—Oh yes, when he was out at the Rock he got a telegram from a mate of his up north. The telegram said: 'What are the studs like down there? They are good up here.' Studs meant Aboriginal women. That people continued to respect him was a measure of how he *was* with people.

The hessian bag

DRIVING AWAY FROM Curtin Springs I can't help thinking of the dark side of the frontier. A man I know who has lived in Central Australia for thirty years tells me a story about some roadside places. On several occasions he had been travelling with Aborigines—friends—and ran into trouble with the dogs. They had pulled in for petrol, or for a drink, and the dogs had turned savagely towards the Aborigine, only to be restrained when their owners signalled the presence of a white man. Each time the dogs had a set against the black man.

—My understanding, my friend tells me, is that the dogs are trained in a special way. —When they are pups they are put into a hessian bag, and inside the bag is some clothing once worn by an Aborigine, some unaired clothing that would make a lasting impression on the animal. Then, with the bag tied up, they beat the shit out of the pup. After that and for rest of its life you have a very useful kind of dog, don't you?

You hear some horrific stories of racism in Central Australia. Some of the time the violence comes through in the casualness of the story, its laconic brutality. On one trip to the Rock I heard Yami Lester, Chairman of the Board of Management of the Park recount a memory of his childhood. The old men used to tell him their dog story—a dogs and horses story. On the cattle station the white man set up riding competitions. When the black man came to ride, he was tested on a horse which had its mane shaven. Shaved and greased, so that the black man might not last long on the horse. Pretty soon he fell off onto the dirt. It was at that point the dogs had their fun. As soon as the black fella bit the dust, the dogs would be on to him, making it all the harder for him to get up.

—It was the way the old people told the story that got me, said Lester, as if it was funny. But they knew it wasn't funny.

Lester grew up in the Yankuntjatjara/Pitjantjatjara country down south.

From the same area Nganyintja has her atrocity story. When she was an adolescent schoolgirl at the mission school at Ernabella, she went with her family to some of the country which was then Kenmore Park Station. The women were gathering food and the men were hunting malu near one of the bores. They did not touch the bullocks but when the cattle were frightened the station owner sent for the police.

The white men came with rifles and the black men were rounded up. They were put in chains, and their women brought in from the hills, where they had seen the men ride on horseback. Into Kenmore Park the Aborigines were marched, and the white men brandished their ammunition, threatening to shoot them all. Later they said: —OK, you can go, but you can leave all your blankets and food and everything here in a heap, spears and all, and we are going to beat you.

This is how the Reverend Jim Downing tells Nganyintja's story:

The white men lined up. The policeman had a stockwhip, others had thick sticks, and some had rifles. They made the men run the gauntlet one by one, and whipped and beat them, chasing them on horses and firing the rifles. Then it was the turn of the segregated lads. Then came the women. Because Nganyintja was alone and the other women were afraid, they made her go first. She ran, chased by the men, who beat her on the buttocks with sticks, chasing her a long way on the horses and firing their rifles. Then all the other girls and women had to go through the ordeal. They camped that night without food or blankets, and reached Ernabella next day. They were bruised and distressed. They had seen the men strike one of the Aboriginal men on the head, felling him to the ground. They thought him dead, along with one other man who failed to return.

The viscous lechery of the bushmen, which was so often idealised, stands out, even in this muted account. As we continue our journey down the Lasseter Highway one bushman in particular comes to mind—Bob Buck. If you want to meet a real bastard from the bush, Buck is your man. A legendary character around the area, Buck is famous for (among other things) discovering Lasseter's dead body. Buck's venture into the hard country in the summer of 1930 is glorified by that mythmaker Ion Idriess (who did the same for Kidman the Cattle King).

Buck owned Middleton Ponds Station, just back there, not far from Angas Downs. Through the 1930s and 1940s, when the Rock was gaining its aura as a reference point to white men, travellers stopped at his place as much as they did at the Littles'. It was with Bob Buck that Severin and Harney travelled beyond the Rock in the late 1950s; and it was at Middleton Ponds Station that young Strehlow as well as Mountford stopped in the 1930s. Young Mountford, who had grown up in the city, made a note of Buck's bedroom, which 'looked like an armoury, one wall practically covered with all kinds of firearms, revolvers, rifles, shotguns, all rusty and dusty. None of them I feel sure, would be of much use in the case of emergency. Even the bed had a formidable looking revolver at the foot although why it was there instead of at the head was not quite clear'.

This is the city man having a quiet dig at the bushman, a view that he almost certainly would not have expressed to the bushman's face. Buck was nothing if not rough: the stoic with a swagger. When his mouth was not filled with brandy it was fired by obscenities. In some quarters his bushcraft was undisputed, even if his reliance upon Aboriginal, or part-Aboriginal companions as he moved through the country went quietly unremarked. (In other quarters, historian Dick Kimber tells me, there were doubts. An old bushman told him that Buck couldn't track a polar bear through soft snow. Then again, the late Bryan Bowman, who managed Glen Helen Station at the time when Buck went after Lasseter, said that Buck was not a good bushman in the conventional sense, but was truly remarkable in quickly gaining the confidence and cooperation of Aborigines.) Buck was also notorious for knowing Aboriginal women as well as the country. Gin-shepherding was his sport. He had an Aboriginal 'housekeeper', a woman he called Looney. He named their offspring Tum who, it seemed, slept with her mother in something less than a chook house on some nights.

Here I am drawing from one of the sharpest books about the Centre, Walter Gill's *Petermann Journey* (1968). Gill travelled with Buck in 1932, in search of, as he romantically declared, an 'unknown tribe'. Less romantic for Gill was Buck. They went to the Rock and, in more ways than one, beyond the Rock. All the way Gill had to contend with the man frontier culture had made of Buck, and the relish with which Buck could savour its barbarities.

'I was working on Henbury at th' time', Buck told Gill. 'It was early in th' morning', Buck said, 'me and me mate was cuttin' up an' dry saltin' the steer we'd killed overnight, when the door of the meat-house opened, and in comes two nigs draggin' two young "qui'ais" [young native girls]. They had 'em by the arms an' the kids were hollerin' and hangin' back for all they was worth. Old blokes, they was, who said they wanted us to break the nippers in. Now in case you don't know what they meant, I'd better explain. By tribal custom it's the old fellas who has th' first go at the young 'uns, and sometimes, when th' crop was a bit heavy, they'd bring one or two along to us. It was like that then, only me an' me mate must have bin restin' or something, because without a word spoken, we upended the poor little buggers on th' butchers block, pulled up their skirts, and did the job with the point of the steel.

'A draw on the cigarette—reflecting on the horrid pathos of the incident. Dinkum, we was both quite serious, but I thought th' old blokes'd die laughin'.

'It was some little time before I got to sleep', writes Gill.

He does not say what he said, if anything, to Buck. That would have involved, I imagine, delving into the hessian bag.

Bob Buck by Mountford, 1935.

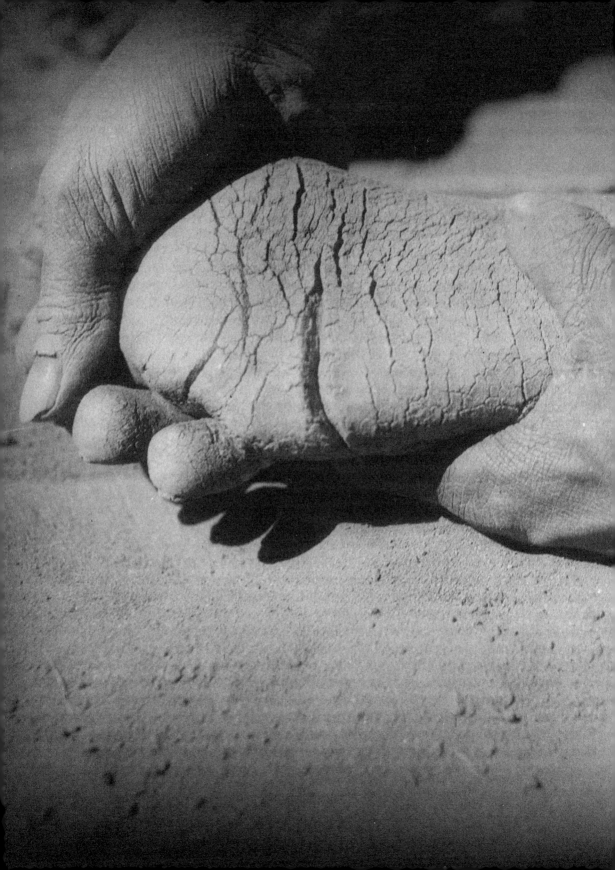

Images and anxiety

There is an image I have come to link absolutely with this part of the country. It is of an Aboriginal foot. The sole. A foot cracked from heel to toe. The photograph was taken by Mountford in 1940 when he was camping at Mount Conner, and is one of many wonderful shots he took in what was to become a long photographic career parasitic upon Aboriginal life. Mountford would become so famous for his still and cinematic photography that *National Geographic*, that neocolonial warehouse of 'natural' images of the exotic would honour him in New York. From thirty years of travelling through this country, on camel and in trundling motor vehicles, he would collect a vast store of images. Many, perhaps too many for the final good of Mountford's reputation, would be taboo today. But many others convey the landscape magnificently. They also affectionately capture spontaneous moments of interaction between black and white, and now stand as grainy evidence of Aboriginal life fairly untouched by white invasion. Many photographs simply record, in a matter-of-fact way that suits the country and its people, earthy details. One of these shots is of the foot.

Mountford took it when he came down from Mount Conner. It had been a difficult climb, a strain to his knees and feet, and he had been struck by the ease with which his Aboriginal companion came down across the rocks. Afterwards he took the man's feet in his hands and inspected the cracks. To his surprise the Aboriginal expressed no discomfort: it seemed that his feet, and apparently the others' as well, were commonly in that condition as they moved about their estate. There was another consideration. The cracks were caused by the Ice Men, the ancestor beings who belonged to the place.

Mountford was immensely pleased to be told the story of the Ice Men. He had come to Central Australia precisely to collect the legends and to record the native art before they were lost. To stop at a major place and not be told a legend or two created in him an anxiety that he might have come all this way for nothing. He had travelled by train from Adelaide to Oodnadatta and then made his base camp at Ernabella, where there was a Presbyterian mission. Many Pitjantjatjara people had been drifting towards Ernabella since the drought of the late 1930s, as pastoralism encroached upon their lands.

At Ernabella Mountford took notes on Aboriginal ceremonies, and observed the children in the mission school at close quarters. He loved photographing children, and once proclaimed: 'They are just as graceful as fairies, running from tree to tree and coming back to us with happy smiles. Their posture and poise just as they are about to deliver their toy spears is a picture of striking gracefulness.'

A maker of tracks, Mount Conner, 1940.

As it happened, Ernabella was different to many missions (particularly the Lutheran mission at Hermannsburg, which was also destined to play a key part in the history of Uluru). It did not inflict clothing upon the children, which pleased Mountford who once observed the consequences: 'clothing that becomes wet and does not dry for perhaps days [s]o colds and other troubles develop, and in less than no time, they are weakened by disease—or dead'.

Ernabella in the 1930s was run by a doctor of medicine, Charles Duguid, who recognised the dangers of clothing, and therefore permitted children to sit at their school desks naked. Mission policy generally was not to separate Aboriginal children from their elders, or the ways of their elders. There were no dormitories. In the mission school which was opened not long before Mountford arrived, children were taught to read and write in their own language. Outside school, they ran freely in the traditional manner. In general the mission had learnt the dangers of a coercive Christian education. Duguid's vision was of 'the missionaries learning the language of the native, getting to understand *their* side of the clash of culture as well as ours'. It was a policy that seems to have served the Pitjantjatjara people well as the next thirty years would show, since, by most accounts, they retained their traditional beliefs and political confidence more than most language groups.

Mountford stayed a month and revelled in the physical skills of the children: he went on picnics with them and set them drawing assignments in class, the better to gauge their 'natural' artistic talents. Out of all this came his many photographs, which were very popular then, some of which have become famous. Today they strike me as somewhat sentimentalised, though universal, images of childhood innocence. At the time, I imagine they appealed to the philanthropic spirit that could inform assimilation policies. Mountford 'caught' the naked brown bodies, white teeth and whites of eyes, while at the same time conveying the idea of benevolence towards *all* of Australia's children. They make the most of Australian sunlight and optimism, and exude the philanthropy behind assimilation policies. In his diary he seldom recorded names, except to note 'Abo child'. Of one girl he did name, he wrote in his diary: 'A young girl Nali about 13, is just a silly giggling youngster, a type that can be paralleled in our own society many times over. I watched her with interest, every hair must be just so, not that she has much brains, but she is feminine enough to know that tidy hair means more attention.' In the same class was Nganyintja, whom he did name, as well as a boy called Tjamiwa.

At Ernabella he had recruited Aboriginal companions: his camel driver Tjundaga and others. It was these people who would guide him, he hoped, across the country to the Rock. The trouble, however, was that as these people travelled with him, they moved further from their own estates where they felt safe and where they knew the

Nantjinin at Ernabella in 1940: a Mountford image of assimilation sunshine.

61

stories. By the time they reached Anneri (Anari today) Mountford was worried that they did not know Mount Conner well enough to help him in his project. So it was a great relief when the man with whom he had climbed the Rock came forth with some stories. The photograph of the cracked foot is testimony.

From Mount Conner they moved out by camel train on the last leg to the Rock. Across the sand dunes into what would become dune after dune, this country has always slowed the white fella in his tracks, and made him confused about distance, the ground underfoot and his reason for being there. The dunes run in great waves aligned south-east to north-west, which means that if you're heading directly towards the Rock as the European has been wont to do (time saving being the essence of purposefulness), each dune has to be met individually, confronted and climbed, one after the other with no respite. There is the ascent, a brief view of the country, then you are in the trough of the wave again, submerged in the desert sea.

So, even when the Rock has been sighted, you can lose your bearings. It is there one minute, gone the next. And how do you, from one dune to the next, keep the line? With relief Mountford notes that his man Tjundaga was travelling straight. 'No doubt Tjundaga had memorised the direction,' Mountford recorded in his book on the journey, *Brown Men and Red Sand* (1950), 'but it was not until the afternoon of the first day (from Mount Conner) that I noticed how simple, yet how efficient, was his method of keeping on a straight course. It amounted to no more than the lighting of thickets of spinifex as he passed along, so that, when he reached the crest of a sand ridge from where we could look back to Mount Conner, the line of "smokes" showed the course he had taken.'

Brown Men and Red Sand helped make Mountford famous as an explorer of sorts, and a diligent ethnologist. The book was a precursor to his other publication, *Ayers Rock*, which was to seal his reputation as an authority on Central Australia, when it was published in 1965 within months of Bill Harney's efforts.

For Mountford dunes were one thing, the risk of arriving at the Rock without adequate informants was another. He started to worry about this when he was at Mount Conner. The Aborigines he was travelling with from Ernabella knew the country, but not necessarily the places they were going to. 'Tommy had already assured me that a man we brought from Ernabella was an Ayers Rock man, but on closer questioning, I found that he had not even seen the place,' Mountford irritably told his diary. It was the first of several disappointments, or 'humbug and disappointment'. He found a man who knew the stories but it was not his country. Then he heard of an old man, thirty miles away, who fitted the bill: a man reputed to be an owner, as well as (therefore) knowing the Rock.

'Two men were agreeable to find him, so I sent them off early to bring him along. I hope to goodness they are successful,' Mountford wrote.

By the end of the next day, the two men returned without the old man. It was a great disappointment for Mountford. They had tracked him for a certain distance and given up. He re-equipped the men with tea and sugar and sent them off again. 'I told them to go out again and not to return until they found him and brought him back . . . So much depends on the success of these men that I hardly dare to hope that they will be successful or to estimate the results if they are not.'

Two days later, the men came back. They had found the old man all right, but he had refused to come. 'They had promised him plenty of food, but all to no avail,' says Mountford. 'This was a very great disappointment, but however it may not be as bad as it looks at present.' It was not so bad because Mountford settled for another man, a young fellow, but you can hear him settling for second best: 'The young man undoubtedly knows some of the myths, he admits that he has made some of the paintings (at the Rock), so I expect I must accept the fact that half a loaf is better than no bread.'

The man's name was Matinya and he would take Mountford around the Rock and out to the Olgas. Mountford made Matinya pose in numerous positions around the Rock, as if he was an absolute authority on the place: we see the young man by Dreaming sites, painting in caves, holding fire sticks by the sacred waterhole at the top of the Rock—an Edenic shot if ever there was one—the results of Mountford's need to create an image of pristine spirituality, of water, fire, Rock and naked man. It is these compositions that made *Brown Men and Red Sand* such an appealing book, since it seems to strike a balance between the images of an Aborigine in his natural setting, and an European sense of the elemental. That Mountford saw his pictures as creations is not so clear from his book, his pictorial wit is clearer in his diary. One shot which was not in the book helps give the game away. It shows Matinya snapped in the company of the instrument taking possession of him and his place. 'Abo with camera' is Mountford's caption in his diary.

Nor does the book reveal the worries Mountford continued to have about informants, Matinya in particular. On Tuesday 30 July 1940 at the Rock he is concerned that the man did not know about the paintings in the large cave near Maggie Springs. The man, however, did know some of the legends, and Mountford wrote them down. Next day, after Matinya displayed more ignorance of the cave paintings, Mountford considered sending for another man from back at Anari. To his relief, he found out that Matinya knew a lot of stories about the north side of the Rock. This went on for a while: the recording of legends oscillates with doubts that last for days, and continues into the Olgas, where it was difficult to get the right information about the whereabouts of water.

Years later, in 1953, Mountford came back to the Rock in the hope of consolidating the knowledge he had shakily gained in 1940. In 1953 the anxiety about

'The most wonderful natural feature I have ever seen', W. C. Gosse, 1872.

informants was still there. No sooner had he arrived in Alice Springs—for he would approach the Rock this time via Angas Downs and the Littles' place—than he contacted Bill Harney who happened to be in town.

Bill Harney introduced him to an Aboriginal man, Fred Maynard, who told him he could 'get an Ayers Rock man'. Mountford notes: 'Next day Fred brings a Pitjantjatjara man back from the Todd who said he was a Mala man from Uluru, and agreed to come with us. He does not look very bright but expect will be of some use.'

Two days later they go out to Jay Creek, the Aboriginal settlement near Alice Springs. There they find another informant, of whom Mountford notes: 'an old Luritja or Pitjantjatjara man, Mick (Aboriginal name Ninin) who said that he knew the myths. So we brought him back with us. It turns out that he is the brother of Carbine, the tracker who accompanied us to Ayers Rock during 1935. This makes me doubtful, because Carbine belongs to Tempe Downs. Still, he seems to know the place.'

A few days later, when he is staying with the Littles at Angas Downs, Mountford sums up his human resources. 'Our Abo staff now consists of Mick, a carpet snake man from Ayers Rock; Charlie, who although he said he was a mala (a marsupial rat) man from Uluru, is nothing of the sort; a young chap Jack (from Angas Downs) and an old man Tjukini, of whom I know nothing as yet.'

Ancient and sublime

THE FIRST GLIMPSE of the Rock. What a sight! All of a sudden, while you are gazing across the undulating dunes, it surfaces on a crest, out of the trough of a wave with the bulk of a whale. You look again, and it's gone. Then around the next bend, there it is again. All rock this time. The *fancy* of the whale subsides. You want to know, what is this thing? Of the earth, yet of the ancient seas.

—Just a dirty big Rock, the driver is saying, in the middle of nowhere.

Very funny. The deadpan bastard does have a point, I have to admit. The image is, surely, all too familiar. Hackneyed. An image made dumb by its over-exposure as an icon. Is this the upshot of our pilgrimage: to be rendered silent? The Rock as a fullstop to eloquence?

'The most wonderful natural feature I have ever seen', said William Christie Gosse, the first white man to come upon the Rock.

Look at the illustration brought back by the Gosse expedition in 1873. The Rock is an edifice of cliff and gashes. It soars above the plains, a gift to eloquence, if not to accuracy!

Gosse was travelling for pastoral interests in South Australia. He had left Alice Springs on 23 April 1873 with a party of four white men, three Afghans and a black 'boy' named Moses. They travelled up the telegraph line towards Central Mount Stuart and swung west. At the far edge of the MacDonnell Ranges near Mount Liebig they came south, through the ranges to Kings Creek, and crossed Lake Amadeus. It took three months to get to the Rock. 'The hill as I approached', he wrote in his journal on 19 July 1873, 'presented a most peculiar appearance, the upper portion being covered with holes and caves. When I got clear of the sandhills, and was only two miles distant, and the hill, for the first time, coming fairly into view, what was my astonishment to find it was one immense rock rising abruptly from the plain; the holes I had noticed were caused by the water in some places forming immense caves'.

The natural feature made a greater impression the next day. Gosse's journal entry is worth quoting in full because it foreshadows so much of the social future of the Rock:

I rode round the foot of rock in search of a place to ascend; found a waterhole on the south side, near which I made an attempt to reach the top, but found it

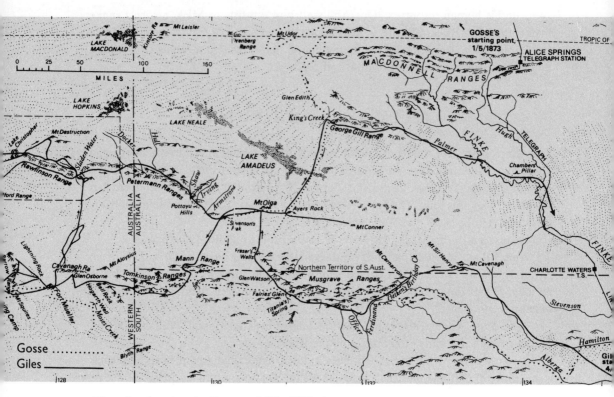

Map of explorations by Gosse and Giles 1873–4.

hopeless. Continued along to the west, and discovered a strong spring coming from the centre of the rock, and pouring down some very steep gullies into a large deep hole at the foot of the rock. This I have named Maggie Springs. Seeing a spur less abrupt than the rest of the rock, I left the camels here, and after walking and scrambling two miles barefooted, over sharp rocks, succeeded in reaching the summit, and had a view that repaid me for my trouble— Kamran [one of the Afghans] accompanied me. The top is covered with small holes in the rock, varying in size from two to twelve feet diameter, all partly filled with water. Mount Olga is about twenty miles west. Some low ranges and ridges west–north-west, one of which I think must be McNicol's Range; part of lake visible, bearing north Mount Conner 96 degrees, and high ranges south-east, south, and south-west, with sandhills between. The one south-east I have named after His Excellency Governor Musgrave; and a high point in same, bearing 141 degrees, Mount Woodroffe, after the Surveyor-General. This is a high mass of granite, the surface of which has been honey-combed, and is decomposing, 1,100 feet above surrounding country, two miles in length (east

66

and west), and one mile wide, rising abruptly from the plain. How I envied Kamran his hard feet; he seemed to enjoy the walking about with bare feet, while mine were all in blisters, and it was as much as I could do to stand; the soil around the rock is rich and black. This seems to be a favourite resort of the natives in wet season, judging from the numerous camps in every cave. These caves are formed by large pieces breaking off the main rocks and falling to the foot. The blacks make holes under them, and the heat of their fires causes the rock to shell off, forming large arches. They amuse themselves covering these with all sorts of devices—some of snakes, very cleverly done, others of two hearts joined together, and in one I noticed a drawing of a creek with an emu track going along the centre. I shall have more time to examine these when the main camp is here. The rock is certainly the most wonderful natural feature I have ever seen. What a sight this must present in the wet season; waterfalls in every direction . . .

The wonder of the landmark. The way it could help orient one to the whole region of the Centre. The seductive power of its climb. The need to explain what it was—its size, proportions, make up. Its value as a watering place. Gosse considered Maggie Springs (Mutitjulu today) the first permanent source of water since Alice Springs (though it was not, no more than the Rock was granite). But with exclamations about the fertility of the spot, and in the telling remarks about the natives and their caves, Gosse registered the Rock's human significance in the vastness of what had been such a harsh country to travel through.

There exists a note of tolerance for the natives in Gosse's response. Art that Giles saw as perfidious, Gosse found interesting, rather impressive. There is no suggestion here that the natives are, by virtue of the white man's arrival, on the brink of dispossession. As Gosse travelled through the country, he refrained from righteous imperial outbursts, and tended instead to note what he admired about them: their skill at cutting trees with stone implements, the fences they built to hunt wild creatures, their fire practices, their use of a poison of some sort to trap emu at watering places. There was also their masterful knowledge of the water places themselves. The further Gosse travelled—he went south of the Rock and named the Mann Ranges, calling them the most beautiful country he had ever seen, and hunted kangaroo in them before running into the dry country again—the more he used natives to find water. Most contacts were friendly, so much so that by the time he turned back and came through the Musgrave Ranges that he had named from the top of the Rock, he was befriending natives and putting Aboriginal placenames on the map. The Alberga *Appatinna* waterhole. The Hamilton *Carpamoongana*. These were water places near Mount Everard, in the Yankuntjatjara and later Pitjantjatjara country around what would become the Ernabella Mission. It was as if at one level of his consciousness,

Gosse felt he should honour the owners, the people physically in tune with the life source, the waters of the ancient land.

Still, it was the land itself, rather than its native peoples, that created the greatest source of wonder for the white man who came into it, and had to manage their journeys through it, across it. When on 13 October 1872 Giles first sighted a grand protrubance from the plains, he made as much of it as Gosse. 'After a long and anxious scrutiny though the smoke and haze, far, very far away, a little to the west of south, I described the outline of a range of hills, and right in the smoke of one fire an exceedingly high and abruptly ending mountain loomed.' Giles tried to 'make a straight line for the newly discovered high mountain'. Alas, the great salt lake blocked him. He did not get to the actual Rock (as distinct from Mount Olga and Gosse's camp) until June 1874, when he wrote: 'There was no water where Mr Gosse camped, but round another turn of the hill we found a very fine deep pool lying in the sand, and under the rocky face of the mount.' Giles found the mount 'most imposing, for it is simply a mammoth monolith, that rises out of the sandy soil around and stands with a perpendicular and totally inaccessible face at all points, except one slope near the north west end'. And he adds his now-famous phrase: 'Mount Olga is the more wonderful and grotesque, Mount Ayers the more ancient and sublime'. While Gosse had struggled for generalities, Giles, a more literary fellow, placed it in the Romantic idiom of his time. If he had reached it first and made it his own by naming, who knows what might have inspired him. To the south, in the beautiful Musgrave Ranges he had revelled in naming Mount Oberon, after Shakespeare's king of fairies.

Ancient *and* sublime, the phrase still rings. It manages, somehow, to connect the scientific with the literary response. Yes, even before we get to the resort, and although all we see of the Rock are glimpses in the middle distance through the tinted glass of the bus window, its physical presence begins to demand an explanatory description. Questions loom: what do I know about it? What should I know (let alone feel)? And, after coming all this way, what have I brought to this place? What is involved in what I say?

Gosse tried to make sense of its peculiarity by recounting some geology of the time. 'This is a high mass of granite, the surface of which has been honeycombed, and is decomposing', he wrote, inaccurately. Giles also mistook the sandstone for granite. When Giles described the Olgas the gaps in his geological knowledge allowed him the space to fill it imaginatively. He speculated: 'It is, I should say, decidedly of volcanic origin, belched out of the bowels and onto the surface of the earth by the upheaving of subterranean and subaqueous fires, and cooled and solidified into monstrous masses by the gelid currents of the deepest waves of the most ancient of former oceans.' This is vivid, muscular talk, made by one trying to enter into the dynamic of this place. A sense of the underworld seems to move Giles, as well as an heroic notion of Rock crags, mountain tops. If he'd been a more literary man or more attuned to the depth of his apprehensions, he might have gone further towards the mythic elements of the land he had entered: Milton's Satan, or Shelley's Prometheus, might have marked the map of 'our' Centre!

The evolving geology story would put Giles and Gosse right about the facts. But the physical presence of the Rock is undeniable, and these first written responses to it were a kind of template of what needed to be known. It rose out of what was once a sea, its composition invoked a wild and ancient narrative of the earth's genesis. Overall it was a weird thing, which called up a language at once expressive and speculative. Rock rather than race and ancestry; matter rather than the archaic spirit of place was what interested these first white men as they encountered the 'natural feature'.

Today, it is the antiquity of *things* that still exercises its fundamental pull. We are here, surely, because of the gravity of the archaic. There is no getting away from this planetary fact. Australia is one of the world's oldest continents: its oldest rocks began to form about four and half billion years ago. It was this Amadeus basin that very largely cradled the mythical, but real, inland sea. The basin formed in Precambrian times, up to three-and-a-half billion years ago, when the first life forms were coming into being. Those stromatolite fossils back at Mount Conner are the clearest evidence of that, and they have been called 'the ultimate living fossils'. As the Amadeus basin was forming most of Eastern Australia was also covered by seas, in which there was an explosion of evolutionary life—the anemones, jellyfish, trilobites and worm-like creatures, all of which predate the jawless fish, the first vertebrates that developed between 500 and 435 million years ago, in the Ordovician period.

The sea then, the old seabed that we sail our minds on as we approach the Rock was the harbinger of elemental beginnings. Is that what we are doing here, voyaging back to all beginnings? And to think that life on land was yet to come. About halfway through the formation of the Amadeus basin land plants evolved from seaweeds, shorelines were colonised by plants and the first fish with jaws developed. It is from Stairway Sandstone of the Amadeus basin that fossils of the most primitive fish have been found, the first vertebrates in the Ordovician in the southern hemisphere. Some palaeontologists will say that these fossils are cousins of the Bony Bream swimming in the rockholes of the Finke today.

It would be another fifty million years before the mountains of Alice Springs will form, and another fifty or sixty before any flourishing plants. Fossil pollens are the fabulous clue to this ancient narrative's growth. Great beach forests flourished here in the heart of what was not yet Australia. In another 250 million years Gondwana will break up, the first amphibian creatures will arrive, and all manner of other armoured creatures militantly thrive. Only after that will the first flowering plants burst upon the earth. How is it possible to comprehend the *slow depth* of such history, and to express

the time that history has laid down in this place? Perhaps it helps a little to tell the geology story in the modern way, as I. P. Sweet and I. H. Crick do.

We are travelling through a Cambrian landscape with over 600 million years of complicated pressure, upheaval and erosion. Mount Olga and Mount Ayer began to find their shape about the same time. Their story is not one of volcanic drama as Giles proposed, but originally one of continuous accretion. The base material of both mountains that geologists call *inselbergs*—a lovely word that catches their maritime prominence as well as genesis—was laid down as alluvial fans flowing out of the Petermann Ranges 550 million years ago. The fans did not meet, though they flowed into the same great basin and had a similar composition: a basement of Palaeozoic sedimentary rocks, igneous and metamorphic rocks. The difference was that the Olga section was built from an ancient mountain of conglomerate, while Mount Ayer had an extensive layer of the sandstone called arkose. This was in the very beginning. Four-hundred-and-fifty million years later, their differences were evident due to tilting and warping, and the differential erosion of water and wind upon the conglomerate and arkose. Thus we have Kata Tjuta and Uluru as we see them today.

And still the giant prehistoric animals have not entered the story. Nor have the great mammals of land and sea, though the sea here has subsided, following the ice sheets that superseded it. As we summarise, time begins to concertina towards modernity, and yet it is only yesterday that the Australian landmass was formed, drifting apart from New Guinea in the north and Tasmania in the south. What is the world waiting for in this genetic story? What happened to the mega-fauna? Did humankind help their extinction, by hunting them out? Was climatic change so radical as to destroy their original habitats? In this process of incessant, inexorable change, what becomes of a notion such as original or, if it comes to that, primitive? For summary's sake we simply say that humans were standing on earth about 1.2 million years ago in Java, probably in China about 500,000 years ago, and that some humans of some kind reached Australia 50,000 years ago.

We speculate to a point. In all that pertains to the archaic, to our precious depth of origins, we are in the realm of conjecture and dependent on what today are the speculative sciences: geology, palaeontology, archaeology. Just north of the point on the map where we approach Uluru, about 260 kilometres as the crow flies, is a rock shelter in the Cleland Hills called Puritjarra. The stone tools found here may be older than 30,000 years. The red ochre goes back 30,000 years, suggesting that the artwork began at least 13,000 years ago, as early as the famous bulls and human figures in the caves of France and Spain. The art has not been dated in detail, but some of the images—enigmatic figures and mysterious heart-shapes in the ancient rocks—inspire

Carvings in Cleland Hills: the oldest faces in the Centre?

me with their gneissic possibilities, as shapes that invoke the beginning of image-making, the fundamentals of the pictorial imagination. These 'smiling' human faces, as they have been called, were carved in a place that has the only permanent water for 8000 square kilometres. Scrutiny of the art as recently as the mid-1980s confirms that Central Australia was inhabited during the ice ages, and that prehistoric human life did not hug the coastline. In geological terms we are travelling through a Cambrian landscape, but culturally we are in a Precambrian place, in a country of archaic human significance. In this light, the Aboriginal presence in the Centre is as elemental as sun, sand, water, rock.

Clinical shots

THE FIRST PHOTOGRAPH of the Rock was taken by Tietkins the explorer in 1889. It did not come out very well, which is one reason why it has never been republished since Tietkins' 1891 journal. Yet it is a striking image, I think, precisely because it hardly attempts a scenic view. The picture is not of the whole rock at all, but of Maggie Springs, the waterhole named by Gosse. Tietkins, a surveyor by training, was in search of minerals and pastoral areas. In the heat of March 1889 he arrived at the Centre and was soon heading west from Alice Springs, out along the MacDonnell Ranges. Four days, and then seven, his camels went without water. Water would be found by his native guide, a man called Billy from the Erldunda area, and to whom Tietkins dedicated his journal, placing a photograph of Billy in the honorific frontispiece. Except for the bare feet, Billy is presented in vest, sleeved shirt and tie, looking for all the world like an Adelaide gentleman. At a time when an Aborigine might be portrayed as a wretch or patronised as a noble savage, this was a compliment.

In the ranges Tietkins noted the least signs of pasture, even when there was no regular water supply to go with it. Dry creek beds were followed by drier gorges. As they moved further west and the season changed, there was more than enough water, it had rained torrentially in May: 'I deemed myself the most fortunate of travellers', he noted wryly, when they were approaching the Cleland Hills, 'to have heard the sounds of running water in country such as this'. Reaching the Cleland Hills, they found running water for two miles in Gills Creek and as well nearly twelve miles of running water in different channels. 'Billy went down the creek with a rifle, and returned with a fine kangaroo.' Tietkins paints a lush picture of the place without speculating on its natural implications for Aboriginal life. In a cave further on he would see 'idle or playful drawings on stone wall representing and signifying nothing in particular'. In

Tietkins' Maggie Springs: the first photograph of Mutitjulu.

the Cleland Hills he noticed nothing of the kind, though those figures and 'smiling faces' were there, continuing to smile as he passed on.

Tietkins went as far west as Lake Macdonald and then turned back towards that confounded obstacle, Lake Amadeus. Billy, forever the water scout, made no contact, it seemed, with other natives. So successfully did the Aborigines steer clear of their visitor that Tietkins did not see any natives for the whole journey of five months. He saw smoke. He saw their signs of camp. He saw where they had burnt 'patches' of country, and across these he directed his camels, who found the hundreds of miles of spinifex such misery. When the camels finally skirted the west tip of Lake Amadeus ('discovering' it was not as vast as Giles thought), beloved Tooroo was so worn and ill from poisonous plants that he had to be left where they camped, at the running water in the gorge of Mount Olga, where Giles and Gosse had rested fifteen years earlier.

They reached the Rock on 9 July 1889. 'Passed round the south base of this mountain of unbroken unfractured stone. At 11.30 I unsaddled upon the spot where I camped fifteen years ago, when here with Giles. After dinner we went out to explore and admire this wonder in solid granite. Many and varied are the wonderful shapes it assumes. In one place the graceful curves and lines upon this vast expanse of rock resemble an enormous curtain turned into stone. In one or two places large caves are to be found near the foot, and these in measure spoil the otherwise regular and graceful lines chiselled by nature upon its face. The rock formation is a course-grained grey granite, the surface all over bearing a reddish colour from exposure to the elements, smooth as glass, and almost polished. It appears to me to be quite inaccessible, except at the one point were Mr Gosse and his companions made the ascent.'

Although the surveyor was drawn to 'improve the rock', he did not climb it. Nor did he ask Billy about it, nor worry the issue of any native presence. He was more interested in signs of his own kin. Next day, 'I made a diligent search for Mr Gosse's marked tree, taking Billy with me. For two hours or more we wandered about, closely examining every tree. I remember it was an unusually large bloodwood, but its exact locality I could not recollect; but quite close to his camp I saw the charred stump of such a tree, and upon the ground was observed a long line of ash and charcoal, and it became evident beyond doubt that this was Mr Gosse's tree. At the time of the fire there must have been a very high wind, for its destruction is most complete, not a twig or spray being left.'

After this Tietkins took his photographs. In so doing he ended an era of exploration in Central Australia. Gone were the days when explorers set down their journeys in words alone: farewell to the exclusively written response with its invitation to the literary imagination and the inner life. Welcome (it had to be) to the modern age of documentation, image-collecting, appropriation. The written record would always involve some wrestling with the process of encountering the county and its inhabitants: photographs simply had to be *taken*.

Five of Tietkins' photographs of the Rock survive: three close-ups of the cliff walls, a view out from a cave, and the shot of Maggie Springs. The overall effect is of a brooding scene, a valley in long winter shadow. Today we might say scene, but it was not really intended as such by the photographer. The shot was taken with a practicality in mind: the valley leads to water. At the same time, the image works in its own right. The valley is conspicuously uninhabited. You can hear the echo in the valley as you look at it—the echo of a single white man's voice as he walks in there, seeking quiet possession of what might be available. Strangely, one senses the larger natural setting. It is not hard to imagine the high winds Tietkins speaks of, the exposure of the Rock to Time's elements. Technically, it is a 'poor' photograph, and yet its clumsy exposure quietly declares the Rock's great presence. The practical explorer seems to have got the image he wanted all right, but it was one that suggested much that he could not take.

The first full view of the Rock so familiar to us today was taken by Baldwin Spencer in 1894. Spencer, eminent Professor of Biology at Melbourne University, was scientist and photographer for the Horn Expedition, the first scientific trek into the Centre. It is a spectacular photograph, taken near the sunset viewing area, as millions of tourists know the spot today. Spectacular, but not necessarily scenic, in that scenic views involve a self-conscious regard for the picturesque. Spencer's shot is hardy, plain: it benefits greatly from virgin privilege of not having a promiscuity of images preceding it. From his camels Spencer unloaded his sturdy cameras and took it in the full light of day. No drama, no mood setting or attempt to accentuate the peculiar appearance of the rock. A factual recording for the scientific record. Its strength is its simplicity, as if the visitor was content to register things with a detachment that did no harm, and did not presume to impose any other view upon a native place.

'Ayers Rock', Spencer wrote in the famous report of the expedition, 'is probably one of the most striking objects in Central Australia. From where we stood the level scrub stretched away monotonously east, west and south to the horizon. Above the yellow sand and dull green mulga rose the Rock—a huge dome-shaped monolith, brilliant venetian red in colour. A mile in length with its sides rising precipitously to a height of eleven hundred feet above the plain, it stands out in lonely grandeur against the clear sky. Its otherwise smooth sides are furrowed by deep lines of rounded holes rising in tiers one above the other and looking as if they had been hollowed out by a series of great cascades down which for many centuries the water in the rain seasons must have poured in torrents from the smooth dome-shaped summit.'

Spencer had also approached the Rock from the north. With Mounted Constable

Baldwin Spencer the naturalist stands back for the pioneering postcard.

E. C. Cowle and his Aboriginal 'tracker' (whose name seems to have gone unrecorded), Spencer made a side trip from their main party. All the way from the range north of the lake Spencer had been applying himself to the bushcraft. The party had been travelling for three days without water over heavy porcupine grass sandhills, and it was no small pleasure to get to the water at the base of the Rock where they could drink and wash. Spencer never pretended to like the roughness of travel in the Centre, though he was stoic at all times. A man confident in his own urbanity, he felt no compulsion to like his camels. He hated their moods and their filthy smell, and the daily arduousness of saddling, loading, hobbling. He spent 100 of the 125 days 'perched high up between heaven and earth' on the back of a beast he called Baron, named after von Mueller. What photographer would be fond of a camel that could sideswipe trees, and throw all the baggage to the ground! Two dozen photographic plates were lost once, while jogging through the scrub—this, after all the trouble a man had to go to keep his plates free of sand, and films from fogging in the intense light.

Then there was the curse of the Centre, the creations made to bedevil all thought and study.

'Being summertime, the climate was rather trying. Even in winter during the hot days the flies are rather annoying, but in summer they are simply exasperating, and all day long you must shield your eyes, ears and nose if you are to have anything like comfort. The only way in which I found it at all possible to make any observations or to collect was by tying my head into a muslin bag and putting up with the irritation on the hands. Long before the buzzing of the flies ceases in the evening, the mosquitoes are humming around in myriads, and when camped out at night the only chance of sleep, unless by good luck a wind was blowing, was to lie in a little coffin-shaped tent of cheese-cloth. If the wind blew, then there were certainly fewer flies, but everything you had—clothes, food and collecting material—was penetrated by fine sand grains. It was often in the summertime an alternative as to whether our meals would consist of bread, meat and flies, or bread, meat and sand. The blacks, whose greasy skin has a great attraction for the flies, do not seem to mind them, and often you will see their eyes covered with the insects which they do not even take the trouble to brush off.'

All knowledge was hard won. A matter of bush perseverance—stoicism— applied, this time in the imperial interests of science. The expedition was successful and added substantially to the store of knowledge. In zoology the record from the region profited with 398 genera (603 species) already known to science elsewhere and 171 new species, mainly beetles, spiders, reptiles and molluscs. Eight new species were added to the botanical record, with 16 other species previously unrecorded in South Australia and 112 previously unknown in arid Australia. In its particulars the expedition was a testimony to the diligence of nineteenth-century inquiry.

At the same time though—and here is living connection with our pilgrimage—it demonstrated a general truth about travel. No-one enters a strange place with an innocent eye, least of all anyone claiming to be educated. For each learned man on the Horn Expedition had a very clear idea of Nature and man's place in it. They were Darwinians, and as such preoccupied with the progressive evolution of things. A 'scientific' detachment was the order of the day, and with it went a morally charged certainty about progress in human affairs. What they wanted were specimens, particularly specimens of the archaic (the past that could explain the future), even if those specimens happened to be human beings.

The Report of the expedition came out in four volumes, with the introduction written by Austin Horn, its organiser and financier. 'The Central Australian Aborigine', Horn told educated readers of the time, is a living representative of the stone age, who still fashions his spear heads and knives from flint or sandstone and performs the most daring surgical operations with them. His origin and history are lost in the gloomy mists of the past. He has no written record, and few oral traditions. In appearance he is a naked, hirsute savage, with a type of features occasionally pronouncedly Jewish. He is by nature light footed, merry and prone to laughter, a splendid mimic, supple jointed, with an unerring hand that works in perfect unison with his eye, which is as keen as that of an eagle. He has never been known to wash. He has no private ownership of land, expect as regards that which is not over carefully concealed about his person. He cultivates nothing, but lives entirely on the spoils of the chase. He is a keen observer and knows the habits and changes of form of every variety of animal or vegetable life in his country. Religious belief he has none, but is excessively superstitious, living in constant dread of an Evil Spirit which is supposed to lurk round his camp at night. He has no gratitude except that of the anticipatory order, and is as treacherous as Judas. He has no traditions and yet continues to practice with scrupulous exactness a number of hideous customs and ceremonies which have been handed down from his fathers and of the origin or reason of which he knows nothing.

Horn predicted doom for the Aborigines, as if extinction was their natural lot.

'Thanks to the untiring efforts of the missionary and stockman, he is being rapidly "civilised" off the face of the earth, and in another hundred years the sole remaining evidence of his existence will be the fragments of flint which he has fashioned so crudely. It was for this reason that I thought it desirable to get some reliable information, supplemented by photography, of this race while there were any of them remaining in their primitive condition.'

This was Darwinism at its most imperialistic, as it is the language of colonialism. While Aborigines were a 'doomed' race and were to be helped when possible, they were first and foremost to be observed in a scientific manner. The attitude towards them is best summed up by Spencer himself, when he wrote to the eminent Sir James Frazer, the renowned historian of myths: 'Australia is the present home and refuge of creatures, often crude and quaint, that have elsewhere passed away and given place to higher forms. This applies to the Aboriginal as to the platypus and kangaroo.'

Later in his career Spencer would be a philanthropic administrator of Aboriginal policy in northern Australia. But on the Horn Expedition, as much as he needed the 'black boys' to help him gather specimens and tell him about their food supplies, individual recognition was neither desirable or possible. 'Here', he wrote in the official narrative of the expedition, 'we picked up a young black boy, who went on with us clothed with a thin hair girdle round his waist and a headband. Of all the black boys with whom we met, this youth was perhaps the most loquacious and anxious to impart information. Having been recently admitted to the privileges of manhood, there was little he did not profess to know with regard to the habits and customs of his tribe, but as such knowledge is only to be gained from the elders, his information, all the more freely volunteered because it was the result of, for a black fellow, a somewhat vivid imagination, was accepted with considerable reservations.'

The black boy's name was Tom, a fact Spencer noted in his published narrative of the report. Peter and Archie also got a mention when Spencer was recording human details for himself, as did an anecdote in the English vernacular told by Tom. But again the eminent naturalist saw no reason to fully acknowledge the social details of his dependence on the natives, whose country he was passing through and whose language he did not speak. 'Difficult to ascertain names of tribes', Spencer confessed to his diary and concentrated his attention on the 'gesture language' of the natives. 'Some had a Jewish cast of face', he added, as if to set a seal upon their full cultural possibilities.

Still, the Horn Expedition did return with an impressive public catalogue of things eaten by the natives. At the level of Nature (as distinct from Culture), here were people intelligently surviving in a place since the beginning of Time. In the fifteen pages of the Horn report you sense a kind of homage being paid to native resourcefulness. The documentation is one of the best records of its kind, and for Central Australia the most systematic tabling, if you like, of the way in which humankind connected with the physical reality of this place. But more of this later, when we get to the Rock, when we encounter the present state of 'marriage' between white European knowledge and indigenous understandings.

In his famous photographs Spencer paid Aborigines a greater homage. In the total collection, group photographs of ceremonies predominate, many of them unpublishable today because of their sacred nature. Among them are images of individuals, 'portraits' of a kind in which the handsome individuality of the Aranda people seem to glow in the Central Australian light. In the beauty of these images lie a positive valuation. (Mountford's portraits in *Brown Men and Red Sand* are part of the same dignifying tradition.) To our eye—even today—they have an aesthetic history that warms Spencer's otherwise clinical gaze. His Aranda warriors could adorn the picturebooks of Homer and Virgil, just as they would invigorate tales of 'noble savages' in the South Seas. Spencer himself expressed admiration for the muscular development of the men: 'You are continually struck with his proportions and physical carriage,' he said. Of the women, he was struck by an equal nobility of form. They are in the image of—to use the phrase of Spencer's inner-circle of male colleagues—a dusky Venus. They are not shot or murdered by the camera. They are sexual beings, and the possibility of relationship seems to lurk there, in the eye of the camera.

But to see them this way is also to lift them out of the larger cultural frame inhabited by men like Spencer. They are still-life shots done with emotional detachment and formally arranged—all the dogs were shooed away, well out of the picture. The photographer pins his subjects to the desert backdrop like any other specimen doomed to extinction. They were collected like museum pieces, and as such are a sign of photographic things to come as far as Aborigines were concerned. After Spencer, and well into this century, other men of science would come to point their cameras at the natives. University parties, mostly from Adelaide, will come to shoot all manner of clinical footage: of the native running, the native sitting and standing, the native throwing a spear, the native hunting, the native painting himself and dancing. The more secretive the ceremony the more valued the 'ethnographic' film. The logic of intrusion would know no bounds with the dying race. By the 1920s the anthropologist Norman J. Tindale would film Aborigines copulating.

Looking into the lucid images of Baldwin Spencer, so ravishingly lit, is rather like looking for too long into the glare of the Central Australian light. You gaze and gaze and a darkness looms. This is the shadow of the clinical gaze, which is devoid of relationship. In the centre of Australia, there is a long history of visitors coming not in order to meet, but to take.

The right way

—WE HAVE COME the wrong way, I said to Endo.

He looked at me suspiciously. I would come to appreciate his intelligence. He knew when I was asking too much of myself.

He smiled. —We should go back, and start again?

—We should be closer to the ground, I said.

—You are complaining again about this wonderful bus?

—I am talking about being on the ground, in the grass, belly in the sand—all the way.

He looked out the window. We were deep in a sea of dune, and almost at the resort.

Endo said, —You make things sound so uncomfortable.

—I am coming here in the manner of *kuniya*, the carpet snake.

Kuniya starts off back there in the sandhills of Paku Paku, east of Mount Conner.

—In the dune, quickly in the dunes, I murmured.

—What are you saying?

In the dunes warm belly in the dunes.
Touching the tree, stretching up to touch the tree.

Endo said, —We are almost there. Soon you will be able to lie down.

Ultjalpara. Ultjalpara.
Touching Ultjalpara.
Touching Ultjalpara till the nectar comes.

I was chanting under my breath.

—This is all your imagination? Endo asked. You are making this up?

I nodded, saying, —How could it be otherwise?

—Well that is something, Endo said. You are at least not pretending to be an Aboriginal.

Digging Ultjalpara
Digging witchetty grubs at Ultjalpara

Eating honey and grub at Ultjalpara
Eating honey and grub at Ultjalpara.

Endo said, —And so, your belly is full. You have celebrated the eating spot, like a good snake. A providing ancestor. And how far have we come with *kuniya* now?

Eggs, carrying eggs around my neck.
Eggs, carrying eggs around my neck.

—But *where* are you?

Kuniya has in fact arrived at the Rock, but I didn't want to tell that to Endo. He was in too much of a hurry. The eggs are tied around the neck by using a grass head pad, the name of which is sacred, and now can be identified by a Rock with a hole in it that can be seen at Mutitjulu waterhole. Then *kuniya* moves out into the dunes again, on the south side of the Rock, near where Bill Harney used to live. The song is sung there, the men are decorating themselves to dance. *Kuniya* dances too, or rises up the Rock face, and is tied together with another snake, in a dance of procreation. The women are wearing decorative fringes around their waists. Then *kuniya* is grinding ochre, and rubbing fat into their bodies to keep warm. The *kuniya* man is looking *kuniya* woman in the eye. More ochre, more fat over their hearts to keep them warm.

—What are you saying to yourself? Endo demanded.

—I am saying that if, even for a microsecond, we had travelled, truly got here another way, then everything would be different.

—Obviously, says Endo.

Heavy tracks

WHY AM I *delaying* our arrival? A reach back into sweeter ancient Time? Maybe. It's also a ruse, I think, a trick I keep playing on myself when I come to Central Australia.

By slowing things up you get closer to the experience of the explorers. But as we swiftly turn towards the resort, which is still out of sight in the dunes, I can hear Endo saying to me:

—You can't properly imagine what you have never experienced. You are either of a culture or you are not. Have confidence in your own. To pretend otherwise is as silly as a method actor trying to play Kabuki. You are travelling by bus. Love your bus.

—What is the present but the past brought steadily forward, an arrival as oddly shaped as a camel?

There is a great tradition of make-believe out here. For example, when Mountford came through in 1940 he was in a way simulating the explorers. Motorised vehicles were to be increasingly attractive in the 1940s, but the camel, if still more practical in the sand country, had the extra charm of being redolent with the adventurer's history of the Centre, especially on a trip that was supposed to be making a unique contact with 'the stone age' people, as the newspapers put it. When you read the contemporary reports and consult Mountford's diary, you find him going on when making contact with the Aborigines as if they are encountering whites for the first time. But this was nonsense, as Strehlow took vindictive glee in pointing out years later, when Mountford's official and honoured reputation as anthropologist and expert on the Rock became too much for him. The lives of the Aborigines had already been massively disrupted by pastoralists, police and mission stations, not to mention the stream of miners who had been coming through the country since the 1920s, and the doggers — the dingo scalp hunters — who had been part of Aboriginal life (and their introduction to the cash economy) before that. It was not simply a matter of Aboriginal lives being disrupted too, they had adjusted, as they had been doing from the start. Why, even in 1874, only four years after the Overseas Telegraph line was laid up through the Centre, Giles and Gosse met natives who knew a word or two of English!

The pace of getting to a place, the stoicism it demanded, is the measure of man out here. You have to be able to survive when you come to a halt, when the country says you have to wait before going on. This is where the bushman, the ancestral hero to the explorer, comes in. That's why no-one really puts the boots into Bill Harney. His credentials as bushman were good. Strehlow knew this and left him alone. Strehlow also knew that because he had to learn that the hard way himself, and knew how difficult it was to become a bushman. When he came back to Central Australia in 1932 he was acutely conscious of having become a 'University Man' and the object of potential scorn from the settlers. He could not ride camels. He had not been into the back country. When he lay down at night under the stars, he had nightmares of being trampled upon by bullocks. He detested the racism that seemed to go with the worst aspects of frontier survival. But he persevered, and, in a few years, after covering hundreds of miles of remote country (and biting his tongue in the face of racist outbursts), he was very pleased with himself, and thus increasingly resentful of anyone who pretended to have done as much. Maybe the harshness of the country hardens the hearts of some men, even as they pretend to travel lightly.

Back in 1935 Mountford and Strehlow had done part of their journey together by car. It's a toss up as to who was less tolerant of their slow progress. It was a matter of getting the machine though salt marsh, sandhills and mulga country. They may get three punctures on the same wheel, and in the sandy stretches, push the car to make it go. Strehlow was the kind of man who diligently recorded details. One day, near the Palmer River (which they had been towed across by Little's donkeys), they left their camp at 12.30, with the speedometer showing 66.2 miles. The pushing began at

72.3 miles (three pushes), and at
72.9
73.8
73.9
74.3

They halted at 2.10 pm. There was more pushing at

76.9
77.3
79.3 and at the 80.5 mile reading of the speedometer.

All up they had come 14.3 miles and it was 3.25 in the afternoon. 'The gear box was so hot that boiling oil and steam hissed out of it, so Percy looked at it, and the universal, and we had some tea.' Strehlow is trying very hard to make light of it all.

Mountford, on another day, merely summarises: 'By one o'clock we had been bogged four times and by half past four had only covered eleven miles having to dig out truck out of the sand seventeen times.'

Better a camel than a Chevrolet. The camels arrived for them a couple of days further on, and it was on the ships of the desert, sailing sometimes on the same ship that Mountford and Strehlow arrived at the Rock. It was to be their historic visit of 1935, one that would create its 'spell' upon Mountford forever, and which would mark in Strehlow's mind the time when Mountford's amateur 'enthusiasm' for anthropology was tolerable, before the likes of Bill Harney got to the point referring to him as 'Old Ego'. Vehicles puncture on the difficult terrain of the Centre; so do many relationships when they compete for pre-eminence in Aboriginal affairs.

In any case, for years after pushing the Chevrolet, Strehlow went by camel, including his early years as the first Patrol Officer in the region. As for Mountford, it was 1950 by the time he conceded to the motor vehicle. He went down to the Rock with a mob of Knox Grammar School boys from Sydney—unashamed tourists, all of them. The days of simulated exploration were just about over. A whole new era had begun.

Tenacious Tuitt

LEN TUITT WAS the man who consolidated road runs to the Rock. He drove Mountford and the Sydney boys on that historic tour. He met the party at the Finke, then took three days getting to the Rock, following the tracks left by Johannsen some years before, at the time of the Mark Foy Expedition. Tracks. Vehicle tracks. Tracks upon tracks. You could write the history of the Centre in terms of who followed whom in difficult country, starting with Giles who got to the Rock for the first time only to find the tracks of Gosse's dray. At the Rock the Foy vehicles came through in 1936, on their way further west. Just before Tuitt in 1949, the motor mechanic Max Cartwright went to the Rock in his Chevrolet truck. Not for tourist reasons, but as the local man for a company on the trail of Lasseter's Reef. Cartwright got bogged making tracks around the Rock—an experience of proud dismay, to judge from his account. Writing as a contemporary chronicler of the road history he also says: 'Later I was to find out that Mark Geale had taken a grader out from Curtin Springs to Ayers Rock in 1948. He had tried to follow tracks made by a couple of army trucks about six years earlier and had lifted the grader blade much of the time . . . I was also told that Stanes of Erldunda Station had taken an ex-army six-wheel drive truck from Curtin Springs to Ayers Rock and Mount Olga a year or so earlier than ourselves, with a group of Geelong Grammar School students. These deep motor tracks over the sandhills would have been made by Sid Stanes.'

In 1950, the Tuitt party stayed in the area for ten days, camping at the Maggie Springs waterhole, climbing and studying geology, and meeting the Aborigines in a way that newspapers reported as if the boys were scientific pioneers. One paper carried a photograph of 'the Arunda tribesmen mixing flour to make damper', getting both the language group wrong, and appearing to suggest that damper was indigenous tucker. Oddly, it was the art collected that was of national scientific interest, a valuation that seems to reflect Mountford's passions. More striking still was the impact their first encounter with Aborigines was said to have on the more thoughtful boys. The school's science master told the press that one boy, before the expedition, had always thought that 'the native could never be right where his ideals coincided with those of the white men'. Coming to the Rock changed that. The master said: 'Since this boy had lived near the Aborigines, studied their arts and tried to understand their outlook, he had been convinced he must do something to ensure Aborigines ensured their full rights.'

The nature of those rights were not spelt out at the time. For the industrious Len

Tuitt the trip was a great success anyway. Already famous for running the mail truck between Alice Springs and Darwin, which he'd recently extended between Tennant Creek and Mount Isa, he saw Rock tourism as the next line of expansion. He tried to interest the interstate tourist bureau in the proposal, but the idea of supporting a venture 280 miles south-west of Alice Springs that still had no regular road for the last 68 miles looked risky. Tuitt campaigned. 'Could the road at least be improved for that last section?' 'No', said the Engineer in town, 'a grader could get lost for several days in that country.'

Tuitt kept coming anyway. In the mid-1950s he brought regular groups down in VW Kombis. Nine passengers at a time. Two days to get there. The Northern Territory Administrator then said he would be granted some land for his resort if he found water and kept the area securely fenced. Little is known about what Aborigines thought of this offer of land in their reserve, or indeed of the first regular visits, as it did not much concern tourist developers at the time for years. Tuitt went after the water. He borrowed an ancient boring plant from Angas Downs Station, lugged it 120 miles over virtually virgin country and ended up 'bogged to the bloody eyeballs of a rabbit warren'. I quote here from the *Inland Review*, which wrote about Tuitt as a local hero in 1969, before the political complication of Aboriginal landrights had established itself (though it was on the horizon). Next time water was found, Tuitt equipped the bore with an air-cooled diesel engine and pump-jack, installed a 5000-gallon squatters tank with a 500-gallon ancillary tank on a stand as an overhead supply. Thus pastoral gear secured the site for tourism. Ex-Army marquees were the store and dining room. Increasingly, people came down, especially school parties in the May and September holidays. They camped in tents or they spent a night under the stars, delivering themselves, one way or the other, to the great space around the Rock. It was an adventure into 'the unknown', all too soon to be known by hundreds and then thousands of people each week.

Laughter and nectar

ARTHUR GROOM WAS the lucky one. His timing, as might be expected from a former Spitfire pilot, was fortunate. The year before Tuitt got the road in, Groom managed to journey in by camel, making one of the last 'explorer trips' to the Rock before mass tourism. In his charming book, *I Saw a Strange Land* (1950) he sketches the state of transport in 1947:

> Camels, donkeys and packhorses are now rare. Cars and trucks grind over
> hundreds of miles of rocky desert, sandy desert or fertile plain; and the average
> man's vehicle is a heavy truck ready equipped with drums of water and petrol,

and food and swag for any long, sudden journey. Many of the old camel and packhorse mail services are now replaced by Eddie Connellan's little planes, centred at Alice Springs, jumping like grasshoppers in a fortnightly service over distances from a few miles up to hundreds of miles, from station to station, Mission depot, or mining field; and many of the native watchers whose keen eyes once saw the ground mail approaching slowly, hours before its arrival, now attune their ears to the sky, and yell at the faintest distant drone of a powerful engine, 'Hareyplane come up sit down now. Gottem mail-bag for ebbrybody!

Groom was travelling for the adventure itself, he says. But he would also look at the country with a mind to the tourist of the future, and consider the fate of what he thought to be a dying race. 'I might find out what was being done to ease the passing of Australia's primitive man.' Groom's Darwinian philanthropy would have sat easily at Spencer's campfire.

The Aborigines who led him across the country and looked after his camels were hardly examples of 'a dying race'. The opposite, really. There was Tamalji, a young Pitjantjatjara man who spoke no English, whose laughter used to frighten the camels. 'I have never seen or heard any man, black or white', Groom says, 'laugh with such physical power or volume . . . His laughter rose up and up, until he seemed to reach a crisis where it could continue no longer; and then down from his amazing high guffaw with a long, drawn, dying scream of finality. It was enough to wake all the skeletons of the desert.' The other young man was Njunowa, who was the silent type, amused and watchful and always hungry. Groom detected a deep wildness in him. Both young men were always running off to chase goannas and lizards to eat and 'pappy dawg' for bushtucker and scalps for sale to government men. Then they would come back, out of the blue, to the camel train, where they would once again adjust to the white man's slow and determined progress towards the Rock. It was the unassailable vitality of their companionship that helped Groom through.

Everything depended on an older man, Tiger Tjalkalyiri.

'I'm Tige', he commenced, patting an expanding chest. 'Tjalkalyiri my name. Mr Albrecht send me—take you Ayers Rock—long way. Kings Creek we go too—right up—cross him—I know good place. Last year I take Ol' Man Thommasin an' Misser Borgell from Adelaide, and Metingeri he come, too—lazy beggar, nearly losem everybody.'

It was Tiger who knew the country like the back of his hand. Little could Groom know the important part Tiger would play in years to come, when traditional owners of the country would step forward to reclaim their land. Travelling with Groom, Tiger was content to gesture towards inhabitants all around. When they got to Kings Canyon they could see 'smokes', mostly out in the great native reserve.

'Tiger and Tamalji and Njunowa held urgent conferences and pointed excitedly to the smokes. They were trying to work out the direction of travel of those who had fired them. Tiger explained some of them: "That one—might belong to half-caste feller—maybe—go out with one camella to get puppy-dawg scalp. 'Nother one—thataway." He pointed directly south. "Maybe Ernabella men go back across desert, and walk-about little while in rocky country, spear kangaroo-euro." He then indicated a line of smokes extending for several miles. "Maybe someone come up tonight from Petermann country—maybe we see 'em."'

The excitement was connected to where they were going. They were coming into Tiger's own country. 'Tiger was proud of his childhood country and patted himself on the chest time and time again with closed fist. 'This one good country all the time. I live here—runabout—when little boy. Good country altogether. Reedy Creek we call Lilla. Bagotty Spring country we call Wynmurra. All good country. *My* country—go all the way across Lake Amadeus and Oolra and Kattatuta. I take you and show you. Tomorrow—we go cross desert? We take them ol' camella—plenty water canteen—we got good tucker—good! WE go three, maybe four, days, thataway—right up by lake country—right up Ayers Rock, we go!'

Earlier on Tiger took a long shot at a kangaroo. He was sixty yards off and saw it stumble. Then he took off from his camel and went after it on foot, disappearing into the mulga. Half an hour later he came back, done in. But here was malu, the carcass of which he tossed on the pebbles. He said, 'Got him—he go close up Oolra (Uluru). I been run—and—chase—him—and just about when I close up fall over meself, him fall over first.'

Tiger the knower of the country, Tiger the joker. Both were to make him famous among white men in the years to come. The malu was tucker for days to come. Its furry carcass was thrown into the fire that night; and the half-cooked meat cooked again the next day, and for days afterwards, carried in stinking condition so that it could be cooked again. It was never eaten before Tiger said grace. This was another aspect of the man, at least when he was conducting whitemen through the country. Tiger had been living at the Hermannsburg Mission under the strong pastoral care of Pastor F. W. Albrecht. Albrecht thought highly of Tiger when he had sent him to work for Groom; and, clearly, Tiger thought well enough of the mission and its food supply to be saying grace even when he was away from the place. One night, when the moon was up and they were in the rangers near the tree which had a big G carved into it—G for Giles, or was it Gosse?—Tiger stood up and sang a hymn. It was a strange night, says Groom, filled with awe for the country and history.

They went Tiger's way around the east end of Lake Amadeus. They encountered bog, mist, an eerie desolation. It had rained, and there was more danger than Tiger expected. All the way, Groom was bursting to get his sight of the Rock, to consolidate his sense of place by seeing as much as he can at the one time. From the Gill Range he thought he had seen it: 'a low faint-blue dome curved a little above the horizon'. Maybe. On the south side of the lake it was a great relief to reach a bare pink sandhill 'where Tiger informed me would be properly good camping place', because 'no more bad lake country now. Tomorrow we all go thataway. *Must* see Ayers Rock soon now. Two more days and we go *right* up—close. Puttem hand on him properly.'

It was days before Groom could put a hand on him properly. The best he could do the next day was climb a sand dune and see the Rock from afar. 'The unmistakable flattened dome, Oolra of the natives, pale mauve against the troubled sky.' On into the dunes. The great red waves that we now know so well from everybody else's travelling! Eventually the Rock is regularly in view. Then not. Hide and seek with the Rock, as you go up and down in the dunes. And then, on one dune summit the great vision beyond the Rock—'the ethereal blue of many domes splitting the horizon like the temples of an ancient city'.

'Kata Tjuta!' Tiger spoke excitedly.

'Mount Olga!' writes Groom. 'The elusive goal of Ernest Giles, and still seen only by few men.'

The closer Groom gets, the less pragmatic his sense of wonder.

'The boys sent up smoke signals; but no answers came back from the Rock. Its solitude was real, and there were times when I felt I was approaching the immense coloured tomb of a dead age into which I had no right to look. The solitude might have been even more impressive had it not been for the continuous bell-call of a bird which surely had beaten place and distance with its high run of notes and contralto base, ventriloquial, distant yet all about, and invisible. Tiger informed me 'That one Bunbunbililila!' and at my attempts at repetition Tamalji threw back his head and laughed aloud.'

(*Panpanpalala*, Pitjantjatjara for bellbird, today.)

Next day, they are within striking distance. And it is as if some dance of nature is taking place to welcome them. 'We got away within the hour,' says Groom with a kind of religious measure, 'our slow approach now accompanied by budgerigars, crows, finches, mulga and ringneck parrots; and a rapid increase of wildflowers on the areas where wandering natives had burnt the spinifex a year or so before, and enriched the sand with ash. One particular bush, about five to six feet high, had golden and green flowers waving up and down in the light wind, remarkably like green parrots in flight. I thought the bush was a type of banksia. Later investigation revealed that it was a type of desert Grevillea. Tamalji and Njunowa left the camels and ran from flower to flower, bending low at each bush, sucking nectar from the flowers, and passing on.'

'I felt', says Groom in awe and in ecstasy, when they finally reached the Rock, 'like an ant at the door of a cathedral.'

PART 2　At Uluru

CHAPTER 1 **Genesis**

Sitting

We are here, after the long journey, and it's hard to know what to say. The Rock is so impressive and such a surprise, even after all this travelling, all this talk, that words fail. The size is one thing. It rises up, out of the dunes like—like what, exactly? Forget the similes.

There it is.

Oolra, as Tiger Tjalkalyiri called it.

Uluru, as the sound was first written on the white man's map earlier this century (naming the place in its own right, quite apart from any person's name which would be tied to it later).

If you stand back and keep it all in view, make it an object of contemplation and wonder, there might be something new to say about it.

Stand then, out in the plains, and see what happens.

Say: 'I will wait out there for a few hours, a day, perhaps. Maybe two. A week might give silence a chance.'

Then move in. As you approach, the silence grows again, the great weight of the Rock's silence increases as you cross the dunes. It *is* approachable, this warm-ochre creation, with its roots deep in the earth, once you adjust to its size. But when you reach its cliffs, words begin to fail again. It towers above the earth, disappearing into the sky. On the ground it curves away in giant strides. After everything, it is now too much of a presence to take in. Too big to be seen as a unit, as Groom said.

At its base stones that were mere stones from afar are boulders. Their gingerbread warmth is tinged with grey. What was smooth is roughly textured, great salty flakes. No, not salty. Leathery, bone-dry leather, a great hide dried out a long time ago. The skin of the Rock is peeling: all around it has lost its scales. Its body has cracked in some places. There are wounds. Up where you have to crane to see, the whole flank is a slope of glowing wellbeing.

Leather. Skin. Scales.

What am I *making* of this Rock?

Do something!

What can I do?

Sit down. Find a rock to sit on.

It is good sitting. Feeling beneath you the connection with the larger whole. Sit quietly now. Let the day pass.

Night falls. The shadow of the Rock presses over you and then, for the duration of the night, you are as dark as the Rock. Morning comes, and you are, astonishingly, still there. The Rock's night has not crushed you into the earth. And the rays of dawn, as they strike the drum of the Rock, are gentle, as sweet as a bellbird. Soon midday comes and it is as solid as the Rock. Sunset is all salt and rawhide. You are still there when night comes again, though the words are not there. The Rock is as severe as Time itself. It will be a long wait, a good wait, what some monks call a good sit before you are inside yourself braced enough to speak truly of the Rock. Give it a year . . .

Do something.

What?

Climb it.

Who said that?

Climb it!

Who is speaking now?

A little breeze has come up. Does it belong to the Rock or to the trees that flourish close to its breathing side? They say that the wind up there can be ferocious, and the ridge of the climb is treacherous, as if, in the erratic scoops and creases up there are microclimates, as local and unexpected as anything in the mountains. I can see a kestrel. It's hovering at the end of a deep fold opening to the sky, and is as composed as the cloud above it. Why not go on up? How much longer must I be grounded here, speechless since my arrival at the base of this Rock?

—Let me go now, I say to the wall of the Rock. Let me leave the footsteps of your side, which so exposes my restlessness. I don't want to climb, not really. Let me come into your cave. Let me wait there.

—Where?

—Into that cavity; see, the mouth is open. The lips of the cave are welcomingly wide.

—No.

—No what?

—An open mouth is no sign of anything. If it's a smile, it is not your smile. A yawning cavity, a wound.

—It is calling me in.

—What do you want to do there?

—Sit.

—What else?

—Look out.

—What at?

—Everything?

—No-one can see everything.

—I want to come into the cave to sleep.

—You must find your own place to sleep.

The moment I saw it, I thought: if I sleep in this cave long enough, inside the Rock, I will, in my speechlessness know where my place is.

All around the Rock there are places that draw you in, but you can't enter. This is a practical world, as well as a place of spirit. This is a world where, as you walk quietly around the Rock, there are caves that you can go under, if not in. They are peculiar, not of the live red earth. On the inside curl of the cave the walls are grey. The colour of sleep? The colour, in so far as colour has substance, is the interior of the Rock when it has not shown itself to the sun. The warmth is gone, it is cool as evening in the fold of this grey wave. What, then, is the Rock's true colour—ochre or grey?

You go in and out of the wave caves, and as you pass around the Rock, walking on feet as yet uncracked, at a pace that the Rock commands, you realise how lucky you are to have arrived at a time when you have choices. You don't have to answer in terms of matter or spirit, no more than you have to say to yourself, after a time, that the Rock is not really that big (or small), or old (or young), or familiar (or alien), or theirs (not ours), but a place that you have come to that belongs to the eternity of metamorphosis.

Climbing

THERE THEY GO, up the Rock, human beings in the first instance, and after they go over the first hump, but before the safety cable, bodies diminish in size to become the

Oriental single file. *Minga*, say Anangu, about the climbers. Ants. All tourists are *minga*, crawling everywhere.

They crawl up the Rock hour after hour. They come back down, less of a crawl for some—a stagger, a reel, a tottering return or a strut. Oh the hard work of tourist compulsions! Conformism is the same the world over: members of a mass incessantly deluding themselves that they are rugged little individuals. You see some people making light work of it, they have their jogging shorts on and the best running shoes and up they go in their performance gear as if they are in a soft-drink ad. These types love being interviewed when they return, although you can see from their empty eyes that all they have done is added something extra to the standing record at aerobics class. The Rock as vanity's training circuit.

There are, though, *less likely people* taking it slowly. Some of them are quite old, people who normally confine their exercise to the golf course or bowling green. They strain for the first few metres, surprised at the rough surface and are flushed by the time they reach Chicken Rock, the first of the testing stages a little way up. The more foolhardy go on, even though their lungs are heaving and their hearts may at any minute burst. It is the heartfeltness that is culturally expressive: the drive to 'triumph by climbing' or to 'mark the place as theirs', after having come all this way. The late-middle-aged Australian men are especially wilful, as if their life has been dormant and elsewhere for so long that this climb in the Centre might revive it. Ageing wives follow on, the men are not be trusted to do such a thing alone. Hindu custom encourages the elderly man to go off and find his way spiritually. Is this the place for Western culture's questing ones? The strain is profound, the agony of some, final.

Since 1968, when the mass tourism made the count of mishaps worthwhile, 25 people have died from some kind of mishap or other while climbing the Rock. If they do not perish from over-exertion, they fall to their deaths. Others fall anyway, breaking legs and ankles. Month after month, people have to be rescued, many of them because they have come all the way without learning or allowing themselves to be told about the physical realities; that the climb is not only steep and arduous; that the sun and wind, and exposure to heat and cold, are matters to be guarded against, dangers to be treated with respect.

Some of those who have paid the final price for their pilgrimage have been commemorated at the base of the climb. Of the five plaques embedded in the Rock, the one that speaks to me most honours a man called Arthur Thwaites of New South Wales, 'who died on top of this rock on 15 June 1972 aged 63 years. The climbing of Ayers Rock was one of his life-long ambitions'.

How can we not celebrate an old man who died having achieved his life-long

Mishaps at the Rock from Ranger's log, January–December 1990.

DATE	NATURE OF CALL	RESCUE	TIME	AGE	NATIONALITY	CLIMBED ROCK
02/01/90	Heat stress		10.00	9	Australian	No
07/01/90	Cardiac	R	10.53	43	Australian	Yes
10/01/90	Cardiac Collapse	R	08.05	75	German	Yes
13/01/90	Abrasions—fall		09.10	38	Australian	Yes
13/01/90	Dehydration	R	09.10	23	Japanese	Yes
26/01/90	R arm—Fractured	R	09.50	50	German	Yes
03/02/90	Collapse Arrest*	R	07.43	79	Austrian	Yes
14/03/90	Heat stress		14.30	58	Australian	No
02/04/90	Leg—Fractured	R	09.50	26	American	Yes
29/04/90	Ruptured tendons L lower leg	R	09.10	57	Australian	Yes
05/05/90	Collapse		07.49	55	American	Yes
09/05/90	Leg injury	R	09.15	55	Australian	Yes
17/05/90	Leg injury	R	11.30	38	Australian	Yes
22/05/90	Hyperventilation	R	10.55	13	Australian	Yes
30/05/90	Deyhydration		13.00	16	Japanese	No
11/06/90	Collapse—Arrest*	R	12.55	72	Australian	Yes
25/06/90	Dizzy and faint	R	12.11	14	Australian	Yes
26/07/90	Dizzy and faint	R	16.45	48	Australian	Yes
04/08/90	Multi abrasions		15.00	28	Australian	Olgas
07/08/90	Collapse	R	11.00	52	Australian	Yes
29/08/90	Collapse	R	12.27	25	Australian	Yes
03/09/90	R Arm—Fractured		09.40	67	Australian	Yes
12/09/90	Collapse	R	11.24	66	Australian	Yes
14/09/90	Collapse—Arrest*	R	09.25	69	Australian	Yes
15/09/90	Collapse		09.50	83	Australian	Yes
15/09/90	Skull—Fractured	R	10.20	15	Australian	Yes
19/09/90	Dehydration	R	10.38	23	Australian	Yes
28/09/90	Skull—Fractured	R	10.48	12	Australian	Yes
03/10/90	Abdominal pain		08.00	23	Japan	Yes
11/10/90	Heat stress		11.10	93	Australian	No
09/10/90	Dehydration		17.50	16	Australian	Kings Canyo
09/10/90	Dehydration		17.50	16	Australian	"
09/10/90	Dehydration		17.50	17	Australian	"
09/10/90	Dehydration		17.50	16	Australian	"
03/11/90	Heat stress		14.00	61	Australian	No
03/11/90	Dehydration		17.00	29	German	Olgas
17/11/90	Dehydration		11.15	48	Japanese	Yes
30/11/90	Heat stress		11.00	50	Austrian	Olgas

goal? He died on *top* of the Rock. What harm did he do by this act of wilfulness? None, his epitaph seems to say, quietly oblivious to the answer history is giving to the question.

Anangu are quite clear about the climb. They prefer people not to do it. They argue with increasing urgency that there are better things to do, as indeed there are, which I hope to indicate in the course of this book, although I will confess to having climbed the Rock myself. There is a time for everything once if you mean no offence, which is why people will keep climbing the Rock for a long time to come. It will also be something that deeply troubles Anangu. For one thing, because people have come on to Anangu land, they feel directly responsible for the visitors' welfare; for accidents or deaths. When deaths have occurred, Anangu have gone into mourning. While they would not have met the deceased, the fate of the deceased near their sacred places resonates in Anangu. Anangu do not put up plaques, but they have helped erect the signs discouraging the climb.

Although the signs do not say this, the route of the climb is sacred. It is the route taken by the *mala*, or hare-wallaby men, when they carry their ceremonial pole to the top of the Rock. We will hear more about the *mala* later, the most public of the myth cycles at the Rock. Suffice to say here that the *minga* is crawling along a path of important religious business: as pride in ownership has been growing since the 1985 Handback, the visitor today is allowed to climb the Rock due to the courtesy of the traditional owners. The least *minga* can do, Anangu say, is take proper care of themselves (think of their families, think of the lives of the rescue team) as they exercise their privilege of climbing in the footsteps of the ancestor beings. It's as if to say (though this is me speaking): 'If you whitefellas insist on planting your ceremonial poles on top of the Rock, please pay more respect.'

When Mountford came in 1940 he found that 'the earliest record was that of W. McKinnon, who noted that he had taken away a match-box left behind by Alan Breadon of Henbury Station many years previously. There were also the names of some members of the McKay party, *all* the members of the Foy party, and of others who sought, but did not expect to find, the fictitious Lasseter's reef.' Breadon owned Henbury Station in the 1920s. The McKay party, which was the first aeronautical mapping expedition to the Centre, stopped at the Rock on the way to the Petermann and Warburton Ranges in 1930. The Foy party came though in 1936. W. McKinnon, who concerns our story of the Rock intimately, was the district policeman. A rugged bushman, he climbed the Rock more than once, and his spirit, as we shall see, casts its shadow here.

'I added my name to that illustrious throng,' says Mountford. 'On the highest point of the Rock some previous visitor had built a low cairn of stones around a glass screw-topped bottle, in which were the names of people, who in recent years had climbed Ayers Rock, and I'm afraid, many who had not.'

It is a nice idea: a list of people who have *not* climbed the Rock. Even by default, it is possible to do the right thing. When in doubt, don't climb, go for a walk around the Rock, take some consolation in the fact that some up there might be naming you. After all, the friendliest T-shirt on sale in the Park is the one that says: *'I did not climb the Rock'*. It goes with the one that says: 'Welcome to Aboriginal Land'.

We might ponder what is involved if we do the climb without the welcome, and not even care whether one is an intruder or not. Again, C. P. Mountford is an instructive example, with his penchant for explorer conceits, and his determination to get Aborigines to do what he wanted. He did the climb with Matinya one bitter morning, as icy wind raced around the Rock. It was so cold that Matinya carried a fire stick and he would light spinifex bushes and stand beside them to warm himself when walking from the camp to the Rock. Mountford was driven by, among other things, the need to see Uluru Rockhole at the summit, the place where the carpet snakes made their first night camp. According to the Aborigines from the east, west and south, it was also where the gigantic, multicoloured *wanampi* lived beneath the surface.

'One the bare surface of the Rock', says Mountford's biographer, 'where it is easy to lose one's nerve from the sense of exposure even on a calm day, the gale was frightening. The terrific wind pressure seemed to buffet the very energy from their bodies. On the crest of the steepest saddle, Matinya shouted that he was afraid that the wind would blow him over the edge. Beyond was space, with the earth hundreds of feet sheer below. Mountford says he was almost inclined to agree with Matinya, but he was on his mettle as a white man, and shouted, "Get on quick, fella."

'A little further on they found partial shelter from the gale in shallow depressions, where they could bow down. "There we rested," Mountford says, "the primitive man and I, each fearful of the dangers around, but each moved by a vastly different impulse—mine, that strange desire belonging to my kind, to discover the unknown; his, not so clear, perhaps a sense of duty as a host to me, his guest. Why else should he have faced such danger?"'

They came down in the afternoon. Mountford was impressed by the surprisingly bare summit with its deep gutters running south-east–north-east, which, as Matinya explained, were the tracks of the carpet snakes as they travelled to Uluru in ancient times. 'In actual fact', Mountford feels compelled to say, 'the gutters were caused by differential weathering of the vertical rock strata.'

Back on the ground they had a meal, and made more intrusions. They went into 'one of the curious cylindrical caves, associated with the initiation ceremonies of the Marsupial Rats [as Mountford mistakenly called *mala*], in which I had seen some paintings on my previous visit. Extending along the back wall, up to about the height of one's elbow, was a dark brown band of human blood which had been poured out from the arms of the men during the secret rituals, and above that band were the primitive paintings of the Pitjendadjara tribesmen.'

When they were in the *mala* cave Mountford had an idea. He had some red ochre with him. What if one of his Aboriginal escorts did a painting so that the primitive technique was fully displayed? Mountford had tried the suggestion a couple of days earlier, and both Matinya and his companion Moanya had demurred: it would use up too much of the valuable ochre, they said. But now the big government man (as he once described himself to them), had *his* ochre. Mountford put the question to them again.

Moanya obliged. He mixed the paints, and with his forefinger drew his fig tree ancestor from the Musgrave Ranges. At the time this delighted Mountford, and in his story of the event, where once again his will had triumphed over Aboriginal discretions, he uses the occasion to essay upon primitive art, telling us that paintings at the Rock were done for their own sake rather than to gain magical control over the elements. That may well be, one thinks, reading Mountford today, but at the time, magic was close to hand. At dusk that day, the children came to camp in an uproar. They had seen fresh blood on the floor of a cave. Everyone knew it was the mark of *kadaitcha*, the invisible spirit that avenges the breaking of the Law. When he hears the wanted person, he cuts his body and allows the blood to flow on to the rock surface.

Moanya knew that the blood was a sign for him, since he had painted in the cave without the owner's permission. From the white camp he borrowed a rifle (no cartridges), knowing that a rifle would keep *kadaitcha* away. That evening the Aboriginal people gathered around the blazing white-fella fire, 'for we had many "cleva" things, and so no *kadaitcha* man would dare come near the place', says Mountford. That night the people had to go back to their camps. It was a miserable night for them, bitterly cold wind raged around the Rock and they were afraid to stoke their fires lest they expose themselves to unseen danger.

Next morning the white man who had created all the trouble was relieved. No-one in the camp thought they had been boned. The children, when they were taken to the cave, could find no blood. Nor could Matinya, even though he said he had seen four drops the night before. Here is Mountford in a final act of duplicitous paternalism: 'Then every man assured every other man he knew that the youngsters had made a mistake—they did not say anything about Matinya—and that they, personally, were not afraid. Tjundaga told me several times on our way back to camp that "They (the aborigines) couldn't put the wind up him." But we were careful not to ask him why, on the previous evening, his camp-fire was as small as that of any other native, or why, at that moment, he was carrying a rifle.'

Walking

IT IS ESSENTIAL to experience the Rock for yourself. You have, after all, come all this way as a member of your own culture, and, sympathetic though you may be to the world of the traditional owners, it is through your eyes, not theirs, that you must first encounter the place. Take it slowly. Be prepeared to be in turns exhilarated, awed, bored and puzzled by the Rock's presence. One other thing: leave your camera at home, and walk alone. Take water and something to eat. If you don't organise yourself, others will over-organise you. Before you know it, before you have felt or learnt anything about being there, the visit will be over. You would have sheepishly followed a party along one or two paths; you may have climbed the Rock, and got back down safely again; but you would not have created the circumstances for anything but the tourist experience you knew about, more or less, before you left home.

Ideally, you should walk around the whole Rock. A circumnavigation is surely as much an accomplishment as the climb. It will take you two or four hours, depending on your pace and number of stops. After one circumnavigation, don't expect to have gained a great deal. In my experience, after one walk around, many details have blurred by the time you get back to your starting spot. Come back the next day and go around again. There is nothing like the pleasure of reacquaintanceship. It's on the second walk that things start to sing. If the Rock is a great chord in the landscape, what you are seeking are interludes of melody you might make your own.

When I don't have the time to walk right around there are two sections of the track I gravitate to, the better to commune with aspects which never fail to surprise me.

The first starts on the east side of Mutitjulu and continues to the far end of the Rock where it turns around to become the north. From this road this is the section where the body of the 'whale' slopes most curvaciously into the sand. This section arouses in me the deepest feelings of kinship between the Rock as an inanimate object and the ancient life of the sea. The shadows along this face are akin to the darkening light that is beneath the sea. It seems to me as you walk along it, that you are closer to the curves and runs of waves; the Rock does not tower so awesomely above you as it does in other parts. It is also the section of track that most invites you to go further into the Rock. If the track permits, you can follow it up to some small waterholes fed by the 'rolling waves above'. But to put this another way—leaving the sea behind. This stretch is the greenest, darkest, and probably most unexplored part of the Rock. There seem to be hidden valleys to your left (even if you do not go up them); in summer there is a delicious respite from the morning sun; in winter, a natural gloom, a reminder that the Centre is not all arc lit, that there are nooks and crannies, places still unknown. If he'd stayed long enough, I can imagine Giles going along the south side looking for a glen to name. To get to know it fully, you would have to camp there at night, and experience the double dark of the Rock once its sun has gone.

But you cannot, as the days of camping by the Rock are over. Be happy that you have sensed something of the south side.

My other favourite part of the track is along the north face, starting at the eastern corner (where you may be already, if you have come along the south side). If you are there before dawn, the sun will come up behind you. I've come to believe this spot is the most welcoming at the Rock. It's where the Rock narrows to its smallest diameter and the boulders seem almost communicative as they start to glow. By the time they catch the full morning light, the north face is a cliff, and you have come far enough to see that everything here has a processional grandeur. You would have seen an aspect of this at a distance from the road. All along the north face a drama of cuts and gashes is being played out, including the great honeycomb shape in the upper reaches near the skyline. From the track, where everything happens at eye level, the step-by-step magnitude and measure of everything makes its mark. You round a tree, and the rock ahead of you seems to make an announcement. You pass by it and see that other brother rocks have gathered by the cliff to say more. And there, behind them is a cavity that seems, in a way, to make more 'sense' of things. It's hard to know why, but the further you go on, an orchestration of rock, wood, earth seems to be happening, with rock the ground of your total awareness of things. What a wall it is. What a rampart you are on! You have started off on the rock apron that seems to be the Rock bursting up from beneath the earth. How far does the Rock go down? You have skirted boulders that seem to have been chiselled from the great face: when, how? At what rate is this whole side of the Rock, exposed as it is to ferocious heat and prevailing winds, peeling off?

Then you come to greener places, ironically, the driest part of the Rock. They are green enough to make a canopy of the trees, which means that technically, naturalists will call them a forest. Yes, a forest at the Rock. A wind has come up. It blows into your face—gusty, cold—even on this spring morning. The wind has come all across the western desert to arrive here in sharp eddies, exacerbated, you feel, by the presence of the Rock. I say spring because the trees along the path are green, the daisies in bloom. At the base, a microclimate created by wind, rain and run-off creates plentiful growth, abundant animal life.

There is a place on the north face where you can walk in and sit by water. Cascades of water from the top have scalloped into a beautiful basin. Looking up from the exquisite pool you see the sky in the saddle. In the middle of the pool the water is crystal-clear, the edges moss green. There are footprints all around the pool. Birds, Euro tracks, dingo paws. A dragonfly cruises at the edge. A lizard track on the slippery verge leads the eye to a rock ledge, where a lizard—no, a goanna—sits, its neck aslant.

You can sit in a place like this for an hour, and be as bronzed and still as a goanna. This is the place to stop the rush of your life. Rock as haven. Rock as sanctuary.

Nearby there is a small cave—a rock ledge really, that you can sit in. On the wall are some paintings—simple and relatively uninteresting, because you find yourself turning your back on them and looking outwards over the plain. You are looking in the direction of the MacDonnell Ranges, but you would need to be higher up to see them. You are high enough to see the green woodlands merge into the greys of the spinifex horizon, where the country gives way to the dunes. Undulations. Rock as vantage point. Rock as lookout.

The Euros love the caves and further along, towards the end of the north face is their favourite place, an enormous gash that runs sideways along the base of the Rock. Even from the road it is an arresting cavity: full lips, the wetness of rock, voluptuous darkness within. On foot, the pull of the place is palpable, and it is not surprising to find as you approach that it is cordoned off and labelled a sacred site for women. Awe. Reverence. The Rock as Mother Place?

Keep going. Walk around the fence that protects the Women's Cave and carry on towards the north-west corner of the Rock. Right at the end is a remarkable vertical slab almost separated from the Rock. You can see the sky through it, but it is fixed there like a pole or the femur, bone on bone, rock on rock. It demands that you stop, not only because the path now changes direction, and this corner creates a double vista of the country, but also because the body of the Rock seems to have changed position. After the drama of the north face, here you have a change of tune to the west. But the striking 'pole' has made an impression, and it seems such an obvious thing to feel that this is a natural place for ceremony, for some kind of men's business.

The point is, by the time you have done your own walking around the Rock the natural features seem to elicit the most natural of questions: do the shapes you see have any kinship with the Aboriginal view of the Rock? You do not want to impose your imagination upon their Rock, any more than the Dreaming, the Tjukurpa, would presume to erase the impressions you have just made. But the walk puts a lovely question into the air: to what extent do the two cultures meet at the Rock?

Time now to go to the Ranger's station where you can obtain a splendid little booklet designed to introduce you to the Tjukurpa, to Uluru as distinct from the Rock. It's called *An Insight into Uluru*, it will cost you a dollar and it's worth its weight in gold. It is a guide to the Mala (or hare wallaby) Walk, and the walk into the Mutitjulu waterhole, the place once called Maggie Springs, which is quite simply one of the great valleys of Australia. Once you have done that walk in the Mutitjulu valley, where the great battle of the snakes was enacted during creation, the Rock becomes Uluru, and part of you will never be the same. The Mala Walk, which is in a different key, and profoundly transformative in other ways, starts at the base of the climb and goes around the Rock to Kantju Gorge.

Only after you have taken these tracks in the right way, with the right company— will your walking mean business, your encounter with Anangu, begun.

101

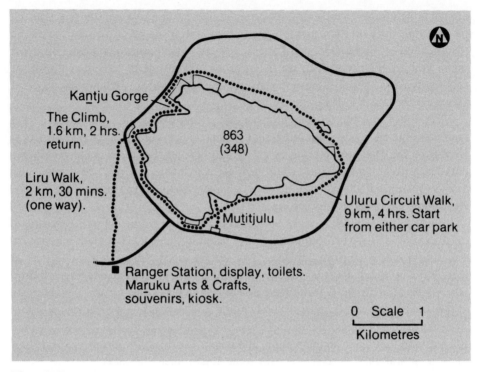

Kantju Gorge

The Climb,
1.6 km, 2 hrs.
return.

Liru Walk,
2 km, 30 mins.
(one way).

863
(348)

Mutitjulu

Uluru Circuit Walk,
9 km, 4 hrs. Start
from either car park

■ Ranger Station, display, toilets.
Maruku Arts & Crafts,
souvenirs, kiosk.

0 Scale 1
Kilometres

Uluru Walking Tracks.

A story remade

MY FIRST VISIT to the Rock was a flying one: an overnight stay, and then the climb.
What I have been saying so far assumes a kind of innocence about the Rock, the better
to see it anew, which is easier said than done. Innocence is a rare commodity in Central
Australia. Too much is known: experience of all kinds is well worn, and so much
experience, as well as incident, seems designed to engorge itself, like a python on its
own tail. Three years later I came back feeling I had developed some connections with
Aboriginal presence (hadn't I been 'initiated' by that malu hunt?). I told this to Tony
Tjamiwa, and I asked him if he knew Ilyatjari.

—He's my brother, said Tjamiwa.

—Is that right? Terrific!

Tjamiwa is, as a custodian of the mala story, one of the traditional owners of the
Rock. Even as I write this, I realise that what I was most hoping for at that meeting
was a walk at the Rock with Tjamiwa, with him telling me that story, trusting me with

102

some of the Tjukurpa. No such luck: I didn't ask because I was too shy, and I am still finding it so awkward that I am not sure whether I could ask. Besides, this was in a way a political encounter: as a senior man of the Mutitjulu community he is frequently a spokesman for the Park. He is a veteran of the 1970s landrights campaigns in South Australia, as well as the land claim for Uluru and Kata Tjuta.

I first met him at Mutitjulu in 1991, at the house of Jon Willis, the Community Liaison Officer. He entered the kitchen wearing a T-shirt splattered with blood. He'd just come back from a kangaroo hunt. Before coming to the table, he washed his face and hands in the bathroom, leaving the red desert sand all around the basin. Willis asked, signalling, about his ears.

—*Uwa*, said Tjamiwa. Yes.

Only after the young white man tenderly put some drops into the old Aboriginal's ears were we ready to begin.

Tjamiwa is a barrel-chested man, with strong hands that move across the table as he talks, picking up the salt shaker, the soda-water bottle, a spoon to make his point. (A gifted rhetorician, Willis had told me.)

We are talking about the legends of the Rock, and how tourists come to them. How the Handback of the Rock to Anangu led to a retelling of the stories and recording them down more accurately. It was then that Tjamiwa made his big statement.

—Bill Harney, Tjamiwa says, had it all wrong.

—In the old days, we didn't have Government rules because the grandfathers and grandmothers were all here looking after it. It was all spoilt by Bill Harney coming along and seeing it and saying: 'what a great Rock'. Bill Harney came here for the government and looked at this place. Bill Harney rode in a motor car. He came here and thought, 'My place'.

Tjamiwa says that Harney got their stories wrong. Not only that, he was careless with secrets (which makes it impossible today to say which stories were wrong).

—He never knew anything, he didn't say anything. He was never capable, he was just a child. He was not an adult, he was a bit of monster, an evil spirit.

Tjamiwa is speaking of the white man as the Other. In so doing he is mirroring the classic European response to difference when that difference is felt as a threat: he is categorising the other as inferior—a child, a primitive in human understanding.

Tjamiwa reads Pitjantjatjara but little English. I wondered how much of the Harney book he knows, and the full implications of what he is saying for white cultural history. For here we have Harney, the kindly, venerable, uncommonly decent chronicler of Australian bushlife accused of disrespect, carelessness, irresponsibility and dishonesty. We all know the bushman is a liar, that's part of the Australian tradition; but to say that the most self-conscious of bushmen, the bloke who did so much to keep the bush legend nationally alive with his stories of Northern and Central Australia, to say that he *wrote the bullshit down*—that's another matter. Tjamiwa, by saying this to a writer and using all the rhetorical skills in his command, seemed to be telling me: go and write this down. *Fix up the story.*

Later on we go into the Ayers Rock Resort (then Yulara) together. He had a meeting at the multi-million dollar corporation headquarters. He had changed out of his T-shirt for the meeting in favour of the monogrammed shirt of the park ranger. He kept his beanie on. It was an odd sight, seeing him wait in the foyer, flipping through a *Business Review Weekly* before disappearing into the inner sanctum of the corporate culture. I didn't ask him about the meeting, but I understand one matter at issue was the decision the resort had just taken to drop the name 'Yulara' in favour of the 'Ayers Rock Resort'. Yulara, which is Pitjantjatjara for 'howling' had been used with Anangu's blessing. It was offensive to drop it just like that. I didn't have to ask Tjamiwa about that because, as usual, he decided what he wanted to talk to me about.

We are having coffee at the Outback Pioneer Lodge, which was then called The Red Centre Motel. There are paintings on the walls. Tjamiwa is agitated and speaking in his language. He has his back to the paintings, but you can tell he is referring to them without wanting to look at them.

They are big, crudely drawn kangaroos, childish cartoons in the manner of the McDonald's icon. One big kangaroo has fallen off its bike, with Uluru in the background. The caption reads: 'Which way to the Rock?'

—They shouldn't make paintings about the Rock like that, Tjamiwa is saying.

—It makes it look silly, that's not a real animal, it makes it look stupid.

The depth of the offence is clear as he goes on. He is speaking of his own blood, the ancestral bond to the place. He has his head down: they are not to be looked at, these images of profound insult.

I felt embarrassed and ashamed on behalf of my culture until he looked up.

—You, he says, are leading your boy in the right way.

He points to Joe, my fourteen-year-old son visiting the Centre for the first time.

—You are teaching him the right way. That's how we teach. And if you don't teach him he won't be able to train you.

This in Pitjantjatjara, which neither Joe nor I speak. But I am moved and flattered to be addressed thus. This seems to be real contact, at last, with Aboriginal life, much better than book knowledge. And what better way than meeting on universal matters of pedagogy: the care of the young, the rearing of our boys.

I say thank you. I boast—Next time we come we'll be able to speak your language. We are starting lessons.

—You'll have to learn it all over again, when you come back here, said Tjamiwa.—You have to learn with us.

I wanted to confess to Tjamiwa that the first time I came to the Rock, I felt a great need to climb it, and had done so, as Joe had done so only a couple of days before. If I'd said that and Tjamiwa had objected, I'd have ventured the rather lame defence that as white visitors wanting to get the feel of the whole place we perhaps had a right to climb it once, and once only. If I'd only known at the time, I might have told him about a Japanese saying about Mount Fuji. 'A wise man climbs Mount Fuji once. He who climbs it twice is a fool.'

Old egos

IT'S A PECULIAR THING to come all this way with the wrong book. Or books. For the next couple of visits I took Tjamiwa on his word. When I opened Bill Harney's *To Ayers Rock and Beyond*, I felt strangely guilty, as well as curious about what was right and what was wrong. How to correct the old bushman's mistakes? The difficulty here was profound. To correct a mistake you have to name it; and then, ideally, put the accurate story in its place. But what if the very act of recording the mistake is the offence, and the correction of the mistake a greater one, if it involves telling more of a story that should be secret? Catch-22, as far as white culture goes.

Harney put his book out in 1963, the same year as Mountford. With Harney you have a yarning, anecdotal account—a kind of ramble around the sacred sites of the Rock. Harney's unstoppable voice runs through it. With Mountford you have something else displayed: his dozens of photographs of the sites are the book's foundation, and the nervous flutter of the camera lens sets the tone to which the the 'legends' tend to be subsidiary. The books fundamentally overlap and probably resulted from some cross-fertilisation well before both men were at the Rock. In 1948 Mountford had received wide publicity for his expedition to Melville Island, where he collected legends and artwork. His guide and general handyman—the practical bushman—on that trip was Bill Harney, who knew the Top End. They became friends, and seem to have remained friends until the late 1950s, when Harney was the first ranger at the Rock, and Mountford came to follow up his research. Mountford had a considerable reputation by then, and Harney called him Old Ego. No-one needed to call Harney that; he was the kind of man who wore his untrained knowledge easily.

Crudely speaking, the books agree on the main Tjukurpa stories at the Rock. Mountford gave readers a charming colour plate of the totemic creatures. They are simply set down:

Liru, The Venomous Snake,
Kunia, The Carpet Snake,

TOTEMIC CREATURES OF AYERS ROCK

A. The Venomous Snake, Liru. B. The Carpet Snake, Kunia. C. The Hare Wallaby, Mala. D. The Spirit Dingo, Kulpunya. E. The Kingfisher Woman, Lunba. F. The Sleepy Lizard, Meta-lun-gana. G. The Sand Lizard, Linga. H. The Marsupial Mole, Itjari-tjari. J. The Willy-wagtail, Tjinderi-tjinderiba.

Mala, The Hare Wallaby,
Kulpunya, The Spirit Dingo,
Lunba, The Kingfisher Woman,
Meta-lungana, The Sleepy Lizard,
Linga, The Sand Lizard,
Itjari-tjari, The Marsupial Mole,
Tjinderi-tjinderiba, The Willy-Wagtail.

I am fond of this illustration because, despite the simplicity of the images (a cut above the cartoons that so offended Tjamiwa), it quietly places each creature in its real physical setting: you look at it and think, 'Yes, this is where such animals live, the Rock is their home.' There is nothing like a concrete image with which to begin a good story. Mountford grounds us at the start: we see what the creatures look like on today's earth, the better to imagine them in the landscape of the Tjukurpa. Having said that, however, Mountford's general outline of the Dreaming leaves something to be desired. Under the heading 'The Universe of the Pitjandjara' he wrote:

> The Pitjandjara believe that their world is flat, and so limited in area that if they travelled to the horizon, which to them is the edge of the universe, they would be in danger of falling into limitless space. The Pitjandjara universe has two levels, the earth, *puna*, the home of the aboriginal men and women, and the celestial world, *ilkari*, in which reside the people of the sky, many of whom once lived on earth during *tjukurapa* times. In this sky world, there is an abundance of food, shelter and water.
>
> In the beginning, that is, before there was any life in the universe, the world was a flat featureless plain extending to the horizon, unbroken by a mountain range, watercourse, or any major topographical feature. Then, at some period in the long-distant past known to the Pitjandjara as *tjukurapa* times, giant semi-human beings, resembling one or another of the creatures in appearance, but behaving like human beings, rose out of the featureless plain where for countless ages they had been slumbering, and started to wander in criss-cross routes over the countryside. And, as they wandered, these mythical people behaved in the same manner as the aborigines of today: made fire, dug for water, performed ceremonies, fought each other, and so on. During the whole of this period, the earth remained flat and more or less featureless. When, mysteriously, *tjukurapa* times came to an end, at every place where one or another of the heroes had performed any task, a mountain range, an isolated hill, a valley, a watercourse,

Mountford's Dreaming creatures for Ayers Rock, 1964.

or some other natural feature was created. The bodies, too, of the *tjukurapa* men and women were often transformed into isolated boulders or piles of rocks.

When the aborigines were asked what brought about this remarkable change, they said they did not know, but felt sure that some wise old men of an earlier generation could have told me. Since these old men had not passed their knowledge on to the succeeding generations, there was no one today who could answer my question.

Today, Mountford's comment on the absence of 'wise old men of an earlier generation' is odd. It is wise older men who, among others, own the Rock, and now speak for it. Tjamiwa never sounded off to me about Mountford, but I understand from Jon Willis that he might well have: the white man who presumes in the way Mountford seems to have done is offensive. At least you don't get any of this in Harney. Throughout *To Ayers Rock and Beyond* the reader retains a sense of the Tjukurpa still being alive. It's as if the vitality of Harney's speaking voice helps things along: his yarn-spinning, and his attitude that was so generally respectful of Aboriginal culture is a boon. In terms of Harney's heart being in the right place, I wonder what Tjamiwa thinks about Harney loving an Aboriginal woman well enough to have married her.

Back to the Rock story. Harney doesn't go in for any sweeping statements about the Tjukurpa. With his lack of formal education, it might have been pretentious for him to try. The Rock that we come to see in Harney's eyes is a series of momentous incidents strung together according to his sense of unifying 'philosophy'. He also says in various ways (and at various times in other publications) that the Rock (overall) was a 'living symbol to the tribes people and a place of food and water, but it was never secret or taboo'. This was his 1957 talk to the 'Bread and Cheese Club', and one can imagine it putting some people at ease. In addition, he said, 'The Rock was uninhabited by the people who so valued it: they had not been there for fifty years.' In other words; his claim to knowledge was privileged and perhaps definitive!

Harney provided his readers with a detailed map. Starting at the 'Climb', he took travellers around the Rock in a clockwise direction, followed the *mala* story along the north face, and then concentrated on the battle of the snakes along the south side. These sides of the Rock were crucial to Harney's understanding of it. For the north side, the 'sun side', he used the Aboriginal term *Djindarlagul*, which he understood to designate a moiety that owned the stories in that area. The south side, 'the shade side', he called *Wumbuluru* moiety. In this way his basic categories linked site, story and kinship—a sophisticated summation, in terms of the Aboriginal sense of place. The shame was—if we judge from recent anthropological opinion—most of it was wrong. Equally advanced in its sympathetic aspirations was the detail Harney put down around the Rock. A glance at his map shows this; the whole place is animated by a

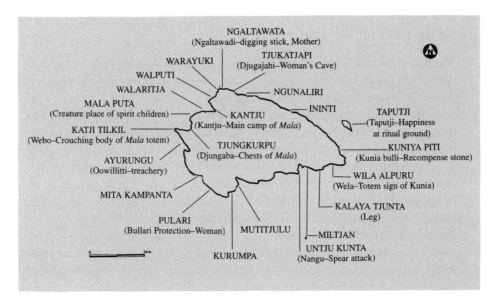

Some A̲nangu place names at Uluru.

narrative sense of ceremony. The links between stories is often missing, but the stories are there, on a map of intriguing richness. Again, it seems a shame that much of it is wrong, massively overstated, or too sacred to be corrected.

The problem can be shown if we put some of Harney's material on a map that is acceptable today.

The Park's official map of the Rock takes in some of the important places, accurately named (the Pitjantjatjara have developed a standard orthography since Harney, the forbidden place name is dropped from public circulation). At a glance you can see 26 sites. Most of them are proper names: *Kalaya Tjunta* (emu thigh), *Ngaltawata* (tree, ceremonial pole), *Mala Puta* (hare wallaby pouch), *Ininti* (bean tree). Some have other meanings that are tied to the site. Of these sites, only 11 places from Harney's work seem to match up (making adjustments for his crudely phonetic transcriptions of Pitjantjatjara). I have indicated the overlap by putting in brackets what Harney called 'meaning in ritual'.

On Harney's map 27 other places are named or indicated as part of one of the myth stories. These are places which are not worth scrutinising today because they are either wrong, offensive or misleading, or any combination of these. This was

109

particularly so with Harney's attempt to itemise sacred details on the north side. Today this area is hard to talk about, as the spaces in the Park map suggest. The scope of Harney's transgression can perhaps be understood by considering his account. Here he is in full flight:

> The mountain of Uluru was, and still is today, the Loritdja people's living symbols of those creative heroes who dwell within it in the same fashion as do the Gods and archangels in other heavens.
>
> As the Earth-mother created the 'shades' (souls) of the spirit-children of the dawn so must the soul of the deceased person return to the mountain to be purified within, so that it can be once more reincarnated to a life upon the earth. Yet these creative-spirits demand one thing from the living. The important one that each and every one of the deceased-one's kin shall be ritually pure in all things during the Kerungra ritual. Failing this the soul of the dead must wander about the land until the next big ritual. All members of a family paint themselves with white clay at mourning rituals—to make themselves invisible so that the deceased shall not steal their soul from their body and thus cause them to die. It is important that the chants of the rituals are correct. If not when they wash themselves at the end of the death ceremonies they will be visible for an angry wandering shade which may cause them harm.
>
> But if everything is correct then the soul is admitted to the mountain and is cleansed. After the purification it will now await the next Kerungra ritual so that it can be 'sung' from the place of the 'putta'—that place of reincarnation which is said to be the point of the ritual Mala-waddi.
>
> Now let us see the story as recorded in the stone symbols we pass by on the journey around the mountain. Not only does the mountain reveal the ritual of the Earth-mother but it was the pattern of their kinship law.

It is hard to know where to start with the corrections. We could begin by saying three things: to speak of Uluru as a Magic Mountain is an European imposition, a crude gloss on the variety of mythological meanings that Anangu bring to it. To expand on this in terms of an Earth Mother, along the lines of Greek mythology, or some generalised version of Greek mythology, is equally fanciful. So too is the rush towards language drawn from medieval Christianity (archangels and heavens) and Eastern religion (the reincarnations of the shades). So keen is Harney on honouring all that the Rock is that he runs a mishmash of meanings, while telling a very simplistic story about the way ritual connects with the afterlife, and Anangu's moral sense of the afterlife. Today few would attempt such a categorical summary without much detailed reference to what his informants had said with respect to particular myths, rituals and symbolic expressions. The religious house that Harney has constructed for his Aboriginal friends is a ramshackle assembly of incompatible materials—a 'she'll be right' hut unfit for the actuality of Centralian life.

Harney goes on to talk about the sun side, and the 'cult of happiness'. He does not say how he got this lovely phrase, and if only it were true. He recounts the story of the *mala* men, and here, it is pleasant to report that he *is* in tune with what A̲nangu are prepared to confirm today. *Mala* are a big part of the Rock story.

Harney strolled about with his Aboriginal informants. He told his *Oceania* readers in 1960 that he did not ask questions, but waited for his informants to chant to him when they reached the right place, where he would boil the billy for tea. It's a picture of ease that he sketches; reading him today I'm envious of the contact he was able to have with Aboriginal people evidently prepared to share their time. Isn't this what many of us want when we come to the Rock: guides who will take us into places and tell us the important things, even perhaps some 'secret' things?

Along the north face Harney and his friends walked, around onto the west side, stopping all the way at special places and sometimes going into what we know today to be sacred caves. The men chant for Harney, just as 'primitives' have done for the white man since the New World was discovered.

They stop at a cave just a few minutes away from the base of the climb. Harney's mode now is that of the great white guide, as if in darkest Africa. His book records: 'This is the kulpi of the "kundji" (meeting place), a primitive form of our present-day vestry before the assembly area. This shelter has wall paintings which represent the 'Kulpidja' beside a smaller one of an initiate ready to be taken into the sacred ritual place. The 'Kulpidja'—obviously a symbol of the Earth-mother—has white radiating lines coming out of a red centre which encloses a black band running through its centre.'

How does Harney know? He sounds so sure, yet he cannot be. Listen closely to the yarning bushman. 'For a long time I sat in that shelter with my chanting mates. Much discussing went on between them and *I was told* that the black band symbolised happiness, the red ochre represented the ritual side of man with white as his belief in the soul and immortality.' (My italics)

'I was told'. Is Harney quietly implying here that there are things that he might not have been told?

'Everywhere is symbolism in words and stones', he says earlier on, 'and here was I in a strange land listening to a new language and trying to fathom it all.'

'Did I do it well? Well, I am pretty sure by the looks on my friends' faces, as I tried to chant it back, that it was "off the ball". Nevertheless, not only were they good translators from the Loritdja to English, but they did an excellent job of untangling my jargon. Fortunately I had been to a Kerungra before with the tribes of the north. This, with my mates' perseverance, helped me out. Yet true knowledge must not be dogmatic. Although I went around the Rock many times with other informants, to check the story, I am sure that those two old men never let me stray. They were good mates to me and if I have gone wrong in the story here and there it is my fault, not theirs.'

This is an unusual admission for Harney, who in all of his books speaks with manly assurance. In *To Ayers Rock and Beyond*, he is not so sure. In a more formal paper published in the then prestigious anthropological journal *Oceania*, he was both more guarded and more expansive about the reliability of his informants. But not here, where, in good yarning fashion and kind of safeguarding candour, he hints that he might be wrong, that he could have been, for one reason or another, misinformed. Though the stereotypical Australian style of yarning does not invite modesty, the skin sense of the narrator can work in the other direction, especially when another culture is involved. To his credit, Harney acknowledged that.

Good boys

FOR OUR CULTURE'S written record, Robert Layton (1969) has done much to table Uluru Tjukurpa for a contemporary readership. From the Anangu perspective, which shapes political correctness in the Park, Layton is one of the 'good boys' of Central Australian history.

Layton takes up Harney's division between the sun side and the shade side. Harney says that the sides belonged to different people, and that a man inherited one of these two sides from his mother. Paradoxically, Harney's position flies in the face of his other big statements about the Rock being *the* unifying symbol for the local people. Layton, however, says that the two sides are in fact generational divisions: that is, all the people in one generation belong to the sun side, all the children to the shade side, and their children to the sun side again. In men's ritual, members of either category may sit and work together, but it is obvious that any of the descent groups owning an estate will contain representation of both.

Layton's focus is on ownership rather than on ancestor stories and cosmic themes such as a 'Mother Goddess', another mistaken concept on Harney's part which Layton puts down to confusion over a Yam Dreaming site associated with a female ancestor, and some parts of the *mala* story. Layton is less interested in making a good story about his experience of the Rock than tabling the social facts about living claims to the country. His informants were Pitjantjatjara men Paddy Uluru and Nipper Winmati, who were prepared to tell him places which were their responsibility.

Both men had responsibility for Mutitjulu, and the Kantju waterhole. After that they named sites that take one right around the Rock (see map of Rock).

Nipper named: Kalaya Tjunta, Wila Alpuru, Kuniya Piti, Taputji, Inintitjara, Mala Wipu (the climb), Walu Kutjuta, Mutjuranpa, Lungkata Waru, Pularinya, Patji, Kapi Yularanya Pulka, Kapi Yularanya Tjukutjuku.

Paddy Uluru named: Kulpi Turrmil, Kurumpa, Alyurungu, Kapi Yularanya Tjukutjuku, Inintitjara, Tjuku Tjapi, Walaritja.

Thus Layton carefully consulted the men who had custodial responsibilities at the Rock and who considered the Rock a unity, though not in Harney's terms. Another aspect to the ownership emerged from Layton's detailed consultations in Pitjantjatjara: Winmati and Uluru's responsibilities for places at the Rock extended well beyond those sites, the sites themselves linked them with other custodial places. Stretching way out into the country, they made what Layton calls 'a chain of estates' that followed the watering places in the Petermann and Blood Ranges to the west, and the Musgrave and Mann Ranges south. None of this means that the Rock is not of prime importance to Anangu. It is to say that it's not of the kind of central importance that Harney proclaimed, and that its significance is inseparable from a sense of the country far and wide.

We might say, speaking as pilgrims of one kind, that the Rock looms large in Aboriginal affairs in so far as people value other places eternally linked in the journey to and from it. We can only come to the Rock in full consciousness via other places, provided that Aboriginal culture has trusted us with the significance of those places and, on our part, a knowledge and understanding—*patience*. Comprehending another culture takes time, more time, I have come to feel, than pilgrims might have.

All this is enough, perhaps, to convey some of my present difficulties. I am steering my way patiently though several shoals here: trying not to make too much of a villain of Harney, but not taking too much of the official view as writ either, since both perspectives have to be seen in their own wider political context, a context that has ramifications for everything, including, it seems, the status and meaning of myth stories.

For example, on a visit to the Rock about a year after Tjamiwa got me going with his story about Harney, I was sitting in Jon Willis' kitchen, out at the Mutitjulu community, when Layton's work came up.

Willis said the thing he liked best about Layton's book was the walking map. I think I had come to know Willis well enough by then to realise that he liked writing that does not try too hard for philosophical generalities; he prefers the low-key work which is close to the actual complexities of daily life, a domain not easily described. Willis, 33, himself is an anthropologist. He was educated at Sydney University, and before that in Catholic schools in Wollongong. As a younger man he was the New South Wales President of Young Christian Students. At one stage he considered the priesthood. He plays the harp, speaks Russian and French, and is fluent in

Pitjantjatjara. You can't hear him speak this language with his Aboriginal friends and not realise the passion he puts into his job. Two years before I met him he had taken up Anangu's invitation to become an initiate, and it is this, as much as his Western cultivations, which inform his life. One part of him seems to operate out of an European fastidiousness, with all of its powers for making intellectual distinctions, the other, out of an insistence that non-Aboriginals cease to presume about anything in Anangu life.

I had been to the Rock three times and still felt as if I was starting out. Where was the end to inquiry? Come to think if it, where was the real beginning?

Anangu have a story—the Wiyai Kutjara story—about the creation of the Rock. This is how Robert Layton tells it.

> Uluru (Ayers Rock itself) was built up during the creation period by the two boys who played in the mud after rain. When they had finished their game they travelled south to Wiputa, on the northern side of the Musgrave Ranges, where they killed and cooked the euro. Then the boys turned north again toward Atila (Mount Conner). A few miles south-west of the Mount, at Anari one boy threw his *tjuni* (wooden club) at a hare wallaby, but the club struck the ground and made a fresh-water spring. This boy refused to reveal where he had found the water and the other boy nearly died of thirst. Fighting together, the two boys made their way to the table-topped Mount Conner, on top of which their bodies are preserved as boulders.

I find this a deceptively simple and puzzling story. Here are the boys, who lamentably remain unnamed (A secret? Because their names don't matter? They remain impersonal identities.) who seem to have done something constructive because they have made the Rock. One might say that, except that there are no terms of evaluation in the passage, except the remark about one boy nearly dying of thirst because the other would not share his water (the imperative of sharing is very common in Central Australian stories). So are they bad boys? What is the connection with the hare wallaby, which, as we shall see, is very important to current Anangu accounts of the Rock? The boy kills what we white people have come to know as a much-valued animal ancestor, and yet it is out of the killing that fresh water springs from the ground.

Stories as cryptic as this can be frustrating, especially when the anthropologist is a contemporary, and has chosen not so say any more. Why? Out of respect for the owners of the story? Because he could not find out any more? Because he thinks the story speaks for itself? What story ever speaks entirely for itself?

Before I could voice any of this Willis piped up.

—That story doesn't belong here.

I was taken aback. Willis thinks well of Layton's book.

—How do you know?

—Because, Willis said, the owner of the story lives here. And *he* told me.

Willis told me the name of man who owns the story, and I made a mental note in the hope that one day I might be able to speak with that person. Then it occurred to me: what would I ask him, exactly?

—Have you read Layton's book, mate? If this story does not say how the Rock was made, what does it say? Do you know any creation stories about the Rock? What's your favourite?

In one move, Willis had brought my attention to an uncomfortable fact: access to Aboriginal stories is no simple matter. Leaving aside how we choose to tell the myth story, there is the fundamental question of privilege. Willis knew the story-teller. The story-teller trusted Willis (I assumed). What more could be said?

We were both waiting for Tjamiwa to turn up. After some months I had come back to the Rock, with the smallest amount of Pitjantjatjara under my belt (and too intimidated by Willis' flamboyant proficiency to say so), and keen to ask Tjamiwa more about Harney. I wanted to know if Tjamiwa would say *how* Harney got it wrong, and what were the most important corrections that had to be made, especially if today's visitors were to be put on the right track.

Finally he arrived, greeted me vaguely—head down, no eye contact, casual handshake—and sat at the table to wait for the tea.

Willis said in Pitjantjatjara that I hoped to talk to him more about Harney.

Tjamiwa made a noise in his throat, and began to flip through *To Ayers Rock and Beyond* which was on the table. Suddenly he stiffened and sat upright. He began to speak.

—I told him, he said, raising his voice (Willis translating)—You're a fish, you're a crocodile!

Tjamiwa was waving his hand, and looking at the figure of Harney who might as well have come into the kitchen.

—What do you know? You know nothing. You're a fish! A crocodile!

Willis was grinning at this re-enactment. It was Tjamiwa putting the first ranger of the Rock to rights. I didn't realise at that moment, because Willis hadn't let on or thought to tell me, that Harney's ghost could well have stepped into the room because the house that he lived in was just behind us. This was the place that Severin built: a rambling five-roomed structure with a cement floor and rickety veranda that looks directly at the Rock, commanding the view that the early motels had before the Handback decision moved them away. I went into it the next day. The place was occupied by white construction workers and was in ill-repair—light switches cracked, dry grass tufting out of the walls, snake infested. A relic of white history neglected by its black owners . . .

—That's right, Tjamiwa said again, you know nothing. You're not from here!

Then he subsided. I was hoping this was a prelude to more detailed talk about Harney, but it was not. Instead he launched into a long story about something else, quite unprompted, as far as I could tell, by Willis. It was the story of the murder at the Rock.

When he had gone, I asked Willis a question. That conversation Tjamiwa had with Harney, what language do you think it was in? Tjamiwa knew some English, that was clear, though he was only a boy at the time he would have been speaking with Harney. And Harney, as we now all know, spoke no Pitjantjatjara.

Willis hesitated.

—The language, he said, of the imagination.

CHAPTER 2 **Murder**

At the cave

BEFORE TJAMIWA LAUNCHED into the murder story, he had been thumbing through Harney, looking at the pictures and glowering at them, as far as I could tell. Harney's version of the event — written a long time before anyone imagined Anangu regaining ownership of the Rock — went like this:

> I heard the tale, as it was told to me by one of the tribesmen, as we sat one Christmas day at Angus Down . . . The aboriginal told me in grim detail of the missing aboriginal and the capture of the prisoners at Middleton Ponds beside the Palmer River. He told me about the digging up of the body of the murdered man. How the policeman nonchalantly shook the skull and, hearing a rattle inside it, found the man had been killed by a rifle bullet in the head. From the tribal business it now became murder, so he chained up the culprits to a large tree, but that night they escaped and were fleeing to the westward.
>
> The road our coach had travelled from Mount Quinn homestead followed somewhere along the path of the escapees with the avenging limb of the law on their trail. They by-passed the scene of the crime at Mount Conner to be off through the night on the long road to Ayers Rock over sixty miles farther on to the west.

He told me how the tired escapees tried to elude their relentless black trackers during the day by covering their feet with cloth and clawing beneath spinifex there to await the night; how the law tried to burn the spinifex country and so flush them out. But the Wonambi spirit of Ayers Rock protected them so well that the fire would not burn. But human endurance cannot stand up against fleet camels that can go long distances without water, and the final story was written in the shelters of Uluru under the watchful eyes of the tribal spirits.

Harney continues, taking us right to the Rock:

Every time I went around Ayers Rock during the time I was Ranger there I looked up at a cliff face called the Mulu (nose) and pictured that final scene...

The trembling aborigines were jammed into a rocky crevice of the 'Nose', listening to the white-man's law climbing up towards them. The policeman, peering into the darkness of the crevice, could see nothing and would have gone away but for his tracker who claimed he could smell the sweat from the unwashed bodies of the wanted men. The aborigine who told the tale to me at Angus Downs went on describe how the four men hiding in the crevice could hear the talking. Then faintly they heard footsteps creeping in, and in desperation, one of the escapees on the outside who was too stout to creep further into the narrow cleft of the mountain, leapt out with a stone in his hand in an effort to create surprise and thus get away.

Now spoke the rifle of the white-man's law and the doomed man toppled on to the floor of the crevice. Then a strange thing happened. The dying man, with a superhuman effort, crawled out of the cave and neither threats nor promises could make him reveal where the others were hidden.

As if this was not melodramatic enough, Harney presses on:

The Mulu with its severed nose looks with passive face over the Loritdja tribal lands and keeps its secret well. Yet what a story it could tell of man's devotion to his tribal kin, even unto death—what a strange scene, the cowering men within the crevice listening to their dying comrade asking for water before he died and the last vision he had on this earth was the policeman's black-tracker pouring water into his parched throat. Thus died a brave man.

It is 1934. The 'brave man' was Jokanana, Paddy Uluru's brother. The policeman was Constable William McKinnon, then aged thirty-two. Harney lays on the brave, I feel, perhaps by way of laying off the police. McKinnon, a man of his times, already had a reputation for brutality among the Aborigines: the shooting at the Rock and other accusations of brutality, including thrashing Aboriginal men at Hermannsburg, were soon to prompt a government inquiry. When Harney was writing McKinnon was probably still in the district, and Harney seems to be doing his best to tame the savagery of 'olden times'. The shooting at the Rock was legally justified, the inquiry reported in 1936, though not warranted under the circumstances. Shooting 'should be resorted to only when all other possible methods of recapture have been exhausted'.

McKinnon had taken Uluru and three others into custody at Mount Conner four days before he walled them up at the Rock. The sequence of action in Harney's version of the chase seems accurate enough but that may be all. For years afterwards Paddy Uluru told his brother-in-law something different. His brother was wounded escaping: when he got to the Rock, and when they heard the police coming, his wounds prevented him from crawling as far into the cave as the others. The men inside heard the footsteps outside. 'Then someone called something from outside. The man in the cave called out, "Wait I'll finish this bastard." The shots were fired. After that more shots were *fired into the cave*, but none of the police party would go right inside into the darkness.' (My italics)

This is Reverend Jim Dowling reporting in 1988, after speaking with Paddy Uluru's brother-in-law, a man called Kantji. Downing cites another Aboriginal who described how the men were sitting on the top of the cave (near Mutitjulu), resting in the sun. The police suddenly came around the rock and began shooting at them. The men dropped through the holes at the top of the cave. The only one shot was Paddy Uluru's brother. They waited a long time until they were sure the police party had gone. Then they buried Paddy's brother and Paddy hid those sacred objects that were too long or heavy to carry. Taking the others Paddy set out for a far country—far south to Mimili Station in South Australia.

While Harney romances the cave, he is vague about crucial events six weeks earlier. Paddy Uluru and six others had killed a young man, Kai-Umen, from Kata Tjuta. Kai-Umen, Uluru told McKinnon when the Constable took him in with four others, had told secrets to white men. No other weapons but sticks and stones were used, the men told McKinnon. The Constable then dug up the body and cut off its head. (How else, a policeman might have said, is identification possible back in Alice if you don't have the head?) McKinnon believed his captive's story until a week later, when, examining the skull, he heard the rattle of the bullet inside. One of his men in chains, Numberlin, then made the crucial admission which brought the white-man's law into full play.

The rifle belonged to a white man, Robert Hughes, a dingo scalper. 'The dogger' had lent Numberlin his gun when they were camping together at Mount Conner. Numberlin said he wanted to shoot kangaroo, and Hughes had let him go off with the gun loaded with two cartridges. Numberlin came back with one cartridge and no kangaroo; Hughes was uneasy. When Kai-Umen's body was found by his wife, suspicion turned to alarm. He hastily packed up from the Aboriginal camp, rode to Ernabella station and reported a murder to the police.

Numberlin had been the first arrested. He denied the charge, but McKinnon caught him by the shoulder, pushed him down and gave him 'just a little knock with his foot, not very hard'. This is according to McKinnon's Aboriginal tracker at the Alice Springs inquest (as cited by Robert Layton, whose diligent narrative I am summarising here). Another captive, Cowarie, gave a confession to McKinnon which he later withdrew; he claimed that 'I told McKinnon that I killed that man to get out of getting a hiding. I had to own up because he was giving me too much of a hiding with a bullock hide.' Cowarie was not committed for trial because he had nothing to do with the rifle. Numberlin had been recaptured two days before the murder at the Rock; Cowarie brought himself in. Nangee, who was also brought to trial with Numberlin, was caught a fortnight after 'the cave incident'. It was Nangee who admitted that Kai-Umen had been executed for revealing ritual secrets to his wife, who described how all the men had carried out the execution, by striking Kai-Umen with sticks and stones after they had shot him. Numberlin and Nangee were both sentenced to ten years' imprisonment by Judge Wells on 21 February 1935, a savage punishment in the circumstances.

The moon dream

THESE WERE THE EVENTS that led young Strehlow and Mountford to the Rock in 1935. They were with the Committee of Inquiry led by the Adelaide pathology professor, Professor John Cleland. The members of the board were Reverend John Sexton from the Aborigines Friends Association in Adelaide, and Vin White, a respected public servant from the Northern Territory. Strehlow, with his excellent Aranda and adaptability in other languages, was the translator. Mountford kept the minutes of the evidence. It was the job of the inquiry to tour the area taking evidence, all the while presenting what might be called the kinder face of white-man's law. In an atmosphere of affable forebearance—hearty bushmen together—Constable McKinnon went with them. On their camels and in their stop-start motor vehicle they made their slow way through the sandhill country to the Rock.

Strehlow's initial feelings are clear from his journal entry for 11 June. What might have appeared a romantic response to the Rock can now be read in its practical context.

> The Rock was reached at last, the goal of my boyhood dreams—the shadow of a great rock in a weary land, and how welcome it was. All hushed tonight, only the moon is shining down union the great black walls of the rock—and one

feels that the Land of God is indeed near. It is like the great silence of eternity. And near by lies the body of the dead man; and that body has brought us hither to this vast pile that shall endure long after our own bodies will be only dim scattered dust, known to no man, forgotten by all save God alone who moulded them first even as He fashioned this great Rock, that sleeps tonight in a still moon dream.

Next day he was obliged to face unpleasant facts more directly:

> The body of Jokonana was exhumed by McKinnon, White and the Professor this morning, and will be taken back by the Professor.
>
> The camels stayed last night, and Walker and Carbine brought them back only about 3 p.m. So no inquiry was held in the afternoon, the party having already dispersed in order to view the Rock.
>
> Saw the scene of the final tragedy today. I was greatly shocked by the way in which poor Jokonana met his death—a poor, hunted creature, *shot callously at least twice in the cave*, without being able to defend his life or to escape. And now he is being taken back—his bones and head wrapped up in a calico parcel; his vitals, lungs, blood, entrails, liquifying flesh in a large billy can. And that is permitted by our white man's civilisation. (My italics)

'Shot callously at least twice in the cave'. It scotches Harney's whimsical version once and for all. It was a brutal killing at the Rock, and Strehlow's note to himself makes no bones about it, even though, as he sits on his swag under the great back walls of the Rock in the moonlight and the great silence of eternity, Constable McKinnon is sitting in friendly fashion nearby. Only six days earlier Strehlow had turned 27 and had been delighted to record in his private journal that McKinnon had 'smilingly given me some of our boiled sweets as a birthday present'. On the way back, McKinnon would have a birthday, and the party treated him to a special dinner of the last of the plum pudding and radishes.

When they got back to Alice Springs the camaraderie of the white investigators held firm. Here they are at the prison, conducting the last stages of their inquiry in a bleak tin shed, as an icy wind chilled everyone's bones, despite overcoats. Strehlow wrote: 'Numberlin, Nantji, [Nangee], Panna, Saltpetre, Munty, and a few of others were re-examined, without results. There was, however, one great dramatic moment in the bleak tin shed, when Numberlin alleged that McKinnon had come to his cell before the arrival of the Board, and persuaded him to give false evidence—to tell the Board that McKinnon had never hit him, and had always been kind to him etc. Old Panna caused some mirth in the court room later on. Mr White asked him why he had told Dr Kirkland a lie about his broken arm. Panna then told the interpreter [Syd Walker]

1935 Board of Inquiry stops for evidence of murder.

how it had happened. Dr Kirkland had come to him and had said to him (here Panna cleverly imitated the agitated tones of the Doctor), 'Tell the truth, tell the truth, tell the truth.' At this Panna got such a fright that he told him a whole lot of lies. This must have happened to most of the witnesses whom the Board interviewed.'

We are a long way from Strehlow's anguish at the Rock. The white man's bantering mirth—an atmosphere of winks and nods about police brutality—is implicit. Strehlow will be glad when it's all over, and afterwards tells his diary that the whole inquiry is a farce. At the time, the conventions of the frontier prevented a man, especially a younger man, saying so. Besides, in a matter of months he would become the first Patrol Officer of the area. His appointment would express the government's way of coping with native transgressions; an increase in local officialdom rather than in police powers and numbers; and soon Strehlow himself would be speaking out with authority in favour of corporal punishment of the Aborigines in his charge.

White retakes

MOUNTFORD ALSO HAD his worries about the inquiry. As well as keeping the minutes of evidence he was writing his frustrations in a little black book. Admittedly, on the first day at the Rock there was wonder of the place, and the awe of exploring it. If Strehlow had tried to still his unease by referring to moon dreams, Mountford had a less settling experience. He was very conscious of his intrusion into a cave. His diary entry suggests a refrain for his life, his tendency to go into depths he was inclined to defy.

'The lamp continually went out,' he wrote, 'and in the darkness one felt dis-associated from everything that was real. It seemed as if I were surrounded by the presence of those who for untold centuries had frequented this cave, painted their strange symbols on its walls, and conducted their secret ceremonies on its floor. I wondered what would happen if one of the Aborigines belonging to the spot should come upon me. Would he attack me as an intruder, as he had every right to do, or would he show me the courtesy so often extended to a stranger?'

Next morning the party slept well after sunrise and woke with a 'really holiday feeling'. It was also the day of the exhumation, after which Mountford noted, 'Cleland did not wish to take more evidence. I wonder why he accepted this position. He is much more interested in the disappearance of the mulga than that of the native.' That night Mountford went to sleep dog tired. 'And,' he scrawled by the campfire, 'savage at J. Cleland's attempt to shield McKinnon, when White had him cornered.' Mountford was even more disillusioned the next day, when they had left the Rock. Cleland called him over to his camp to take dictation. 'He, however, dictated to me, the whole report relating to the shooting (without consulting either of the members of the board).'

Mountford never publicly cited his little black notebook, but years later, in 1948, he had the courage to make an unprevaricating statement about the shooting at the Rock: 'The policeman stayed with the camels and sent the armed tracker to search for the escapees. The tracker came on them sitting on top of an outcropping boulder, fired and hit him. The unfortunate Aboriginal, unarmed and twice wounded, tried to conceal himself in a crevice, a little larger than his own body, under one of the huge fallen boulders. There the native was shot by the policeman, who claimed that his own life was in danger.'

This is the account that Harney, who befriended Mountford in the year it was published, must have read, and decided to gloss over.

It was to be some years before T. G. H. Strehlow was to be as public on the matter. In 1950 he noted the severity of the sentences received by Numberlin and Nangee. 'Tribal killers,' he said, 'were normally acquitted by the Northern Territory courts till the 1950s. The "unusual severity" was without doubt due to the grave concern felt by members of the European jury that a rifle borrowed from a European dogger had been used to shoot the victim. Had the latter been speared in the normal way, no alarm would have been aroused.'

As for the 'farce' of the inquiry, Strehlow seems to have kept the force of his judgement to himself. Instead, in 1935 he furnished the Board of Inquiry with a general article on 'Notes on Native Evidence and Its Value'. It is a firmly written anecdotal piece that argues by implication. Drawing on several of his own earlier experiences with natives, Strehlow says that when it came to telling the truth, or giving evidence, what a native says depended on the trustworthiness of the white person, the relative stranger asking the questions. If the stranger is held in esteem or respect, well and good, the native will be candidly informative. If not, then it makes common kin-sense for the native to lie, to dissemble or evade, to employ without any qualms of conscience all their skill as 'born actors of a very high order'. Strehlow also sought to advise the Board that 'the natives are naturally suspicious of the good intentions of strange white men because they have been frequently deceived and exploited and robbed by unscrupulous whites'.

Did Strehlow and Mountford share these worries at the time? It seems not. Certainly, there is no mention of Mountford in Strehlow's journal (his private diaries are still unavailable to the public), and only a brief mention by Mountford of him. The Mountford entry does not concern the murder at the Rock, but, in retrospect, we might say that with regard to the subsequent reputations of both men, it had deadly portents, since Strehlow would, in years to come, do his best to mortally wound the body of Mountford's work.

They had returned to Bob Buck's place at Middleton Ponds, and after tea they went to the Aboriginal camp to get man called Nukulupi to explain some drawings. Strehlow came as interpreter. 'It was an unsual experience,' Mountford recorded. 'Mick (whose Abo name I have forgotten for the moment) was poring over the drawings, whispering details to the interpreter and five other natives around him. Each one was very interested, each endeavouring to make clear to Strehlow who spoke Aranda perfectly the meaning of various complex designs. The firelight on the faces of the natives, the rapt interest as they explained the drawings to Strehlow was something which we will not forget for a long while.'

Mountford is touchingly open about his dependence on Strehlow, and there is a natural envy for the university man whose knowledge of the language gave him such

Strehlow and Mountford shadowing each other's careers in 1935.

an entry to Aboriginal trust. More the pity then for Mountford when Strehlow turned on him years later, claiming that not only did Mountford depend on him for native knowledge more than he fully acknowledged, but that when it came to the stories at the Rock, and the myths that belonged to the Pitjantjatjara people, Mountford got them atrociously wrong. At the time however, in 1935, who knows what the proud young Strehlow was saying to a PMG technician so glowingly keen to enter the Aboriginal world. My guess is that Mountford was then too humble to say much to the scholarly mission boy, but kept his eyes open and took one shot that showed how the camera can outwit words. It is of the shadows of both men on the same camel. Strehlow and Mountford rock in slow time with each other, in an image that gloomily foreshadows their attenuated relationship.

The hunt

TJAMIWA HARDLY LOOKED at me as he told the story.

—*Out there*, he said, facing his translator Jon Willis—*near Atila, two fellas borrowed a rifle from a dingo trapper. Said they had some hunting to do.*

—*There was a man there who had broken secrets by telling them to a woman. But it wasn't hunting, it was shooting a man. They aimed and they aimed and shot him.*

There is a growl in Tjamiwa's voice, and Willis seems to be picking up the gravity of the story. Tjamiwa pauses.

—*Later, his wife said to them, where is he? They said, perhaps he's gone somewhere.*

A note of mischief in the voice. Tjamiwa shrugs, as if to say, 'We're sorry, but we have no idea where your husband is.'

—*She went looking for footprints, for 2 nights and 2 days, and found the body, where they men had put it, in a cave. She went back to McKinnon at Angas Downs.*

—*They* (McKinnon and his aide) *went to get horses—rather than camels. The men had got away, they had gone north to Lake Amadeus, they didn't know they were being chased. Then McKinnon came upon them—they heard the horse coming, wheezing and panting. So they took off, they went very fast.*

At the mention of the wheezing horses, Tjamiwa shows some satisfaction: men are better than horses, Aboriginal men in their own country.

—*McKinnon had a man with him . . .*

Tjamiwa pauses to remember this man. He can't, and is annoyed with himself. He is thinking of the police aide who did the shooting.

—A nasty man, who later went to South Australia.

Willis can't recall the name either.

— They chased the men. They chased them right out around Atila, where the men hide. McKinnon went back to get horses.

— He went back to the dead man and he cut him—he cut him like this— Tjamiwa made a short, strong and savage gesture, which flashed me back to the malu hunt.

— Then he came out again, down after the men. He caught one of them and tied him up, and left him there, in the sand.

— He went after the others, they can see him, from the top of the dune, and go (quick movement) *like this—up the dune. The horse goes up the dune, but the dunes are like this* (steep) *and the horse gets tired.*

There is a grim pause at the mention of Numberlin left buried in the sand, followed by glee as Tjamiwa returns to the chase. He slows the narrative down, waves his hands—like this, up the dune, while the Aboriginal men keep ahead. White hunter labouring in Anangu country.

— They—the men on the run—come right across here, around to Uluru, arriving at the mala, the women's cave.

— Then they come around the rock to the south-west face and go up in the rocks, where they hide in a ledge (the 'cave' just north of Mutitjulu wall).

— They are hiding there and McKinnon and his aide came along. Then one of the men (there are four) *shows himself and goes back under the ledge. They were trying to get out the back of the wall of the cave.*

— McKinnon and aide start shooting from down below. They can't see what they are shooting at, but they keep firing.

— They killed the man. He was dead in the cave. The others are there, lying back in the cave. Nobody can see them.

— McKinnon can't see the others, so he waits.

— He makes a fire and lies down for the night—on his back, his rifle across his chest. Like this.

Tjamiwa leans back as if to lay the gun across his own chest. His face shows a slight pout of ignorance; a skilful actor's mockery of the white man.

— McKinnon was waiting and waiting.

— When he is asleep, one of the men came down from the ledge. In the dark he crept towards the policeman with a rock in his hand. Right up . . .

Tjamiwa paused.

—. . . but then chickened out. He went back to the others, and they all took off!

A sweep of the arm now.

— They went to Mantarur, right around, then south to the Mann Ranges, then through the ranges down to Mimili where they stayed, for the next forty years!

Tjamiwa's telling ended there. As if to say: see, understand now what it means to come back to this place, what it is to own this place that we were driven away from.

I should add, in the interests of strict documentation, that this is the gist of the telling. I wrote it down afterwards (and checked it with Willis) because, to my horror, the tape recorder did not work—as so often happens in Central Australia, especially during moments of some significance in Aboriginal encounters. Verbatim, it would have been a longer story, and somewhat more dramatic. The experience of listening to it with the emotional weights hanging in the air as Willis translated was extraordinary; the narration of the chase carried one across the country and it seemed to go without saying, as Tjamiwa recounted the shooting at the cave and Paddy Uluru's near attempt at murdering the white policeman, that all the colonial details documented above were known absolutely to him, though that would have been impossible. Tjamiwa was speaking imaginatively out of a broad sense of family history, of the blood brothers and sisters he grew up with down south, because they fled there out of necessity.

Tjamiwa's brooding anger seems to me to be evident in what Paddy Uluru had to say years after his escape. This is Paddy Uluru as reported in 1977, when the campaign for regaining the Rock gathered momentum: 'The whitefellows having frightened me, chased me away—having gone from that place—I wandered around—having left my things (sacred) there, I moved around . . . yes, I went around here and there—finished! The policeman having frightened me, chased me away from there . . . It is my camp. Uluru is my camp. This is mine, this holy cave; my fathers and grandfathers entrusted me with this cave. This holy cave. And girls have broken (the sanctity of) this thing of mine. And I have become very sad. This is my great ceremony, my great camp with its holy tree [ngaltawata, the ceremonial sacred pole] and mutitju [cave] on this side is holy. Ayers Rock is holy. I am Uluru and these things are mine . . .'

No wonder then that the story of murder at the Rock is still alive. Tjamiwa wanted to—had to—tell it because it was told to him down south, because Paddy Uluru (now deceased) was a custodian of this place before him and would have told him the story himself, just as Cassidy Uluru, Paddy's son, would have been told by his father, and so, is telling the story today to the camera, which any of us can see on the video *Uluru: an Anangu Story*. That video, I must say, is the one you should be watching on the way to Uluru if you have to watch anything on a bus trip. It is a splendid film which involves much imaginative re-enactment. It re-creates from the Tjukurpa as well as from historical incidents; the murder at the Rock has an important place. It is used in the way that Tjamiwa used it with me: as an instructive tale about the brutality of dis-possession. The tale has the status of a modern legend that is gradually being worked with the resonance of myth, since it begins almost at the historical beginning for

Anangu, when many of them were making first contact with the white men. It involves a banishment from the homelands, a painful exile that is followed by a return, a just and deserving homecoming. It is a story that has classical proportions and a power to evoke that is now independent of white culture's social memory. And like all myths it can be told with twists and turns of emphases—the snake of revenge showing its fangs one minute, the great coils of resolution settling at their watering place the next. In so far as it belongs to the place in a way that animates past, present and future, it is in a way a Tjukurpa story, a contemporary Dreaming.

CHAPTER 3 **Snakes**

Snake consciousness

WHEN I BRING MY imagination to bear on the Rock I get tangled in all manner of things. There is the question of what the Aboriginal myth means—a task for the imagination if ever there was one. A myth is, of course, much more than a fanciful story—what Willis calls a cutesy tale when disparaging how the Aboriginal myths are sometimes treated. Myths are not merely 'made up', a notion that approximates a myth to a lie. If we must speak of lies (and bush tradition demands that we can't forget about them) we should think of Plato's idea of the noble lie, a story created by society for the honourable purpose of moral instruction. In all cultures myths are narratives that carry weight, they are the exemplary tales. They usually deal with the great themes of life: birth, death, war, marriage, loyalty, provision, survival—although to say this much is not to say that their meanings are always apparent. As stories, myths have an element of mystery, which adds to their power, their hold on the imagination. In effect, myths call upon the imagination in the most concrete ways, which is the reason why myths are often inseparable from *inma*, ceremony. The story is married to a rite, and at the heart of the rite is the chant, at the centre of which is the convergence of music and meaning we call the poem. Myths are deep chords for our poetic sense of reality. If the Dreaming is the poetic bow of reality, the string to the bow is the myth, and the arrow is the chant, which aims at the heart of the body's movement in the poem.

130

To discover, when I came to the Rock, that there was a dearth of public poetry and ceremony was a blow to my imagination. But that is how it is, how Anangu now are. There are few chants on show because Anangu gained control over their own culture in time enough to head off people writing their chants down. Those who have, as Robert Layton did for the Uluru land claim, have been obliged to maintain a tactful silence, and for Land Commissioner Toohey Layton only summarised the verses he had. They were parts of the song of *Kuniya* and *Liru*, a story that involves a battle of snakes. The main battle (though not the whole story) took place at Mutitjulu waterhole, and today you can't stand in that magnificent valley without feeling something of it because it is all part of what Anangu want to present to tourists. The bold narrative, once your think about it, is as wide as the sky. But without its chants, and without being Aboriginal, the poem that we can find in them is a matter for our imagination. And yet, what is more galvanising and concentrates the fearful western mind more perfectly than a snake story? Through many cultures, it is the snake story that seems so fundamental, so exemplary of great themes.

The Park is a paradise for snakes. There are ten species, and even their scientific names stimulate the imagination.

The Yellow-faced Whip Snake.
The Hooded Snake.
The Half-girdled Snake.
Narrow-banded Snake.
Desert-banded Snake.
Ringed Brown Snake.
The Mulga Snake.
Woma, the python of sand dune and sand plain.
Stimson's Python, which lives around the Rock.

From the names we can see where they live, and certainly know something about what they look like. Appearances are deceptive, however, there are several legless lizards in the park that can be easily mistaken for snakes. From an Anangu point of view, the classifications seem to be quite straightforward, to judge from the weightings given to the myth story. There are the pythons and there are the poisonous snakes. With regard to the epic battle in the great valley of Mutitjulu, *Kuniya* is Woma, and *Liru* is either the very deadly Western Brown or a Mulga Snake.

We seem to be dealing with particulars here. The battle was conducted between *a Kuniya* and *a Liru*, although, as the story is often presented in our language it takes on an allegorical reality. It is *Kuniya* at large (in some kind of sense) in battle with *Liru*, generic poisonous snakes. I don't mean that the snakes are representative but rather that the story is told as if they are in essense larger than themselves. In this lies their ultimate truth. Earlier I used the analogy of Plato's noble lie to point to the narrative purport of myth stories. A more comprehensive analogy (as Susan Woenne-Green pointed out to me) is Plato's idea of forms. With the ancestor creatures of the Tjukurpa it is the particularity of their form that endows them with their timeless, abstract truth as the ultimate enablers of reality. Their reality is furthermore evident in things. Indeed, in ancestor times they were so gigantic that they left these in the landscape. As a result, large, important areas of the Rock—much of the walking route—is resonant with the sounds of battle. To me, a generalised notion of 'snake' has become part of the whole place. This sense is heightened by the knowledge that there is another snake of importance to Anangu, a snake which has no direct counterpart to the Western classifications precisely because it is a mythic creature. It is called *wanampi*, and it guards the Uluru waterhole in the upper reaches of Mutitjulu gorge. Anangu fear it. Arguably, it might be thought of as a Rainbow Serpent, a creature known in many parts of the country. The Rock and the Park powerfully integrate with what I would call the snake-consciousness of the country.

Imagine a snake map of Australia. It would record all the species of snake in the most snake-infested of continents, from the fat pythons and water snakes that abound in the monsoon lands to the innumerable reptiles of the desert, snakes as profuse in reality as they are in mythology. Is there a domain where earthly reality intersects with the mythic more than the snake's? The map would have to show snakes which are dangerous to humankind, and snakes which are not; it would indicate the natural as well as extra-terrestrial habits of snakes and it would suggest the ritual deeds that belong in the kingdom of snakes. A coloured map, from the silvers and greens and night inks of tropical snakes to the honey and gold and bronze of desert snakes, with each colour band having a rhythm and perhaps a song attached to it. In total our map would resonate snake, though each species would be separately delineated while at the same time displaying its affinity with its neighbour, just as stories do, when one story unravels out of the other. Thus an imaginary snake map whose presence could not help but be larger than life, as myths are, when they are brought forward with their ancient powers.

Harney's 'mythology'—*his* imagination poetically at work—put the serpent at the base of the Rock. Of the serpent he pronounced: 'The mountain itself must be regarded as one complete ritual-stone because it is the abiding place of the all-knowing "Wanambi—serpent who lives in the valley of Uluru". He is the presiding spirit of the tribe who understands their ritual and judges their way of life. He is called the "all-knowing one" because he knows each tribesman's secret. His footprint can always be seen in the sky during the rain time because it is a rainbow's arch across the heavens.'

Then, as if this was not grandiloquent enough, he went even further into his own imagination by giving the great serpent powers over himself. 'Wanambi growled at me sometimes, I knew this by the way he hurled his angry breath against where I live. Then sometimes I knew that he and I are friends. To him—as with all Gods—is the power of reading people's minds. Thus does he know that I am with his people as I record his story for the white people who visit his domain.'

Few ancestor beings have loomed larger in white imaginations than the Rainbow Serpent. Indeed, to say 'Rainbow Serpent' is to automatically speak *the language of the imagination*. According to white records there are hundreds of Rainbow Serpent myths. They stretch the breadth of Northern Australia—across the top from the Kimberleys to Cape York, and run down through the Centre as far south as the Bight.

When the eminent Radcliffe-Brown surveyed rainbow myths in 1926 he found that they had four main 'elements': a conception of the rainbow as a huge serpent; it perennially inhabits deep, permanent waters; it is associated with rain and rain-making; and is connected with the iridescence of quartz crystals and mother of pearl. He was inclined to represent the Rainbow Serpent as a sort of guardian spirit, and its regular association with water suggested to him that the Aborigines conceive of it as the Spirit of Water.

May we come to the Rock then, alert to the universal presence of *wanampi* coiled beneath it? It is an arresting thought, except that the limited generalisations of anthropologists must check our powers of imagination. Half a century after Radcliffe-Brown, R. M. Berndt cautiously ventured two general statements which said that the myths bear upon such vital issues as seasonal fertility, and the renewal or maintenance of life-sustaining resources in nature. Beyond that, there are differences according to the part of the country we are in, and the Aboriginal custodians of the story. The serpent is sometimes male, sometimes female, a creature whose offspring calls it father (especially in the coastal areas) or mother (in the inland places). Differences of climate and weather seem to turn the serpent stories to different accounts.

And yet, there seems to be a third generalisation implicit in the Berndt account: the great creature expresses the relative place of men and women in religious life, especially in the matter of initiating boys into the sacred affairs of men. In Northern Australia the serpent stories often link with the story of the Old Woman, a kind of ogress. In another variation, women, often two sisters, enter the story by offending the standards of conduct required by the larger force of the snake. The snake devours and then regurgitates the offenders, tribal youths survive the snake's swallowing and emerge as initiates. Indeed the swallowing and the regurgitation are there, even in the first white recounting from the *Wiradijeri*.

My general point is that the story has many dramatic twists and turns, and these variations are essential to the meaning and significance of each place with each telling. This was the direction of Stanner's response to Radcliffe-Brown's overview. Stanner, whose fieldwork is testimony to the need to consider each Aboriginal society on its own terms, worked through the details of what the Murinbata people were able and willing to share with him. After this he said Radcliffe-Brown's elements were of secondary importance: 'Their main usefulness is taxonomic. The Rainbow Serpent does appear to be a kind of guardian spirit, and to say that he is The Spirit of Water is not inapt. But the quiddity of the myth transcends such characterisations. What it narrates is a religious world drama: a *drama* because it tells of events that follow in sequence to a unison which is a consummation by catastrophe; a *religious* drama because ultimate things of human beings and existence are the concern throughout; and a *world* drama because the import is cosmological.'

Stanner was writing in the early 1960s, drawing on fieldwork done in the Top End in the 1930s. Harney must have known of the work, even though he was not the kind of man who would have read the fine print of Stanner's fastidious essays, with their superb blend of analysis and observation. Speaking of 'mythopoeic thought as probably a continuous function of Aboriginal mentality', Stanner went on to make the point another way. He said that in selecting what version of a myth fits a place and circumstance the anthropologist is under 'a moral and intellectual duty to decide what is representative. *But his duty is also one of art.*' (My italics)

A modest proposal

WHEN MOUNTFORD WAS on the way to the Rock he was writing down the legends (his term) whenever he could. In 1940, between Mount Conner and the Rock he was told two serpent stories. One of them he recorded in this way:

In Iridi times, near Henby, some rat people Puraia went out hunting and came across the tracks of what they thought was a carpet snake, but it was really *wonambi* that had left Itjurka—ala—kwanaga water hole in the Finke and was out looking for food. The rat men found it in a hole, and pulled it out. The body of the snake was carried some distance away and the men prepared to cook their meat. First, they made a fire of Dubrosia, but when they placed the snake in the coals, the water in his body put the fire out. They then tried broom rush from the corkwood tree but with no better results.

Thinking that something was wrong, they collected a large heap of dry desert oak wood, for they knew this would give a hot fire, but when the snake was thrown on top, the fire all went dead, and the snake still moved about. An even better wood was that of iron wood, but even though the fire was so hot that the men could hardly get near, the moment the wood fell in the midst of it, the bed of red coals all blackened and lost their heat. As a last resource one of the men lit a fire and the dead wood of samphire which, in itself, particularly the leaves, is very full of water.

To the surprise of everyone, the fire kept its heat and soon the snake was cooked and everyone had their fill. But the snake was so large that they could not possibly eat it, so shouldering the remains, they set off back to camp.

To reach their camping place, the party had to pass over two sandridges. As they were crossing the first, they noticed their legs were becoming stiff and painful. They rapidly became worse, and by the time they had reached the next sandridge, they were becoming rigid in all limbs. And all around there were little snakes, running everywhere. Every little snake was surrounded with a rainbow colour.

The hunters were of course unaware of the cause of their illness, and were just able to struggle into camp and drop their load of meat and lay down. When the people and the doctor reached the hunters, they were stiff as if dead for some time.

When the 'doctor' saw the 'meat' that the hunters had brought in, they realised what had happened.

They killed all the young snakes straight away and then started to cure the hunters. First they opened up the abdomen of the men, and found them stuffed full of water grass (probably algae). This they cleaned out, sewed the men up, then they became conscious.

The doctors then lit a series of fires and placed a man between two. This caused a profuse perspiration, and the water (absorbed by contact with the *wonambi*). The men had to endure the heat from the fire until all the water had been taken out by the heat.

The 'doctors' then made a large fire of samphire wood and totally destroyed the remains of the *wonambi*. A large pile of black stone can be seen on this spot, evidence of the time when man tried to kill and eat the *wonambi*, the keeper of the rainbow and the waterhole.

Mountford does not indicate clearly who told him the story. Although he wrote it down while camping at the Rock, he does not, in his rather artless diary, leap to conclusions about 'rainbow serpents nearby'. (His Harneyesque inflation of *wanampi* came later, in his book on the Rock.) My understanding is that *wanampi* should be referred to quietly, in the context of the presence of water, with the emphasis very much dependent on the season of the year, which is to say, the availability of water. In other words we should, in our minds, decentre the drama. *Wanampi* is there, here, in this place we value for water. But that does not make him (it, her) an all-embracing topographical presence. As there are many baby snakes in Mountford's story (what a stimulus to our imaginations that is!) there are across the country many *wanampi*, one presence after another, and no one of them is necessarily more important than another.

It is in this kind of light that the Park presents *wanampi*. In the invaluable walk guide, *An Insight into Uluru*, we simply read: 'On the approach to Mutitjulu waterhole, you are walking the same path Anangu have always followed. As we near the waterhole, Anangu always show respect for Wanampi, an ancestral water snake. The Wanampi has the power to bring or stop the supply of water if it has any reason to be angry.'

A little more is said about *wanampi* in the 'Tour Operator's Workbook', notes prepared as a background to the walking guide. An entry under 'Sounds' says: 'Like other kinds of ritual behaviour, some sounds are particularly associated with *Tjukurpa*. For many Central Australian peoples, for example, the bull roarer is a sound particularly associated with men's ceremonies, and the sound of bull roarers is considered frightening and dangerous. For this reason, Anangu are disturbed by the sale of bull roarers to tourists. Other sounds are associated with particular contexts. For example, in pacifying *Wanampi* (water snakes from Tjukurpa) such as the one that stays above Mutitjulu spring, Anangu approaching the spring call out "Kuka kuka kuka".'

Another note from the 'Tour Operator's Workbook' draws on the work of Robert Layton. The anthropologist is describing how he sat down with Paddy Uluru, who spoke about the Mala Story and that of *mirin mirin* (the cicada). Paddy Uluru illustrated his point as he spoke. Layton reports: 'Another legend describes how Pantu (Lake Amadeus) was made by a *wanampi* (Water snake). Paddy Uluru (now deceased so use his name with care), explaining how the *wanampi* had dug out the ground with a stick to form a lake, drew concentric circles in the sand.'

Nothing closer to the Rock than this is drawn or publicly spoken about. But we get more details about the *wanampi* further west at Kata Tjuta:

> *Wanampi* is a mythical giant serpent. *Wanampi* is not like the totemic beings of the *Tjukurpa* time, as he has not created any of the topography of the land, but remains the same today as he always was. Mount Olga is the permanent home of a dangerous, highly coloured *Wanampi*. *Wanampi* live and guard waterholes.
>
> During the wet season this Kata Tjuta *Wanampi* lives in one of the waterholes on top of the mountain, but during the dry season he makes his home in a waterhole in Olga Gorge. If these dry up he retreats inside the rock itself.
>
> A wind blows constantly in Olga Gorge, sometimes gently at other times like a hurricane. This is the breath of *Wanampi* when angry. Anangu will not light a fire in this area or drink from his waterhole.

There is enough drama here, I suppose. *Wanampi* is a presence rather than a dramatic agent. The lesson for us is to recognize the cultural respect warranted by *wanampi*, just as we might learn to esteem the presence of water.

Snakes up front

THE MORE PUBLIC SNAKE story at the Rock is the battle between *Kuniya* the python and *Liru* the venomous snake. The booklet that does so much to introduce us to the Tjukurpa treats the snake battle as grandly as the Rock itself. *Kuniya* came to Uluru from the east, from Erldunda (where we took our morning tea). All along the Lasseter Highway we were on track with *Kuniya* as she carried her eggs to the Rock. The booklet reports what Anangu want to say today:

> She has been away for a long time, and has become an adult and a mother. She misses her home. She wants her children to be born in her own country and she wants to bring her children there.
>
> She begins her journey aware that with no arms and no legs she is vulnerable to predators. She carries her many heavy eggs in a bundle around her head. Her journey is long and hard. Each night she must stop and curl up around her eggs to keep them warm. Each day she resumed her journey west. She is burdened and dispirited, because being low to the ground she cannot see very far ahead. Each time she reaches the top of a sandhill she peers carefully over it, looking anxiously for a sign of home. Finally Uluru appears on the horizon but there is still a long way to go. She must go snake-like up every sandhill and down the other side.
>
> Finally she arrives. . . . She is exhausted and starved but she has brought her children to be born in her country. She is home where her body and spirit will be renewed.

It's near Taputji, on the eastern side of the Rock that she arrives, one of the places, as it happens, of special responsibility to Paddy Uluru. In the video *Uluru: an Anangu story*, we see this arrival re-enacted. A handsome woman, naked to the waist, carries a basket of eggs on her head; she weaves her way delicately towards the wall of the Rock and very gently sets herself down, her eggs down, in the shade, under a ledge of the Rock. There she tucks herself down to sleep—curls around the eggs if she would, having arrived in the fullness of time for the eggs to hatch so that later, as the film says, 'all the little *Kuniya* grew up, at Uluru'. A deep sense of maternal power, and of the beauty and strength in female responsibility comes through these images. Watching the video with all the stories out of my culture running in my head, I could not help thinking: 'Yes, *Kuniya* has arrived, eternally, with her great powers of procreation'.

Kuniya's opponent in the great battle is *Liru*, the poisonous snake. It is as well to know that 'in Nature' (as if this mythological is not *in* Nature as well, in its own way!) the python likes a meal of *Liru*, eight species of which are in Luru. She curls around *Liru* and constricts, suffocating them until devouring time. In the great battle, *Liru* has come from the west, though the arrival and location is not as specific as it is in Kuniya's story. This, at any rate, is how our booklet recounts the drama:

> In the beginning, the female *Kuniya* becomes very angry with the lack of respect for proper behaviour shown by her nephew, *Liru*. She attacks him in a great rage, and the battle becomes a disastrous encounter.
>
> As *Kuniya* approaches *Liru* in her righteous anger, she performs a ritual dance to make it publicly known that a woman of power is seeking to punish the person who has offended her. *Kuniya* is furious, and in an attempt to control the dark forces that her ritual anger is unleashing, she picks up a handful of sand and lets it fall to the ground. This is to settle the forces she is disturbing, so that they will not harm others.
>
> However, *Kuniya*'s rage is too strong, and a great battle takes place. *Kuniya* strikes *Liru* and he receives a small wound as he deflects the blow with his shield. Then *Kuniya* delivers *Liru* a second strike and he receives a deep, long and fatal wound. *Liru*'s shield falls with him to the ground.
>
> *Kuniya* has avenged her honour, but in her furious rage every plant near the battle has become poisoned. The spearwood bush here is particularly poisoned.

The story has led us into the valley of the Mutitjulu waterhole, one of the grand sites in Australia, no question about that. Before any words from Anangu, the valley creates its own drama. You walk in with a natural sense of ceremony and awe and some trepidation as you do, say, at Delphi, where the archaic oracle held court in the cliff faces, among the eagles. And so the spectacle of that wound up there, the long fatal gash that *Liru* received which is still visible on the Rock valley wall makes sense, perfect sense. To realise that the plants around you have in some way been cursed by the excessive rage of the great female anger, that also falls into place as you seem to naturally adopt a ceremonial approach along the valley towards the waterhole. The booklet sums it up: 'You will not just be looking at rocks and walls; *you will be walking in the midst of creation.*' (My italics)

Yes, you think when you get to the watering place, that's right. I am.

The grand fit that exists between the snake battle and the grand site, together, they grip your imagination. On reflection, though, there is something missing. An incompleteness, a sense of unfinished business in the story that is so neatly summarised in the booklet. That is part of the problem, I think—the drama is so speedily rendered that much of its power is lost. The most powerful myth stories do not have to be long, as we have seen with some of the Rainbow Serpent stories. But to work on the imagination they have to be told with a minimum of explanation and resort to summary. The verbal gloss has to be avoided. Particulars in the story have to be allowed to sing. This is a basic rule of narrative as it works in white culture, and—to judge from most of the records we have of Aboriginal culture—in indigenous narrative as well.

Besides, our booklet starts the snake story in a puzzling place. 'In the beginning', it says. In the beginning of what? What made *Kuniya* angry? And what brought *Liru* to the Rock in the first place? Need these two 'people' fight? We are told that *Liru* is *Kuniya*'s nephew. What brought relatives to such a tragic state of affairs? How far does the story go back? Is the beginning related to the beginnings in other Tjukurpa stories? To interpret this story of battle, I can't help but reach for other about struggles between kin—the *Bhagavad Gita*, for instance—but if I developed that thought I might sound like Bill Harney. Perhaps there is no entry into the story, especially as it is severed from *inma*. The esteemed anthropologist Clifford Geertz once said that he would understand a culture when he knew what a person meant when they sincerely said: 'I am a parakeet.' Is that what a walk into Mutitjulu involves? That I go there with someone whose whole being is involved in the battle between a great female serpent and a tenacious male, a poisonous snake?

A walking meditation

BARBARA NIPPER, a custodian of the *Kuniya* story, is a heartily large woman. Nearby, her voice is rich and low, contralto; from a distance—I have heard her shrewishly call to Tjamiwa, with whom she likes to competitively show stories of the Rock—she is as pitched as a cockatoo. She wears gaudy colours. She walks with a lopsided swish, as if she has learnt to put a limp to good use. All skirt, hips and shoulders carry her forward. Her dark look, which sweeps the ground, makes me nervous, but she has a laugh that ripens berries.

It had been suggested that if she was going to do the *Kuniya* walk for me, I might show my appreciation with gifts. She liked fruit and fruit juice. Orange juice would be nice. She was also fond of chicken. I could get some roast chicken from the Resort supermarket. She would like that. So I arrived one morning at the Ranger's Station with a shopping bag, not quite sure whether to hand it over to her straight away so that she could have a breakfast as we walked, or whether it was more appropriate to offer it afterwards. Also: should I pay cash? No, I was told: Park Management would reimburse Barbara; she would get about fifteen dollars an hour for the job.

My go-between was the Ranger Julian Barry, who is responsible for training the

Aboriginal rangers in the Park. As such, he is probably the white person closest to Anangu after Jon Willis. He is fluent in Pitjantjatjara, which he learnt in other advisory jobs in South Australia and the Central Lands Council, where he worked as an anthropologist. On anthropology as a professional practice Barry tends to make scathing remarks. He speaks of himself as a practical person committed to the day-to-day business of living with Anangu, rather than a bookish person. But as it happens, our talking point is the excellent thesis he has just finished for Deakin University. It is a critique of Fred Myers' distinguished book *Pintupi Country, Pintupi Self* (1986). The Pintupi were the last of the Central Australian Aborigines to leave full-time hunting and gathering for all the consequences of whitefella tucker and settlement, and to this extent are a different group to the Pitjantjatjara, who 'came in from the desert' much earlier. Barry argues that Myers' whole approach is coloured by his need to make of the Pintupi a purer case of 'pre-contact' Aborigine than they are. But what Barry does not dispute is the finesse of Myers' description of Pintupi society, especially as it connects with the Tjukurpa. For Myers the Tjukurpa is not so much a Law as a 'symbolic projection into space of various social processes'. As to those social processes, Myers stresses the immediacy of Pintupi life, and the high priority given to the maintenance of social relationships. 'There is, in Pintupi life, both violence and enormous concern for the welfare of others.'

I mention this now as earthing gesture: I had not arrived with a wishbone for Barbara so much as the flesh of the chicken. This is the real world, the practical world of concrete exchange, so far as telling stories go. Who knows what kind of story will be told in what situation? Narratives are negotiable, but at the same time—using Myers again—the Tjukurpa is by no means mere pragmatism. Myers speaks of the Tjukurpa as a mode that clearly marks out the difference between the visible and invisible.

'A late arrival to a conversation', Myers writes, 'often asks a story teller about the status of a narrative: "Are you talking about The Dreaming?" "NO", he may answer, "not Dreaming; I'm talking about the visible" (yuti), or "not Dreaming; I'm talking about what really happened" (mularrpa). Since the word mularrpa usually means "real", "true", or "actual" as opposed to "untrue", "fictitious", or "lie", its contrast with the concept of The Dreaming may seem puzzling. However The Dreaming is not viewed either as a fiction or a lie. In fact there is no category of fictional narrative in Pintupi. A story either happened or it did not; if it did not occur, the story is a "lie".'

In Pitjantjatjara there are some differences in these equations, but the frame is the same. 'From The Dreaming it becomes real', as Myers has the Pintupi say it. And it is true, because proof of the truth is the seeing of the place where it happened.

All of this then, I had in mind that morning. 'Snake' is one thing. *Kuniya* is another. Finding my way into the *Kuniya* story was more than a matter of going for a walk with a powerful woman. There would be levels of truth, levels of narrations—all true—and somehow, even though I was a witness from another place, I would be implicated in them. Rather than think about any of this, what I had to do was listen.

And so we set off: Barbara Nipper, her friend Nura Ward who was visiting from South Australia, Julian Barry and me, in brilliant morning light. The sun had come over the Rock and settled in the valley of Mutitjulu. The waterhole, above which *wanampi* slept, was still in shadow, but the high southern rock face was lit, so that you could see the signs of battle and the stains in the rock below, where the bush had been poisoned forever. The sky was blue. The sky was empty. An expectant silence seemed to hang above us, so that the crunch of our footsteps into the valley was dramatic, and even when we stopped at the most banal of places—the tourist's sign—tension remained.

I had to read the sign. A reminder for this *minga*.

Julian Barry waited with the women. They seemed to be girlishly in league as well as bonded in adult authority as we moved on.

Barbara stopped to indicate the cliff to the right of the valley. We regarded the gash, high in the great wall.

—So *Kuniya* . . . Julian said, after listening to Barbara.

—So *Kuniya* picked up some sand. She was really angry at the *Liru* because the *Liru* had killed her nephew . . . After the fight over there, where her nephew was speared, she got really wild with one of the *Liru*—she got down, she was so furious—she got down and picked up some earth and threw it down . . . To settle things down she got the sand, the soil, she was really really wild—she hit *Liru*, the man, on the head and killed him.

This is what Julian said to me. The breaks indicate the points at which he stopped to ask more of Barbara. I had no idea what was said in-between, although it sometimes appeared that Barbara said more than Julian translated to me.

—How did she kill him, I asked.—With the sand?

—With the *wana*, the digging stick.

—Was the sand sand or what?

There was a quick exchange.

Julian said:—When she was spreading the soil she was doing it as *inma*.

As he spoke Barbara raised her open hands shoulder high and made a swaying movement. She started to chant. As she did, Julian went on:—People did this, this is an *inma* that people do, before turning once more to her.

—What was the chant she sang? I asked.

He consulted.

—She'd prefer not to say that.

Another question, and again Barbara answered by singing. A short refrain.

We had to move on. A few tourists approached. As we walked Julian explained to me that Barbara was shy of conveying the chant; it was a man as well as a woman's story.

When we stopped again, Barbara raised her hands and swayed. We were talking about the sand again.

—Willis probably knows this, there are a couple of words I'm not familiar with.

He spoke to her again, but then we had to move again to avoid some more tourists on the path.

There was more talk. Barbara breathed heavily.

Here was another sign. It was the one on the path, right in the middle of the valley.

Barbara spoke in a long burst. In the middle of it Julian spoke English to her: —And *Kuniya* put her eggs safely somewhere?

—Yeah, breathed Barbara, to Julian.

Then more in her Pitjantjatjara. Speaking softly, as gently, I felt, as a woman handling some eggs. She had thoroughly warmed to the telling.

There was a pause. All was still in the gorge. I found myself looking at a bloodwood tree as if it had a personality of its own. Barbara spoke again, Julian translated.

—So after putting down her eggs, she came up here and said 'Hey, they've hid my . . .?' Maybe killed him. She came here, she went up, she started doing *inma* . . .

Barbara did the dancing gestures again: she said more.

Quickly Julian said: —I don't really know what she's talking about here.

He then resumed: —So she grabbed a bit of red gum tree, she grabbed her fighting stick —made out of river red gum. (The question was to Barbara.)

—Uwa, said Barbara.

—And . . .

More loud talk from Barbara now, and singing on a higher note, one, two lines . . .

Julian listened again, and queried.

Then to me: —She vomited.

More talk from Barbara. High level, then low and emotional.

—OK, said Julian, she vomited —Perhaps in rage, perhaps to make the . . . And her *ukari* came round here.

And again Barbara murmured softly in Julian's ear.

—Then she hit *Liru* on his shield. It fell. And then, she killed him.

Here Julian seemed to have picked up Barbara's solemnity. The announcement of death. He inquired some more in the same tone. There was a long to and fro before I was told any more.

Barbara pointed to the Rock. A sweeping gesture as if to indicate 'right over the top'. With that sign she seemed to dismiss everything that was visible before us, invoking all that was invisible at the Rock.

142

—*Ukari* did it. She was really missing her nephew. She killed him!

Barbara softly again.

—Barbara's saying that's the Aboriginal people's law, that's the way it happened . . . So if somebody kills your nephew . . . it's the same Law today . . . If Barbara's nephew gets killed then she'll get a big digging stick, she'll get really wild and she'll go and finish off that person . . . This is another example of people looking into the Tjukurpa for their Law . . . And it stands strongly, our Law says . . . we look after this Law, we practice it, we sing the songs, we do the *inma*, and all our lives we do that Law.

It was OK then for me to ask a question.

—The sign about the *Kuniya* story spoke about the virtue of controlling anger. How did this fit in with Barbara apparently talking about acting on anger?

Julian replied,—Yeah . . . maybe it's more like focusing than controlling from what she's said. He checked: after another to and fro he spoke.

—It [the story] is [about] a way of doing *inma*, and fighting.

Barbara was moving her hands above her head and chanting.

Julian said:—Waving the digging stick, a way of . . . Do you have another question?

But before I could speak there was a lot more talk . . .

—Barbara was saying, some parts of the *inma* men look after, some parts the women look after. And she's saying to me I should go and ask the men and they can teach me about the men's side . . . Barbara was saying, before landrights, they might have wanted to come here and take the rocks away . . .

Julian and Barbara's voices fell away as they spoke. Then Julian said, very sensitively:—Barbara's just saying that her deceased husband, Tjamiwa's brother-in-law, before landrights, looked after that site, and was involved in whatever that fight was at that time . . .

—Where did the *inma* take place? I asked.

Barbara spoke, and then sang.

Julian inquired. She chuckled. She spoke.

Then he told me:—I'm not sure. Often, I don't think there is any specific place, it might put people under a bit of pressure to ask . . . Any more questions?

—What happened to the eggs?

But there was another interruption.

—We should maybe move over on the grass eh, Julian said.

So we did. Tourists had arrived; they paused to listen, stare and looked as if they might take a photograph of these white men in intense conversation with two Aboriginal women.

We sat on the ground, in the grass among the bloodwood trees. I took a minute to find a spot because I was wary of *minga*. Nor was I sure where to sit in relation to Barbara. By now I was very conscious of her not talking to me at all, but rather to

Julian, where her signs of communication rested. Julian sat beside her and I felt superfluous to the dialogue, though it was all for me. As the conversation resumed I was struck by Barbara's ease there, on the ground. Huge enough to spread, she none the less arranged herself with impressive poise and decorum on the earth. As if she had planted herself lightly, a flowering root plant that belonged there, on the ground and had been there for a long time.

As her voice rose Julian cut in: — Barbara's saying I think it's men's business.

—Noooo, she moaned.

Julian, with a smile in his voice said: — No, everybody's business? . . . So Barbara's saying everybody here's . . . we might talk later about that later, but at the moment . . . any more questions?

—Is there any part of a song that Barbara can say?

—She was saying men and women do it together so she . . .

He paused. Barbara was chanting and Nura had joined in.

Julian said, — That last part is where *Kuniya* is getting ready to strike.

Barbara sang some more, explained some more.

Then both women were singing again, in enthusiastic unison.

Julian cut in. And still they sang, then stopped, and Barbara's voice went up: a shout.

—She [*Kuniya*] threw sand on her own stomach . . .

Singing, talking, singing. Their voices dropped, but the strength of the chant increased as they did. Barbara's voice went out across the ground, one syllable after another, one phrase unfolding after another, across the ground before us with all the sinuous strength of a snake.

Julian translated quickly, urgently: — Yeah, I'm a bit reticent about recording stuff, anyway, I can see it backfiring in the future, and besides, I can't understand most of it . . .

At this point Barbara's singing was a high croon. The chant asserted itself, as if Julian's qualms were neither here nor there; they seemed to have become as displaced as my need to know what they meant. Now that Barbara had begun the song and its connection with this place, it seemed to be exercising its own power. Then the key she was singing in rose again and left the ground. The chant was head high and travelling, rising towards the rock face.

Suddenly she stopped and spoke to Julian again.

—*Uwa*, he said.

More talk.

He told me: — I've got a really good painting done by her daughter, at home.

A lot more talk. Oh, the talk, like running water, like parrots taking off and landing, like the clatter of sticks on rocks. The women's voices were so high, so exclamatory, that I thought they would break into the chant again. And for a moment they did. And then silence in the gorge again, as if it was there so all the invisibles could be visible again.

We had stayed well out, I saw, from the waterhole. No one had to break the silence with the *kuka kuka kuka*.

Julian cut in:—She [*Kuniya*] was living here. And she travelled around a great deal. Went really fast. And she got married over near Imanpa. Over at Wallawa dam, near the National Park. And she went around near Erldunda, and then she came back with children . . . She came back carrying the eggs . . . Necklace . . .

Cries from the women at the mention of necklace.

Julian said:—It appears to me she made a necklace out of the eggs.

The women were singing again at the thought of the necklace. A deep, rhythmic song, with laughter, then trills . . . High talking and laughter at the idea of the necklace . . .

After a while, during which Julian confessed to difficulty, he said:—So she [Barbara] is talking about carrying eggs and meat and stuff like that on her head . . .

—OK, *palya*, said Julian.

—Had I finished? OK?

Oh no, I thought. Time has come to an end.

—What about the track, I said, I need to be clear on the route of *Kuniya*.

During the exchange Barbara let out a scornful laugh.

—They travelled around a lot of places, said Julian.

—I understand, I said, it started at Erldunda.

—It started here, went to Tempe Downs and right around, Julian said.

Much talk between the women.—I should ask Willis, Julian said.

More high-pitched talk.

But we were coming to an end.

—So they're saying she [*Kuniya*] travels around, she lifts her head up, and looks after the eggs when she carries them, to look after the children.

And then we were all getting up from the ground. We started to walk back, the women ahead of us. This was the end, unless the story broke out again as we walked away from the Mutitjulu waterhole (which we had never really approached), heading along the path towards the Toyota.

Shedding the skin

THIS IS A SLIGHTLY simplified version of what happened in that hour or so. I haven't mentioned the way Barbara and her friend, Nura Ward, kept talking and breaking off to collect things: plums on the way, figs on the way back. The story was not just a story, it was a stroll used for food gathering as well, and the sociability that went with it. The women's pleasure at being there in the morning was apparent (and made me feel a bit better at taking up their time). Nor have I fully mentioned the way in which they moved and gestured to different parts of the telling. Barbara made a big thing of that *inma* with the sand; and then later with the digging stick that had become the murder weapon. Her body had moved insistently and it was about the only time she addressed a communication directly to me. As if the body spoke louder than words, as if the chant—aimed straight—might be a better means of communication than anything Julian could transmit. Maybe she felt that 'the poem' was something that could cross cultures?

Her movement with the imaginary digging stick was striking. She had her hands up and was holding the stick above her head as she swayed. The tempo was hard to tell: if it was a slow swaying dance, or something more urgent. It had the rhythm of seduction, and yet . . . When we got back to the Ranger's Station Julian consulted his dictionary to find the word he had written on the back of his hand.

Akutarinyi
do a kind of skipping dance-step. Women use this in ceremony, and also as a challenge to fight; minyma tjuta akutarinyi, pika pungkunytjikitja 'women do the skipping dance-step, when they want to fight'

I had also been impressed by the difficulty of getting the narrative straight, and of fleshing out the story in a way that creates—for white culture—a vivid narrative of the kind that Berndt had been able to produce. What time this must take! What time, and what skill. On my little walk there were the constant interruptions (what I felt to be interruptions, at any rate), and the departures from the sequence of action. None of my questions, as far as I could tell at the time, had been answered directly, some of them not at all. The story had been presented, rather than told, and in so far as it was told, the part of the story that I had been given was only a small part (I knew this, if only from the *Kuniya* verses Robert Layton has summarised for Justice Toohey at the landclaim). What I had been told or shown had been determined by several considerations, not the least of which was the time I had been granted and had available (the full *inma* takes days), and the social obstacles expressed by Barbara. There was the absence of men, who also owned the story. There was the memory of Barbara's husband, whose presence was felt when she brought the Tjukurpa story into the present, by referring to his recent death. It was on the way back in the Toyota that Barbara told me (through Julian) that for the purposes of this book she preferred to be called Barbara Nipper.

Then there was the matter of the chants, which are so important to *inma*. In some *inma* the chants go along with the action, they are the necklace of the dance. In others, it seems that the chant is the backbone to everything, in that they are the sacred words. To the chants I had no access, not only because I could not even pick up the words that were sung in my presence, but also because, even if I had been able to speak Pitjantjatjara, it is possible that I would have not understood. The sacred chant is a concentrated linguistic item. When Strehlow brought all his years' work together in *Songs of Central Australia* he made much of this: in some sacred chants phrases and words are used in a way that mask meanings so that only the senior people recognise them. The song itself requires a high level of initiation before it can be understood, let alone fully entered. To appreciate this is to realise in yet another way that the difficulties of getting a full story written down for white Australian culture are profound, if not insurmountable.

I tried to say cheerio to Barbara. I was reaching to shake her hand as she was turning away. Then she had turned away. Gone. I thought: I cannot even acknowledge her, her diffidence (indifference?) had put a fullstop to that. At every step of travelling in the Centre I discover that the serpent of presumption must be avoided in favour of insignificance, ignorance. Impossible to really grasp anything here, not even a woman's hand to say thank you. Then she turned. She saw me through the back of her head. Her hand was limp, her fingers tucked together. Eyes down, then away, with that lurch, a flick of her torso. Away she went with the tuckerbag of juice, fruit and chicken.

CHAPTER 4 **Marsupials**

Invisible rituals

THE SUPREME MARSUPIAL in Central Australia is malu, the Red Kangaroo. How could we have come all this way and not seen malu? The answer is that malu is there all right, but it chooses not to travel by the Lasseter Highway, or sleep under mulga trees near the Ayers Rock Resort. But malu is the strong story through all of this country. The places where malu ceremony are held are some of the most sacred sites in the Centre, and the line of malu, as it goes from north to south (roughly) is the Dreaming track that links all language groups in ceremony. That ceremony is men's business of the utmost importance because it deals with the initiation of boys into manhood. The presence of malu is absolutely integral to the maintenance and transmission of the Tjukurpa.

That is why, I realised well after the event, Tjamiwa was so upset about the pathetic cartoons on the wall of the Red Centre Motel. He was not simply making a point about tactlessness: he was implying that his culture had much to affirm about malu. The tact required with respect to malu is such that the line it follows through the country cannot easily be drawn. T. G. H. Strehlow claimed to have mapped the strongest malu sites in Aranda country thirty years ago; but that was a time when the white man thought he had a right to do so. Some twenty years later naturalist John Newsome pursued his passion for the Red Kangaroo by travelling through the country

148

using Strehlow's material as his map. Newsome reported that he had found the actual sites where the great 'increase' ceremonies for malu were held. To read his report today is to notice his excitement that he had, like no other white man besides Strehlow, probably arrived at the sacred sites to which he had not been invited. The other dimension to Newsome's 'discovery' was less worrying: he was there out of an interest in the natural habitat of the sacred sites. He observed that they were places of striking fertility, exactly the kind of spots that would—perhaps not surprisingly—sustain a good population of malu. Today we might say that Newsome's achievement confirmed a truism: an Aboriginal ceremony made deep ecological sense.

When the traditional owners of the Rock were making their legal claim upon Uluru, they had a problem with malu. They had to affirm its presence, while for Tjukurpa reasons keep details out of the public eye. Robert Layton's map of the Dreaming lines is fairly explicit about some ancestor creatures, but not so much malu. It comes from the north-east down through Purrarra Well to the soak at Patji. The other malu line comes down through the Petermanns from the north, and continues far south to Mount Davis. On the map malu does not come to the Rock. It is not *at* the Rock, any more than it is *at* Kata Tjuta. That is not to say it is not there, especially in the case of Kata Tjuta. When I said, earlier on, that there is a snake consciousness in Australia, I was stretching a point of imagination in our culture. To say there is malu consciousness all about here is not, I understand, stretching the point for Anangu. Malu is here, a strong line through the area.

Baldwin Spencer was lucky at the Rock. When he came with the Horn Expedition, he sat in on a malu feast. He was much moved by it, though, in retrospect, quite uncomprehending as well. It happened when it was 'quite dark', and he dramatically makes the most of it, since the natives were in a 'genuinely wild state, none of them having seen a white man before'.

'Sitting round there fires, two of the men prepared the kangaroos for cooking', begins Spencer. 'First of all the two large tendons were extracted from each hind limb. To do this the skin is cut through close to the foot with the sharp bit of flint'. And so on: tendons, teeth, hitches, bindings—the account of primitive practicality.

'The hole [of the belly] is stitched up with a short pointed stick, the limbs are dislocated, the tail cut off at the stump, and then the animal is ready for cooking.'

Australians know this routine by now. It is the standard and ritualised dismemberment of the malu, if senior men are present, just as the white man has described it for two hundred years, just as anthropologists felt compelled to describe it as late as the 1950s (when Frederick Rose was down the road at Angas Downs), just as I self-consciously avoided describing it out in the Mann Ranges, when I was still shaken by the fate of the baby malu.

Spencer continues with a kind of blind relish. 'After lying here (on the hot ashes) for an hour it was supposed to be cooked and was taken out and placed on acacia branches. It was then cut open and first of all the liver and heart were taken out and eaten. The carver took the burnt skin off often using his teeth to tear it away and with a yam stick cut the body up roughly into joints, helping himself as he went along with such dainty morsels as the kidneys. Everyone, women and children included, had their share of the meal, and if not done enough it was well rubbed in the hot sand and cooked therein to suit the taste of the eater. *It did not appear* to be any special portions given to any individual, but the men were served before the women and the children received pieces from the men and women.' (My italics)

'It did not appear'! Today we can only cringe at the rush to generalise on the basis of such limited and distanced experience. The method of science flounders in the heat of the white man's mixture of awe and condescension towards 'savagery'. Spencer should have said: 'I did not know'; in all consistency he might have said: 'The treatment of this carcass is absolutely methodical. The method of eating it may be too. As may be the meanings attached to the hunting, the feasting and speaking about the animal.' He expressed nothing of the sort, not because he was a man without sensitivity or devoid of any sense of ritual (as his subsequently famous books would show), but because science as he understood it was not to involve acts of imagination into other forms of meaning in the world. When he came to the Rock he saw the natives feast and then sleep, 'sometimes waking during the night and raking together the embers of the fires around which they slept'. He leaves the Rock after that, as if the natives are in their crude state still sleeping, whereas in fact, the sleep was Spencer's: he and the Horn party never quite woke up to the lived complexity of the 'Nature story' they had been so close to.

Real things

MALA, THE RUFOUS hare wallaby, is one of the big public stories at Uluru. *Mala* is as big in Anangu imagination as the Red Kangaroo seems to be in ours. It is one of the many medium-sized Central Australian marsupials that have almost completely disappeared from the desert in the last fifty years. Nocturnal, grass, herb- and seed- (and ant) eating, *mala* have suffered from the arrival of four outside forces: white man's cattle, which does damage to the undergrowth; white man himself as he has populated a hitherto sparsely inhabited region; feral cats—the 'pussy cats' as Anangu call them; and rabbits, that once-innocuous larger mammal introduced on the coast of South Australia at the turn of the century, which had eaten its way to Central Australia in plague proportions by the 1920s. What seems to have happened is that when *mala* have not been eaten by cats or foxes, they have had their food devoured by cattle and rabbits. As a result they hardly exist in Nature, although they have survived in myth.

Spencer spotted some small marsupials, especially the spinifex-hopping mouse, but he did not register *mala*. It was the splendid naturalist H. H. Finlayson, who loved 'The Red Centre' (also the title of his famous book), who put *mala* on our scientific maps when he came through in the late-1920s. Finlayson travelled rough and survived bush hardships with gusto and none of the disdain Spencer wrote into the Horn Report. He made few observations at the Rock, but further south, in the country toward which the *mala* fled in ancestor times, he made great chase with the most interesting of the smaller herbivorous marsupials (*Lagorchestes hirsutus*).

Here he is in 1932, having come into dry country, a long way from water. He travelled with four camels 'taking along three of the bucks and two "weeis"; bright boys of about fourteen'. It was a matter of finding the right patch of spinifex—in this case one about ten square miles and surrounded by dense mulga. There were plenty of mala tracks, and burrows everywhere under their arching pincushions. Anangu with him said they were experts, which they were, but it turned out they could not catch the *mala* by one method, 'which is to follow the freshest tracks to a squat and then, while two or three stand ready with throwing sticks, another jumps upon the tussocks and breaking down the shelter, sometimes exposes the mala, which has no time to use the burrow.'

Hope in the party dwindled when this did not work. But the next day was ideal for their favourite method of hunting. It was a scorcher, with the wind in the right direction. A *mala* drive was possible, the method perfected by 'age-long repetitions'. Finlayson continues:

> Firstly runners are sent into the wind with fire-sticks. They diverge from the starting-point along two lines, and, thrusting the torch into spinifex clumps at intervals of about fifty yards, they soon have an open horse-shoe of flame eating into the resinous and almost explosively inflammable vegetation. The extent of country fired depends, of course, on the size of the party operating, but in the present case when the runners were recalled, the arms of the horseshoe were nearly two miles long and the extremities of the open end which faces the wind, were nearly a mile apart. The country outside the horseshoe is left to its fate, but matters are so arranged that the areas where maala tracks are thickest are within the lines of flame, and upon this space attention is focused.

> The subsequent events form three distinct phases, during each of which some kills are made. The fire, of course, makes rather slow headway against the wind, but as it creeps on, all life forsakes the tussocks well in advance of the flame and a steady concentration of all living things is effected. As the flames advance into the wind, the party recedes from them slowly, keenly watching for a breakaway

151

from every likely looking tussock, and should a maala break cover within range, his chance of dodging the throwing-sticks is slender. This is the first phase, and it occupied most of the morning. But while this has been going on the extremities of the wings of flame have been closing in and when at last they meet, the action suddenly quickens and the second phase is ushered in.

With the wind full behind it, the closed line of flame now rushes back towards the starting point, and to the steady roar of the leeward fire is added the sudden menacing boom of the windward one, changing from time to time to a crash, as some isolated patch of mulga or corkwood is engulfed, and swept out of existence in a second. The party now gathers up the spoils already taken and dashes through the leeward fire to the safety of the burnt ground beyond, and there, in line, await the meeting of the double wall of flame, when every living thing which has remained above ground must come within range of their throw.

It is a time of most stirring appeal. The world seems full of flame and smoke and huge sounds; and though the heat is terrific, one is scarcely conscious of it. In the few tense moments that remain before they break into frenzied action and frenzied sound, I watch the line of blacks. The boys can scarcely control their movements in their excitement; the three men, muscled like greyhounds, are breathing short and quick; they swing their weight from foot to foot, twirling their throwing-sticks in their palms, and as they scan the advancing flames their great eyes glow and sparkle as the climax of the day draws near. It is their sport, their spectacle, and their meat-getting, all in one; and in it they taste a simple intensity of joy which is beyond the range of our feeling.

Mala saga

SMALL FURRY THINGS that they are, *mala* might seem closer to our domesticated imaginations than snakes. For Anangu not so; and therefore, potentially not for us either, if we are able to get a bearing on the story. The power of the *mala* is integral to the culture of the Rock, but the components of that power—the events and 'meanings in the *mala* story—are easier to point to than narrate. Finlayson spoke about the joy in the *mala* drive being 'beyond the range of our feeling'. What feelings are appropriate to the *mala* story? What feelings are, by virtue of the Park's authorised version, permitted?

The park booklet, *An Insight Into Uluru*, tells us:

'a simple intensity of joy which is beyond the range of our feeling', H. H. Finlayson on the mala *hunt*.

Mala men, who come from the west, carry the ceremonial pole, Ngaltawaṯa. They scramble quickly to the top of Uluṟu and plant the pole in the ground at the most northern corner to begin the Inma . . .

The Mala men are happy and busy. Suddenly people from the west come with an invitation to join another Inma. The Mala must refuse, as they have already started their own ceremony. The people from the west return home in great anger at the insult. They plan to wreak vengeance upon the Mala in a terrible way.

Across the land comes and evil, black dog-like creature: Kurpany. He has been created by these people in the west to destroy the Mala ceremony. Luṉpa, the kingfisher bird, cries a warning to the Mala. It is ignored, and Kurpany attacks and kills many Mala men, women and children. In terror the remaining Mala flee to the south with Kurpany chasing them all the way.

The official brochure seems to give a clear interpretation of the *mala* business. It is an orientation to several things—to the direction from where the *mala* people came, to a commemoration of ceremony; and to the drama of retribution when ceremony is disrespected. Cryptic though this version is, I find it powerful, a concentrated narrative with the power of tragedy.

And yet, there is not much of a story here, is there? It is very cut back, and I feel it does not have the imaginative fullness it might have. It was Malinowski who insisted, under the rubric of functionalism, that all myth served the purpose of being social charters for customs, institutions or beliefs. I can see that about the *mala* story as it is told here, while wondering if, it would have other dimensions if told differently, and on the basis of other aspects of Anangu material. Having said a myth is about ceremony, we can still go on to ask what that ceremony is about. No openings to that question here, any more than there is material to ponder on other aspects of the myth: its connection with ritual, for example, or the extent to which it might be a story fundamentally about origins, or about nature, or psychic conflicts, to name some of the basic ways of approaching myth. I'm not suggesting it is the job of the Park to provide myth theorists with grist to their mill. I am, though, expressing frustration at the thinness of the cautionary tale as it is on the page, and drawing attention to the secular blandness of the booklet. Anangu are possessive and cautious about their own culture; Pitjantjatjara people will only say so much, which is their right. Having said that, what can we say about white culture's processing of their stories?

The booklet exists because people like Tjamiwa got fed up with tourists who keep coming and 'never see anything'. Tjamiwa said this to Susan Woenne-Green when they were walking the Rock in *mala* precincts. All around there were rocks, trees and other things to do with the *mala* story. These marks, these tracks is where they *really* were,

Tjamiwa had said in one of the many exchanges that went into the production of the booklet.

We should not underestimate the work, the labour of cultural exchange, that went into *An Insight Into Uluru*, which was produced by the Mutitjulu Community in collaboration with the Australian Nature Conservation Agency (then Australian National Parks and Wildlife Service). Tjamiwa was a principle informant; Woenne-Green, then Community Liaison Officer, the principal interpreter and recorder. Many walks, many tellings of different experiences each time. The booklet went through several drafts of consultation with the designer as well as owners of the stories. The task was to place the story properly in the context of the walk itself; to position the narrative in the landscape in a way that oriented people towards the story in a way that fitted Anangu's. But none of this, despite all the walking, talking and consulting is to say that the myth we have is *as it is* in Aboriginal culture. It has been, on the contrary, sufficiently removed to be able to list what has been lost.

Drama, in the version we have on a page—the enactment of ritual, is barely suggested. This is because we have story without ceremony, *inma*. Also lost is the Aboriginal 'style' of the myth. Again we must mention that the prose we have is not song, not the chant, not the drama of concentrated, incantatory poetry. There is, in the *inma* and chanting, the characteristic repetition of Aboriginal narrative. Such repetitions are both an aid to memory and a part of the natural rhythm of the talking; they are rhetorical and energising. Recall the way Tjamiwa recounted the murder at the Rock. The plot of that story was linear, but the style of telling was circumlocutory. Indeed, Tjamiwa's general strategy (telling me that story rather than the one I asked for) was oblique. Often, with the unfolding of story in *inma*, and in the chant, a narration can take hours and sometimes days and weeks to complete, assuming that the idea of completion is appropriate, which is not always the case.

All this is to say nothing of other performative aspects that are integral to the meaning of a myth. There is, as I've mentioned before, the sacred layering in the poetry, the masking that is there in syntax and rhythm; but over and above that meaning is also a matter of what kind of singing it is. There is, for example, the matter of voice modulation: the whispering and backward inhaling that call up, invoke and evoke, the Great Events of the Tjukurpa, things that can hardly be spoken, let alone written down in a potted prose summary, albeit a judicious one. Admittedly, we might feel that in the summary we have something like a core meaning of the myth. It has the beauty of succinctness, and the virtue of adjectival coherence, but what it cannot have because of all of the above, and more, is the manifold power and extension of the Tjukurpa 'story'. The Tjukurpa sings deep, travels wide. Ideally, the booklet should be a scroll a hundred kilometres long, a scroll in braille, so that we can move our hands across Aboriginal English spoken for days in ceremony; it should be a document (since our culture demands written things) designed to be read while walking into the country, through dunes and ranges, along wide, dry riverbeds to waterplaces, travelling through whole seasons of the country; a document that creates as you read it, and allows time for us to touch the song.

Alas, we read. We have the written word which, in order to save time, abstracts. That is the way for a written culture. The word creates an idea of *mala* for us, almost by way of reminder of the distance that exists between our imaginative understanding and an active entry into *inma*, which is grounded in the invisible worlds that are of the body, giving us a promissary note to Reality. Out of our written forms we can only sing thinly, ethereally. Even a good little booklet containing words set down with integrity becomes as distancing as a camera. And yet Anangu would not see the booklet as being so distant from the Tjukurpa. 'Anangu feel quite strongly', Susan Woenne-Green writes to me, 'that this sort of literature makes the visibility happen. They've had years of apparent experience of Harney *et al.* demonstrating just that. A *major* point is that people like Tjamiwa are very aware of the power of language and how the importance of metaphor, poetry, 'good quality expression in English, and want this aspect to be enhanced in the tourist material (as opposed to two-bit ethnography)'.

Well and good then. *An Insight into Uluru* embodies a potent paradox. For the Western mind, it gives abstract clues to the presence of *mala*, while being for Anangu close to Tjukurpa's concrete reality. Still, I need to say that while I know Uluru pulsates with Aboriginal song, the lines I have in the walk booklet leave me wanting.

Willie wagtail history

STRANGELY, OUR POSITION at the Rock can't help but be enriched by taking a larger bearing on what our culture has previously tried to say about *mala*. What follows is meant to suggest the richness and sanctity of the Tjukurpa story, while tracking the competitive song and dance white culture can make of it.

You can approach the *mala* story from any number of directions. We can enter the story at various points because it depends almost as much on our topographical focus as it does on the narrative. *Where* we enter the story (this where of time and space) determines the ancestral creatures we will be talking about. For it is important to bear in mind that to call it the *mala* story is, to some extent, misleading. As we've already realised from the simplest summary, the narrative is in a way a saga: not only does it involve the approach, arrival and tragic departure of the *mala* creatures themselves, other creatures are implicated: *lunba*, the kingfisher woman; *panpanpalala*, bellbird; *lungkata*, sleepy lizard; *tjintir-tjintirpa*, willie wagtail; and *kurpany* the evil black dog. Not only that, some of the totem ancestors play parts in more than one story. In effect, we can talk schematically about the *mala* story, only to discover that it intersects with the snake story, and that in various places around the Rock the narratives entwine. Strehlow starts with the *mala* men before they got to the Rock:

> A large party of *mala* men and novices (*maliera*), led by a leader called Lungkatatjukurba (*lungkata* is the sandhill blue-tongued lizard), came south from the Pintubi-Kukatja country to Ayers Rock. At various places they put down brush-fences called *pirmalta*. Mala hare-wallabies were then driven by the young *maliera* novices towards these *pirmalta*; and other hunters who had been crouching behind the *pirmalta* slew these hare-wallabies when they came within reach . . . Just before reaching Inintitjara, a left-handed mala man called Tambu saw a *tjintir-tjintir* or *tjintira-tjintira* (willy wagtail) woman sitting on the travel route leading to the water. Incensed that a woman should have dared to remain sitting near a trail which was being followed by a group of *maliera* novices (who must not see a woman during their initiation period), Tambu killed the woman and left her body lying at the side of the track. The party then went on, and put down a large men's camp at Inintitjara. Some time later an ancestral kingfisher (*lunba*), seeing a *mamu* (man-eating monster) approaching from the west at midnight, tried to rouse the sleeping *mala* men and novices in their camp. But the sleepers woke only after the monster had already come into their midst and ripped two of them in pieces. The *mala* men and novices immediately fled from Inintitjara, and the monster raced after them in relentless pursuit.

Strehlow's account dates from his stay at Hermannsburg way back in 1933. The occasion for resurrecting that record was his essay on Mountford, which was written in 1968, but remained unpublished for some years because some colleagues saw it as such a devastating assault. The subject was Mountford's already published book on the Rock and his new book, *Winbaraku* (1968), in which Mountford travels the route of snake story that starts in northern Aranda country and runs south. The song cycle Mountford first recorded was from a Kukatja/Aranda man, Patika, better known as police tracker Paddy, on his 1935 expedition. Mountford had in fact sought Strehlow's help in interpreting Patika's crayon drawings. Mountford's errors in the snake story are Strehlow's main target, but he attacks on all fronts, including Mountford's claim to knowledge about Ayers Rock. Strehlow's informants were the Yankuntjatjara men, Tjonkiti and Kapuluru. Through the Kukatja translator who was fluent in Yankun-tjatjara and Aranda, Strehlow wrote down and discussed 28 verses of the *mala* song. Bear in mind here that Strehlow does not claim to be an expert on the Rock. His 'domain', if we think of white fellas appropriating Aboriginal culture in the act of recording their stories, was Aranda country. 'Why should I', he says superciliously, 'have focused on the Rock, when it is only one of a hundred or more major totemic centres in Central Australia?' Thus the onus is on Mountford to be properly informed, even if, as Strehlow claims, he makes basic geographical mistakes about tribal boundaries, vegetation and rainfall. Mountford's named informant in his book on the Rock is a man called Balinga ('probably this is Mountford's version of Paljingka', sneers Strehlow), who may well have been initiated into the *mala*, but was one of the many Pitjantjatjara or Yankuntjatjara men who no longer lived at the Rock. Strehlow claims is that if the man had become a visitor he could not be completely reliable and his knowledge of songs and ceremonial acts would be limited. It is a strange claim, especially in the light of his own reliance on non-residents for his informants, and the fact that he, no more than Mountford, could not speak to them in their own language. But leave aside the deadly tussle over informants; let's return to the story.

Having surprisingly conceded that his version of the myth closely corresponds to Mountford's on most points, Strehlow aims at what he says is a key difference. He has *tjintir-tjintirpa*, willie wagtail woman killed by a left-handed *mala* man but Mountford tells readers one thing in *Brown Men and Red Sand*, and another in his *Ayers Rock*. The snake does the killing in the former; the death is evaded in the latter. Strehlow makes a test of the question: Who killed willie wagtail woman?

The answer, Strehlow says, is to be found in Harney, who writes: 'To the left as we stand before the Mother-stone is a boulder which is reported to be the left-handed *Mala* of the creative ritual—he who speared the Djindra women of the willy-wagtail totem, who now lies prostrate a little to the right where she fell from her rock-hole camp in the crevice above. A small hole on her side is the central feature of the legend and it is repeatedly pierced with a spear during the ritual chanting.'

'Mountford could have done worse than to consult Harney's book on Ayers Rock', says Strehlow, 'a book well worth reading carefully.'

No questioning of Harney's sources, no anxiety expressed about Harney's unfamiliarity with this part of the country or the local language. Strehlow's worries about Harney were to be expressed later and not here, where he applies double standards by pitting Harney against Mountford. How can we judge the substance of the difference today? It is difficult, if not impossible. Caution is advisable, especially when we come to Harney and the Great Mother. In the previous passage he is in full flight about the Mother, which should make us wary of everything else. Why does Strehlow accept this at face value, when he had never recorded anything like it in Aranda, or the other language groups he had worked with? Pinning Mountford to error was the all-important thing.

In any case, Harney also seems to have told his *mala* story with the kind of poetic comprehensiveness Strehlow liked. Harney included the chant:

Loonba sits amid her droppings on high.
Her magic tells us an evil approaches.

We might want to quarrel with the quaint diction, which is akin to the style of bush poetry Harney wrote, rather than anything translated these days from Aboriginal language. Leaving that aside, the dramatic focus is strong: *lunba* is calling her first warning at the approach of *kurpany*. She is high on the rock on the north face, and to the west of her, the *mala* women are at ceremony in that great woman's cave he calls Dundajabbi (Tjukutjapi today). The dramatic focus is strong partly because it is a chant. Sharp and to the point, the chant acts like the call of a bird. Furthermore, since we are still wondering how we might approach the feeling of the *mala* story, it gives us some kind of direct access to the drama. Here it is, the bird on the cliff face, crying out with feeling. Although this verse is a report of feeling ('Her magic tells us') it seems, does it not, if we exercise out imaginations, a short step inside the drama?

Harney's moves around the Rock have a general virtue in this respect. He was in his own mind following the chants. He tells us in the *Oceania* article (from which the lines are taken; they are strangely omitted in his book) that was the way he worked. He would go out with his informants, Kundekundeka, a *Kuniya* man, and Imalung, a *Liru* man, both born at the Rock. He says he had plenty of time with them to go around the Rock; they would walk together and he would stop at the places they wanted to stop. There he would light the fire and put on the billy, and there, if the men were inclined, they would sing him parts of the story. So what we get as we move around with Harney is a potential sense of the movement of the story, and of its resonance in the song of ceremony which is the poetic key of the reality that is the Tjukurpa. The narrative fragments as we read while we walk with him, and becomes a confusing assortment of items: ceremonial details in one place, an item of verse or verse summary in another, a cross-over of stories here, a return to *mala* there. If Harney had not found 'his Mother' at the Rock his account would be quite incoherent.

With Mountford, nothing is presented in verse form, and very little is presented of the totemic ritual and the sacred ceremonies at the Rock. For Strehlow this is the indictable offence: 'Mountford maintains a complete ritual silence on Ayers Rock; and the question presents itself—is this inscrutable silence the result of solemn warnings issued during tribal initiation or merely an indication of complete ignorance?' It is a ruthless question. Somewhat hypocritical, too, since Strehlow himself had already published much sacred material in his *Songs of Central Australia*, regardless of his own solemn knowledge about problems of access. But there is no way out for Mountford on this. His text lacks the poetry.

Nevertheless, leaving aside Strehlow's highly motived criticism (so fueled was he by envy of Mountford's academic honours), there are virtues to Mountford's version of the *mala* story. In Ayers Rock he offers us an extensive and clearly expressed prose narrative. It is fuller than summaries we have today, and is less convoluted than Harney's grandiloquence about religious meaning.

Unfortunately, Mountford tells us little about his informants, and his manner of shaping the story over several years of fieldwork. It is, however, extensively tracked topographically, because the real story he tells of *mala* and, indeed, of the Rock is done photographically. The formidable and formidably ambiguous achievement of Mountford at the Rock was to subject the sacred places to the camera, the lens that characteristically invites our culture to see but with detachment, which permits us to approach the inner life of another culture with chilling and sometimes obscene detachment.

Here is some of the *mala* story through Mountford's eyes. The first image we get is two small rocks on the ground near the north face, with an unnamed Aboriginal (Matinya from Mountford's 1940s visit, Balingal from his later trips?) sitting beside them, posed in contemplation. The caption is: 'Where Liru man raped Mala woman', an event that, once again, does not seem to fit into the sense we might have of it as *mala*, as distinct from a snake story. Turn over and you'll see a magnificent photograph of what is almost a valley on the north face: the face is gorged from the rush of waters, and at its base is the waterhole I mentioned much earlier, where it is possible to sit in a forest at the base of the Rock. Caption: 'The hare-wallaby, Mala woman and poisonous-snake Liru man: water-course where Liru man returned to companions on southern side'. The snake story again, and the place where the snake man most implausibly (in Strehlow's view) left his battle on the south side for vengeance on willie wagtail. Whether this is true or not, we admire the photograph's rendition of what seems to be such a natural connection between landform and narrative. Yes, there are the marks of snake in retreat, see it go up the Rock!

Much of Mountford's appeal is to seduce us in this way. The Aboriginal myth frequently accords with what we think we can see in and at the Rock. And so to the next photograph, the sacred woman's cave, Tjukutjapi, which Mountford does not put an Aboriginal name to but which Harney called Dundajabbi, proposing the translation 'vulva open'. We get the shots of the camp of the *mala* women from the outside, that wide, beautiful aspect you can see from the road as you come around the north face. There are several such shots, and the captions do little to carry the *mala* story along. Then the camera starts to penetrate the story. We go into the opening. One caption reads: 'Breasts of Mala women'. The next takes us outside again: 'Boulders, mother nursing sick child'. And then, back inside again: 'Clitorides of Mala women'.

If fecundity is an aspect of the *mala* story, Mountford certainly brings that out. There are many more children and breasts to come. His camera shows no respect: it enters where, it seems to me, angels would fear to tread. Some of the shots are dramatic: they conjure the grandeur of the place and the story—the stories. In general, though, they lack awe, the kind of awe that informs the religious chants, the *inma*. Strehlow made his complaints about Mountford's omission of verses in order to reveal his rival's inadequate knowledge. We might add, in considered retrospect (restraining ourselves from unfair advantage) that Mountford's sustained exploitation of images

160

Tjamiwa and Rock (see Introduction).

Minga *(ants): tourists all year round (see Genesis).*

Walking the base of the Rock is a finer feat than climbing it (see Genesis).

Barbara Nipper looking into Julian Barry's lens
(see Snakes).

Land Commissioner Toohey with Nipper Winmati, 1979
(see Stars, Land, Love).

Jon Willis translating for the tourist industry on a mala *walk (see Sharing).*

'Desert Abstract' by Peter Latz (see Beyond the Rock).

A sign in Lasseter country (see Beyond the Rock).

from the Tjukurpa deprived Anangu reality of its poetic integrity, the very allusiveness and secret coherence that sustained its sacred order. At one level, we are grateful for Mountford's 'good' photographs of the Rock. But at another, our deeper poetic sense tells us that sympathetic respect for the Tjukurpa is not to be gained in this way. It is as if Mountford's camera has, despite his best intentions, systematically violated the sites. I never fail to look through the visual stories in Mountford's *Ayers Rock* without feeling that I have seen everything and know nothing of the place.

Pouches

ON THE WEST FACE, halfway along the *mala* walk as it is marked in the brochure, you come to a beautiful conical cavity in the Rock. It is a small cave of the most inviting aspect. As soon as you see it you feel that in a few steps on those boulders you could be up there, tucked inside like the happiest of marsupials.

It is clearly signposted: Do not enter. Do not photograph this place. (Astonishingly, Mountford did not photograph it. There is no Mala Puta in his book, and I saw none in the shots pasted into his diary. Perhaps he had, despite Strehlow's jeer, been warned off?)

The Park booklet says: 'This is Mala Puta, the pouch of the female hare-wallaby.'

And nothing could be closer to the truth.

With reverence for the nurturing powers of the female you walk reverentially past.

One day, however, as I came through the trees with Julian Barry, two figures were up on those boulders. When they saw us they scurried down. It was a middle-aged Japanese couple, each with a camera around their neck.

—Please, said Julian firmly, no photographs. He pointed to the sign.

The couple looked awkward, smiled at us, and hurried on. Their demeanour was that of people who may not have been able to read that sign.

—They speak English, said Julian.—I heard them before, when they walked past us.

I cursed the couple. Julian kept quiet.

Witness to this was Endo, who was walking with us. I had bumped into him at the base of the climb. As we walked in the steps of the Japanese couple, he seemed to be angry, but I couldn't tell whether it was with his compatriots, or with me for cursing them. It was only later, when Julian had finishing showing us the *mala* walk that he let loose.

—I don't see, he said, why a person should be so upset when the photographers are almost certain to know nothing, or next to nothing, about what they are shooting.

—That's not the point.

—What is the point?

—The point is that it is a sacred place, then people have a right to ask that it be respected.

—How exactly is taking a photograph an act of disrespect?

—Exactly how I don't have the Anangu knowledge to say, I told him. — But prior to that, it's respectful, surely to do as people request.

—We are allowed to look at *puta*. Is that right?

—Yes.

—We are permitted to do a quick sketch of it in our notebook?

—Yes, I suppose so.

—Then what is it about a photograph?

—It might be numbers. So many people would take pictures from all over the place if they are not restrained. Anyway, I thought you were in favour of Anangu not selling their culture short. You don't like the artefacts sales. Pictures are more artefacts, no?

—I objected to *their* marketing of *their* cultural goods. Here we're talking about visitors quietly making theirs, harmlessly.

—It is harmful if it's taken against the owner's wishes. That's what must matter, even before we wrangle over anything else.

—If it's the case, he said, already the spirit of the place has been stolen by the camera, then it's happened! There is no turning back. The image is out, the spirit abroad. It is no longer exclusive to here. The circle of innocence, this Eden of images, has been broken.

—We would be better, I said, without our culture's promiscuity of images.

—What you really object to, Endo told me, is people souveniring from this place. You feel that even images are possessions, or property that should not be removed. As if we are taking away 'meanings' or secrets without permission.

—There is some truth in that, I said. — Photography as theft.

My Japanese friend smiled as if he had won the lottery.

—Therefore, he said, they cannot be of *religious* significance to the visitor. If you are not yourself part of the Tjukurpa then it is merely an image you have collected. Once you get that image home, once the photograph is developed a long way from here, and shown to others a long way from here, it's as meaningless, as neutral as this.

He stopped. He picked up a stone from the track. He held it in his palm a moment, offered it to me, then dropped it in his pocket.

It's one thing to respect another culture. It's another, surely, to adopt medieval rules for *thinking* about it. How on earth are we going to consider indigenous cultures if we have to bite our tongues all the time?

162

We have come to Kantju waterhole, where the wind whispers through the trees, and the brochure calls for a quiet approach. We stopped talking for a while.

About the Mala Puta, Harney was his usual blunt slapdash self: '*The cavity is the symbol of reincarnation. It was here that light came upon the earth*', he says with his 'world religion' gloss, before going on about sacred food, the fruit of the Mother's quivering body, and spirit children.

Compare the restraint of the brochure. 'This is Mala Puta, the pouch of the female hare-wallaby. It is very important spiritually . . .'

—What could be simpler? What could be more deserving of respect? I asked.

—The American Indians, Endo said, once made a fuss about the camera. The camera was stealing their soul, all that. Then things changed. Step by step they grew to realise that very many of the images taken of them were intended as homage. Now, of course, now that they own the images as part of the general American Heritage, they are proud to show them. Where would we be in terms of our appreciation of the strength of their culture without photographs of people like Chief Seattle?

Endo had started to chant.

The air is precious to the red man.
For all things share the same breath
—the beasts, the trees, the man, they all share the same breath.
What is man without the beasts?
If all the beasts were gone, men would die from a great loneliness of spirit. For what ever happens to the beasts soon happens to man. All things are connected
. . . Whatever befalls the earth befalls the sons of earth.

—That's one of the great statements, I said. —Indigenous belief, universal credo. It's kin to the ecological philosophy of Anangu.

—I wonder about your Anangu 'ecology', said Endo. —With regard to Seattle, it would be greater statement if the Chief had actually said it.

—What do you mean?

—It is, Endo said, the most quoted single statement by any native American. But it does not represent the mind of the old Chief. It was worked up by the well-meaning Southern Baptist organisation in Texas in 1970—more than a hundred years after Chief Seattle was supposed to have spoken. Your chief indigenous ecological statement was penned by a white scriptwriter.

Endo waited for me to respond.

—You're kidding me, I said.

—Why would I kid you about this? It's a simple story. There is native narration. There is native narration carried on by another culture. There is poetry, there is prose, there is the poetry of prose. There is the contemporary need to locate traditional truths

163

that work. But culture is a complex place that seldom allows for simple truths. That's what I like about it. This is *the* poetry of the present.

—Maybe you should be writing my book, I said.

I wondered about the booklet. That was a product of goodwill? Of tinkerings also? I don't mean to imply here that any of the brochure, as restrained as it is, is anything but 'true' to the beliefs of Anangu. But it is brief, and self-consciously limited in scope. 'It is only meant to give tourists accurate information at a limited level.' I quote here from notes made by Susan Woenne-Green in the course of producing the brochure. A question then is: how limited is that level? By what criteria is it decided that some matters be public, others private? The question must be asked because we live a culture that happens to value knowledge for its own sake.

I confessed to Endo:—My mind swings to and fro. On the one hand, the last thing I want to do is commit any kind of offence against Aboriginal culture. Too much of that—and worse—has happened already. On the other hand I want to know and understand, and as far as is possible be trusted to understand. So much of what has been written about indigenous culture in Australia is wrong. Now we have a chance to set some of it right. So I don't want to push my way into anything, yet I'm dying to know, to be shown.

—So occasionally, Endo jeered, you might need to take a photograph, just for your own records.

—No. I never travel with a camera. I don't like the distraction of having to stop for the shot. I hate pointing it at people. I don't like intruding. Besides, don't we have enough photos of Aborigines and their places already; if anything, we need them taking shots of us. That might give a new angle on cultural relationships.

Endo said:—That fellow Mountford. He was fond of the native people. You're not telling me he took all of his photographs, those lovely portraits, without permission.

—Well, with his cinematography, he didn't tell them what he was doing. That's how he got such 'natural' shots, and why they were so popular in the States, especially with eminent anthropologists craving for images that suggest first contact. With still photographs, it's hard to know what he let on. There is that photograph he set up out here, with Matinya standing at the tripod. 'Abo with camera', Mountford calls it in his diary. The joke seems to be on the native, who is trying to make head or tail of the strange instrument.

—Don't worry, said Endo, the day will come when the natives are filming us, in all our cultural confusion.

—It's still a good way off, I said. The only image I know that points in that

'Abo with Camera', as Mountford captioned Matinya in 1940.

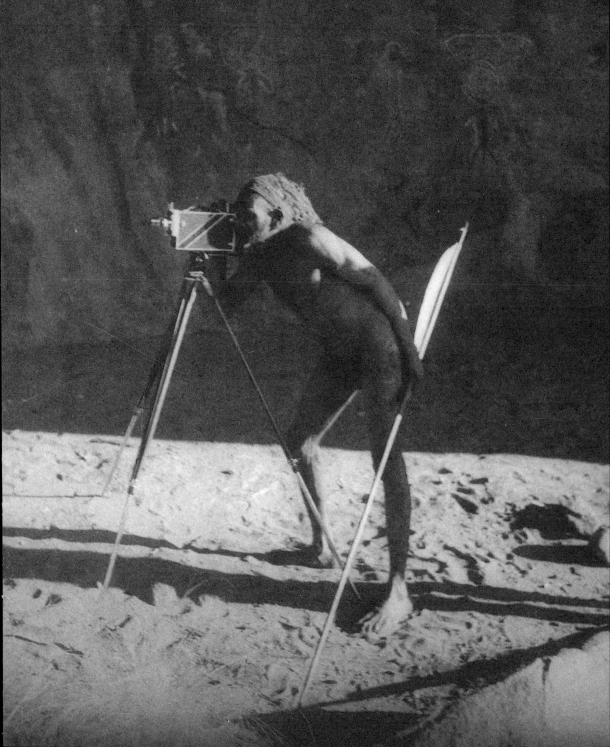

direction is David Haigh's shot of Tony Tjamiwa taking off with the tripod. Mind you, with Mountford Anangu had their fun. He had the camera but he did not have all the power.

—What kind of fun?

—Not letting him get—*take*—the pics he wanted, maybe. Subtle sabotage.

—Where was this?

—Out at Kata Tjuta. It was the stories he wrote down from there, as well as the photographs, that created great offence with his last book, so much so that his most sumptuous publication was withdrawn from the market.

—Tell me about the sabotage.

—It's only my reading of it, I said.—I'll show you when we get back to the Resort.

Conscience rocks

I WONDERED WHETHER that rock would burn a hole in Endo's pocket. What I couldn't say when he souvenired that small portion of the Anangu estate was what had happened a few months earlier, when David Carter, a Ranger at the Rock, had made it public knowledge that tourists were compelled to return such things. Carter told the local paper that each year, two or three people returned pieces of rock to the Rock. The piece came with an apologetic note, and the request was that it be returned to the spot from which it was taken. And the note might include a story, a tale invariably of the ill-fortune that had befallen travellers since they had transgressed by stealing the Aboriginal stone. Once the traveller had gone home—back to a distant part of Australia, or to England or Greece or Scandinavia—it was as if the power of the Rock had reasserted itself, and along with it, in the traveller's imagination, the potency of Aboriginal beliefs about place.

Mention of those few cases in the Easter of 1993 prompted a rush of good conscience from all around the world. In the next three months 150 letters arrived at the Ranger's Station, 465 parcels containing nearly 400 kilograms of rock, three crates' worth. When I wrote about it for *Time* magazine I called it a 'downpouring of respect', albeit one which showed that travellers to the Rock were as uncertain of their own lives as they were of Aboriginal spirituality.

'As a young fool back in 1976', wrote a self-thwarted pilgrim who preferred to remain unnamed, 'I took this timeless relic from atop Ayers Rock (near the Book).

Tjamiwa with some of David Haigh's equipment.

Could someone PLEASE return it to its rightful place and may I be forgiven for disturbing the spirit of the Rock. It (the stolen rock) has caused nothing but bad luck since I had it. I had lost a couple of jobs, had poor health and my wife took off with another fella. Worst of all, even my dog won't have anything to do with me.'

'My stupid father', wrote another pet lover, 'thought he was being clever stealing a piece of Uluru. Since then we have lost 3 beautiful pets (after 14 years without a single death). A fortnight after he returned with the rock, the first death occurred, since then the serious illness and deaths seem to be endless. Maybe we are just being superstitious but it's a risk I no longer want to take. Our animals are the most important things in our lives. We can't bear to lose any more.'

Heart attacks, untimely operations, blindings and falls seem to be the order of the day for elderly couples who have come back with the red earth souvenirs. Wives bemoan the recklessness of husbands. Husbands take stock of things and suddenly mend their ways. 'Would you be kind enough to return these small stones back to Uluru, which my husband took last year. It was after watching a TV program one morning that he decided to return them.'

Stealing a rock was worry enough, accepting a piece of Uluru as a gift could be just as bad. An Australian living in Hawaii, working in Earth Sciences for the government, wrote: 'I have had this rock since 1985 and have had the worst "luck" in my whole life ever since. It might be the Rock maybe not. Who knows? but I'm through with it . . . In a brief breakdown these are just some of the things that have happened to me. Coincidence . . . maybe . . .

1985 My marriage of two years broke up and bad news about a family
      member.
1986 My father died at age 50.
1987 My grandmother died and so did a young woman I was friends with.
1988 My son and I nearly died due to childbirth. Emergency C section — I then
      had two more operations for no apparent reason.
1990 My marriage had recovered but broke up again.
1991 Found out my sister had typhus and fibrosis.
1992 My young son, four years old, had to have a throat operation — no
      apparent reason. I then divorced.
1993 Another car accident — not my fault.
*1989 was rear-ended in a car accident and broke my back in two places.

'This is a fraction of what I have been through. I don't want the rock any more. I've had enough chaos and trauma. Thank your for your assistance in this matter. Again, I respectfully request that it be returned to Ayers Rock and no legal action against me for returning it, honestly.'

In the dramatic litanies of bad luck speaks a common faith that inanimate objects from Aboriginal Australia can threaten the health of households.

'I am sending them back so the spirits calm. A note of reconciliation for past deeds might be struck.'

'Indigenous tribes', said one passionate traveller, 'particularly Australian Aboriginals, American North-Indians and Pacific Islanders, know a great deal more about the *essence* of life than "white" people. I am of English/Irish descent . . .'

And so on. The stories, even in summary, speak worlds, working the material of myth: of life and death, fate and magic, chance and retribution. The big difference is that the spiritual base of the white storytellers is either unclear or fragmented, and is expressed from the point of the view of the solitary ego, the individualistic letter writer; whereas, the mythic ground at the Rock is the Tjukurpa, communally known. There is much ignorance in the white attempt to contact that communal spiritual ground at the Rock—ignorance and pathos. At the same time it's as if the act of trespass has served some good. It points to at least the idea of a meeting between the two domains of story-telling.

The dim magician

WHEN MOUNTFORD is telling us about himself at Kata Tjuta in 1940 he sets the scene by quoting Giles who found it truly wonderful, with its 'rounded minarets, giant cupolas and monstrous dome . . . huge memorials from the ancient times on earth' where 'Time, the old, the dim magician', had toiled. Mountford then laboured with photographic equipment into the landscape. Sharp stones cut his boots to ribbons and he slipped and stumbled in canvas shoes. On their fourth day, when they had less than a gallon of water in the canteens, he was set to make a cine-shot of the remarkable spire of rock called Pupiana that overshadowed their camp.

I told Endo:—As you read his account it is essential to realise that the Tjukurpa stories at Kata Tjuta are private; so much so that today, Anangu prefer their nature to remain unnamed, except to the most trusted members of another culture.

Mountford wrote:

I asked Tjundaga to lead his camel-string along the valley at its base.
Meanwhile I took a short cut through the hills, so as to be in position when he arrived.

I set up the camera, then looked for the string, but it was nowhere to be seen. For a while it was not unduly troubled, for the short cut would have put me well ahead of Tjundaga; but, after waiting for a half an hour in a strong, icy wind, I was vexed when I saw by the smoke signals that the camel-string was well on its way to Ayers Rock.

It turned out that Tjundaga, having gone hunting with Lauri, had forgotten to pass my instructions on to Nibiana [the Ernabella woman much prized by Mountford], who had set out blithely on her way, totally oblivious to the fact that she had left more than half of the party behind.

As the absence of the camel-string made the first position unsuitable, I had to find another—no easy task on steep slopes covered with masses of broken boulders, dead trees and spinifex.

Meanwhile old Tjalerina was wandering aimlessly with a blazing fire-stick in his hand, trying to keep himself warm. Just as I had found a new place, and the clouds and lighting on the subject were ideal, some embers, which had dropped from his fire-stick, lit a bunch of spinifex on the windward side of me. The flames, driven by a strong wind, came towards me with the speed of an express train, barely allowing time enough for me to carry the camera out of harm's way, before the fire swept over the place where I had stood.

I was more than annoyed, for surely that was the last straw, and relieved my feelings considerably by telling Tjalerina—in English—my candid and immediate opinion of him. The poor old man was most contrite. He had already tried to put out the fire, but had about as much chance of extinguishing that explosive blaze, in such a wind, as one would have of putting out a burning oil refinery with a water pistol.

Again I had to find another position, and was just about to take the much delayed photograph when I noticed the aborigines, whom I had placed in the foreground, were laughing. For a moment I was puzzled as to the cause of their merriment until, on turning round, I saw old Tjalerina, his face wreathed in smiles, telling his companions on the hillside, by gesture and hand-signs, about the incident of the burning spinifex, and my subsequent behaviour.

For a while the old man was so busy with his story that he did not notice I was watching, and when he did so, the speed with which his fingers stopped their movement, and the smile left his face, was so ludicrous that I forgot my annoyance and, much to Tjalerina's relief, laughed with the rest.

Endo put the book down.

I said:—This is farce, I would suggest, possibly engineered by Anangu. Mountford says he had the last laugh, but my guess is otherwise. He goes on to say that the picture turned out well in 'glowing colour'. He can't mention the glowing things Anangu used to distract him from transgression.

—How do you know? asked Endo.

—I don't know. I'm only trying to imagine what might have been going on between the lines. It's only in recent years that the white culture has been able to really admit that they might have missed something.

Mountford came back to the Rock ten years later, and a photograph he took then well illustrates, it seems to me, the kind of relationship he sought with the place. In 1935, on that first visit which left him with the lure of the Rock, he had entered a cave. There he was greatly moved by the presence of untold centuries, strange symbols, the thought of secret ceremonies, while all the time feeling that he was an intruder, and deserving of attack if an Aborigine belonging to the spot should come upon him.

This time he is considerably more self-assured; not only does he enter an important cave all over again, he does so without any sign of trepidation as an intruder. Furthermore, he goes with two others, sets up a table and executes their portrait in the place.

The cave is the sacred cave at Mutitjulu. In the full uncropped photograph, paintings fill the whole wall. The men are behind the table, looking out at the camera. The table has a couple of leatherbound books on it; they hold down a cloth that drapes to the front, so that the symbols on it are clear. The formality and the ceremony of the whole photograph is strong: here are white men marking their spot, fully inscribing their presence on sacred Aboriginal ground. At a glance the transgressional image makes climbing the Rock look like light work in sacrilege.

What was the religion that Mountford had imported to Uluru, into sanctums at Uluru? I did not know the symbols on the cloth. At first I thought I was looking at some ceremony for a Masonic Lodge. Surely not? What could it mean? That the ghost of explorer Stuart, who thought Aborigines were giving him Masonic signs, was playing a trick on the Rock? The Northern Territory is full of gothic tales: was this another twist?

But then, on closer inspection, some research on the signs on the cloth—the compass, protractor—reveal Mountford's own little ceremony to be of the secular kind. We are looking at the trappings of the Explorers' Club, of which Mountford had been a member for many years; indeed it had been the Explorers' Club, along with the officers of *National Geographic* magazine, that had feted him in New York a couple of years before. Explorers! As if the Rock was still being 'discovered', and could be claimed by camera. It is 1950, the sounds of mass tourism are coming over the horizon, but Old Ego does it again. He had made the lure his own.

I showed Endo the photograph.

—You worry too much, he said, it's a local tea ceremony.

—His tea ceremony came to an end in 1976, I said.—His last book *Nomads of the Western Desert* (1976) was an affront. Its cover showed men in 'secret' malu ceremony, as did many others inside. Sacred acts, and sacred sites abounded in the

White rites in the black cave. Mountford's branch of the Explorers' Club meets at the Rock.

sumptuous production. As soon as senior Pitjantjatjara men set eyes on it in Adelaide, in the bookshop in Alice Springs, they called out. Anguish! Anger! They wanted it burnt. Then they discovered, when their white friends explained, that thousands of copies had already gone out across the country. White people who knew the Tjukurpa were also shocked. How could the book go so far without the consent of the authorities in the administration of Aboriginal arts? My understanding is that

172

whatever doubts there had been were eclipsed by the wishes of the author. Yes, the venerable C. P. Mountford had insisted that this great collection from his otherwise admirable collection be published. The Pitjantjatjara Council took the publishers to court. They won judicial suppression of distribution and the publisher Rigby withdrew the book from sale, to Anangu's relief. The suppression, which brought a tragic end to Mountford's well-meaning but strangely careless career, helped shape a militant vigilance on questions of Pitjantjatjara culture.

Symphony

WHAT MORE, THEN, can be said about *mala* beyond — or apart from — Mountford, Strehlow and Harney? Perhaps some credit is due first. Both Mountford and Harney set down a lot of detail that is more or less accurate, if you take bits and pieces of events in the *mala* story of ceremony, invitation, retribution. Their bits and pieces overlap and are compatible with each other. They had different informants as we have seen, most of them men who did have relationships with the Rock, and who must therefore have honoured the Tjukurpa by saying what was real to them. At all times these informants would have weighed up what they said; at some times they might have dissembled, the better to protect what was sacred. In any case, it was then that the white men wrote things down, the bits and pieces and sometimes what sounded like a whole story. Beyond that, what?

Beyond that the writer had to trust that somehow, overall, he had the shape, the idiom and the movement of the Tjukurpa story right: that the 'music of his rendition' was adequate. Was that possible? It is a question of expectations. Susan Woenne-Green draws the analogy of the symphony. For symphony read Tjukurpa, which is a complete score, the full sound of which is known only to very senior people. Having said that, even Anangu only know the whole symphony to different degrees. As for the scribe who belongs to another culture, it is possible to play the tune of particular stories while getting all the music wrong.

Today, it can be argued that it is perhaps possible to get more accurately oriented to the cosmic music of the Tjukurpa. Politics makes that possible (and what an unusual circumstance that is; politics making the poetry of the music possible). Because Anangu own the Rock, they want to ensure that the public aspects of Tjukurpa are set down well. As informants, they are more voluntarily engaged than before: just as their scribes are more accountable to them than before. And so it is possible to say ourselves, when we turn to the work of say, Robert Layton, that while the symphony is by defintion out of earshot, some of the authentic melody might well be there, and that its *movement* draws us into the country in a way that deepens our cultural sense of the place.

I like the way that Layton, who was writing before the production of *An Insight into Uluru*, takes us out to where the *mala* story begins: the MacDonnell Ranges. *Mala* travelled south from near Mount Liebig, arriving at Uluru at Katjitilkil on the north face. There the dancing began: the men at one place, the woman at another, with the women's camp at Taputji, that place on the north-eastern corner which I described earlier when I knew none of the stories, the place where it seems the whole Rock wants to push up through the ground, and not far from which, we might also remember, *Kuniya* arrived from Erldunda with her many eggs.

The *mala* are dancing. Then the invitation comes from the West, from Kikingkura, near Docker River. *Panpanpanala* the bellbird is the messenger from the Wintalka men at Docker River. Layton continues:

> But the Mala were already committed to their own celebrations, so they refused to leave, and the Bell-Bird returned to the Wintalka in the Petermann Ranges, calling 'Pak Pak' ('They can't come, they can't come'), the call he makes today.
>
> When they heard that their invitation had been rejected, the Wintalka men decided to send a malevolent dingo-like *mamu* (an evil spirit) to punish the Mala. This creature, called Kurrpanngu, ran eastwards until he had picked up the Mala track at Mulyayiti (Mount Currie), then turned south and followed them to Uluru. He crept up to Tjukutjapinya, where the Mala women were dancing. The hair skirts, or *mawulari*, worn by the women were transformed into pendant cones of rock at Tjukutjapi rockshelter. Kurrpanngu peered over a projecting rock spur, but the women drove him off, and he continued around the base of the Rock to Inintitjara [sic], where the Mala men were sleeping. Lunpa, the Kingfisher woman, was with them, and she called out a warning but was too late to prevent Kurrpanngu leaping into the camp. At Inintjitjara, Lunpa is transformed into a boulder, looking up at the paw marks Kurrpanngu left in the side of the cliff.

Thus Layton's version of the drama, admittedly truncated but evocative enough. He gives an 'ending', which he leaves uninterpreted: that the *mala* fled southwards and, further out into the country, split into two lines, one heading towards the northern spur of the Musgrave Ranges and onto Ulkiya, the other past Altjinta, near the present site of Mulga Park homestead.

Layton's telling sweeps us across the country: from the north to the south, from west to east, and then from the Rock to places further south. So the moment we consider *mala*, we're drawn into a story that connects one place to another and which seems to demand in its telling particular emphasis. There is, for example, the vivid place that *panpanpanala* occupies as the messenger, a creature whose 'natural' call today fits the tale that is out of creation times. The bellbird, a male, is the messenger that will bring the news that creates the bad fate for the *mala*. By contrast there is *lunba*, the kingfisher woman, who gives the warning of the dingo *mamu*, but to no avail. Both birds, in their own ways, equally ineffectual against the malevolent dingo spirit which is the dominant presence in the story; it is his (or its) wild pounce, his invasion from the west and his ferocious pursuit of *mala* down south that creates the sweep across the country.

Mountford had much more to say about the evil dingo spirit than Layton. But notice here, before I go on, the subtle changes in register. The brochure speaks of an evil, black dog-like creature. Layton says a malevolent dingo-like *mamu* (and evil spirit). Harney called it a ritual dog *Kurapinni*; Mountford a malignant being called *Kulpunya*. Not only does the spelling change through the decades according to social circumstances, but so do the different stresses upon the 'dingo-aspect' of the creature, and its dimensions of malevolence. My own 'evil dingo spirit' is meant as a summary of the narrative implications of the other tags, not as an alternative to the authorised booklet. The point is twofold: to show how the music of this story can be subtly cued by the language of description, and to remind us, yet again, of what might be left out in summary.

Given that the evil dingo spirit dominates the story in the Layton version, it's interesting to see what Mountford did with the creature. After two days at the rock in 1932, and a week gathering stories in 1940, Mountford confidently published in 1948 this picture of mulga-seed men making their malignant being:

> After they had laid out the skeletal frame—a mulga branch for a backbone, forked sticks for ears, women's hair along the back, the teeth of a small marsupial at one end and the tail of a bandicoot at the other—the medicine men spent the rest of the day chanting songs of magic to fill their creation with the spirit of evil. Then, from sunset to sunrise, they left it alone, for it was only during the hours of darkness that such a creature could develop.
>
> The following morning, the evil thing was already showing signs of life; hair was growing along its back, the teeth had increased in size, and the feet were sprouting. Again the medicine men sat round Kulpunya and chanted songs which were so effective that during the next night it actually crawled some distance. The creature was brought back to camp, and the final songs were chanted, to imbue it with hatred and malice toward all strangers.
>
> On the day fixed for the attack, Kulpunya was fully developed. He was about the size of a dog, but had no hair on his body, except along the back and at the point of the tail. The transplanted teeth had grown to formidable dimensions, and his malevolence had greatly increased.

This is splendid stuff: Australian gothic. The white fella's relish is clear: *he* is telling a horror story that we, out of our literary tradition, are meant to receive as such. No wonder the 'little' *mala* fled in horror. The force upon them is an archetype of darkness according to *our* story-telling.

This, of course, is going a bit too far. Some Aboriginal tellings laid the basis for the description. How exactly, we do not know, because none of the authors we've been concerned with tell us the full story of their fieldwork. We can, however, say that in the weaving of the *mala* myth the stresses would have varied according to the Aboriginal storytellers, some of whom could have told the story in such vivid, powerful ways that left the men from white culture so well served that, no matter what the limitations of time, language, understanding and artfulness in second-hand narration, we now have what is, in fact, a reliable version. The same applies to the saga of *Kuniya* and *Liru*, or any other myth subjected to the processes of translation, which is to say, varying degrees of truncation, elaboration, emphasis. In each of these stories other stories intersect, or seem to. As the *mala* story has 'minor characters like bellbird and kingfisher woman, the *Kuniya* cycle involves the willie-wagtail woman and blue-tongue lizard, among others. Depending on the custodial responsibilities of the teller, and the time and place of the telling, and the identity and attitude of the recipient of the story, these details will modulate in the music of the telling, in the whole rhythm and composition of the story cycle. The general composition is, one might say, a movable feast, a banquet of narrative riches that varies, while staying the same through time.

CHAPTER 5 Science dreaming

Fire (i)

—I HAVE A DREAM, I told Endo, of knowing all that scientists know about the Centre.

He said:—That is western culture's Dreaming. The idea that science, if only we know enough of it, will give us the whole picture. And of course it is an illusion, it is opium for the educated class. Science itself is a set of fragmented pictures. Only ecologists, themselves often ideological dreamers, aspire to knowing everything at once.

—My dream includes Anangu, I said.

—How can science include Anangu? Indigenous cultures have no science, came Endo's reply.

—They have understandings, wisdom, I said.

—That is not science, Endo said.

—It is knowledge of Nature.

—It is knowledge of a kind.

—Our science is superior, is that what you are saying? I asked.

—Yes.

He was so adamant about this that I felt that I had to put him in his place. I said:—There is a big thing you have missed in your whole trip so far.

—What is that?

—Fire. The experience of camping by a fire.

177

—What's so special about that?

I told him that one of the first lessons in the Mann Ranges was to look after your fire. Don't put rubbish in your fire. Anangu always keep their fires clean. To learn about fire is to learn several things at once. Apart from the art of keeping warm, there is the business of cooking and tool-making.

—Oh I've seen a bit of that tool-making, said Endo.

—Where was that?

—On the *Liru* walk. You go out from the Ranger's Station through the bush, with a couple of Aboriginal women. You stop here and there while they show you some of their very basic skills. The making of their glue, for instance. Out of the resin of the spinifex. It involved starting a fire, which needed a lot of giggling and laughter.

—Fire, I said, is the most natural place of reverie. It is where contemplation began. Fire is matter and material power over the Natural world. Fire is also the element where matter and spirit meet. Fire itself is the incarnation of matter and spirit.

Endo said,—All you are saying, surely, is that fire has been an important part of Anangu technology, which without fire would have been very limited indeed. Besides, from what I understand, despite everything you have said, the mastery of fire was limited. Was fire not often handled carelessly, so much so that whole tracts of country went under to bush fires? Campfires were left burning, and a big fire would start. Or a firestick might be thrown away, and the bush would be ablaze in a second. What damage to the sacred county must have been done. I believe whole forests were burnt. That to me is a strange application of knowledge, a weird ecology.

—Through the country, I replied, there are Dreaming stories about fire. Invariably, they speak of fire with respect. They are stories of controlling fire, and the responsibilities of mankind having fire.

—Prometheus stories? Endo asked.

—If you like, I said hesitantly.—Or stories where fire has a balanced place in the whole scheme of things.

Endo was suddenly at his most unpleasant:—You're not suggesting they had a science of fire?

—Fire, I said, was a key element in their practical wisdom.

Ants and men

THE HORN EXPEDITION travelled into the Centre with little ecology. Darwinism was still new, speculative. Our nineteenth-century men of science, who were compelled to study fellow human beings of a different culture as natural specimens, had a rudimentary understanding of the arid zone. Knowledge of climate, water systems, flora and

The Horn Party, 1894: scientists and their generally unnamed helpers.

landforms was as much in a state of infancy as 'savages were to the history of man'. The party had come into a great area they called the Eyrean subregion, which they subsectioned as Lower and Higher Steppes, Desert Region and Ranges, which suggest some knowledge of the landscape. That was not saying a great deal though, as the reason for coming was to know much more. All the important relationships in Nature were either incipient in the minds of the Horn party, or entirely forthcoming.

179

Still, Baldwin Spencer was an impressively observant fellow, and his narrative constantly hints at the makings of an ecological understanding, including the subtle relationships that existed between Nature and Man in Central Australia. When you read his general narrative you can't help stopping and starting with pleasure at the way all manner of things come to his attention.

'Many animals', he tells us early on, 'remain under shelter during the heat of the day; along the grassy flats kangaroos may be seen feeding, and on the Porcupine sandhills the Rat-kangaroos (*Bettongia lesueuri*) are constantly dodging in and out amongst the tussocks. The Jew lizard (*Amphibolurus barbatus*) is often seen sunning itself, and other allied species dart into their holes when disturbed. There is a great contrast in this respect between different lizards, and it is the Skinks which appear to be the most susceptible to heat. One day in summer, out amongst the hot sand in the bed of the Finke . . . the blacks came up with a number of lizards, and amongst them, a fine specimen of *Tiliqua occipitalis*. Having my hands full of specimens, I asked a blackfellow to look after it and not to let it escape, when to my surprise he simply put it down on the hot sand. It was perfectly alive when put down, having been captured in its hole, and when placed on the ground it began to travel at some rate, but after going five yards, its movements became slower and before ten yards had been traversed they ceased and the animal was quite dead—simply apparently baked to death by contact with the hot sand.'

Ants were not beneath a Darwinian. 'On the sand', he tells us after moving from lizards to acacias to a discussion of how resin was obtained from the porcupine grass, 'were little crater-like pits and track of ant lions (*Myrmeleon*). The way to find the animal during the day time is to follow up a track leading away from a crater until it comes to a sudden stop, which indicates that here the larva is at rest at the bottom of the little craters, which are probably used at night. At first we had searched unsuccessfully below them but a black boy on being asked to show us where the ant lion "sat down", as he called it, at once started away from the crater and followed up the track which is a very distinct groove on the surface made by the animal as it drags its body along.'

There is much more about ants, but only after vivid entries on rats and mice and other natural features. There was the curious little black ant, *Hypoclinea flavipes*, which could be called the porcupine grass ant. It digs galleries for long distances along the surface of the ground and also went a long way up the trunks of gum trees. Then there were the honey ants to be found out in the mulga scrub, where they had dug their deep nests.

'A native woman', Spencer tells us, 'armed only with a yam stick will dig down to a depth of a few feet in a surprisingly short space of time, breaking up the earth with the stick held in the right hand while in the left a small potichi is held and used as a shovel to clear the loosened earth away.

180

'The honey ant nest is not indicated on the surface by the mound. There is simply a hole perhaps an inch or more in length, and from this central burrow which is about three quarters of an inch in diameter runs down vertically with horizontal passages leading off at intervals after a depth perhaps two feet has been reached. In the nest which we dug up that afternoon, a few honey ants were found in each of those horizontal passages. They are quite incapable of movement, their small bodies looking like little appendages of the swollen abdomen, which has the appearance of an almost transparent bladder with the hard terga and sterna forming dark bands across it on the upper and under surfaces.

'When the nest was disturbed the workers made no attempt to hide the honey ants,' Spencer observes. He does not go beyond that as an eyewitness. He was unlucky: there were few ants in that burrow, and it seems to have been too hot to go after more, even if the native women were doing the digging. So our scientist seems to have missed the ecstasy of eating the honey ant, the unique Central Australian pleasure of devouring the feasts of honey pots stored in the earth. If Spencer had experienced that explosion of nectar on the palate he would have had a special introduction to the pleasures of the native diet, not to mention the relationship Anangu have with the remarkable species.

Short of first-hand experience, Spencer sometimes falls back on other scientists. Mounted Constable E. C. Cowle sends him specimens, two species of ants in fact, after his journey: two of the thirty worldwide! When Spencer notes this we get our first glimpse of the profusion of life that might exist in the desert, even if we speak only of ants. He tells more of the honey ant from hear-say: 'When required for the use of other ants, ants are *said* to come and tap the sides of the swollen abdomen with their feet, and in response to this stimulus the honey is passed in drops out of the mouth of the modified honey ant and is then eaten by the others.' (My italics)

The authorities for this vivid detail of antlife—who eats what when—are cited as Mr W. Wesmael of Mexico and Mr H. C. McCook of Colorado. It is just the kind of detail that might have come from elsewhere, namely, the natives themselves. 'The aid of the blacks is simple indispensable', Spencer says when ants are first mentioned, 'in procuring specimens, sometimes they are at a loss, but very seldom, and as a general rule they not only recognise each individual track, but from the appearance of the marks at the mouth of a burrow, will at once tell you whether the animal is in it or not.'

For decades white men had lauded native powers of observation. But Spencer's is a strong statement, an acknowledgement that partially compensates for his otherwise condescending references to 'black boys'. As he develops his narrative he reveals a growing interest in what the natives are about. The ants, he had already noticed, harvest a resin from the base of the porcupine grass. He thought it odd that the blacks said they did not use the resin already massed there, but made their own by burning the leaves of the grass. 'They could not tell me why', says Spencer, 'but only said their fathers had not and they never did, which is a typical answer to the question "why" when put to a black.' There is a certain truth to Spencer's observation which we will come to, but this is not to say that the attitude to the western question 'why' was necessarily an example of 'the extreme difficulty with which they [the natives] bring their minds to bear on abstract ideas', the Darwinian observation made in the general chapter on anthropology.

The resin puzzle contrasted with the flexible native approach to the Pituri plant, *Duboisia hopwoodii*, a small shrub used by natives as a narcotic and item of trade, although for trade there was a preference for the native tobacco, *Nicotiana excelsoir*. Native tobacco leaves were rolled and chewed with ash, and the plug tucked up in the hair when not in the mouth. The chief use of the Pituri plant *Duboisia* was as a decoction for the purposes of stupefying emus. The leaves were pounded in water and put in the watering place where the drugged emus became easy game.

It was by way of these kind of observations that Spencer's party drew closer to native life. Insects, flora and fauna pointed to an indigenous sense of interrelationship so that when the expedition summarised its findings, it was possible to table an authoritative-looking section on how the natives survived in nature. The final report has twelve pages on native foods that begins: 'There are few living animals that come amiss to the Central Australian Aborigine. To mention the names of all that are eaten would be largely to recapitulate the zoology of the district and I believe entirely so on the case of the mammalian fauna.' A list of many things known to be eaten follows, from lizards and frogs to numerous seeds, fruits and roots. Admittedly, some of this list is not first-hand; it drew upon the work of non-scientists such as Pastor Schulze of the Lutheran Mission in Hermannsburg, a man who had been compelled out of Christian necessity to note the phenomenon of 'cannibalism'. On that particular horror Dr E. C. Stirling for the Horn Expedition reserved judgement; but when he came to write up what it was that the natives ate, he created a picture of a savage, voracious people eating their way across the country. While their list of plant foods and powers of observation show their knowledge of nature, the uninhibited breadth of their tastes places them in beastly fashion *in Nature*. As served up by Horn, the native menu is yet another implication that blacks lacked certain basic—fully human—powers of discrimination.

The entry before 'Cannibalism' is about food restrictions. Stirling says: 'With regard to the rules observed concerning food restrictions amongst the natives, I was personally unable to obtain any reliable information, and I must, therefore, refer the reader to Mr Gillen's paper, in which he alludes to certain restrictions of the kind as affecting animal food.' This at least hints at cultural restraints, which Gillen was in a better position to know since he lived in the area and spoke some of the native language. It thus opens the way to a reflection on the special relationship the natives might have had with animals and plants, if only they had been 'able' or willing to say, which they did not. So the 'restrictions', the active discriminations, remained a closed book to the Horn men of science, even when they were close to the kind of eating which brought them into play.

Fire (ii)

DECADES LATER, in the early thirties when Finlayson came to the Red Centre, he underlined the dynamic and interactive relationship Aborigines had with their habitat. The *mala* drive, where fire was used as a tool for hunting, was a dramatic example. 'It might be thought', he reflected, 'that such a fire would wipe out every living thing in its path, but that this is by no means so, can be seen from inspection of the ground afterwards, when fresh mammal tracks are in plenty; it follows also from the fact that the whole business has been carried out systematically for untold generations and over enormous areas of country. At such times the burrowing habit is the salvation of both mammals and reptiles; and as there is not massive smouldering debris as in a forest fire, it is only a matter of a few hours before most forms are on the move again, looking for pastures new. But the prickly vegetation having been swept away, the sites of the burrows are exposed and the subsequent digging operations much facilitated. The maala, which makes only a shallow pop hole, now falls an easy victim.'

This was a perceptive comment ecologically, with its sense of habitat, and anthropologically, in that it credited Aborigines with a knowledge of what they were doing. An earlier, patronising image of Aborigines, expressed by Professor J. B. Cleland, had been of an unchanging people in an unchanging environment. This was the same Cleland who led the Inquiry into Constable McKinnon, whose prejudicial insistence on the white order of things was such a disappointment to young Strehlow and Mountford. On the impact Aborigines had on the environment and the changes the natives had produced in the vegetation of Australia, Cleland wrote: 'It would seem that they have produced singularly little . . . There was no need to destroy large areas of natural vegetation. In fact it would have been contrary to their interests to do so. They fitted naturally into the ecology of the land they inhabited and might have continued to do so indefinitely.' As to the fire: 'obviously the frequency and extent of bush fires must have increased greatly since fire-producing men arrived . . . I know of nothing to suggest that such firing by the Aborigines has altered the covering of vegetation, for instance, by open grassy areas replacing forest, or by the burnt country being especially subject to wind erosion.'

Cleland's 1957 statement, which moved the focus from eyewitness local realities to macro-considerations of the origins of Australian flora, was slow fuel to a controversy.

How had fire, including the fires naturally ignited by lightning, and not merely the 'black lightning' of the Aboriginal firestick, affected the landscape? The eminent anthropologist N. B. Tindale argued in 1959 that 'man has had such a profound effect on the distribution of forest and grassland that true primeval forest may be far less common in Australia than generally realised.' Ten years later, the pre-historian, Rhys Jones, claimed that 'through firing over thousands of years, Aboriginal man has managed to extend his natural habitat zone'. Jones was thinking especially of Tasmania, but his argument was akin to Hallam's, who looked at Western Australia in 1975. What we had by the mid-1970s was the Tindale/Jones/Hallam thesis that Aboriginal fire had crucially shaped the habitat of the continent. It made less sense to talk of a natural habitat than to think of aspects of the landscape as being, arguably, 'man-made'.

It was Jones who used the dramatic phrase 'firestick farming', which put the Aborigines centre stage as actors in the landscape. Seen thus, so much anecdotal material seems to fall into place. There are observations that predate first settlement, when men like Flinders saw smoke for miles along the coast as they sailed along it. The range and often the rhythm of the fires would have been explained if they had a phrase like firestick farming. Admittedly, one observer on the *Beagle* noted that the natives deliberately engaged in burning bush and that they distributed fire 'in sections every year'. Major Mitchell, that pioneer of settlement into the temperate grasslands of the continent saw, as ecologist Stephen J. Pyne beautifully puts it, that 'fire fused Aborigine and bush into a special weld'. Mitchell wrote: 'Fire, grass, and kangaroos and human inhabitants, seem all dependent on each other for existence in Australia.'

Fire made an impression on most of the explorers of the Centre, and they made glancing blows at explanation. 'The natives were about, burning, burning, ever burning', exclaimed Giles, 'one would think they . . . lived on fire instead of water.' Giles wrote of hills where 'the natives had recently burned all the vegetation from their sides'. Gosse noted that Aborigines had 'burned the grass all around' the key water at a place called Daly's Gully in mid-October 1873. These entries did not explain the thinking behind Aboriginal fire practice, but they hinted at a method. For how could there not be a method? If fires had been lit in uncontrolled ways, Giles and Gosse would have ridden into a landscape of charred stumps and ashes. Unmitigated conflagration would have been a dominant feature of the Centre. Lightning, of course, was the uncontrollable fire agent; large fires did blaze at sporadic intervals across arid Australia, but seldom, it seems, to the point of general devastation. Some kind of balance was there between Man and Nature. But what kind of balance was it?

The contemporary debate has turned on the macro-effects of fire. Many parties, it seems, have overstated their case, a point best made by D. R. Horton in 1982, when he reviewed the biological evidence of flora and fauna, the pattern of which would have been the same whether Aborigines practiced firestick farming or not. Horton argues that if firestick farming had been as dramatically practised as the phrase suggests, it would have been counterproductive, especially on the smaller animals. This makes a certain kind of sense. The real expert on the mammals, H. H. Finlayson, had seen the vulnerability of the *mala* with their shallow 'pop holes'. There is no real suggestion in Finlayson that Aborigines were likely to destroy what they most keenly appreciated, an argument that only makes sense if the finesse of local knowledge is ignored. Horton seems to ignore the full implications of a little key study done a few years before his own paper. Investigating the demise of *mala* in the Tanami Desert, where the main culprits were cats, rabbits, foxes and the depredations of cattle, Bolten and Latz found that the colonies of *mala* that had survived were from parts of the country with a distinct fire pattern. In places where there were extensive, hot, summer fires started by lightning, *mala* had gone. Along the stock routes, where cool, winter fires had been deliberately lit, and which had produced a tight mosaic of different vegetative states, the colonies of *mala* had survived longest. So the question becomes: what kind of balance was it that the Aborigines knowingly sought?

Horton, while trying to put the grander claims of 'firestick farming' in its place, ('There is no such thing as partial farming') gives Aborigines credence for understanding long-term effects of fire: 'It is clear that there was this understanding—come back after a fire in woodland, and there will be kangaroos, and many plants with fruit, two years after a fire and wattles are beginning to produce seed and native rodents are beginning to become abundant. After about five to ten years some small wallabies will be available, and wattles will be mature and in native woodland, after perhaps twenty years small wallabies, possum, and bandicoots are available.'

Beyond that, what did—do—Anangu know? The closer the fire debate gets to the ground of particular areas, the more the sense of Aboriginal practice emerges. The key contributor here is Dick Kimber, the Alice Springs-based historian. Kimber's 1983 paper, 'Black Lightning: Aborigines and Fire in Central Australia and the Western Desert', recounts the basic pattern of fire practices as glimpsed by the early explorers and confirmed by himself in the 1970s, when he lived with and travelled with Warlpiri and Pintupi people. 'Burning appears to have increased in frequency and extent in August–October and continues until major rains came in the December–February period. Although this in part reflects that spinifex-dwelling animals could best be hunted by firing the grass at this time of reason . . . I believe that it also indicates that Aborigines viewed more extensive burning of the country as desirable during these months. Although the evidence is not entirely clear, it seems that large scale increase in burning often occurred immediately prior to the onset of rains, suggesting a close link and therefore planning and control.'

So again the question becomes: what did the Aborigines know? Kimber tackles

185

this question in the most direct and humanistic way: by recounting what it is that
Anangu say about fire. Because his report goes to the heart of fire practices near the
Rock, and indeed to the whole business of two cultures agreeing on the ecological
management of a Park, I quote at length. He is talking about Aboriginal management
of fires of moderate size:

> Important reasons for the lighting of such fires have at times been volunteered.
> Thus on 15-1-75 L. Tjakamara, a Warlpiri man, commented on a bushfire
> that had started while an old man had been cooking a kangaroo, 'Good fire.
> We got too much dry grass . . . Bushfire burn it all off. Like olden times.' This
> view, which was widely shared by the Aborigines at Yuendumu Setttlement,
> contrasted markedly with the attitude of white workers, one of whom was
> organising fire-fighting groups. More specific reasons, reflecting the need
> to burn, have been given by Kukartja, Warlpiri, Pintupi, Maialtjara and
> Winanba people. On 16-8-75 mention was made of a bush tucker hunt bushfire'.
> U. Tjangala expanded on this on 5-2-76 when he said that the bush tucker plant
> foods would 'shoot-up' and 'make it a little bit easy (to collect)'. J. Tjampitjinpa
> reiterated this view on 31-3-76 emphasising the importance of 'cleaning' of the
> country. This 'cleaning' of the country is often stated: it will 'make the bush
> tucker come up'; it allows very easy hunting of goannas as their tracks and fresh
> mounds of earth at the entrance to their holes stand out; it permits easy travel;
> and it gives clear view when hunting larger game. In addition, cleaning of grass
> about an important native well or other site is viewed as caring for the site in a
> way that the mythological creature figure or figures, viewed as ever present, will
> recognize and appreciate. And finally, 'cleaning' of the country is viewed as
> method of promoting fresh plant growth for animals, a point succinctly made
> by J. Tjungurrayi on 7-12- 76 (and reiterated by J. W. Tjuparrulla on 29-4-80):
> 'Burn 'im off, rain fall, grass coming up, plenty of Kangaroo.'

Malu, emu, mole

ANANGU HAVE A WORD for the Red Kangaroo habitat.
Ulpuru.
Malu country.
And for green country regenerated from a fire, *nyaru.*
To the Horn scientists Red Kangaroo was *Macropus rufus*, which was sufficiently
majestic in the Darwinian scheme of things to get the first entry in the list of mammals
in Central Australia. 'It was seen everywhere in the plains from Mt Olga, lying south

'from a collector's point of view the camel is the most unsatisfactory of beasts', Baldwin
Spencer, 1896.

of Lake Amadeus, to the Burt Plains, lying north of the MacDonnell Ranges, and in
all the intervening country.' Physiological notes follow, on the basis of two skulls
brought back.

Ulpuru means more than merely 'the plains'. *Ulpuru* is the country of open plain
with no spinifex or prickles, which supports lots of grass, though not any kind of
grass. *Ulpuru* indicates green grass and herbs, since malu hardly need water as long as
their feed is green and moist.

To say *ulpuru* is to distinguish it from *puti*, the plains in general where the mulga
and acacia trees grow. Here the country might be a little stony, which malu do not like,
any more than they like the boggy ground after rain. Malu come onto the *puti* when
the feed is good and it is not too boggy, but the *ulpuru*, the area open enough for the
wind to come through, is what malu prefer.

Out from the Rock, towards Kata Tjuta is a spot known as Malu Katu. This is *ulpuru* country; and if you're trusted enough in the language it's possible to stay there and be told a little about malu. You might be told, for instance, that Anangu used to use fires out here to hunt malu. This was in the days before the wireless!

You'd light a fire, this Aboriginal man is saying, and then look around for another one as an answer. You'd know where the others were, and where your friends were. Or others might light the fire. They will be telling you where malu was, and so on. Local knowledge is like nothing else because it is part of life, lives full of practical knowledge, and with meanings that have a deep connection with the country. This is talk of the country while you are in it. As I see Anangu saying: 'It is OK that you can put the names on this paper (notebooks), keep them in this machine (tape recorder) and look at all these things (illustrations in books) but they are all in back of the Law, just on the very surface. None of them is real, they are white-fella things, ideas about Anangu idea. I can't properly talk about the country, teach about the country unless I am in it, walking on it, touching it, looking at it.'

A crucial point—malu is so important to the Law that not much more than this can be said about it anyway. *Ulpuru*, a category of what we call landscape has an accessible dimension to it, rather than as described above, a description that fits in with white ways of describing habitat. Beyond this, however, Anangu will not go. A silence sets in so that to our minds *ulpuru* remains a kind of open country itself, where the wind of the imagination must blow through.

It is in this way that Spencer's species of knowledge about *Macropus rufus* can be buttressed: by particular physical details and a sense of ceremony about malu. The bigness of malu can, however, be suggested another way. In Anangu terms the zoological classification of malu is revealing. For them, malu is 'all the same but a little bit different' to *tawalpa*, the crescent nailtail wallaby, *mitika*, the burrowing bettong, and *waru*, the black-footed rock wallaby. In other words back in ancient times, in Creation times, there were events that related them in some kind of evolutionary way. We don't know that way because this notion of evolution is not designed to be as public as Darwin's. But it is there in the Tjukurpa, and just as vital to Aboriginal culture at the Rock as scientific evolution is to ours.

Emu.

Kalaya.

They were once everywhere too.

Spencer got close to the hunting skills of Anangu, and had his clearest glimpse of the zestful conception with the 'wildlife' when three of his black boys suddenly came to a standstill:

after carefully examining the ground they became very excited. On seeing what was the matter they told me that there was an emu about with six young ones.

The three then separated and commenced to track it up. Then went on a trot the whole time; not a word was spoken but where the scrub was thin they communicated with each other by signs. After two miles run, during which it was quite enough for me to do to keep up with them and to look after my collecting material without troubling to look after tracks which I could not detect, they came to a sudden halt, and there in an open patch in front of us was the mother emu with its six young ones. The mother at once made off, but, shouting and laughing, the blacks soon caught the young ones and we brought them back to camp and carried them alive for some hundreds of miles on camel back.

(Memories of malu. Was Spencer the first white man, I wondered as I read this, to write down this evidence of Anangu 'cruelty' to the young wildlife?) He concludes: 'Their keenness and suppressed excitement when on the track were worth seeing, as well as their childish glee when they were successful.'

Today we might say, in the Anangu way, that they were in *karu* country, an area with creeks and banks, where there might be waterholes after rain. This is what *kalaya*, emu, like. Not for them the *nyaru* country either, the area of burnt and regenerating country. There is no cover there, no protection from eagles, and no hiding place for their eggs. *Kalaya* lay up to ten or twenty eggs, the hatching of which is a protracted business. One or two hatch a day until all are done, and the male sits on those that have arrived.

These eggs are a delicacy, and the feast to be had from *kalaya* is very tied up with the whole Anangu pattern of burning the country. This is what your informant is likely to talk about when you are out in the country.

'When the little emus are on the ground you do not burn.' 'It may be two days between the hatching of eggs, so you have to wait till then, too.' 'Emus stay in one place or close together until they are grown up, which is all the more reason, perhaps, to leave their habitat alone.'

Your informant might tell you more details of *kalaya*'s survival habits, such as the parent emu carrying excrement away from the nest in order to remove traces of the nest while they are camped in one place. No sign for the eagles, no scent for the dogs.

At the Rock, *kalaya* comes into the tale of *lungkata*, the blue-tongued lizard. This is the story of the two brothers far south of the Rock (in South Australia), two bellbirds, *panpanpalala*, who were stalking the emu, and drove it to Uluru where it was killed by another two brothers, the lizard men. With a stone axe they cut up the emu, and you can still see the sides of the butchered bird on the west side of Mutitjulu today. The thigh bone the lizard men buried, and that is the spur on the south-east face of the Rock. It is this hidden part of the bird which causes trouble when the lizard men give the bellbird brothers a skinny bit instead. The bellbird men set fire to the lizard men's shelter, burning them to death. Today you can see them as half-buried boulders.

And see what distance, what ground we have covered, to get from Spencer's sense of the emu and what comes through Anangu communications today. So *kalaya* does not seem to be a big story for the Rock, but this is not to say that all reference to *kalaya* is uncomplicated.

It is a feature of the Tjukurpa to have several and shifting names, depending on the dialect and the speaker's time in human history. The emu is widely called *kalaya* throughout the Western Desert, and it has the Ngaanyatjara synonym of *tjakipiri*. Something of Spencer's problem of access can be gained by considering this contemporary note on the business of naming:

> a senior Anangu woman . . . volunteered the information that the 'old name for Emu is Ngaanyatjara's Amalyara. That name, she explained, fell from use because of someone's death a long time ago and was substituted with Tjakipiri. Amalyara was no longer sensitive: it was just not in common use. Nowadays, it was said, *Kalaya* is what all Anangu called Emu, even though all three names are known to apply to the same animal. Except for a young Anangu woman who was present, everyone indicated that they knew Amalyara as a name for Emu, even though on numerous occasions it had been asserted that there were 'two names' for Emu. Clearly, in the circumstances of all but this occasion, Amalyara was not the name for Emu.

Itjaritjari.
The blind, burrowing, marsupial mole.

We met this creature, remember, on the *mala* walk. Just north of the base of the climb, there are the signs of her building a shelter. Our booklet tells us: 'Itjaritjari has always lived here at Uluru, in close harmony with the Mala. She is a playful old woman, and has busily tunnelled in the boulders above the cave. You can see the holes in these boulders where Itjaritjari can poke her head out.'

Spencer was very taken by the mole (*Notorcytes typhlops*). Marsupials were of great interest to Horn generally, from the skeletal remains of the *Diprotodon*, which was as big as a rhinoceros, to those skerricks of mice that jumped from tussock to tussock in broad daylight, apparently surviving even in drought. How did the mole fit in?

The curious thing was that the mole, although blind, spent part of its time on the surface. 'The complete loss of eyes externally is, no doubt,' Spencer said, 'to be associated with the fact that it is constantly burrowing in loose and often hot sand, the grains of which would, if it had eyes, be a fruitful source of irritation.' The zoological affinities of the mole were obscure to Spencer, as he was to its geographical origins. After much reflection he thought it may be 'the one (as far as yet known) surviving representative of a once more widely dispersed burrowing and mole-like marsupial,

190

which, for some reason, has been left stranded in the central region and elsewhere disappeared.'

So that was one mystery, something to be solved by western science, as more of the great continent was understood. A mystery of another kind was mooted when Spencer moaned about Dr Stirling's difficulty in catching a blind mole for himself. It was only after the expedition got back that samples were sent from Charlotte Waters. At the time this was the trouble they had:

> The blacks say that they catch them best when there has been a fall of rain, as then their tracks are more distinct. They do not make a permanent run like a mole does, for the obvious reason that the loose sand near the surface simply falls in and obliterates the burrow as the animal passes along, so that it is necessary to be able to follow their tracks on the surface, and this the blacks always tell you that they can only do after rain. It must be confessed that this is not an altogether satisfactory explanation, but it is one always given by the blacks. The latter will follow any track up on dry or wet sand, and there can be no difficulty whatever in their detecting the track of Notorcytes however dry the sand is. I fancy that the real explanation lies in the fact that the blacks catch the beast on the surface when they happen by chance, to come across it, and that, for some reason, it is most frequently seen on the surface shortly after rain.

Spencer's reason for doubting his Aboriginal helpers are unclear, unless it was for their own reasons that Anangu did not wish to catch *itjaritjari* in particular places, or at particular times. But this kind of rationale, which might have led to another kind of understanding of the mole in the natural scheme of things was beyond Spencer at the time, as we saw with the malu feast.

The Western naturalist got one thing quite right though. 'They live in the sandhill districts'. This is the habitat Anangu call *tali*—the kind of country out around the sunset viewing area. *Tali* is where most of the small mammals live, *itjaritjari* among them, along with the striped skink and the frogs that dig into the sand on the moister side of the dunes, waiting for rain. *Tali* is *not* the best hunting ground for Anangu and *itjaritjari* is by no means a much coveted food, at least not at the Rock where it has clear associations with tjukurpa. The depth of that association is hard to gauge; all *we* can say here is that the bit on the *mala* walk is all that we get, perhaps for good Anangu reason. *Itjaritjari* is a presence, but the resonance of her presence is hard to see, surfacing as she does a little bit, before going underground, as in the myth story.

If Anangu had felt like it—if Spencer thought to ask—they could have said more about *itjaritjari*'s physical habits. She eats lizards, insects and seeds, especially mulga seeds. Some Anangu say she has a sweet tooth, that she likes honeydew, nectar, and the sugary scales found on gum leaves.

191

The dance of categories

IT HAS TAKEN scientists some time to get a comprehensive understanding of habitat and flora fauna in arid lands, especially when that knowledge has been acquired in relationship with Anangu. The literature of acknowledgement (of Anangu) begins problematically with Spencer, and runs through this century with increasing richness and complexity. Finlayson is a landmark. Many scientists—too numerous to mention here—follow him. With a few exceptions when writing up their findings, Aboriginal knowledge has, according to the conventions of western science, taken a back seat. Our good fortune today is that joint management of the Park has nourished something new: it is a literary product that honours indigenous knowledge side by side with scientific understanding. 'Uluru Fauna: the Distribution and Abundance of Vertebrate Fauna of Uluru (Ayers Rock–Mount Olga) National Park', is the work of CSIRO in Alice Springs. It is the product of social trust and tenacious cultural intelligence by both cultures. Conventionally speaking, its principle authors are the scientists J. R. W. Reid, J. A. Kerle and S. R. Morton. With regard to Anangu knowledge, the key contributors are the scientist Lynn Baker and Susan Woenne-Green. Their chapter in the report, 'Anangu knowledge of the vertebrates and the environment' was researched over three years with the the the Mutitjulu community. Baker and Woenne-Green pay special tribute to Edith Richards as a crucial informant, and list those who shared their knowledge.

Ruth Connelly	Puliya
Wally Curtis	Ruth Sitzler
Trigger Derek	Awulyari Teamay
Kakali	Malya Teamay
Peter Kanari	Norman Tjakaltjiri
Billy Kayapipi	Tony Tjamiwa
Kayu Kayu	Barbara Tjikatu
Kata Kura	Willie Wamantjangu
Elsie Malpangka	Tommy Wangi
Jimmy Muntjantji	Alan Wilson
Maureen Nyantuny	Billy Wilson
Nyinku	Nipper Winmati
Bernice Panata	Nancy Yangarra
Martha Protty	

I repeat the list for several reasons. The written work flowered from the traditional soil of the oral culture: in effect, Anangu are co-authors of the historic chapter, which had aimed was to gather up-to-date information for Park Management. How else to look after a National Park without knowing, as extensively as possible, the delicate balance that exists in flora and fauna; and how to penetrate that delicacy without also knowing the connections with patterns of topography, rainfall, fire? This is the compass of the overall report, and as such, although it covers only terrain within the Park, it amounts to the most detailed ecological survey of vertebrates in any part of arid Australia. But before the Anangu contribution, a sketch of the Western listings:

There were birds in abundance, 117 species recorded for the survey. Due to recent rains, there was a massive influx of the wide-ranging nomadic species early on in the survey: budgerigar, white-winged triller, the crimson chat, masked woodswallow and the honeyeaters. And there were the rare species:

Scarlet-chested parrot.
Striated grass-wren.
Grey Honeyeater.

Three additions to the park list were:

Forktailed swift.
Little corella.
Peaceful dove.

I would love to cite all of these birds; their names fall down the page like feathers; they make a glorious plumage of nature knowledge. I look at their names and feel that the Park sings with immemorial life.

Of reptiles, seventy were recorded in the park. Uluru as a nest of slither, flickering tongue and scales of all colours in the sunned rock and sand. The dragons included:

Black-shouldered ground-dragon.
Military dragon.
Central netted dragon.
Canegrass Two-lined Dragon.

Among the geckos:

Spiny-tailed.
Fat-tailed.
Bynoe's Prickly.
Jewelled.

The goannas:

Short-tailed pygmy.
Rusty desert monitor.
Sand Monitor.
Perentie.

With mammals, however, profusion abates. In ancestor times there were 46 species of native mammals in the Uluru region. We know this from the skeletal material in cave deposits around the Rock and Kata Tjuta. Among the species that have gone are:

> Mala Rufous hare-wallaby.
> Black-footed rock-wallaby.
> Brushtail possum.

Bandicoots:

> Golden.
> Desert.
> Pig-footed, and the
> Bilby.

The survey found that 22 of the present 25 or 26 species still inhabit the Park. An impressive contemporary fauna for an arid Australian district, says CSIRO, of high conservation significance. Welcome, then, to the:

> Hairy-footed dunnart.
> Ooldea Dunnart.
> Fat-tailed Dunnart and the
> Desert Dunnart.

Yet be found in the sandhills, or spinifex where the mice still are are the

> Sandy Inland Mouse
> Desert Mouse and
> Spinifex Hopping Mouse

as present as it was to Baldwin Spencer, when it leapt about him in broad daylight.

And the survey found:

> Echinda.
> Marsupial mole.
> Mulgara.

with bats, the

> White-striped Mastiff.
> Yellow-bellied.
> Hill's Sheathtail bat.

These names, our ascension and descent of calling, make up white culture's song of the

Park. It is a song we sing, even those of us who have never seen such creatures, out of trust in the tune of science, even though we know that some scientists have never seen the things that they name either. It is a song partly composed on this continent as naturalists have made their way across it, collecting and naming, and realising as they went that not everything was as upside down as they first thought. Or as alien as even Darwin thought when he said: 'Surely two Creators have been at work.'

It is a song that has its origins in Europe, where the epic journey of naming began. Darwin's naming was of course parasitic upon the repertoire played by Linnaeus. Before that we had the meditations of Pliny The Elder, whose 'Natural History' is the first elaborate play with the naming of things that have been seen and accurately observed, which exist on the earth, with those which have been imagined, and exist only by naming, born of the mind of Man, if not God. Pliny's science oscillates between the intent to recognise an order in nature and recording what is extraordinary and unique. Nature is eternal and sacred and harmonious, but it can issue forth with inexplicable, prodigious phenomenon. Better-known animals are mentioned with imaginary ones. While speaking of elephants, Pliny digresses to inform us of dragons, their natural enemies; while telling of wolves, we hear of the werewolf.

Of fish Pliny was able to say: 'Fish that have a pebble in their heads; fish that hide in winter; Fish that feel the influence of stars.'

I have used the phrase 'dance of categories' as an invitation. Put the profusion of names from science beside Anangu's. What happens? One culture gazes at the other, and sure enough, if the music of the imagination strikes up, each might step out with the other in way that enlarges the consciousness of everyone in the Park. What else is ecology but the ability to describe how all systems and classifications relate to each other?

To the tune of mice

THE CSIRO TEAM had marked out 13 sites throughout the park, places of various habitat where the survey would be conducted according to conventional sampling methods. One site is at the Rock itself, and it is to this place that Susan Woenne-Green and Lynn Baker go one day with Barbara Nipper and Nipper Winmati.

It's October—spring time to us. Blooms. Scent. Warm, sweet earth.

Anangu call the season either *Piriya Piriya*, after '*Piriya*', the warm consistent wind that comes from the north and west, or '*kaliny-kalinypa*', after the flowering of the honey-suckle grevillea (*Grevillea eriostachya*). A focal time of the year for Anangu.

Woenne-Green and Baker went into a valley just east of Mutitjulu, which opens out onto the alluvial fans that come out from Rock's run-off. A rich and various habitat, a combination of what Anangu might call '*puli*', rocks and rocky country, and '*wanari*', the mulga country.

Baker explains to Barbara and Nipper how the white fella sets up the pit traps and fences. She is told that there is a lot of everything in the valley, in this place where Anangu once lived.

Nyii-nyii. Finch.
Kalaya. Emu.
Ngintaka. Perentie.
Tjilkamata. Echinda.
Waru. Wallaby.
Kanyala. Euro.
Patiny patinypa. Long-nosed legless lizard.

They caught three *patiny patinypa* that afternoon. When they did Nipper sang part of the *inma* in which it appears:

Patiny patinypa is a whistling lizard; its whistle is related to the *inma*. A long time ago it had legs and could bite things. But now it is legless, noseless, fangless—due to an event in the Tjukurpa.

Today it lives in the *tjampi*, the spinifex country, and sometimes shallow burrow, *milyinytji*, especially when it is near a fig tree. It lays its eggs in the burrow, and when they hatch the little ones come up, and eat the figs that have fallen to the ground.

There is the yellow *Patiny patinypa*, which lives in the sand hills. This is still the same name as the one . . . 'like a snake colour but not a snake'. And there is a red one, which is short and stubby and lives in various places.

All this was told to Woenne-Green and Baker as they walked around with Nipper and Barbara. Walking around, in bits and pieces, stopping and starting, in the wind.

There are geckos to speak of too. *Papangaurpa* and *matjanya* are both like snakes but not snakes. Neither has legs. *Manjanya* is also brownish in colour; *panakur* is stubby, short, reddish. Both are associated with Tjukurpa.

Nipper gives the danger sound for *papangaurpa*. He says that another name for *ngawurpa* is *warura*.

Barbara gives this some thought.

Nipper says Ngaanyatjara speakers use *warura*, while Pitjantjatjara use both. They are walking again, and the wind is getting warmer all the time. *Papangaurpa* lives in a little hole, Nipper continues. They dig it and then block the entrance with a little bunch of pebbles, as frogs do.

There is another gecko called *pirurpa*, which lives in tree bark. This is a little one.

They don't eat him. Only devils eat geckos.

On second thoughts—hawks, *kurkinpa*, do. As do birds.

Anangu never eat geckos, perhaps because the reptiles eat all the things beneath the bark, and give off something undesirable or unpleasant from this.

'An exudate of some sort,' says Woenne-Green in her field notes.

Over many weeks and months Anangu came to share their nature knowledge. Always, for the white person, it was a drawn out, teasing exercise. Not only did it call upon considerable linguistic skill with words heard for the first time, words used ambiguously, words lost in the wind; it demanded a patient acceptance of Anangu's order of presentation, and systematic reluctance to say everything at once. 'It is clear to us that a sophisticated system of classification is in operation among Anangu', Woenne-Green wrote at one stage, 'but at the moment we do not understand it.'

Easier to appreciate were the ways in which Anangu knowledge seemed to supplement some of the white-fella stories about animals. It was an enormous help to have the incredible tracking skills of Anangu, especially the steady work of women like Edith Richards, whose skills were a constant source of amazement to those who went out with her. This added to field information around traps, and sharpened knowledge about such rare species as *tjakura* (giant desert skink, *Egernia kintorei*), as well as the whereabouts of the increasingly rare marsupial *murtja* (mulgara, *Dasycercus cristi cauda*). Equally refined was local knowledge of habitat preferences. Anangu knew which animals were flexible in their habitat requirements, and which were not. Thus a certain mouse, the scientists will be told, prefer the fire-regenerated area rather than mature spinifex; the tree-dwelling geckos prefer this kind of bark, not that.

We call this life history information. To Anangu it was information bound up with a 'naturally integrated' view of the species.

Here is Anangu on *tarkawara*, the spinifex-hopping mouse that so intrigued Spencer:

> *Tarkawara* live together in large groups. They dig a burrow system that runs steeply, deep into the ground. There are many exits and entrances. The main entrance is covered over and a number of remote escape holes 'katata' exist. These holes are blocked off by sand or small pebbles when the animals are inside or when adults have left young behind whilst they forage. These blockages can be easily broken though if *Tarkawara* needs to leave or enter in a hurry. There is a special chamber for breeding which is filled with chewed spinifex.
>
> The offspring generally move out to build new burrows, though sometimes the males will stay with the parents and breed after the parents die. Male

offspring may bring females into the nest, while female offspring move to a new burrow with a mate.

Tarkawara move burrows constantly to stay close to their food source. During drought they collect food and store it in holes. They live nearby even if there is no water. When there are good seasons they breed quickly and there are lots of them running around.

This was an addition to scientific literature; hitherto there were no records of arid-zone mice storing food, and the survey confirmed Anangu reports. Less resolved was a difference that emerged between the scientists and Anangu. The subject is the eating habit of the dasyurids, the subset of *mingkiri* known by scientists to be carnivorous or insectivorous. Not so, says Anangu. They eat seeds and plant material.

The scientific certainty is based on stomach-content analysis, scat and detention. On such hard evidence should Anangu claims be dismissed? Not necessarily, say Baker and Woenne-Green, certainly not without asking some basic questions about Anangu grounds for perception. Do Anangu make their judgements from the animal tracks leading to the plants? Do they spot the nocturnal creatures too infrequently to really know? Or are the stated diets of these creatures 'determined in the non-public areas of the Tjukurpa'? Or, finally, *do* these creatures *sometimes* eat seeds in their natural habitats? What we seem to need here is closer study of the collaborative kind initiated by the survey.

Time and again though, the overlap between life-history knowledge and what can be sung from the Tjukurpa became apparent. It was one thing to get the titbits of information about legless lizards and their previous condition in the Tjukurpa, details of which were not spelt out. It was more forceful to get the story of the species which play a part in the big stories at the Rock. Thus scientific knowledge about *Kuniya* (*Woma*), the rock python, comes in part directly from the Tjukurpa.

As the fauna study summarises: 'Anangu state that a characteristic behaviour . . . is that they lay their eggs on a little circle of grass or other ground debris and then coil their body around them 'like a nest' to keep them warm and to protect them. This behaviour continues until all of the eggs are hatched. The behaviour of the female Kuniya is described in the song-line celebrating her travels as an ancestral being to Uluru from the east.'

So what happens when we put the scientific play of categories beside Anangu's?

Well, as I have been trying to show from the CSIRO's Fauna Survey, at least two basic things are apparent. First, there is a remarkable overlap in the way the two cultures 'see' the observable habitats. The sand, grass, rock, scrub and tree areas are similarly perceived, with both cultures having their particular refinements, depending on their purposes. Anangu took pains to mark off the habitat of the Red Kangaroo (*ulpuru*) and pointed to claypan and saltpan areas (*tjintjira* and *pantu*), not that our scientists could not see these habitat zones; for this survey's purposes they did not have to name them. Similarly with the seasons: there is enough overlap to fit ours into theirs. So in looking at the topography—as in undergoing its seasons—we are, to a degree, one culture rather than two.

Secondly, there is a general overlap with regard to the classification of fauna. There seem to be broadly similar groupings of animals according to structural features, as well as colour and markings. There are some major similarities between our use of 'family', 'genus', 'species' and 'subspecies'.

Beyond that, differences begin to show up. In some ways Anangu knowledge is more specialised. Some terms, for example not only classify an animal, they economically indicate its behaviour in a way that might take us a sentence to describe. The words *wanitjunkupai/yuratjunanyi* describe the act of hibernation by reptiles. The terms do not apply to mammals. There is also a specific verb to the action of *ninu* (bilby) rubbing its forepaws together. And there are two words for young emu. *Yakalpa* for the still-striped young. *Tjampuni* for the baby emu still travelling with its mother. Remember Spencer's zealous report of the emu hunt, and the precision of the hunters? The conversation that Spencer heard but could not understand must have contained these distinctions.

There is another significant difference with the scientific system of classification. The criteria for naming does not seem to be constant. There are immediate social factors that come into play, which cause the naming of a species to vary according to the speaker and his or her state of knowledge, and also be determined by prohibitions on a name if someone has died. Some things have multiple names. Over and above this, it did appear to Baker and Woenne-Green that naming was much determined by the object's status as a food item: edibles within a group have individual names, the non-edibles not. Following this rule, tracks, burrows, markings, size and habitats were specifically but not always named and not always consistently.

Take the mouse, *mingkiri*.

It lives all over the park. In scientific terms we are talking about seven species:

Sandy inland mouse. *Pseudomys hermannsburgensis.*
Desert mouse. *P. desertor.*
House mouse. *Mus musculus.*
Wongai ningaui. *Ningaui ridei.*
Ooldea dunnart. *Sminthopsis ooldea.*
Hairy-footed dunnart. *S. hirtipes.*
Desert dunnart. *S. youngsoni.*

Now with the House mouse, which the white fella brought into the area, Anangu's perceptions present no great puzzle. It is different to the other indigenous mice for a simple reason, though they were shy of saying so at first. When pushed a little, and when they saw the white fella trying to phrase the question without being too prying about Tjukurpa, one of senior men laughed and came out with it. 'White-fella *mingkiri* have big balls.'

But what of the other *mingkiri*, since *'mingkiri'* includes all the smaller rodents and dasyurids that do not have large or distinguishing features, and may also be used as a general term for all small mammals?

Distinctions are made, Baker and Woenne-Green point out, by reference to teeth, nose, tail, pouch and, yes, genitalia. But the naming may stay the same, while also being different. They write: 'During discussions about Mingkiri, informants generally appear to be discussing rodents rather than dasyurids. Occasionally female dasyurids are called Murtja/Arutju due to the presence of the pouch. At times Mingkiri appears to be restricted to rodents as classified by the position of the nipples and the absence of a pouch. Some informants have suggested one of the reasons for the physical differences between animals within the name Mingkiri is that some are capable of interbreeding with Murtja/Arutju. At times people describe small pouched animals as Mingkiri but a different type of Mingkiri.'

The Desert mouse is at times called *wiltjinypa* rather than *mingkiri*. This distinction seems based on the size of the animal and the size of its hind feet in relation to other members of the *mingkiri* category.

Mingkiri is pale coloured, not dark like *anula*, while *tarkawara* have white feet or at least feet that are paler than the rest of the body.

One senior informant using an analogy to explain the relationship of *mingkiri*, *tarkawara*, *anula*, *murtja* and *ilypalya* stated:

> There are numerous names of plants that are seed plants and for lots of fruit plants with certain sized fruit or seeds or size of plants when they actually bear edible fruit/seeds. [He then continued about birds.] There are lots of birds that live in nests, lots that live in tree hollows. Over these two categories are those who build nests in trees and those who live in hollows in the trees. All these live in trees (not on the ground). All have different names.
>
> Then there is *Puntaru* (Little Button-quail) and *Marupunpu* (different bird), all of this type live on the ground. Within this category are some that have nests and some that do not, although they are still ground layers. Then there are some that excavate little holes in the ground. They are still on the ground but different from the others. This is like when Anangu talk about *Mingkiri, Ilypalya, Anula, Wiltjinypa, Murtja, Tarkawara*: they all make burrows and dig like crazy to have their young inside comfortable and safe quarters unlike other

things that do not do these things. Five names are *Mingkiri: Ilypalya, Anau, Wiltjinypa, Tjurtja, Tarkawara.* They do not just make holes for their young in any which way. Some animals just forget their kids such as *Ngiyari* (Thorny Devil), *Lungkata* (Blue-Tongue Lizard). All five however, work very hard to make everything well built and safe.

The elder went on to say where these species were now living and where they used to live. As Baker and Woenne-Green point out, there is much movement in this system of classification. Much of it seems to be on the surface, involving various observable details. But the logic of that play goes deeper. It springs from basic considerations within the Tjukurpa. All Anangu knowledge ultimately interlaces with the private Law, and the ways of speaking and thinking about *mingkiri* are no exception. Its differentiation from *murtja* (mulgara), *arutju* (fat-tailed antechinus) and *tarkawara* (spinifex-hopping mouse) 'appears to derive from the Tjukurpa. All of the above are related to malu (Red Kangaroo)'. So say Baker and Woenne-Green after their sympathy dance with Anangu categories.

Any wonder then that they have long wondered about a scientific paper they might write, the better to play the tune of the problem: *When is a mouse not a mouse?*

Taxonomies have various presuppositions built into them, depending on the interests, values and purposes of the classifier. Categories dance in and out of focus, depending on the degree to which the system is intellectually self-conscious, and what the classifications are supposed to do. Let us assume, at the highest level of generality, that all systems of knowledge are part of humanity's attempt to answer the two basic problems of existence: survival and meaning. There will be systems seen as answers to the question: *how to survive*? There will be others oriented to answer the question: *Why* survive? And there might well be systems that coverge on both. This seems to be the case with the kind of 'related whole' of Anangu knowledge described so painstakingly by Baker and Woenne-Green. By contrast, science in our culture generally prides itself on being able to separate the questions; indeed, on being able to refine the 'how' question in ways that give deep(er) explanations to the way Nature works. Linnaeus's hope of revealing God's order of Nature is still there, in the wider quest of science. That realm of ultimate meaning is our Tjukurpa, we might say. But science itself works with classifications that are more disinterested and impersonal, which proceed according to finer questions and observations about how living things function and came into being. This has been the case since Linnaeus, as systems of classification have grappled with processes of change, with the evolution of life forms rather than still-life classification. Before Darwin we had static categories—tables, lists, charts, all the 'definitions' on a geometric model. Since Darwin, classifications contend with dynamic processes, and point towards 'related wholes' that we have come to think of as ecology.

And yet, taxonomies since Darwin have neither brought a stable order to the natural world nor managed to expunge the kind of cultural value judgements that loaded pre-scientific classifications. The whole business of framing the world remains a cultural one. There is no natural order that is not in some way a product of the purposes, conscious or otherwise, of the classificatory system. Even modern biology has no one 'correct' taxonomy of living things, though it can be said that its classifications dig for the underlying evolutionary history of organisms. Still, everything depends on the criteria we wish to bring to bear. Thus we might focus on similarities of anatomy, function and the ecological role of a species. We are then dealing with shapes, morphologies evident on the face of the matter. What of the natural *history* of things? What, exactly, is a species? As soon as we ask this, other criteria come into play, much of it as invisible to the naked eye as anything A̲nangu might want to hint at in the Tjukurpa. For we are then considering the 'fine print' of genetic structures, matters of great refinement and precision. If you take the morphological criteria, there are, for example, three species of zebra on the planet. If you take the genetic, there are two, since in evolutionary terms the mountain zebra is closer to the horse.

Imagine A̲nangu saying, your categories are all over the place, how do you decide between the two?

The question is bemusing, and we answer: It depends. It depends on how many distinctions we want to make, and the circumstances we are in. Sometimes we want to know how things came about, and as much as we can of their ultimate constituents. At other times we are classifying for different purposes, and it makes no real sense to put too fine a point on 'difference'. Here we pick up the great maestro of evolution, the man who plays fine music with scientific categories. Stephen Jay Gould gave us the example of zebras. Gould also speaks of the evolutionary ordering of lung fish and the coelacanth, which are genealogically close to the mammals: 'the lungfish must form a sister group within the sparrow or elephant, leaving the trout in its stream . . . At this point, many biologists rebel, and rightly I think . . . must classifications be based only on evolutionary information? A coelacanth looks like a fish, tastes like a fish, acts like a fish, and therefore—in some legitimate sense beyond hidebound tradition—is a fish.'

Fire (iii)

ENDO HAD COME at last to the Tavern, the cockpit of dubious narrative at the Resort. I'd never had a good drink with a Japanese, although they have a reputation for enjoying one. But Endo did not like the beer, and had sat with a Scotch, overweakened with water.

—It's bore water, I teased, you ought to go on the rocks. He was unmoved.

It was three o'clock on a Saturday afternoon, time the young manual workers of the Resort came in. The atmosphere was rowdy. A few young women leaned at the counter tables with their men. What was nice about the place was, at that time, the absence of *minga*. They were out in the sun touring the Park. The clientele laughed and leaned against each other as if it was their club. The Tavern is really the only watering place for the thousand or so employees of the Resort, and it shows: the place can develop a hot, in-house atmosphere of people who feel the pressure of working in an isolated outpost. These are young, mostly single people, earning a dollar as quickly as they can, in order to move on. They come from all over the country, attracted by some vague idea of the Centre, and after a visit to the Rock, consider that they have seen it, and settle down to their work, and their play after work. It's hard to know what some of them do at night, but one can imagine. In the remote white community, it's party time. About eighteen months is most people's limit of tolerance. In-turned, generally ignorant and indifferent to the owners of the Park, the place burns with time-consuming, hedonistic passion.

—It is, Endo said, a bit like a beer hall.

—No it's not, I said, it's a league's club without the pokies. Drinkers here have taken their punt on the Outback.

—You're over-looking the glamour spots, he said.

—I am, I said, remembering the smarter-looking young people who did the front of house at Sails and Desert Gardens. Where did they go for a drink? They had to make their own fun. Spot fires, out of sight.

There were no Aborigines in the tavern, but a few were hanging around outside. The bolder, drunker ones wanted money, or they'd ask you to get takeaways for them. Their own community at Mutitjulu had put the tavern off-limits, and the six-pack limit had put a stop to easy purchase. From where we stood you could see the steps of the concourse where they intercepted innocent *minga*. The face of the white person was sternly recomposed by the time they reached the Tavern. Hard to know if they knew about the drinking rules (although it was printed up in most hotel rooms), or what they felt about the locals begging. *Minga* plunged into the air-conditioning, as if the unexpected heat of 'race relations' was too much for them.

—The fires in 1950, I told Endo, fed by the fuel grown during the previous twenty years, wiped out about one-third of the Park's vegetation. The same again in 1976, when 76 per cent of the Park was burnt. Then in 1990, a fire came from the south, travelling thirty kilometres in one night, and reached the park with a rush. But it stopped, it didn't get into the Park.

—Why?

—Lack of fuel, because the spinifex had been systematically burnt off. Since 1985 the patch burning, the mosaic of burning every few years depending on the life-cycle of the spinifex had been done in the manner of Anangu, in consultation with Anangu. The same again in 1991, when a huge fire swept down from the north. It stopped when it got to the mosaic. You can see it exactly from the Landsat photograph. The great swath of burnt country to the north, fingering out as it reached the Park.

—Anangu, Anangu, crooned a voice behind me. Know what the blackfellas should do when the fire comes?

—No, what's that? I was answering a bony young bloke in a navy singlet.

—Piss on it. They should get out there with their fucking big beer guts and piss until it goes out.

He was carrying five pots and, with the aplomb only the drunken have when they are carrying drinks, moved around the back of Endo's neck without disturbing the foam. Endo looked unimpressed.

He said—My understanding is that your CSIRO have put a lot of work into fine-tuning the fire program. Their detailed scientific knowledge of grasses and fuel loads and that kind of thing, comes into the Park Management too. It's hardly a matter of the Park being saved by traditional knowledge, least of all what you have been calling traditional ecological knowledge.

—It is a matter, I said, of the two things coming together. That's what I'm saying. And I don't really understand why you jeer at the ecological. It's your shout. If you're doing Scotch I'll have a double with my pot, thank you Endo.

When he came back I had my speech ready.

—Knowledge may be demonstrated in different ways. Take the idea of 'cleaning the country'. It is a key term for Anangu, one that gives us an idea of what is in their mind with fire practices. You are 'cleaning the country' when you are doing any number of things: burning for hunting, for new growth, for ease of travel, and for the sake of the Tjukurpa ancestors, *who are ever present*. Think about the last reason, because it is a reason. You are burning the country with enormous care precisely because it is matter of sacred trust, part of your responsibility to the creation and continuous maintenance of the whole place. So the idea of regeneration comes in, as does the idea of balance.

—So you're saying that they are ecologists. Natural ecologists.

—I am.

Endo smiled.—This morning, he said, I was in conversation with a most informative Ranger out at the Rock. He said that up in the Tanami Desert, where the last colonies of *mala* lived, there is another marsupial called the *mulgara*. Evidently it is an endangered species.

—So?

—And yet, Endo said, the Aborigines there think nothing of eating it.

—I can understand that, I said.

—You mean you excuse it for the present time. Meanwhile you are giving medals all round for ecology. And what about your malu, how do I know that I have not seen a malu on my trip because Anangu have shot too many of them? Being in balance with nature when you hunt on foot, and use fire as a tool, is one thing. Charging cross-country in your Toyota with a rifle is another matter altogether. And what about the emu, that wonderful great bird so conspicuous for so long around here? Where is that now? Am I right in saying it is an endangered species here also, and that Anangu have not helped matters there either?

—Kalaya is not mentioned as being at risk by the CSIRO report.

—I wonder, said Endo knowingly.—It is not what my ranger led me to suspect.

I wondered if I would take exception to his snide dogmatism, but I could see, with some relief, that he at least had a stiff drink in front of him. If he got a bit drunk he might loosen up. In any case, the issues he raised—the extent to which Aboriginal ecology was entirely consistent with ours—could not be swept aside with wishful politics. Besides, I had to admit (if only to myself) that the idea of balance had to be seen historically. Before the white man, the balance struck by Aborigines may well have fitted in with current ecological principles. After white contact things may have been different. Strehlow speaks of Aranda and Kukatja tribesmen burning wisely in pre-white contact days, while remembering what the Sydney University party saw at Ajantji in 1934 when Pintupi and Ngalia people lit spinifex fires 'everywhere in the rough country south of the (MacDonnell) range'. The fires blazed for a fortnight, ruthlessly burning many square miles and euro, emus, wallabies and rabbits were slaughtered in profusion. The hunters gorged, and the time of food scarcity began. It is a sad ecological picture, a bizarre example of maladaptive human behaviour, until you realise that this was a period of drought, when the hunters had been driven in from the desert. The country was also already out of kilter because of the rabbit, the depradations of which exacerbated the drought. Overall the context of fire practice *had* changed. That is Strehlow's point about the Aranda and Kukatja tribesmen: their country was being carelessly burnt by hungry immigrants. Similarly perhaps with the slaughter of emu, the 'joyful slaughter' that Finlayson saw out in the Petermanns in 1931, before the drought had set in. Then, Strehlow speculates, an abundance of game must have existed, since bushmen like Billy Liddle and Bob Buck had, in 1927 and 1929, seen gatherings of three hundred Aborigines. Balance, like everything else, keeps changing. Ecological understanding for everybody has to change with the times.

—Let me ask you a question, said Endo.

—Fire away.

—What if, he said with a smirk, a great reserve of uranium is discovered beneath the Rock?

—Beneath Uluru.

—Right under your Rock.

My Rock.

—Your 'Sharing of the Park' Rock.

—You can't mine in a National Park, I said, too tartly for my own good.

—Cheers, I added.

It was fine beer. Sweeter by the minute. We needed nuts.

—What are you drinking to?

—Debating skills. Rhetoric, I said.—OK, listen. I will admit that there is no alliance between the Greens and Anangu, necessarily. That was shown in the Top End, when traditional owners agreed to mine uranium. Or rather, when local politics had it that the black–green alliance did not really come together. It must also be said that many Aborigines have personally financially benefited from that decision, as has their national organisation, the Australian and Torres Strait Islander Commission (ATSIC), from the royalties of the uranium mines. Contrary to the propaganda from much of the mining industry, Aborigines are not automatically opposed to mining on their land. Up in the Tanami they benefit from one of the oldest gold mines in the Territory. Over at Hermannsburg, just north of Lake Amadeus, they profit from the Meenie Oil deposits. On behalf of traditional owners the Central Land Council is certainly very careful about giving mining companies permission to explore on Aboriginal land. But once the consultations for that permit have been done, it is on the cards that Aborigines will say yes to mining if they see fit.

—Yes to uranium-mining in the Park?

—Not here, no, I don't think so, I said.—I mean: even if it wasn't a National Park, the owners here are very strong on their law. The Tjukurpa would stop them. The extent to which the Rock itself—or the places at it—is sacred would stop them.

—Not like that case I read about recently. Where the sacred site was moved, so that mining could take place.

—Not like that, no, I said. Endo was referring to South Australia, where negotiations between owners and mining companies had reached such a compromise.

—There would be no deal where everyone agreed to move the Rock, Endo said. —The Rock as a movable feast. A nomadic Rock, better than a hard place.

We laughed. We were getting pissed.

—There is a big new word in Aboriginal Studies, I said.

—What's that?

—Negotiable. Mining rights. Aboriginal identity. Landrights. Traditional claims on land. The price of a dot painting. All negotiable. But there is something that seems not to change. There are some fixed points. And coming back to fire.

206

—Tell me a fixed point about fire.

—I found Dick Kimber's wonderful article, 'Black Lightning'. I read from the beginning: 'The boulders are glowing coals in the late afternoon light, Lungkata the Blue-Tongued Lizard huffs on his firestick. The firestick glows. He touches it to a bush and the bush explodes into flame. The flames leap from bush to bush, pursuing Lungkata's sons, for they have broken the law and kept meat from their father. You can see the glowing coals. You can see the fire path running south from the Ngalia country to the Kukartja, then south and south again to the lands of the Pitjantjatjara. Lungkata lives.'

When I had finished, I said,—Some of the stories don't change. That's where the deep knowledge is. The deep ecology is what is of value in the Tjukurpa.

Endo said,—That's not deep knowledge. That's myth. Mystery does not equal depth.

—Don't you realise, I said, that until very recently even our ecologists had to admit to the mysteries, that systematic knowledge of the arid lands has only just begun.

—There is a lot I don't realise. That is one reason I like to learn one thing at a time. I like measurements. I like experiments. I like objective truth. I can at the moment see that your whisky glass is empty. That is a fact. It has nothing to do with whether you deeply value another drink or not, or whether you feel like singing about it. You do? I'll get you another then, and myself too.

I felt this was the most intelligent thing Endo had said for the day. When he was at the bar, the stick in the navy singlet came and sat on his stool.

—You don't want to take any crap from that Nip, he said.—My old man hated their guts.

His expression suggested parody, but the depth of his irony was uncertain. I took a punt.

—Piss off, you racist bastard, I said.

—No worries, he said, and left.

—Are you all right? asked Endo when he came back.

We are crowding up.

A busload of Germans have come into the Tavern. They stood in a pack. One of them put his camera to his face and photographed the bar menu with a startled cook beneath it, then, after a barking exchange with their tour guide, they marched out.

—I was speaking with a German tour guide in Alice Springs, said Endo, and I believe that although the Germans are perhaps the best-educated group who come to the Rock they also have some odd ideas. That police here can still shoot Aborigines, for example. That black babies are born with extra large fontanelles. What did your visitor say?

—He said his father's Dreaming was on the Burma Railway.

Endo went quiet.

In the pause, and with the new drink, I felt entirely lucid.

If you want to talk about clear understanding of arid Australia, I wanted to tell Endo, think of the wonderful work of those CSIRO men, Steve Morton and David Stafford Smith. For the first time now we have a model of how things interrelate, a 15-proposition schema that illuminates *our* arid lands, the so-called desert that Anangu have survived in for millennia. You start with basic truths about the physical environment (the rainfall, soils), and you go to the unique dynamic features of plant life (soils, fertility, carbohydrates and fire) and then to the consequences for fauna. Proposition 1 happens to be 'Rainfall unpredictability'. Proposition 15 is 'Consumer stability is surprisingly high'. In-between is the web of relationships that are the survival strategies of all living things, right down to ants, who are consumers like everyone else, as good old Spencer noticed a century ago but was in no position to explain. Take Proposition 8, 'The importance of fire' and you get the scientific statement that 'fire is an important driving force in the arid zone because of high perennial biomass, slow rates of decomposition and plentiful carbohydrate tissue. Although it may be infrequent, fire plays a crucial role in maintaining plant species diversity at a site by removing adult plants and recycling nutrients.'

Think about Proposition 8, I wanted to say to Endo, and ask yourself the question: did Anangu know this? The answer has to be yes, though they would express the knowledge differently. They know it mainly because they live here. It's local knowledge. This model for arid Australia is exciting and deep because it is local knowledge. What counts is knowing the different patterns of variations throughout the region, the better to survive, whether you are an ant, hare, wallaby or human being. It is those patterns we are on to now, we being the mob coming to it a bit late, on the cracked heels of Anangu.

—What are you thinking about now? Endo asked.

—Ants.

—Ants?

—Proposition 11, I said, 'Infertility favours termites'.

—Cheers, he said.

—Where the biomass won't run herbivores, the ants move in. And I bet there is, in some Anangu song, some understanding of this.

—I have no idea what you are talking about, Endo said.

—Take the honey ant.

—Where to?

Endo had looked away. A backpacker had come into the bar. She had long blond hair and the seat of her denim shorts was torn. A sweet brown buttock showed through.

—Do I have your attention, Endo?

—What nationality, do you think? said Endo.

—*Camponotus inflatus*, I said, the singular thing about the honey ant is the swollen replete, commonly known as the stomach, which distends to contain that fat jewel of honey, which is not so much glucose as fructose.

—Glucose, fructose, Endo said, as the girl returned with her drinks.

—You have been in America too long, Endo. This is not television.

—Somewhere, said Endo, I have seen her on TV.

Waiting at her table were three other backpackers, all male. I had Endo's attention again.

—There is, you will be pleased to know, a honey ant in America. Honey pots on the honey ant undoubtedly serve as storage organs for the whole colony. The workers go out and bring fluid back to the nest and feed it to the repletes, and then, in hard times, it is food for all. Living storage organs, yet another example of the great variety of survival strategies that are here. Intimate knowledge of which Anangu have, although our understanding of the honey ant has progressed very slowly indeed. For millennia they have known exactly where to find them, which is in dense groves of mulga. But what we have only recently been able to ask is: why has only this species of ant been able to develop its storage capacity to such an extent?

—OK, why?

—Steve Morton says it's to do with its special adaptation to the infertility of mulga soils. The mulga soils are deep and infertile, and do not store ground water particularly well. Paradoxically, however, the rains are sometimes very good. In those times the honey ants boost production. They lap up the bounty of sweet debris from plant and other animal life. Then, when hard times come, they are ready for survival in the special locality they live in. Other ants, you see, might live elsewhere, in spinifex country, or rocky areas. Each ant to its own infertile locality, you might say, and each ant, to go a little further, doing its bit to rework energy systems at the micro level.

—Oh, *minga* do all sorts of work.

The bar, we could see, was filling up with *minga*. Trust the backpackers to be the forward movement of the swarm.

—I would go even further in the ecological model, Endo said.

—You would.

—I would put *minga* at the centre of it all.

—You would.

—Without *minga*, the whole natural economy out here would collapse. It would not exist. There would be hardly anybody here. No visitors, no Resort. Without the Resort, and all that it stands for in the unreliable economic system of your country, there would be little interest in the whole place. Without interest, there would be little gathering of knowledge. Take away the *minga*, and your CSIRO boys would not be as busy as they have been. Our elders, the men who know, whose love of their knowledge

209

helps bind us to our 'laws of Reason', they make their honey because the tourist industry puts this place on the map. That's the big picture. Without *minga* as energisers, without the whole Park Biz, the ecology wouldn't go.

—But there would be, I said, the Honey Ant Men's Love Song.

—You can chant what you like, laughed Endo.—Is this another one of your make ups?

He departed with thoughts of home
He departed with thoughts of home
He departed towards another place

He rose to go
Joyfully he went
Sank down when he was tired.

It was a chant of sixty-five verses by Thomas Jangala, recorded in Warlpiri country in 1971. It is a strong poem, beautiful in its economy and refrain as it sings of courtship. I love it for its passion and obliqueness, its narrative cunning and depth. What deeper ecology there than the ecology of love, that system of systems.

Red Bird Messenger
Aroused her, as Honey Ant approached.
Walking slowly, the woman aroused.

Red Bird Messenger
Saw the Glistening desiring
On Honey-Ant glistening.

—I think you should stop soon, Endo said.
But I thought some verses demanded gusto.

Admired her shapely legs
Admired her loins and eyes

Eyes looked at the visitor
Lovesick

The woman left
Her country,
Heavily

Suddenly, the young fella with the navy singlet was beside me. He and Endo seemed to be exchanging grins, like old mates.

Singlet said:—You want to go quiet a bit, mate. They'll take you for a blackfella and put you out.

CHAPTER 6 Stars, land, love

Stars

—WE SHOULD, ENDO SAID, take our political bearings from the stars.

We were out at the Resort, and Endo had just come in from a 'star tour'. Of the smorgasbord of things you can do—the Harley Davidson rides, the joy flights, the sunset cruise in the white limo—'the stars' is one of the better things, since the night sky in Central Australia is unsurpassed. There are more stars here than anywhere else in the world, and they are the brightest stars. The colour of the large ones stand out, and the smaller ones which you can't usually see come forward in clusters as if they belong to our own solar system that is, planet by planet, palpably close. In Central Australia, when you are lying back in your swag, you can touch the stars. And between them, the blackness is blacker than anywhere else. It's as if you can see the breadth of all light in the cosmos, and the depth of its night. It's as if, while being on earth, you pulsate with the heavens, entirely lit by them, while being in the night.

I said to Endo:—Take the long view, you mean?

—More than that. Realise, everytime we look into the night sky that we are gazing at the horizon of time.

—What I'm most aware of, I said, is how much I can see that I have never seen before. Things are so clear and bright. I feel as if my eyesight has gone native or something. I mean, Anangu make incredibly precise observations. Not just of the major stars, but of the smaller constellations and their patterns. They know the nightly movements, and have a complex calendar which they use for all sorts of food-gathering activities. That's a horizon of time, I suppose.

—You know, Endo said, I paid fifteen dollars hoping to get some indication of how your Anangu saw the night sky. I have heard of the Sky People. I have heard of their stories of what are called Creation Times. I have heard it said that they have a story for every star.

—And what did you get?

—We got eaten by mosquitoes. Apart from that we were told bits and pieces about the night sky as it is known to Europeans. And even then, the guide didn't know enough, but he talked like—what is your Australian expression—a 'bloody know-all'.

—That's the one, I said.—Were you told about the settler who, when he met up with any Aborigines, went through the routine of shooting at the moon?

—For what reason?

—So that when the moon went into eclipse, he could be seen by the blackfella to have power over it.

—I believe, said Endo, that as far as stories go, something else is reversed.

—What?

—The moon, in many, many myths in other parts of the world, is female. Here it is male. The sun is woman.

—That's right. You could say, especially if you have northern Australia in mind, that the sun comes up in the morning with her heat and warms the earth all day before sinking like life itself into the ground at night, while the moon, with its cooler watery light comes and goes with the tides, is her male escort, waxing and waning like death. Anyway, did you see the Pleiades?

(In Greek mythology, the seven daughters were pursued by lustful Orion: they begged to be delivered and were turned into doves. The least brilliant of them was Merope, who, having married a mortal hides herself in shame.)

—We were two hours too early, Endo said with disgust.

—In Aboriginal myth, I ventured, the Pleiades story may be similar to the Greek: a group of young women flee from an amorous hunter, and one way or the other ends up as a part of Orion. There is a lot of running away and great emphasis on illicit advances. It all seems to be about conquest and submission, or, if you look at them as object lessons in conduct, they are about love and support.

—That's right, said Endo, but you should not be so schematic. The Pleiades story is all through tropical America, and goes up into North America. But sometimes the Pleiades is really a man dressed as a woman, or a grandfather or even a woman trying to catch her husband.

—In this country, I said with silly pride (as if the story was mine!), you can follow it from the Southern Ocean to Arnhem Land.

—In tropical America, there does seem to be a basic link with the seasons, but everything else varies depending on the region and society. In one place it may be linked with summer, in another, to winter, or to the dry or wet season, settled or unsettled weather, work or leisure, abundance or famine.

—Here, I have read that the arrival of the Pleiades in the dawn sky in autumn is the sign that the dingo-breeding season has begun.

—In tropical America, Endo continued, the Pleiades do have something in common. They are named as constellations of something. 'The kids'. 'The chicken coop'. 'The parakeets'. 'The swarm of bees'. 'The tortoise nests'. 'The handful of spilled flour'.

Kungkarangkalpa is the Pitjantjatjara for a group of Ancestral Women. They keep a pack of dingoes to protect them from a man, Nyiru.

—Against these terms for the constellation, Endo went on, are the singular terms for the parts of Orion. Belt. Sword. Shield. In this way the Pleiades and Orion complement each other.

Nyiru, I continued, raped one of the girls who died, but he kept chasing the others with a spear. When the women changed into birds and escaped from him, he defied their dingoes and went after them, ending up as Orion's belt. The two small stars, which you really have to be in Central Australia's brilliant clarity to see are his footsteps as he pursued *Kungkarangkalpa*.

Endo brought fingertips to his forehead:—Maybe the heavens are filled with tragic desires.

—Fertility ceremonies, I said, were performed for the dingoes, when Pleiades were sighted in autumn. After that Anangu would raid the lairs for dingoes, culling and feasting on the young pups.

—So the Pleiades story is 'big women's business', as they say.

—That is my understanding, I said.—But listen, what is this business about darkness and the horizon of time?

Endo said:—If all the stars that ever existed were still there the whole sky would be a blaze of light, correct?

—I suppose it would, I said.

—So the darkness is the space where stars have died, said Endo.

—I am lost, I said.

—Otherwise their light would be still there, with us.

—I see.

—So the darkness that is there is either the space where stars have ceased to be or where there were never any stars, the space of the Universe *before* the Universe existed. The night sky between the stars is the space that exists on the edge of time.

—That is a grand way to see it.

—You can thank Edgar Allan Poe for the insight. He saw it like that before any scientist.

—And politics, how do you get that into the picture?

That's like asking how dingoes get into the picture. Or any Ancestor Creature. The dingoes are there because they complement the women in some way in the story. Maybe there is a myth where the dingoes eat the women? What matters is the interchange between nature and culture, the balance that is struck. There is starlight. There is the darkness between them. What is politics—the stories we need to tell when we gaze at the stars—or the darkness between them?

—Time I went to bed, I said.

—You're welcome, he said.

Density of the night

YOU CAN GET some idea of the Aboriginal presence at the Rock before Handback from the settlement map the time Lindy Chamberlain lost her baby in August 1980. At the south end of the Rock there are three motels: the Uluru, the Inland and the Red Sands Motel. Further around near the air strip to the north is the Ayers Rock Chalet. Between the Red Sands and the Inland Motel beside the bus-camping area is the Ininti store and the main camping site. There were a few houses for the white men who helped run the park. The 'Roff Residence' is the house that Peter Severin built for Bill Harney.

It was, in a way, a charmingly ramshackle settlement that had flourished, as things do after desert rains, in the tourist boom of the 1970s. A place like the Red Sands had its own swimming pool, a massive indulgence of water that scummed over each day and in which lizards thrived at night. It was the kind of place where a traveller might find a deadly snake under the bed or in the toilet block at night. There was a certain lack of definition about relationships with Nature. This was the Outback, a frontier.

On the terrible night baby Azaria was snatched by a dingo, there were two-thousand people camping in the park. About 150,000 tourists arrived each week: many walked around the Rock, many climbed it, all were witness to some of the Aboriginal life, which was most conspicuous near the general store, less so at the 'blackfella' camp over in the dunes at Bore 29. About 50 or 80 Aborigines might be living at the Rock at any given time, depending on the seasons of nature and ceremony. Men such as Lively, Captain No. 1, Nui Minyintiri (who worked with Bill Harney) and Tiger Tjalkalyiri, who were friends of Senior Ranger Derek Roff, acted as tourist guides, answering questions as the tourists poked around the boulders and caves, including, whenever a visitor felt like it, the sacred caves.

214

'What do they do in that cave?' an American tourist is said to have asked Tiger, a man renowned for his knowledge and his skills at story-telling.

They were standing near what is now known as the Mala Women's cave on the north face.

'Oh', said Tiger, 'puggin.'

'What did they do?'

'Lota puggin', said Tiger, as the titters in the group started.

Tiger was a man quick to realise the complexities of a social occasion. For here was a tourist whose genuine interest in Anangu culture, it appeared to him, was somewhat limited. And here he was, an elder of Tjukurpa, in the compromised position of an adjunct to the Ranger who did not really belong in the place.

'They do puggin?'

'Puggin?'

'You don't know puggin?'

Puggin? What ceremony was this, said the look on the tourist's face. Perhaps a secret ceremony, you show me. All this on the face of the traveller seeking the 'real thing'.

'I show you,' says Tiger. 'Come over here.'

When the woman came to his side, Tiger leaned in towards her conspiratorially, while ensuring that the others could see. His forefinger and thumb made the suggestive circle, and the forefinger of the other hand the unmistakable action of copulation.

All this in one little joke, a joke that raised the question: whose joke at whose expense? Tiger's Aboriginal English made for moments when the tourists might appear to come out on top.

'It's remarkable', one of them told a Ranger, 'how they have cigarette caves.'

'Cigarette caves?'

'Caves for smoking in on special occasions?' ventured the traveller.

The Ranger twigged. 'You might say that, special caves, yes.'

What Tiger had said in all seriousness was that place there was a 'sig-a-red' cave. Sacred indeed!

What a joke. The sacred goes up in smoke. Why didn't these people learn to speak the Queen's English, for God's sake?

Because they were lying around on the grog, wasn't that as plain as day? Well yes, even to the visitor who did not want to make such sad observations there were drunken Aborigines out there at the rock. You could see the empties, you could see the drinkers hanging round the store and the motels, even though they were discouraged from doing so. There were drunken women as well as drunken men. Some of them would do all manner of things to get another drink, including, if necessary, walk around the Rock answering stupid questions about it.

One authoritative woman, for example—genuinely so when she was sober—

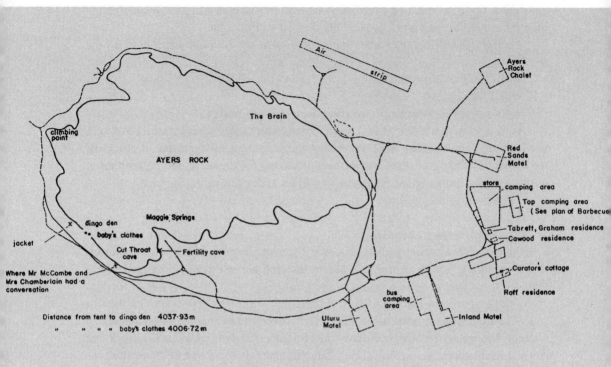

AYERS ROCK AND ENVIRONS

White settlement at the Rock before Handback.

would come out with a busload of visitors. On the way she would drink the beer provided by the tour operator. Once they were at the Rock the beer did the talking. Those tourists heard all variations of the *Kuniya* story, the Rainbow Serpent, and the Great Mother business, even though the latter was mostly a product of Bill Harney's more excited efforts. The Aboriginal was at once an attraction and at the same time an embarrassment, an ambiguous 'feature' of the Park.

During Harney's time, the welcome extended to Aboriginals at the Rock was ambiguous to say the least. Harney once remarked that the people at the Rock were a 'greater lot of vandals than the unthinking tourists', what with the mess and smell they made with their dogs and camels. At the same time, though, Harney greatly relied on his Aboriginal guides, just as many tourists greatly appreciated something as 'authentic' as the Aboriginal presence. From the 1950s to the late 1970s this ambivalence continued. It took a white-fella crisis like a lost child to illustrate again how useful and problematic they still were.

On the fateful Sunday of 17 August, the Chamberlain family had done all the tourist things: they had driven around taking photographs of the Rock, they had walked the stretch between Mutitjulu and the climb, and taken photographs there. Altogether, Michael Chamberlain had taken countless photographs of the place. They did the climb: or rather, Lindy had started up the face expecting to be able to carry Azaria in her backpack, but found her legs not strong enough yet (after the birth) to keep going, but Michael went up easily and came galloping down, scaring the daylights out of his wife at the recklessness of his descent. In her admirable account of family loss and punishment, *Through My Eyes*, Lindy Chamberlain remembers the Rock as a girl: she had been there and climbed it at the time when there was no chain to assist the windblown or the trepid, and when the book you could sign at the top had to be replaced every few years rather than every couple of days. When Michael reached the bottom, it was their young boys' turn to climb: the father took Reagan a little way before he had to bring the four-year-old down; he then had to go up again after Reagan latched on to a group heading towards the top. By the end of the day Michael Chamberlain had conquered the site two-and-a-half times, and that night it was a happy, though weary, tourist family that settled contentedly at their campsite.

At this stage, the Chamberlains did not seem to be especially aware of the Aborigines. Back in Alice Springs they had camped with them in the caravan park at Heavitree Gap and sadly noted the drunken disorder and litter. At the Rock it was the dingoes which made an impression. That afternoon, when Lindy was walking with the baby on her shoulders, a dingo had stood steadily gazing at her. The young and healthy-looking creature remained unperturbed by the boys who were playing, but took off when Michael arrived. Later, at the campsite, a tourist noticed a dingo fossicking near the barbecue shelter. When Michael tried to throw it some food, Lindy stopped him. Some signs warned:

DINGOES ARE WILD.
Feeding and touching wild animals
breaks down the natural gap
that separates them from humans.
Dingoes CAN and DO bite.

For your own sake and to maintain
the dingo's integrity as a wild animal
PLEASE DO NOT TOUCH OR FEED THEM.

There was another detail on the sign in the toilet, which Lindy wrote about later: 'The faded typing indicated the main reason for not feeding them was that they were considered sacred by the Aborigines and it would be a pity if tourists changed the dingoes' habits so much that they became pests and had to be shot because they were a nuisance to the public.'

Some things were out of balance in the Park. The signs had only recently gone up because Derek Roff was worried about the growing number of incidents with dingoes and/or dogs (there were many dogs in the Aboriginal camps). Children had been bitten, tourists' clothes stolen and torn, campsites and sleeping spots intruded upon, and in one case only a few months before, as a Ranger was to report at the first inquest, a child was dragged by the throat from her parents' care by a daredevil dingo. That Ranger, one of three who supported the dingo explanation for the death of Azaria at the first inquest said he shot that dingo. I say 'daredevil' by letting my mind go to the spectacle of *Kurpany*, the horrible creation of the mulga-seed men, when they sent the beast across the dunes to punish *mala* at ceremony. It is a fanciful connection at one level, yet one which suggests the lurking unease of many tourists at the Rock when they realise that these were *wild* dogs wandering nearby by day and prowling around by night, all the time testing the claim tourists had on their habitat. So menacing was this presence that Senior Ranger Derek Roff had already written to park authorities that 'children and babies can be considered possible prey'.

So the inevitable happened. 'The dingo's got my baby!' The cry that Lindy Chamberlain let out as she came into the tent about 8 p.m. that Sunday night, when she saw a dingo turning away from the tent flap and shaking its head as if it had something in its mouth—that *cri de coeur* that was to become the slanderous bone of contention which has left its lasting imprint at the Rock. Rumours defending 'the dingo' at the expense of the mother seemed to have begun as early as the morning after the search: whispers at first, murmurs in the motel bar that were to surface into a nationwide mockery of the cry 'The dingo's got my baby!' Not the dingo, no. It was the mother who had done away with the baby, slaughtered it, cut its throat, beheaded it in ritual sacrifice, and in an act of religious mania or ritual or both, murdered her child minutes before pretending it was alive in that tent. All the time its dead body has been stuffed in Michael Chamberlain's camera bag that was on the blood-stained floor of the family car. Another myth adhering to the Rock had begun.

It would take two inquests, a trial at which the Chamberlains were convicted and a Royal Commission which absolved convictions before the story worked itself out. With the hindsight of Lindy's innocence, we can see now what helped rumour coalesce into witchhunt was the treatment of Aboriginal evidence. At the first inquest the work of Aboriginal trackers carried weight (although problematically, as we shall see). In general it pointed to the real possibility of dingo as culprit. At the second inquest, which led to the trial of the Chamberlains, the evidence was cast aside in favour of the now-discredited forensic evidence. At the trial Aboriginal evidence made no appearance at all, and was only brought back into the picture by Royal Commissioner Morling when he re-examined the case. Thus Anangu, in and out of view, the blackfella featuring this way and that, depending on the vicissitudes of white authority and its imagination.

The legal saga opens a sharp little window on the cultural situation at the Rock only a decade ago.

They were brought in very quickly, the 'black trackers'. No sooner had Derek Roff arrived at the Chamberlain's tent about half an hour after Lindy's cry than the word was in the Aboriginal camp. Barbara Nipper, Nui Minyintiri, Captain No. 1, Daisy Walkabout, and Kitty Collins were the Aboriginal group that arrived as the 300-strong search party got underway, walking as a chain up the dune to the east of the camp. They were held back at first: Roff thought it best to keep the trackers separate from the chain for them to be there when prints were found. Lower down there were tracks everywhere. Towards the top, larger tracks were found by another camper, Murray Haby, who had gone with his torch ahead of the big party. There were not just tracks, but a depression in the sand as well. It was these tracks that Nui Minyintiri picked up in turn, when Roff and Haby called him in.

Minyintiri had his own torch, he had twirled spinifex into a stalk and made a firestick.

John Bryson, in *Evil Angels*, places this part of the story so:

'Here was the depression Haby had found.' Haby said: 'There's only the one,' but it wasn't long before the old Aborigine pointed to another, and then a third. 'Mmm', he said, a syllable which infected the others with disquiet. Perhaps they were now standing at the very point where, after flight, this dingo was considering behaviour of quite a different kind.

The size of the prints impressed the tracker. 'Big fella,' he said. But Roff was more interested in the imprint of the bundle in the sand. The pattern put him in mind of crepe or a knitted weave, perhaps. 'But is it the baby?' was what he needed to know.

'Maybe, maybe', Minyintiri said, He held a palm upward to indicate the weight of the body. 'Something like'. Then touching the unfussed periphery of the mark with a finger, sad and gentle, he indicated something they had seen but not yet recognised.

'Not move any more,' he said.

Bryson is writing from evidence that Roff and Haby were able to give at the inquest. But reporting of the Aboriginal perspective was less straightforward. A major complication set in the next day, when the results of the black tracking were taken by the police. The group were joined by another Aboriginal, an older senior man with a white

219

beard and poor eyesight, Nipper Winmati, Barbara Nipper's husband. According to Bryson, the night before was too cold for the ailing Nipper to be out the dune, yet as a mark of his seniority, it was he who assembled the results: he was the custodian of the information. As Nipper spoke Nui stood quietly by.

Nipper said it was a big dingo with a damaged front paw. From the top of the dune it headed, criss-crossing, in an arc towards the west face of the Rock, in the direction of Mutitjulu waterhole, or Maggie Springs, as it was called then.

It was in this area that baby Azaria's clothes were found a week later. Nipper Winmati was one of the tracking party then, along with his wife Barbara Nipper and Daisy Walkabout. The police asked them to comment on the dingo tracks in the vicinity. The Aborigines laughed; there were so many tracks there. Then the women set out. Nipper called the policeman to a cave. Bryson reports it thus: 'Daisy Walkabout was there already. She was pointing to a low rock, on which he could now see stains. He (the policeman) felt his pockets for a clasp knife to scrape away a sample. Blood?

"Blood". Although this was the Cave of Fertility, the possible origin of these stains was evidently not one Daisy Walkabout might have expected here.'

At the inquest in Alice Springs some weeks later it was Nipper Winmati who stepped forward to give evidence on behalf of the trackers. Stepping forward is perhaps a misnomer: for it was to the man's embarrassment, and to the patronising delight of the local press that he arrived at the court after a heavy night and went to sleep on a bench in the court foyer. He would not come into the court until he had a clean shirt, and when he did what he said was confusing.

Nipper told the court that the tracks 'he' had seen started at the tent.

—When did you see the tracks? asked Macknay for the Coroner.

—In the morning time.

—Which day?

—Monday, said Nipper.

—Did you see any other dingo tracks around the tent?

—One big track. A big one.

—Which way did that go?

—I was going up the sandhills. There were two tracks and one cut short and the other went further into the bush.

Nipper went on to say that the big tracks went up the hill and came out on the road, before heading west towards Maggie Springs.

The questioning went backwards and forwards on this point, as if Macknay did not understand or as if Nipper Winmati did not know what he was saying himself. Later the question was:

—When you saw the tracks on the sandhill, did you see any other marks apart from the paw marks?

—I saw one track, I saw one dingo.

—Was that dingo you saw on the hill carrying anything?

—Yes. I tracked it halfway and I saw it put it down and left it and then after that carry it again but after that I cannot find it. Too many have been there at night time. There has been no track because the marking is gone.

There was then a very confused and confusing exchange about which dingo went one way (south) and which one went the other (west). Two dingoes near the tent was common ground in the evidence by then. But which dingo did what? The conversation moved in Luritja that was translated, and then in English. Tracking the misunderstandings was difficult then as it is now, when one reads the transcript. But it was the next exchange that seemed to stymie the otherwise clear logic of the tracker's perspective.

—Nipper, have you ever known dingoes to take babies from Aboriginal camps?

—No, said Nipper.

—You have never heard of that?

—No, I have never known about the baby.

—What about camp dogs?

—Camp dogs cannot take away. They cannot take them, camp dogs.

What exactly was Nipper saying here? From all accounts he was very uneasy. Was it simply because of his concern for their own camp dogs? Did he mean to be as categorical as 'no never'? (This is odd considering the extent of the Ranger's stories, the evidence that Derek Roff would give about a child had been taken at Papunya.) Was Nipper simply worried about the camp dogs? Was he answering a question that had not really been spelt out, just as he had been reporting, according to his culture's custom, in the first person when he had not been there as an eyewitness? What was the legal status of his evidence, since it was, strictly speaking, hearsay?

On the issue of whether Nipper had actually taken part in the search on the Sunday night, stories differ. According to one account, which tries to fathom the two-dingo confusion and solve the problem of possible human intervention with the jumpsuit later found near the Rock, Nipper had been up and about tracking the dingo as far as the backyard of a ranger. According to another account, Nipper's glaucoma made him half-blind, a useless tracker, even in daylight.

Lindy Chamberlain says, quite rightly, that Nipper Winmati was uncomfortable for several reasons. For one thing his interpreter was a woman: this was not the way to conduct a conversation with a senior man (unless she was his daughter-in-law, or dealing with women's business). For another, he was being asked about dingoes and babies, which was a private area.

At one point the Coroner asked,—Using Luritja dreaming, could you tell the court the Luritja dreaming of dingoes and children?

Translator Pamela Harmer said,—This would be hard to say in Luritja, but I know for myself.

—See if he can recall the Luritja dreaming of dingoes and children, the well-meaning but tactless Coroner insisted.

Harmer said,—For an Aborigine to have twins who both die that is taboo. So they keep one baby, the strongest one. And the Dreamtime story is that children who leave the camp, the Dingo Spirit will get them. So they leave the weaker twin out bush. For the dingoes.

It was an insistence for which the Coroner was to later apologise to Nipper, but only after an angry Pamela Harmer reproached him during recess. He had, she said, shamed the senior man. He could not speak freely of the Dingo Spirit. Perhaps this makes sense of the Nipper's utterance, 'No, I have never known about the baby.' Aboriginal women did not go on the record.

The real speaker at the first inquest was white ignorance of Aboriginal culture and etiquette. As a result Aboriginal evidence did not stand up as it might, and was easily shoved aside at the second inquest, when another narrative was forced to take its place: stories based on the forensic evidence. Thus the eyewitness account from oral culture was eclipsed in favour of the documentation of the written culture. That itself involved a rather typical positioning of the Aborigines in the park. A painting by Pro Hart says it all. It shows the trial judge blindfolded, and the jury that would convict Lindy Chamberlain of murder wearing masks, sunglasses and dunce hats; while outside the court, looking in with a piercing gaze, is the 'black tracker'. It is a definitive image of the knowledgeable Aboriginal locked out.

The trial took place in an atmosphere of frenzied myth-making. A satanic version of 'Mother Business' seized at the throat of the cheap mass-media. Alongside were the bizarre stories of the dingo, the creature maligned by the very idea of the woman's innocence. The pro-dingo stories, which seemed to turn the realm of Aboriginal taboo inside out, were shockingly popular. The jokes played upon puppy-like dingos, maternal cannibalism, and 'baby food'. Baby food became white culture's sick refrain. The logo of the T-shirt offered by a national newspaper said, 'Save the Dingo' and showed a dingo absconding with the can of Baby Food. By the time of the trial Lindy's dingo account was a national joke laced with obscenities, some of them repeatable, most of them not. Whenever one told a dingo story, the hiss of the joke said: the wild creature was not the culprit, but the nurturing mother, culture itself.

The point is that stories, tales and theories all conspired as a myth to obscure the particularities of the local, eyewitness and human truths of the case. The result was a trial charged with the malevolent aspect of myth, which is to say myth in motion was a lie rather than an instructive tale. When, in the early part of the trial a photograph of a dingo was held up and described as 'the dingo blown up', the jury laughed. Some sniggered and giggled for the rest of the proceedings. 'I have to satisfy you', said prosecuting counsel Ian Barker, 'that a dingo did not take the child. . . . The story is incapable of belief, and you cannot believe it. We are dealing here', he mocked, 'with a man-eating dingo who raided the tent like a tiger in an Indian village.'

That night, when it was absolutely clear to Lindy and Michael Chamberlain that their baby had gone, and the thought had occurred to Lindy — who had once made a study of dingoes when when she was a student — that their baby was probably already dead, they did not fully appreciate the extent to which others had sprung to their aid. There was enough light around the tent to see it was a dingo all right, a fine, 'beautiful' one, Lindy was to say, and you could see somewhat beyond the campside, if you had been there since dusk, and 'your eyes had slowly grown accustomed to the density of the night'. But you could not see far out into the dune, so the Chamberlains could not appreciate the amount of activity that built up in the area as the search party grew. Only when the morning light spread over the hill did Lindy know: people by the score, Aborigines among them. The sight was a blessing.

The Chamberlains stayed another night and decided to go. They would say goodbye to the people who had been most helpful. Derek Roff they found at the Aboriginal camp. They didn't realise it when they turned up, but Roff was there with a rifle. He had come to shoot the camp dogs; he was about to break the sad news to Nipper Winmati. There was a policeman there too, one of the first to cast savage doubt on the Chamberlain story. The policeman would soon barge into the house of Toby Nanyinga and Ada Nangala, two old citizens of the area. He would get into the kitchen and empty the rubbish bin, rummage, and search for what he would not say. The Aborigines trembled in alarm and anger. Toby would raise his arms: 'You think I ate the child?' The policeman left when Roff rushed in and pulled him out.

—We were told, Lindy said to Roff, that you wanted us to look at the camp dogs.

That was true, and Lindy did. These bitzers were nothing like the animal she had seen at the tent.

Michael asked Roff: — You shot some dingoes. Last night, I believe.

Bryson tells the rest of the story with ominous clarity:

'Roff agreed that they had. Last night and this morning.'

Any chance of a photograph of one?

'Of a dead dingo?'

'The jaws', Michael explained. 'Someone ought to write a book about all this. My wife and I are thinking of writing one ourselves.'

It was a request about which Roff felt instantly uncomfortable, though reasons didn't readily come to him. 'No, that wouldn't be possible'.

Michael had another question. He had seen plaques set into the base of the Rock, memorials to the dead. Could the Chamberlain family provide one in memory of Azaria? 'I couldn't authorise that myself,' he said. 'You should approach the Conservation Commission.'

Perhaps his refusal of two requests prompted Roff to concede the third. It was for a photograph of the trackers. They stood, while Michael lined up for the shot, and shuffled more closely together: Winmati in old bone slacks, the vast Barbara, Daisy Walkabout, and little Kitty Collins. Roff agreed to tack himself to the end of the line, all not intent on looking serious but pleasant.

This is the photograph Lindy put in her book, *Through My Eyes*, as a mark of gratitude to the Aborigines.

The Chamberlains left. They drove away from camp and the Rock, out onto the road that would take them back to Alice Springs. The further they went from the Rock, the faster Michael drove. He had his foot down way beyond Alice Springs, and it was way north on the road between Tennant Creek and Mount Isa, where the Chamberlains lived, before they encountered Aborigines again. They had pulled in for petrol, to make sure of their supply of fuel because Lindy did not want to travel in the dark, when a carload of Aborigines came in.

They were a friendly lot, and young Aiden was friendly to them. They were talking about cars, when the man who seemed to be in charge spoke to Lindy:

'You're the people with the little baby that's lost at Ayers Rock?'

Lindy's story goes:

'We said, 'Yes, how do you know?'

He said, 'My people, they tell me.'

'Oh, you read the papers?'

'No', he said, 'not yet. We've just come in from the mission now.'

We said, 'Well, how do you know?'

He said, 'My people, they tell me. In my head they tell me. We know.'

Michael asked, 'And you recognised us from that?'

He said, 'Yes, the little boys, the car, you, I know. And Jesus, He will look after your little girl. You be all right. You don't worry. My people, they keep looking till they find something. Maybe next year, maybe the year after, maybe nothing, but if they can, they find.'

We said, 'Thank you.'

He said, 'Jesus loves you. He look after you, after your little boys. He be with you, you travel tonight. You be fine and you not worry about your little girl, you see her in heaven'.

Thank you lord, I thought. That angel had a black face.

224

Anangu did keep looking, but they did not find. Legalities, investigations unfolded, and their view of things was corrupted, abused, tossed aside and then rediscovered. One day, three Christmases after Lindy Chamberlain had been sent to prison, a tourist named David Brett slipped while climbing the Rock and fell to his death at its base. His body was found several days later, partly decomposed and with his right arm chewed by goannas and dingoes. Nearby, partly protruding from the ground was the matinee jacket: the garment Lindy had always said her baby had been wearing when she disappeared. The case was reopened: Lindy was freed and 'pardoned' by the Northern Territory government (which even then did not have the grace to completely exonerate her). Bryson's *Evil Angels* came out in 1985, the year of the Handback; and Fred Schepisi's film crew visited the Rock about two years later, by which time Anangu would have no more to with dingo and the baby business. What were they expected to do—play, *act*—all over again, 'be themselves'? No, the day had come when you couldn't get 'black trackers' that easily.

Land

THE MOTELS HAVE gone now. If you want one clear sign of the difference before and after the Handback ceremony of 1985, this is it. In the old days visitors could stay at a motel and camp just about anywhere. You could, if you felt like it, walk through one of the blackfella's camps; photo opportunities everywhere. Now you are kept at bay: visitors can't stay within twenty kilometres of the Rock. Aborigines have a community with a school and a clinic and other services, and like all other citizens of the nation, have established their rights to privacy. Their settlement, Mutitjulu, nestles in the dunes at the east end of the Rock, where the motels once were.

Few legal changes have happened so quickly as the achievement of Aboriginal land rights in the Northern Territory. Before the late 1970s, you could say that the philosophy of *terra nullius* applied, that is, life went on *as if* the first Europeans to occupy the country in 1788 were right when they declared that as the indigenous people neither had title to the land nor resisted foreign possession of it, it was unoccupied—an empty place. This immoral blend of legal nicety and social absurdity was demolished by the Northern Territory Land Rights Act (1976), brought in by the Commonwealth Government on Australia Day 1977. Under the Act, land that was once Aboriginal reserve, the poorest pastoral country, automatically became Aboriginal property. The Act set up statutory Land Councils as vehicles for Aboriginal land claims for the vacant crown land that could then be contested—as it was immediately, and has been since in claim after claim opposed by the Northern Territory government on the militant behalf of pastoral, mining and tourist interests. At present almost half

225

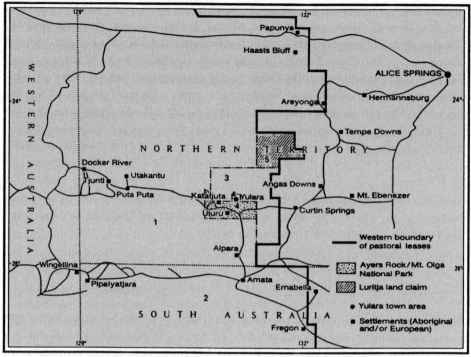

Settlement and land claim maps.

of the Northern Territory has been, or is being claimed by its traditional owners. In South Australia, the Pitjantjatjara and Yankuntjatjara peoples regained land titles in 1981 and 1984, and they now own 18 per cent of the land, mainly in the northern part of the State. Nationwide, *terra nullius* was in principle expunged by the 1992 Mabo decision of the High Court.

The Uluru land claim of 1979—a historic moment for the Aboriginal people as well as the nation's iconography—was the fourth claim under the Northern Territory Land Rights Act. Politically, it was a victory for the Central Land Council on behalf of traditional owners, but it was a victory that began with a major setback and ended with part of the land claimed unwon. The initial setback concerned the Park itself, the area immediately around Ayers Rock and the Olgas (as they were called then). The Park had been extracted from the Aboriginal Reserve in 1958. On the eve of the claim, in a political maneouvre by Prime Minister Fraser's Commonwealth Government, the land title was vested in the Director of the National Parks. As such, it no longer fitted the definition of unalienated Crown Land under the Northern Territory Land Rights Act. Traditional owners therefore had to confine their claim to lands around the park;

in particular for the Aboriginal estates that were not on crown land but the sacred sites which were intimately inseparable from those at Uluru and Kata Tjuta. Here the Aborigines were successful. All but an area debatably Aranda country north of Lake Amadeus (the claim for which was adjourned) was granted to the Pitjantjatjara/Yankuntjatjara people. When the Labor Government came to office in 1983, a further agreement was reached between traditional owners and the Commonwealth: the Rock—the Park—would be handed back on the condition that Anangu lease it back to the Government. Thereafter the Park would be jointly managed by Aborigines and federal park rangers.

To come to the Rock today is to reached a historic monument, one of the many landmarks of recent Aboriginal history. To say 'history' here, as we reflect what makes this kind of visit possible, is to be sharply reminded of the term itself: that history is *made* of stories which are a continuous matter of official and unofficial narration. The land-claim process turned out to involve the difficulty of getting stories straight, so that the traditional owners could, to the white man's legal satisfaction, be left to tell their own! Hearings for the claim lasted sixteen days, and produced more than a thousand pages of transcript which still does not have its fully fledged social historian. In the absence of a major account, let us travel awhile through the transcript, the better to view some of the rough country that has always been part of the Centre: the country of cultural misunderstanding.

Magic words

LOCATION: Ayers Rock
Time: 25 April 1979

It is the first day of the land rights hearing out at the Rock. It has been going on for six days in Alice Springs, since the beginning of the month. Out here it will go on for five days if all goes well, and then return to Alice Springs for the final round.

Presiding is His Honour Justice John Toohey. As the first Aboriginal Land Commissioner Toohey had already presided over three complex land claims and decided in favour of the claimants in two of them (the third at Boroloola only partially so, much to the gratification of Mount Isa Mines and to the chagrin of traditional owners). In years to come he will be promoted to the High Court of Australia, where he will be one of the authors of the Mabo judgment.

Acting for the Central Land Council and the traditional owners was barrister

227

Geoff Eames and his solicitor Ross Howie, Melbourne men who had come to live in Alice Springs. Anthropologists Daniel Vachon and Robert Layton acted for the claimants. For the Northern Territory government and other interests was Mr Ian Barker QC (soon to play his part as Prosecutor in the Chamberlain case). Counsel Assisting the Commissioner was Mr Graham Hiley, and anthropologist and linguist, Susan Woenne-Green.

They are in a wooden hall attached to the Ayers Rock Chalet.

When things get going, Daniel Vachon will act as interpreter.

But things are hardly moving because it is still raining, as it has been for days. So wet has the 'desert' become that Toohey and his crew barely made it to the Rock at all. The airstrip was closed; the roads were closed. Only by virtue of an intrepid driver of a 4 × 4 drive bus-charter company did they make the trip from Alice Springs: 14 hours of solid driving, sliding and plummetting into immense puddles, the windscreen wipers having ceased to work a short distance out of Alice. The very arduousness of the journey perhaps served to remind them of the traditional remoteness of the Rock, of the pilgrimage involved in reaching this 'Centre'. It was, however, not at all clear when they got there if the Aboriginal informants could or would arrive. *All* the roads were difficult and the people from Ernabella had left a day late because they wanted to stay for a Church service. With regard to the Aboriginal claimants at the Rock, the question for Land Comissioner Toohey on 25 April 1979 was: were there enough of the right people present to go on with the hearing?

—Yes there are, Mr Eames told His Honour.

Early on, Peter Bulla was heard. Bulla is the custodian of Kata Tjuta. He told of his children and the matter of learning the country when they do not live at Kata Tjuta. To the question what might happen if they did not return to learn the country he tells the interpreter:

—Them family could take a stick what their idea of Kata Tjuta.

There was some unspoken amusement in the court. (You can often hear it between the lines, as you move through the transcript.) Bulla's reply was taken to mean: the kids would be firmly obliged to learn the ceremonial business of their country.

The interpreter said:—Can I ask something?

—Yes, please, said Eames.

Interpreter:—If his grandchild does not learn Kata Tjuta—I cannot remember how he said it—I used the word 'still', would his country still be Kata Tjuta, and he said 'yes'. Then I said your daughter's son and he said, yes my daughter's son. Then I said, from his grandfather—that is him—and he said, yes from his grandfather.

His Honour:—Mr Eames, what I think I will do is just break for a few minutes and give you perhaps an opportunity to talk with Mr Vachon, Mr Hiley and Miss

Woenne and see whether there is some magic phrase that is an acceptable one which might help proceedings.

Interpreter:—Excuse me Your Honour, what do you have in mind when you say magic phrase?

His Honour:—Well, this is one section of what we are trying to do. We are trying to meet the concepts and the definitions of the Act in the course of which it is necessary to find out not only what country a person has, whatever that may mean, but also this particular hearing seems to be complicated by the existence of more than one estate or at least the situation in which a person can have an interest in more than one area of land. Also, we want to know whether both can be held and in what circumstances, or whether one is lost and, if it is lost, how it is lost and if the country in which a person is not born can be his or her country, is it because his or her mother or father belonged to that country, or is it something else that has to happen. All that sort of things. The words magic phrase were not meant seriously but more of a form of question, I think.

It had been raining for so long that many things have become difficult. For some weeks, the lawyers Eames and Howie had been stranded at the Rock, staying at the Red Sands Motel until an unpleasant incident occurred, the kind of thing that happens, perhaps, when people are confined to their quarters. But then again, it possibly said a lot about race relations at the Rock, especially relations with people uppity enough to make a claims for ownership.

Nipper Winmati, one of the traditional owners, came into the bar. He wanted a drink.

—No, said the proprietor, you can't.

—And why not? asked Geoff Eames, on the black man's behalf. It was the question troublesome characters from the south have often asked in such circumstances. Besides, Nipper was the lawyer's client.

—Because he has no shoes, came the reply.

Down pat. No argument.

To which Mr Eames rose to the occasion. No magic words, but a passionate speech about racism. Then the lawyers, Howie with Eames, marched out. They checked out into the rain, unsure as they did whether other accommodation would be available, or indeed, if they would be admitted if word of their stand on principle got about. Fortunately for everybody there was a place for them at the Chalet.

On that first morning, Justice Toohey heard the testimonies of three Aboriginal men: Bill Okai, James Severn, Tiger Tjalkalyiri.

Bill Okai had taken some time to list his children and their whereabouts, and their need to learn about Kata Tjuta when Tiger makes a sign.

Mr Eames:—Tiger,were you wanting to say something then?

—Yes.

Tiger wanted to add to the list of children who pertained to the country. These children were born at Jay Creek (near Alice Springs, in the MacDonnell Ranges).

—Do those children hold Kata Tjuta?

—Yes.

—What about now, when they are still young ones? Maybe you other men, if you want to talk about that one?

Interpreter:—I said, I made a statement, I asked the question I suppose: your children, their country of birth was Jay Creek, and he said, yes. I said, if you bring your children here and show them Kata Tjuta from that would it be their country, and he said, yes.

A discussion followed between His Honour and the interpreter about the distinction between 'being at Kata Tjuta and talking about it'. Again the questioning went through Tiger, as a senior man.

Mr Eames:—Right. Firstly just to restate the situation, Tjalkalyiri, did you take Kata Tjuta through your mother?

The answer was yes.

—Where were you born?

—Ayers Rock.

—He was born at Ayers Rock, Eames told His Honour.

—So does Tjalkalyiri talk for Ayers Rock and for Kata Tjuta too?

—He said all the old people when they used to live here they used to go round different areas around Ayers Rock, where the peripheral water is, clay pans and things, and they used to go for bush tucker, but they use to always come back to Ayers Rock because of the water situation and life there at Ayers Rock.

His Honour:—What was the word that was repeated all the time?

Eames:—Tjalkalyiri, you have those two countries then, your have Kata Tjuta and you have Ayers Rock, what we want to know now is what you want for your children Leo, Rose, Antamara and Nellie.

—His children's country, Eames relayed, is Ayers Rock, from his grandmother. But he has just previously said that Ayers Rock is a unit with Kata Tjuta in terms of what he has said before: eating, foraging, and that kind of thing in terms of water resources. And he named Valda, Rosie, Bruno, Leo . . . as being in that situation, their country being Ayers Rock through their grandmother. And Lilly.

—Lilly or Nelly?

—Nelly.

230

—Could you just ask and try to make this as non-leading as you can, whether these children only belong for Ayers Rock or whether they are also proper owners for Kata Tjuta as well.

—They can see Kata Tjuta and they can choose Kata Tjuta. They are choosing Kata Tjuta.

—They are choosing Kata Tjuta?

—Yes.

—Well, we had better establish what that means too. Ask him what he means by 'They are choosing Kata Tjuta'.

His Honour:—Perhaps you could tell us what you think. You drew a distinction yourself between?—you are using some sort of continuing process, are you, by the term 'are choosing?'

Interpreter:—Well I never said 'choosing' in my question, I should tell you what I said. Is that all right?

Eames:—Yes.

Interpreter:—I said, 'You said previously that your children's country is Ayers Rock. Is their country Kata Tjuta as well?' And he said, 'They can see Kata Tjuta' and then he told me to tell you that they are choosing Kata Tjuta.

Eames:—Is it possible to ask what he means by 'they are choosing'?

Interpreter:—I asked him what he meant by . . . which means choosing, which I think means choosing and both men were saying 'teaching', and then I asked 'learning the country' and then I asked, 'Well, who takes them to that country and teaches them?' and then Tiger said . . .

His Honour:—Somebody mentioned you were pointing to a man at the back of the hall.

Interpreter:—That is Leo. Leo is sitting back there, his stepson, or his son, he calls him his son in the language. I asked 'who showed Leo Kata Tjuta?' and Tiger said he did. Tiger did.

What are we listening to here? Many things at once, that much is clear. The white fella—even 'clever' elders among the white fellas like Justice Toohey—have to apply all their intelligence to make sense of so many things mixed together. To this extent what was going on was like 'life itself', a matter of social exchanges organised less by abstract principles than the particular demands of the situation. Some of the complex fabric of Aboriginal life was obviously there, alive and speaking in the court. But it demanded an ongoing interpretation, no easy feat at the best of times, even for trained ethnologists. Justice Toohey, along with most of his colleagues, were in positions not unlike those early travellers who came into the company of very different people and who have to make sense of it all. You could know some of the language. You could have an interpreter, but you still had to find your feet in the company of strangers.

Eventually it had stopped raining enough to go outside. The hearing adjourned to Kata Tjuta, where traditional owners were keen to show the sites they were claiming according to white-man's law. From the Aboriginal point of view talking about places in the abstract was a strange business. Being there—being shown—was crucial to ownership and understanding. But being there also demanded some tactful under-standing on the white man's part. This the lawyers had to learn on the spot.

Mr Hiley, for instance, blundered into a strange question of Toby Nangina.

—Toby, he asked, can you tell the judge what the malu *did to you?* (My italics)

—What did he do at this well?

—Might be water, says Toby.

—Water, yes.

—And camp here, in the creek.

—Did he drink much at the soak?

—No, said Toby Nangina.

Eames, apparently rescuing Toby from the bind of being asked so directly about the sacred malu, said:—And whose country is that kangaroo?

—Kata Tjuta country, him come up. Malu . . . no more. I decide by this finish.

The issue of what malu did to Toby was dropped, but certain things still had to be clarified for His Honour. There was some more blundering on the visitors' part, at the end of which Robert Layton was obliged to tell His Honour details about the location of ancestor beings that otherwise would have remained private.

It was all very delicate, very difficult. One minute the white fella was on the firm ground of being told about the Dreaming track and having it physically indicated. Next minute either the language broke down or a word that was taboo had to be dropped out of the conversation (and the transcript). Part of the strain was the white convention of having to write things down. Indeed, the adversarial system which was more or less in operation, even out in the damp winds of Kata Tjuta, was intended for that purpose, even though it was, in this case, being applied to members of an oral culture. An issue out there and right through the hearing was: how far should one go in the mode of interrogation? For the sake of clarity you had to go so far: but too far might challenge the spiritual foundation of a man's being.

In terms of cultural difference, a question could go backwards and forwards, round and round. A tiring process for everybody, not the least for the claimants. For what they had to say to His Honour, they had often said many times before: to their lawyers before the hearing started, to the lawyers with the anthropologist before that, to their anthropologist for weeks, months and perhaps years before that.

How did Anangu feel about that?

Like telling your story to a waterfall. Everything you said seemed to get washed away. What there something wrong in the heads of these white fellas? How many times must a knowledgeable man of the Tjukurpa say what was TRUTH even before anyone said it? What was proof that you owned the country when you were already in it, and had always been in it since time immemorial?

The political reality was that everyone had to fit in with the Act. It defined Aboriginal ownership in a particular way. Section 3 said:

> traditional Aboriginal owners, in relation to land, means a local descent group of Aboriginals who—
> (a) have common spiritual affiliations to a site on the land, being affiliations that place the group under a primary spiritual responsibility for that site and for that land; and
> (b) are entitled by Aboriginal tradition to forage as of right over that land.

The question was: who was going to be the master of such words as 'local descent group', 'common spiritual affiliations', and 'primary spiritual responsibility'? Not to mention the notion of 'rights' to forage.

The Act itself has a prehistory that foreshadowed difficulties. Conceived out of the difficulty of defining legal land ownership when Justice Blackburn ruled against Aboriginal landrights in 1971 (when Nabalco wanted to mine on the Gove Peninsula), it was born out of the Federal Government's 1972 Aboriginal Land Rights Commission as a means of shaping a law workable with Aboriginal culture. That was easier said that done. 'On inquiry', as Mr Justice Woodward pointed out, 'it soon becomes clear that the social organization of Aboriginal people is highly complex. The problem of understanding it is made worse by a number of factors. These include, firstly, the difficulty of expressing many Aboriginal ideas and arrangements in English terms . . . Further, some Aboriginal concepts related to land-owning have no parallel in European law . . . Yet another difficulty arises from disagreement among anthropologists as to the exact nature of the relationship between Aboriginal organization for landholding and land usage.'

The Act with these criteria was the best that Woodward could do. As it turned out, it was not a poor best, but it would take a number of landrights cases for the difficulties of definition to be refined; and, in due course, Land Commissioners would rule that it was more in the spirit of the legislation to interpret claims of ownership from the claimant's point of view rather than tangle in negative legalisms. In narrative terms we might say that stories of claimants, while being scrutinised, also had to be heard sympathetically.

Or put another way, and without wishing to pluck the jewel of 'truth' from due legal process, the root issue was that of tolerance: tolerance of cultural difference, tolerance of the Centre's often-shameful social history, tolerance of the limits of white-fella knowledge. At the Uluru Land Claim everyone had their story, and it was up to the good, clear-thinking Justice Toohey (whose heart was in the right place, the Aborigines had no doubt about that) to take in as many strands as he could and out of them weave his own song of judgment.

Sayables

OF SOME THINGS there could be little argument. One of them was the nature and extent of the Dreaming tracks. To lay them out and link them with an important site was by definition to make the spiritual claim; they could either be specified or they could not, and when they could not, silence reigned. It only made sense for an anthropologist to be able to say what he could, as Robert Layton frequently did on behalf of the claimants, who once again believed that the details of their private Law would not go far.

Suffice to say here then that the routes of the ancestor beings were noted, including, as it happened, the presence of honey ants at Purrarra Well, one of the places which opponents of landrights like to insist had no significance to Aborigines at all.

Layton told His Honour about other Dreaming tracks. *Mala*, Devil *Kurpany*, the Two Boys—each was in turn introduced to the man of white-fella law.

—Shall I pass on to the *Kuniya* track?

—Yes.

And so on. Layton did not spare the details that could be said. He spoke of tracks and sites until His Honour thought fit to say:—Have you *exhausted* the Dreaming tracks that are relevant to the vacant crown area? (My italics.)

Can Dreaming tracks, those lines of cosmic fecundity, ever be exhausted? Toohey was not making a cultural comment, he was trying to do what his own culture has long tried to do well: *complete* its lists.

—We have got one more, said Layton, which is the track of the *Wanampi* or water snake which runs along the route of Aparanya Creek which is inside the Petermann Reserve, goes underground and takes the underground route through vacant crown land and it emerges at the surface again at Katiti in site that is attributed to the Aparanya estate. This *Wanampi*, as I have learned since compiling the claim book, was actually one of the snakes involved in the fight at Ayers Rock, who then, from the fight, went down to Apara, and then we trace this route—just incidentally *Katiti* means tooth—he was still arguing when he got to Katiti and he argued so hard that one of this teeth fell out. That is how the site got its name.

But that did not exhaust the Dreaming tracks (or the narrative possibilities of place) either. When the historian Dick Kimber gave evidence His Honour heard not only more about ma_lu, and of its *critical* significance to the whole country and the Rock, but also passing reference to bush turkey, firesticks, hawk, native cat and cormorant dreaming. Kimber was at pains to emphasise that these tracks were more than extrapolation from what people said. The rituals and songs belonging to them were regularly enacted; the ceremonial life from Papunya to the Rock, from Mount Conner to the Petermanns, was still strong. Furthermore, the Pitjantjatjara people were renowned among other Aboriginal groups to be particularly strong on ceremony. Senior Pitjantjatjara men had a reputation for that. Kimber said, using an Aboriginal expression of the Alice Springs people when they looked south to the Pitjantjatara, 'they standing up, that other mob are lying down'.

That was all very well as far as generalities went, but how much 'standing up' was there, and who were the people really doing it? It is a poignant question at a time of rapid social change, especially when the senior men were lamenting the modern lives of their young fellas. The key legal question was, *who* owned the land? That question, to white-fella ways of thinking, tended to focus on hearing witnesses as 'individuals' in the European sense of the term. Already, however, it had become clear that the Aboriginal sense of identity is complicated by profound social considerations. As a way through those complications an odd question was put to Dick Kimber. He was asked whether there were 'physical signs' that one could look for in identifying who was in charge of a certain site: could you tell, for example, by seeing who started the songs that belonged to a site?

— I suppose normally I would just ask, Kimber began (as if to say, if you trust these people you would not be looking for 'physical signs': you'd been talking with them, and taking their answers seriously).

He continued: — But above and beyond that, in a case of a ceremony it is not absolutely clear-cut because sometimes the enthusiasm that is engendered at these, a young man might start off who has got some responsibility. Now if initially if that was all you saw and you had to go away you might pick him, but what will normally happen is he will be put down and say someone else will then start off the singing and on a couple of occasions, only, I have known when everyone is ready and there is an old man who is trying to get it exactly right in his head because there has got to be a right order, you might get another very old man who respects him, will start it off although he has not go right to, and that will give the other man the clue really, he is trying to edge him on a little bit, get him going, and so then everyone will stop that old man too and you will get another personal lead off. *It is not always as clear cut as it might appear to be on the surface* . . . (My italics)

Kimber's answer is wonderfully first-hand. And it is a cameo of *communal* vitality. When I read it my heart leapt, this was the fireside I'd wanted to be beside, singing and witnessing with some intimate understanding. Earlier on Kimber had said he had often been encouraged to sing by the men, and that as music, the refrains were designed to be remembered and to be carried easily in the mind from one language group to the other right through Central Australia. He was, as he characteristically does, speaking judiciously out of particular experiences, and that was the strength of his statement.

It was also strong in another way. In retrospect, you can see it pointing to the heart of several problems the land claim had to work out as it went along. When, if ever at all, was an individual speaking for himself, and not for or through his sense of community? How could the outsider know? How much contact do you have to have with the country/people/an event to be qualified to know? As Robert Layton puts it,

> Listening to the Aboriginal evidence I realised that the list of places belonging to estates that I had collected during my field work were not ones that the speakers had learned like multiplication tables. They were thinking them out, as they spoke, on the basis of their lifetime's experience. When they said, for instance, 'Puntitjata belongs to Aputjilpinya because we used to go there from Aputjilpi,' or 'Yulara belongs to Uluru bcaue we always went there after rain.' it was clear that they were thinking about a country (estate) as an area focused on a permanent water but including peripheral waters as far as those accessible from other base camps. When, on the other hand, people said Yulara belonged to Katatjuta because the dreaming track came from Katatjuta, it is clear they were thinking in terms of *ngura inma nguru*, 'country from the songs'. Because of this, members of adjacent estates sometimes both claimed ownership of certain peripheral sites and there were inconsistencies of detail between different lists. . . . Whether or not sites were said to be shared depended to some extent on the form of the question. To answer, 'which places belong to Uluru?' it would not necessarily be relevant to say that some such places also belonged to another estate. The broader question, 'Who sings the songs for Wakuliyannga?'—a peripheral site on the Mala track between Uluru and Aputjilpi—is likely to evoke a general answer such as 'everyone' or 'we all do', because this kind of question reminds people of shared ritual responsibility.

'It is not always as clear-cut as it might appear to be on the surface', as Kimber said. What did getting below the surface consist of?

Take the matter of 'a local descent group'. It was one thing to know the songs, to be invested in passing them on, and to confirm visits to the sites to which the songs be longed, but quite another, in the face of opposition counsel, to clearly establish the kinship lines.

Part of the initial trouble was that 'a local descent group' was thought to be patrilineal, a matter of rights and responsibilities passed down the father's line. This was because it fitted best with the work of Stanner and Ronald Berndt when they were advising the Woodward Royal Commission. And it was thought to be so because it fitted the experience of Justice Toohey in three of his other cases (with the Warlpiri, Alyawarra and Yanguwa peoples), where the evidence accepted fitted the anthropologists' patrilineal model.

Not so, however, with the Uluru claim. Robert Layton argued that the Pitjantjatjara people were different: spiritual responsibilities could be inherited from the mother's side as well as the father's. Layton used the term 'ambilineal' when he uttered this term before Justice Toohey. It was by way of saying that as the hearing progressed the model of Pitjantjatjara ownership became fully clear to him, and that he might have been able to make it clearer as a model if he had been able to write it down for the hearing. Pitjantjatjara people did not have a generic name for clan; nor did the group associated with particular estates have a proper name. And there was no Pitjantjatjara word equivalent to 'ambilineal'.

Consequently the ambilineal concept had to come out of painstakingly sifted evidence from Aboriginal witnesses. Even then, as Justice Toohey remarked, the principle did not emerge with complete clarity, although he did find it 'quite clear that the claimants recognized that country need not be acquired patrilineally'.

For example, Leo William's country was Kata Tjuta, his mother's country. His father's was Piltati in the Petermanns, but Leo transmitted membership of Kata Tjuta to his children. Some witnesses claimed membership of Ayers Rock group through their father, but Napala Jack took membership from his mother. Pompey Whistler took his membership of the Apara group through his mother, as did Pompey Douglas and Billy Kaypipi of the Apararanya group from their mothers, though they transmitted it to their sons. In general fathers were still of central importance, since 79 (or 69 per cent) of the 114 people connected with the claim transmitted membership to the land-owning group that way. It was the 23 people (20 per cent) who transmitted through their mother that made the Uluru claim distinctive from the point of view of what the anthropologists had to say about Aboriginal society. (Another 8 and 3 per cent of the claimants transmitted through parents' siblings and grandparents respectively.)

There we have the question of how exactly the land was handed on. How to get beneath the surface details of that? What if a person had not been living in the place for long? Children, for instance. 'Then family could take a stick,' Peter Bulla said about the obligations to teach and learn. But this was hardly a general principle and it was not much clearer when Bill Okai commented on Bulla's evidence: 'Those children who go and live somewhere else, they still think of Kata Tjuta and Ayers Rock. A long time ago a person's mother or father might have taken them away from this area but they will still think about this place as being their country from their mothers and fathers.'

Again it took an anthropologist to help with a concept that cut into the surface of the social fabric. Susan Woenne-Green, advising the Commissioner, reminded the hearing that in the Pitjantjatjara language there was a distinction between *kulira* (understanding), the word that described having been taught about a country without visiting it, and *ninti* (knowing), to do with first-hand knowledge of an estate. Only having *kulira*, Woenne-Green contended, did not disqualify one from the rights to *ninti*. Only death would do that. Entitlements, in other words, along with responsibilities, lived on.

Knowing and understanding. Death and life. Kin and country. At almost every turn this is what the land claim was about. The inseparables. This was the communal thrust of everything, no matter who was in the box. And yet there were some things, which should have been simple and concrete, which were hard for the court to know what to do with. Imagine the consternation when it could not be established where exactly a key witness was born.

This was the case with that strongman of the Tjukurpa, Tiger Tjalkalyiri. Everyone knew Tiger; so many people admired his power and skill in story-telling — who would have thought there might be any confusion about the criteria for him standing up as a traditional owner.

Tiger was in the box for some time before they got to this point. He did not seem to mind, and rather liked to talk about himself. He knew he was a character (in the European sense of that term), just as he knew how to play with the social context he was in, as all characters do.

Tiger was old enough to have travelled in many parts of the country. In the early days he was at the cattle station at Tempe Downs. Then he lived at the mission at Hermannsburg.

Eames: — When you were in that country, Tempe Down country, your family, they still know the songs from their country, still sing the songs from their country, know their country?

—Oh, yes, yes.

—What happened when you go over to Hermannsburg? How did it go then?

—Some of us we became like learn like mission, like Christianity and we became Christians.

—You became Christians when you went across to Hermannsburg. Did those ceremonies stop when you went to Hermannsburg?

—Yes.

—What happened about the ceremonies in Hermannsburg?

—I think they still . . . I know the brother still remembers, said Tiger, evidently going quiet.

Earlier on Peter Bulla had said they had kept the songs in their head, unbeknown to the mission. Exactly why Tiger went quiet is impossible to say, sometimes there is no getting beneath the surface without great presumption. What can be said is that he was still living at Hermannsburg, at an outstation away from the Church. He came backwards and forwards from there to the Rock by way of looking after the country, and, it seemed, for a more practical reason.

—I want to watch the place, he said of Ayers Rock.

—And that is what you do, go back and forth, back and forth like that?

—No house I could live here, said Tiger.

—You have a house in Hermannsburg, but you have not got a house to live here, have you?

—Yes. I would like to see Ayers Rock now.

When then, had Tiger been born? Place of birth was supposed to be a key criteria for belonging to descent group.

—Ayers Rock, he had told the hearing.

This had been Layton's understanding. In the two years' fieldwork Layton had done with him, Layton had always understood that Tiger had been born at Pularinya, on the south side of the Rock. Trouble was, as Layton wrote afterwards, others claimed that they had never seen Tiger around the Rock when he was young, and that he had been born at Wintawata, in the Musgraves. How to settle the matter?

Harold Groom—if you recall—had come down to the Rock with Tiger thirty-three years earlier. 'My country', Tiger Tjalkalyiri is supposed to have told Groom, 'go all the way across Lake Amadeus and Oolra and Kuttatute.' Uluru and Kata Tjuta is what Groom meant Tjalkalyiri to mean.

But on the other hand there were written records to the contrary. Susan Woenne-Green told the hearing that Tiger had been born at Wintawata. How did she know? She had located census records compiled by T. G. H. Strehlow. In this case, however, the anthropologist did not record how his information was obtained.

Woenne-Green was reporting material that came from Strehlow's archives. Strehlow's widow was assisting the Northern Territory government in contesting the traditional-owner status of some claimants, including Tiger's and Bulla's.

How to resolve the matter? Pit one white-fella's record against the other? Where did the competing oral claims fit in when they were not made a fuss of in court? If Tiger stood up unopposed an owner, on what 'final' authority could white culture challenge that? Normally, of course, you would *just ask*.

The white culture did ask. And then it left the matter, rightly so, in the totality of the political circumstances.

Map making

WHEN IT CAME to the matter of maps, the issue became who made them, and for what purpose.

As it happened His Honour spoke about maps in a way that might have made an anthropologist vulnerable.

—Do you mean, His Honour asked Layton, the actual map was in each case drawn by you?

—Yes.

Layton had been talking about the map of the estates. Out in the 'field', he had sat down with the claimants and they had drawn the sites on the ground. Whenever that happens, he explained, north always lies in the same direction as north is from that locality. 'In this instance', he said, 'of course, to preserve these things and to write in the names—they have been drawn on paper. It just happened the way things worked out, that I was not always sitting on the south side of the sheet of paper. So, in order to clarify things we can tender the originals and also one that I have redrawn and reoriented the names so that in each case north is at the top of the page.'

—You drew them from a map on the ground?

—I put the sheet of paper on the ground and said, 'Now, suppose Ayers Rock is here and Kata Tjuta is there, where are the other sites?' Then people nominated sites and pointed on the paper and I drew a circle at the point they indicated and wrote the name in beside it.

Mr Hiley had some fun with Layton by drawing attention to a piece of the map that had been torn off in the field, with names added later. He cross-examined Layton on the people who had contributed to the information on the map. The point that he missed was the way in which the map-maker had to a degree begged the question of the centrality of the Rock and Kata Tjuta: he had made them the coordinates, when, from the multiple Dreaming tracks and their many sites, this was to some extent arbitrary.

This was as far as the fieldwork was scrutinised in court, but it was far enough to snidely imply other questions: how much orienting did the anthropologist go in for when he was gathering his data? After all, the anthropologist was an advocate, and not merely a dispassionate ethnologist. To what extent was he actually acquainted with the sites? Layton named 169 sites and did not venture to suggest that he had walked all of them. That would have taken ten years of field contact rather than two. (Come to think of it, how many A<u>n</u>angu had walked them, in this era of the Toyota?)

The map by Strehlow was used to query boundaries. From fieldwork done thirty years earlier, he had drawn a boundary between the Matuntjara language group to the north of Lake Amadeus, and the Pitjantjatjara and Yankuntjatjara speakers to the south. His line went through the middle of the lake, imposing an exactitude entirely inappropriate to his own understanding of the mutual agreements people had for foraging and ceremony. Strehlow knew what had been well established by the claimants: that in the seasonal life of desert people's relatively peaceful struggle for existence, territorial 'boundaries' overlapped. This had to be pointed to the opposition counsel, but throughout the case, Strehlow's work continued to represent an 'opposition anthropology' to the Pitjantjatjara claim. Strehlow's material had in fact much informed Commissioner Toohey's decision to defer the part of the claim that extended into traditional Aranda country.

At the same time though, Strehlow's work, which was complex material gathered over many years, could be turned around, and used another way. Hiley put it to Layton that people as far away as the Pintupi had a 'sort of interest in Ayers Rock' (apparently implying that if they did the Pitjantjatjara people had in some way less interest).

To this Layton responded: — Well, the Tingari track that runs through Kikingkura country and links, sorry Docker River, and links Kikingkura with Ayers Rock, comes from Pintubi country, I believe, but that is of course outside my specific competence.

— So you would read down the word 'part shares' would you, to refer to an interest in the common dreaming perhaps, rather than an interest of a proprietary nature?

— That is correct, yes.

Part shares *versus* common Dreaming. Common Dreaming *versus* proprietorial claims. These were indeed cut-and-dried categories: they made the kind of mental maps that drew hard lines through lakes. The paradox was that Strehlow had shown the relative importance of the Rock to Aboriginal people all through the country. He offered a perspective that put Pitjantjatjara claims in context, while not necessarily refuting them. Much can depend on how an anthropologist is used, on how we find our feet with them.

Sightings

WE HAVE BEEN stopping and starting in the transcript as if there was an articulated opposition to the land claim throughout the hearing. This was not so. As soon Justice Toohey ruled that the Park around the Rock could not be claimed, Ian Barker, who

241

was acting for the Northern Territory government, decamped to Darwin. Thereafter there was little direct challenge to the claim. There remained, however, the legal necessity for clarifying the basis of the claim under the Act, which meant that an anthropologist or a witness could be cross-examined in a way that might, to some, imply the weakness of his or her case. Critical questions had to be put, if principally to satisfy His Honour that all the appropriate Aboriginal evidence was in. The rhetorical structure of the proceedings seemed to imply an oppositional logic.

It was one thing, for example, to worry about the issue of maps; it was quite another to challenge the ways in which traditional owners inhabited them. A key legal issue was 'strength of traditional attattchment' to the country. A white man's common-sense might suggest that a crucial criteria of attachment was the degree of a person's residency on that land. But how could the strength of that attattchment be gauged when people had dispersed, either voluntarily or involuntarily? As His Honour pointed out in his final report: 'When the movement of Aboriginal people from their traditional country has been forced upon them, it may seem especially ironic that their claims should be weakened by absence of traditional settlement.'

Justice demanded that the irony be corrected. Besides, the dispersed people were there anyway, coming and going across their country. Toohey made a strong point of this. He looked back to the 1930s, when large numbers of Aboriginals inhabited the Pitjantjatjara lands. Admittedly many of these people were off their claim area, which is not surprising given the facilities on the cattle stations and the harshness of the country (the disrupted ecology which made it harder to survive in). Out on the reserves—in the Petermann Ranges—up to 500 people might gather for ceremonies; at Curtin Springs 180 Aboriginals had gathered for red-ochre ceremonies.

For Curtin Springs His Honour was drawing on Little's estimate, Bill Harney's host at Angas Downs. Toohey referred also to Harney's many references to people around the Rock, as he did to Professor Rose's observation of the many people regularly travelling to and from Uluru and the Petermann Ranges. Although the sightings of large Aboriginal groups diminished in the 1940s and 1950s people kept up continuous contact with their country in and around the claim area. This, despite the attempts of welfare officers to keep them in their settlements, was a matter of considerable bureaucratic frustration throughout the 1960s. 'In 1972, about 100 men, together with women and children, attended the Rock for the purpose of ceremonies,' Toohey reported. He went on to squash the logic of oppositional irony by citing Dick Kimber, his principal informant on the matter of population movements:

Speaking of the pressures that operated to move the Pitjantjatjara from their traditional country, Mr Kimber commented: 'The fact that they have retained any interest at all in the area is probably remarkable enough, yet in that which follows I believe one can see that the strength of the attachment to the claim area is certainly strong.'

This is a quiet understatment by a historian acutely conscious of the history of white invasion. In 1873 Ernst Giles declared that the Great Designer of the Universe intended that natives be dispossessed. One-hundred years later they are still in ceremony at the Rock, despite all attempts to keep them away. Less than a decade later, they gain a legal title to their land, and along with it, the right to exclusively inhabit the site again, for all the world, one might argue, as if the doomsayers had never spoken. In the light of the *political* history of the Centre, this achievement made Anangu look as solid as the Rock.

'Tough love'

HERE I AM out at the Mutitjulu Community, at Jon Willis' place. From his kitchen window I can see the Rock. It is one of those views that take you by surprise. The monolith humps narrowly at its tail; you might easily walk up the slope of its tail, sit on its haunches and climb onto the top, which would give a splendid view of the country back to Mount Conner. From this angle the Rock is narrowest, and yet, perhaps because of that, it seems to be heavier than ever. The mass through the trees out there has a creaturely presence. You might wave to it.

From the window I am also looking across the grounds of the settlement. I can see the houses, the cement structures with their cement porches. Windows are painted or boarded over. I can see the scrawny trees that might shade part of a house, and the dead tree sticks up from the dry ground. Beside the houses are motor vehicles with bent fenders, broken windshields or a missing wheel. I can see a basketball court and a building with a wire fence around it. Just outside the window, on the ground to the left, is a humpy. I say humpy because *wiltja*, in this built environment, looks like one. Anyway, Willis' neigbours seem to have camped in his front garden.

Mutitjulu is tucked away in the scrub, out of sight from the tourist road that rounds the Rock. To visit you need a permit because it is on Aboriginal land. You have to drive some way in towards the first of the big dunes before the settlement appears. Then buildings become visible through clearings littered with paper and plastic. A left turn takes you down to a cluster of square rooms linked by a walkway: the community adminstration block, which looks scruffy, down at heel. Further along is the store, opposite is a disused-looking petrol station. One bowser. Then, in a wide crescent, the road loops through the community, on both sides of the road are the residential structures built for Anangu since Handback.

Rubber tyres lie in the dirt. Mattresses are out of the house and on the ground. Here and there, the mattress, or a blanket, or a chair, is part of an outdoor camp. A little fire has been lit, and beside it are several women, half-dressed children and dogs. Between the camps and houses there is not much movement: it is as if the stationary human figures in this dilapidated physical environment have created a scene of profound immobility as heavy as the Rock itself. Occasionally a car might trundle away, low slung and overloaded with black bodies. Or a dog might trot. Yes, it is the sudden decision of a dog, spotting another mangy dog, that creates the occasional frisky element. The rest is still, watchful. The young children lean against the wide, slack bodies of their mothers. Adolescents languidly lope, as if they have time to burn.

Is it the heat? Is it 'the life'? Are my first impressions of poverty and ennui accurate or not? In creating these images I am well aware of negative stereotypes. They are true enough, yet how much weight should we give the visual? 'It is this kind of depiction', remonstrated Jon Willis (when he read my words), that makes Anangu wary of outsiders. They do not like being characterised as dirty squalid people. It is an incredibly bourgeois preoccupation we have with the surface of things.' True, true, I say to myself, even now, even after visting Mutitjulu many times in the course of writing this book. Inside these houses that *smell* of poverty (that rancourous odour with the burnt tinge) live people with complex social lives, lives as rich in allegiance and meaning as any visitors'; lives still animated by one of the great cultures of the planet. The *social depth* of life at Mutitjulu can't be captured by a snapshot, I know that. And yet, living here in the run-down houses, and outside, on the ground, in the dirt—their *own sacred ground* littered with the material debris of white culture, the scene contrasts so greatly with the multi-million dollar Ayers Rock Resort that it has to be set down.

It also requires description for another reason: as a way of starting to gauge the social reality of Anangu nearly ten years after Handback. I've been here for a couple of days now, waiting to meet more of the Aboriginal people this time, even though I'm still shy of them, and never quite know how to converse without feeling like I'm intruding in some way, imposing myself in the form of a question, that mode of interaction endemic to western culture. Each day Willis goes off to and each day I have run of the place, which is a privilege, since you are so far from the Rock when you stay at the Resort. Here I can get to the Rock whenever I like, and experience being so close to the Rock right round the clock: in the early morning when it seems to have risen out of the ground to meet the sun; at noon when its bulk bakes like some deadweight; at dusk when it seems to lighten and prepare itself for the invisibility of night where it belongs. You can feel as you sleep the immensity of outer space, when its mass belongs to that darkness between the stars, and it becomes the Rock that defines our border with Time.

Yes, it was 'invaluable', staying out there at Mutitjulu. As days passed, I came backwards and forwards from the Rock. Around and around. Marvellous. Getting to know it. Being burdened by it. And bored. Returning in awe. Round it all over again. So familiar, yet different every time. The Rock is a presence unto itself. If I could only meet more of the people who owned it, and lived beside it. Who were they? What were they like? I knew them only from books.

Four days have passed, but I have not, I have to confess, talked with anybody yet. Each day Willis comes back to the house without having been able to make an appointment for me. It is frustrating. I tell him I hate intruding in people's lives and am embarrassed at the whole imposition of the interview. But my project demands *some* personal contact.

—And you *should* have it, he agrees.—Maybe Tony Tjamiwa will be around tomorrow.

—Great.

—And I would like to speak with Cassidy Uluru, the nephew of the man who was murdered at the Rock in 1932, and Maureen Natjuna, who travelled to the place when she was a girl, before the days of the motor car, across the red sands.

Willis agrees.

I was out the evening the two women came over. They sat in the kitchen for two hours, to no avail on their part.

—They were keen to talk, Willis said.

Barbara and Maureen were not to be found on Wednesday or Thursday. By Sunday I had still not met up with them.

—This is how things are here, says Willis, it's very difficult to make arrangements.

On another note he said:—You can't establish trust with people coming and going quickly like this. Your brief is as big as a PhD and a supervisor would laugh in your face at the amount of time you have allowed for contact work.

—Life is not, I said, a PhD. And I'm relying on you to help me towards some understanding.

—What kind of understanding?

—Well, what people think about the future, for example. How they see themselves in, say, ten years' time.

—What if they have no view of the future?

—Then, that in itself is interesting, something to reflect upon, surely.

—The last time I was here, Tjamiwa complimented me for travelling with my son. He was pleased that I was teaching the young man, just as he was, within his culture, busy transmitting worthwhile things. Thus we spoke as patriarch to patriarch, and so we might, I suggest, converse together about the future.

Willis thought for a minute.

245

He said, — You may not have understood Tjamiwa. He was complimenting you on travelling with your son, moving around the country with him. That does not mean he has a view of the future, necessarily.

That afternoon Willis came back to the house with Tjamiwa. It was then I heard the murder story.

When I was fed up with the Rock I sat around the house. It was too hot to sit outside. In the air-conditioned room were the radio and books. I could also look out the window. The fires went all day, people sat there all day, and the litter was blown about by the wind. Occasionally you could see a person walk from one house to another, or move from the shade of a tree to the shade of a building. There is not much movement, except perhaps further across the compound, near the store. The dogs were the travellers. I was getting to know some of the dogs!

The heat pressed itself across the dry ground. The air itself looked weighted, pressed by the sun over the Rock. The Rock, as the hours passed, changed its moods. A brooding hump is an object lesson in patience. Becalmed, I started to read Lévi-Strauss' marvellous travel book, *Tristes Tropiques* or the *World on the Wane*, as it is called in English. 'I hate travelling and explorers,' begins the jaded romantic.

The great anthropologist hated travelling because so much of the reality of life in the field is a loss of time involving hours of inaction, the full recounting of which can only concern trivialities and insignificant happenings. 'The truths which we see so far afield only become valid when they have been separated from this dross.'

'What struck me', he writes of Sao Paulo in 1935, 'was not the newness of the place but their premature ageing . . . that they should display such signs of decrepitude with such a lack of shame, when the one adornment to which they could lay claim was that of youth, a quality as transitory for them as for living creatures.'

Each day Willis comes home for lunch. One day, as he came in, the room suddenly filled with people. In his wake shuffled ten young men and a couple of boys. A few I knew. They had wandered into the place to speak with Willis, and two of them were trainee rangers who had been here the afternoon before, watching a video (and accepting some of our curry and rice). Now they were back in force, to watch their video again.

The Awakening, the 'archaeological thriller' by Bram Stoker, author of *Dracula*. Scene: Egypt. Plot: heroic archaeologist (Charlton Heston) disinters evil Egyptian lady at a time when the Seven Stars are doing their millennial turn in the Heavens. His own illegitimate daughter is reincarnated as the ancient Dark Lady. What follows is the threat of incest, and much destruction as the spirits seek vengeance for modern man's bungling, egoistic lack of respect for ancient rituals.

In this saga of primitive magic, the Pitjantjatjara audience is rapt. Daughter kisses father on the lips: consternation in the black camp. The intruder into the tomb

dies a terrible death: horrified glee. Evil forces climax: palpable pleasure all through
the room. And then, when it is all over, when the story is done, the young men get up
and head for the door. They seem to get out through that door all at once. No
backward or even a sideways glance, nothing, no word—gone.

Willis is standing up and aware of my astonishment at the rapid exits. Grinning,
glancing at me, he calls out:—Bye. Thanks for coming.

—That's one of the funniest things I've ever seen, I say.

—I used to get offended, but I don't anymore.

—What was happening, I'd love to know what was happening in their heads, all
those young men, school age, or not long out of school.

—I didn't see the group like that at all, he corrected me, instantly making me the
object of observation.—For me they are a group of *watis* and a few boys who are
getting ready for initiation.

—OK. But what were they thinking about the film?

—I have no idea. A lot of what they said was slang. Some jokes—repetitive
verbal things—did the rounds.

—They know about Egypt, where it is?

—They'd know about Egypt, not where it is exactly.

—What about when the daughter kissed the father on the lips? What did they say
then?

—Oh, he's the father, isn't he? Oh, they know about that. And later they said,
when he was holding her hand in the hospital—they said he's mad.

—The black magic stuff, the vengeance?

He shrugged. The phone rang. When he came off the phone, someone came in.
Another interruption, another distraction. Then he had to go. He left saying he would
try again to get me an interview. I was alone again, free again to wander in the books.

'Journeys', writes Lévi-Strauss, 'those magic caskets full of dreamlike promises,
will never again yield up their treasures untarnished.' He is lamenting the inevitable
modernity of the Indian culture he comes into contact with in Brazil, the way in which
we—the West—have changed them since the first encounter. Savagery is no longer a
pure state, it cannot be; and so it is impossible to 'see the full splendor of a spectacle
that had not yet been blighted, polluted and spoilt'. And then his classic statement of
contemporary nervousness:

> I have two possibilities: either I can be like some traveller in the olden days,
> who was faced with a stupendous spectacle, all, or almost all, of which eluded
> him or worse still, filled him with scorn and disgust; or can I be a modern
> traveller, chasing after the vestiges of a vanished reality. I lose on both counts,
> and more seriously than may at first appear, for, while I complain of being able

247

to glimpse no more than the shadow of the past, I may be insensitive to reality as it is taking shape at this very moment, since I have not reached the stage of development at which I would be capable of reviving it. A few hundred years hence, in this same place, another traveller, as despairing as myself, will mourn the disappearance of what I might have seen, but failed to see. I am subject to a double infirmity: all that I perceive offends me, and I constantly reproach myself for not seeing as much as I should.

Opposite Willis' place is the school. One morning I walk across to the wire mesh that surrounds it. The teacher, a young man from Cairns, is starting his first year there (no teacher has lasted more than a year since the school opened five years ago), and tells me he's considering barbed wire for the top of the mesh. The new bathroom facilities inside the school are attractive to the community during after hours, and the teachers want to keep them in good nick for the kids, who, as soon as they arrive at school each day are showered and fed, and (I see from a sign on the blackboard) made to blow their nose. A bundle of towels is stacked in a washing basket under the table. After the shower comes breakfast, which the teacher and his Aboriginal aide prepare. They have arrived hungry, and want more, and settling down to lessons afterwards is difficult.

—I feed them up without adding to obesity, the teacher says, because they eat so much junk from that store.

Thirty-four kids are enrolled at the school, but the average attendance is the baker's dozen, such is the mobility within the community, and the restlessness of teenagers, especially the older boys in line for initiation. Most of the kids—all of the young ones—are coming into the school to speak English for the first time. A curriculum guide from the Northern Territory Education Department advises the teacher to speak English all of the time, which is just as well since he speaks no Pitjantjatjara. A TV teaching aid comes from the BBC.

—Still, the teacher says, some of the parents are interested in the school, and what it might provide. He hopes to build on that.

One mother, an influential woman in the community and park business, did a painting for the kids. The painting tells a traditional story, and she brought it to the school with an audio-casette recording of herself doing the appropriate chants. It was a welcome addition to the school resources for which she expected payment. The teacher was nonplussed at this expectation, but rather than embarrass the mother, money was found from the Maruku craft centre. The school now has the picture as part of its permanent resource. Since then the woman has made a submission about what the school should be doing. She listed help with the writing of Pitjantjatjara (as well as English), with learning traditional stories, with dances, and with traffic control.

—What does she mean by traffic control?

—Training so when the kids go to the town, or a big city, they don't get run over.

There was a gentle knock on the door back at the house the next afternoon. The young men, especially the two trainee rangers, tend to knock and walk in. Now someone was standing outside, waiting.

It was two women in their thirties.

—Willis in?

—No. Jon gone out—Docker River.

—Phone, said the the woman with the direct gaze. Her friend looked away, shy, in the usual manner.

—Where's Jon? she asked as she stepped in.

—Docker River.

That Willis was so far away seemed to settle her as she moved across the room.

—You get this number for us? Perth. Hospital.

I rang two hospitals before finding the whereabouts of their relative, the shy woman's husband.

—Ask 'em, the shy woman said to me, when he coming home.

The nurse said that their patient had checked out for the day with friends, and would be back that night to sleep.

I relayed this to the women in the room.

—Let me, said the wife and spoke into the phone. Her English was quietly effective.

—Tell me, sister, who he go with, you got their names, when he coming back.

She listened intently as I answered the door to a small naked black boy. As soon as he was in the room he was plucking Willis' harp like a two-string guitar and spinning the TV controls. His mother chased him around the couch and he returned to behind the TV set with glee.

—No, no, she yelled, and tipped him outside. She came back from the TV set—slinking—towards me. The Abba video was in her hands.

—This good one.

—Yes, I said.

—Not very long one.

—No.

—Very cool in here, she said. This was a black woman who had mastered the art of looking the white man in the eye.

—Watch some of this, a good one.

—I don't think so, I said.—Tomorrow, when Jon comes back.

—Just a little bit, she said.

—No, this is not my house, I said.

She shrugged understandingly, I thought. Then they were gone.

Willis had disappeared. Gone suddenly on initiation business. Earlier that day a couple of men had rushed in, their spirits up. One I knew from the night before. I had given him and his wife a lift into the Resort to get some petrol. He was a strongly built man skilled in odd jobs, who had once worked on Yami Lester's property down south. His name was Andy. His wife Molly rode silently in the back seat while he made competent conversation in broken English. Where was I from? he asked, and seemed to know where Victoria was when I told him.

—You're the second person to ask me that on this stretch of road, I said.

—Yeah?

—Yeah.

I told him (in words different to this) that as I was leaving the community a boy had waved me down. He had ditched his bike and asked for a lift to the Ranger's Station a few kilometres away. Thinking this a harmless request, I let him in.

—Get your bike off the middle of the road, I said, before we go.

The boy did that and we were off. But a minute later he said, —Yulara, you take me to Yulara, my mother's there.

The boy was saying Yulara because the new name, Ayers Rock Tourist Resort, had not caught on yet.

—Yulara, I said, dubiously. He was about fifteen, a sturdy kid with the makings of a swagger, the cool that characterises the American black who must develop such a front against prejudice and his own vulnerability.

—What's your mother's name?

—Carol, he said, she's a ranger.

I knew of no Carol who was a ranger, but there were still many people I had not met.

—You go to school?

—Tomorrah, he said. His name was Tigger.

When we were out on the highway I pressed on with more questions about his mother, whether she was really there, and what he might do if she was not, and who else he knew out there.

—I'm hungry, he said.

After a while, he asked, —Where you from?

—Melbourne, I said.

No response.

—Know where that is?

A shrug.

We were coming to the gate of the park. He stirred now, suddenly squirming in the seat, all the cool fallen away.

—My mother, he said, holding a finger to his temple, she shoot me, she kill me.

—OK, I said, I don't think your mother is out there. You should go back. Look (to my great relief now), here is a Ranger.

Just up ahead was one of the Ranger utes, driven by an Aboriginal with four Aboriginal mates. I did a U-turn and pulled up beside them with their black relative. They got out quickly and peered in.

—This fella is looking for his mother, I said.—It's best that you take him back home.

—No-one said yes, no-one said no, but the boy got out and they drove away with him.

—Do you know that boy? I asked Andy.

—No, said Andy.

When we got to the Resort, Andy pulled me back for Molly to walk ahead.

—We have a talk, he said. I felt the grog request coming and headed it off. Quickly he adjusted to this and we arranged to meet later on for his lift back. He was still dependent on the white fella for transport, urging Willis to lend him a vehicle—quickly quickly for some important business.

With the initiation ceremony, a message stick had to be carried to Ernabella. The spanner in the works was that the community at Ernabella were so fed up with their mob of boys: so delinquent had they been that the community would have none of the message stick and the ceremony for them. So the route of the stick had be diverted to Docker River—out west, where some preparatory ceremony had to be done.

—You can't take the white car, it's got one light. The other one is stuffed, it's leaking oil and you can't get in under the bonnet, said Willis.

Andy was a man who knew when mechanical facts could not be argued with. The men went away.

I don't know what note—in their language—they parted on, but a little while later Willis was rushing around himself.

—What's up?

—I'm going to Docker River, won't be back till tomorrow.

He had been called. As a *wati*, it was the kind of 'invitation' that could not be refused, no matter how short the notice. Already he had some camping gear thrown together. Hat, face net, swag. He had his big ball of red 'Pearl' wool for the headband. And he had—after rushing back into the room for them—his credit cards.

—What do you need those for, I laughed.

—Food, the phone, you never know, he said. And then he was gone.

Alone again, I switched on the TV. Blur and roar of the dislocated set. I switched it off, cursing the little black tyke.

What kind of story am I telling here? I am driven, partly I know, by the distance

251

that divides me from these people. I would like to get 'inside', but a travelling stranger can't do that. Even if I lived here for three years, for the term of a PhD, I might be no closer in the long run. What can we really know about another culture? How do we know when we know?

All that is entailed in the delicate issue of access and what we bring to the other culture is splendidly set down by Clifford Geertz in his *Works and Lives*, a book that leaps off the shelf of Willis' fine library. Geertz scrutinizes anthropologists as writers. Lévi-Strauss is very much a writer, yes, a kind of fabulist of fact. *Tristes tropiques* as myth; in its own right, a story of lost illusions. Evans-Pritchard, famous for his study of magic and government in an African tribe is endemically replete with colonialist certitudes, that Oxford common-room tone that admits to no uncertainty, and which appeals to right-minded readers in the know of upper middle-class English culture. Malinowski, who worked not so far from here, in New Guinea, was endlessly industrious with his accumulation of field notes, but was also the Conradian dreamer who gave the game away in the confessional diary published after his death: 'On the whole my feelings toward the natives are decidedly tending to "Exterminate the brutes".'

What is it to be on the inside of another culture? Geertz on the problem of the 'total immersion approach to enthnography': 'There is the landscape. There is the isolation. There is the local European population. There is the memory of home and what one has left. There is the sense of vocation and where one is going. And, most shakingly, there is the capriciousness of one's passions, the weakness of one's constitution, and the vagrancies of one's thoughts: that nigrescent thing, the self. It is not a question of going native . . . It is a question of living a multiplex life; sailing at once in several seas.'

Willis was out there on his seven seas, to Timbuktoo and back, with credit cards. What kind of book would he write if he ever sat down to write it all—if these people allowed him the peace and quiet to settle to such an isolated and isolating task?

It is tough sailing these days for the narrative self, that 'I' which is the author on the page. Nervous self-consciousness keys the modern attitude. Younger ethnologists are riddled with doubts epistemological, political, moral. Strip the text of its rhetorical illusions and what do you have? 'Violence', says one maker of what Geertz sardonically calls 'author-saturated texts': 'Some form of symbolic violence', as 'inherent in the structure of the situation.'

It grew dark as I read. What was I doing here, how long could I tolerate my own voyeurisms?

There was a knock on the door. A gentle one. It was the wife of the sick man in Perth coming to ring the hospital again. She had another woman with her who carried a torch. When the wife had contacted her husband, the other wanted to ring the police.

I got on to the hospital. Our patient was not back in the ward yet.

—There is family here, I said to the nurse, let me check about messages.

—Wife! said the woman, wife!

I corrected into the phone.—It's the wife here, I said.

She took the receiver from me.

—Tell me sister, who he go with? What her name?

I could not tell whether the information coming to the worried was good or bad news. She put the phone down and left. For some reason, her friend no longer needed to ring the police. I stood by the window for a while but could hear no car.

It was the next night that things broke loose. Willis was out to dinner and I was alone again. From the darkness outside, there was yelling. I heard the next morning that it was a trainee ranger rowing with his wife: she left him that night, taking the kids south to Amata. But this yelling was more than a single family blue: the whole community seemed to be erupting and on top of the explosion were—to my ears—the distress calls of women. The bedlam continued for fifteen minutes. At last came the knock on the door.

It was the Abba fan with a man in tow.

—My husband, she said, as they pushed into the room.

—Ring the police, said the man, heading for the phone.

He knew the number and made the call as his wife said:—Old woman hit a girl with a *nulla nulla*. The girl is down on the ground. Old woman, she go mad.

—Is the girl unconscious?

—Down on the ground, with the *nulla nulla*.

Her man was talking in very broken English to the police.

—You should get a doctor, I said, for the girl.

What good could the police do, I wondered.

The woman nodded vaguely.

—Is there doctor?

—Nurse over there, she indicated.

—On the community here?

She nodded.—Maybe go over, she said, but I did not feel that she was about to.

—Are the police coming? I asked her man.

He seemed unsure.

A few minutes after they left there was more shouting. I could hear the raised voices of older men joining the women.

The couple came back. The man headed for the phone.

His wife said,—They use axe now.

It was a short call, rather as if the police had already got the message and were on their way. The man and his wife went back into the rowdy dark. I waited. Then the man came back again, this time with a rather drunken mate. They came to door, as if to make another call, and stood there.

—Jon come back?

—Not yet, I said. And then ventured to say,—You're a couple of strong blokes, what do you need to ring the police? Can't you get the women to calm down?

I have no idea what they thought of this opinionated outburst. They drifted off towards the yells that seemed to be subsiding. The ructions must have lasted another five minutes and then, all of a sudden, stopped. Only little fires hissed and snapped in the clearing. The door swung open and Willis came in.

I told him the story, my version of events. He cursed the Abba-loving woman, who always slunk in when he was out, when someone else was using the house.

—They knew, he said, he would not have allowed them to ring Perth. Or let a young kid in the place.

We were facing the window, gazing out on the night that was now so still.

—What about the damaged girl, the one hit by the old lady?

—I don't know of any old lady out there who could do such a thing, Willis said.

—It was distressing, I said, hearing the women yell and scream with such anger and fear.

—Do you find it distressing, he mused, I don't. I just wish they were a culture that had other ways to express their anger . . . or that they would be violent more quietly. And that when this kind of thing happens the police come and take someone away into protective custody.

It did remain quiet, and the police did not come. The only remaining violence that night was perhaps my own words, as they issued from my efforts to at least sketch the possibility of manifold stories.

—Is the health of these people better than other communities in Central Australia?

A moment's hesitation from Willis.

—No, he said.

This cryptic answer implied that Mutitjulu, despite some things in its favour, was part of the nationwide scandal of Aboriginal health. That is, among Aborigines in Central Australia, the life expectancy was twenty years less than the national average; seventeen less than the NT population. The crude death rate was three times higher than the Australian population. Aboriginal men in the Centre die mainly from diseases of the respiratory and circulatory system, external causes such as accidents, poisons and violence, and infectious and parasitic diseases. Among women, respiratory and circulatory diseases are also the main causes of death, along with neoplasms, diseases of the genito-urinary system, external causes and infectious and parasitic diseases.

Much later Willis told me:—Some things are much better at Mutitjulu than in other communities. Some things are worse.

He referred to a good record on child health and aged care. On the other hand, there was an unnaturally high level of diabetes. The figures for sexually transmitted diseases looked worse than some communities, but this was probably due to higher levels of detection: Anangu here were more cooperative about the education program. Renal failure rate was very low. The trauma rate from alcohol and stress related to alcohol was high. Willis put this down to geography: Mutitjulu was an isolated community, but grog was easy to come by, and people came from far afield to get it.

These details came later. Willis seemed reticent initially; and it took us a while to get on the same wave length. I would visit in the spring, wonder about what I had been told or seen; and come back in the autumn to think again. Each visit was a matter of hanging out—for information, to meet people. Each visit shifted the focus of the snapshots: I recognized familiar faces and could sometimes put names to faces, and every now and then, say hello to an Aboriginal person who was not too shy to acknowledge me.

Waiting—the ability to stretch yourself through time, the desert trek of fore-bearance that is patience, the essential virtue for survival in the Centre.

'Tough love'. A phrase I heard for the first time back in Alice Springs. At a Chinese restaurant I met two indigenous people from North America. Bob, a battered-looking seventy-year-old in a cowboy hat, and Buck, a smiling younger man with a jet-black plait. They were in town helping Aborigines run a self-help project against alcoholism. Previous alcohol programs in the Centre have been set up by white people. This one is based on a North American scheme managed by the community itself.

Bob personally remembers the prohibition era for the American Indians, days when white man ruled that the indigenous people could not drink. In California he pretended to be Mexican so as to get a drink.

Alcohol became legal for indigenous Americans in 1964 (only three years before it did in Australia). Disaster struck: individuals and whole communities couldn't handle it. Both men remember the before and after. Now, with the self-help programs beginning to work, the Indians have made their own rules to stop the drink. Voluntary dry areas—as Mutitjulu is, in theory.

—It has been a slow return to community health.

—When would a community be well enough to run their own grog shop?

They shot me looks that said: No, never.

They patiently explain:—Once the health comes back through the *tough love* that is applied in the programs, some communities might consider it. They have debated the economic benefits of selling their own grog and so far have not. They want to consolidate the health. Saying 'yes' to grog might be a generation away.

Meanwhile all kinds of people are becoming 'experts' on Indian culture.

—Why, said Buck, there was that guy who wrote that famous book about the Blackfoot. White fella, wrote the old stories down. A best-seller among Indian supporters in the 1970s. His book was taught in universities, but when young Indians took the book back to the elders, what did they find?

—They found that the stories were wrong. They found that the elders laughed. The stories were half-truths, spun for the benefit of the white scribe!

A white Australian at the table exclaimed with delight.

—See, he said, forcefully, that's the bloody thing about the written word. Once it's put down it becomes GOSPEL! You and I can tell each other things like this (he gestured to mean we give and take, we allow latitude, we see the *unspoken* as we speak), but once it's *written*!

The Americans nodded.

Another Australian at the table said:—Look, no-one knows what Barry is going to write down about this conversation. It could be anything!

Soul

SIX MONTHS LATER, I am back at Mutitjulu for a special reason. The community has a church. Yes, the other side of Bill Harney's old house, there it stands in all its prefabricated glory. What a surprise it is—my naivety again? Or should I be surprised at the Park officials who have taken so long to mention this Christian aspect of the place? Anyway, there is the church in all its glory. The light bounces off the galvanised iron roof and shines on the big silver box high in the front, the vented tower that will soon house the air-conditioning unit. On top of that more glinting in the new day's light: the crucifix. Against the blue sky the crucifix is a sharp ikon over Mutitjulu.

It's Sunday morning. The service will be out on the ground where it usually is because the building inspector has yet to approve the church. A congregation of about twenty people: men, women, children, dogs, has gathered near a bush beside a tap. One group, the women with most of the young kids, in an eiderdown, another on the ground near a person on a kitchen chair. A few paces away against a wall are some young men and boys. When Willis and I come up room is made for us. I find myself on a mattress and bed base beside an old man wearing a red headband. He and two women have moved along for me.

—*Palya*.

The preacher is Tony Tjamiwa. He is well into his sermon, the kind of sermon he has been giving each Sunday morning for a few years now. This one, as we will discover later, he had started earlier on, but it was interrupted by a reveller. Now he is speaking again from the Good News Bible. He gesticulates. An arm reaches behind him in the direction of the Rock. An arm goes out, to include the congregation before him.

He is wearing dark blue trousers with sneakers and a knitted beanie. Bare chest. You can see his ceremonial scarrings. Beside him is a plastic chair, his leather briefcase and the two or three dogs that come and go. They sometimes stand as if they are guarding his bag, or they flop onto the dusty ground, where they pant to the sermon.

Tjamiwa is resonant preacher. This is Pitjantjatjara that seems to make every word count. His gestures are those of a preacher who has embraced the world. His congregation are attentive, though they look down and about as he speaks. No child speaks. The beautiful baby girl in a fresh blue dress has not made a murmur; she smiles up to catch the composure of her elders. When a wayward blue heeler pup waddles into the group it is scooped up by a grandmother and sent on its way.

The sermon comes from the Gospel according to John. 'Before the world was created, the Word already existed'. It is the gospel of miracles, and the gospel where everything—water, bread, light—points to spiritual realities.

Tony Tjamiwa's prayer goes:

> God the Father is up there. God is in the sky looking down. God is everywhere, caring about all of us, the whole family, hearing what we say. Everyone should keeping asking God to continue taking care. You should all stay with God.
>
> Thank you God.
>
> You should all stay with God by staying on the right path, with the right behaviour. God lights the light in your spirit. God is always listening to what you want. God is always taking care of everybody.
>
> God is the sacred spirit in all of us. We also have the same sacred spirit in us.
>
> Stay with God. Stay with God.

Throughout the service Willis had been sitting on the ground in front of me, all ears. Afterwards he says that in parts he had trouble following Tjamiwa in detail.

There had been, for instance, some pronouncements about wine. Tjamiwa had said it was not just some white fella's stuff. It was the blood of Jesus. So you have to use wine properly. And in his language he had used the ceremonial word for blood, which is not often used in public.

—And had he been talking about the Rock?

—Yes, he had been talking of God who had made the world, and in particular God had been responsible for making Uluru, but in a way I did not quite understand. He was kind of saying, it was a joint project of making the world.

Willis gave a little laugh, as if to say: 'It's ridiculous, this process of translation, the meanings can sound so strange.'

Like 'joint management' of the Park.

—You know, said Willis, God working with Aboriginal people.

—Including the Rock.

—Yeah, and then he said a whole lot of stuff: that God knows everything about us, and he wants us to pray to him, and he sent our older brother down to teach us, to inform us.

—Older brother?

—Yeah. If God's our father, and Jesus is his son, Jesus is our older brother.

—Right.

—And he told that story about when Jesus was lost as a child, when his parents were frantically searching, and found him in the temple and Jesus finally saying: 'Why were you worried for me, I was in my father's house.' He was talking about God's Law with the older men, which sounded really strange. He took pains with the way he phrased things, and said that the Tjukurpa and God's Law work together.

Tjamiwa came over to Willis' house for a cup of tea. He had a shirt on now, two in fact, and he was sweating under his beanie. But he left it on as we sat in the kitchen. Out of his briefcase he brought the Bible, and as soon as I spoke to him about his sermon he solemnly read all of John 17. 'After Jesus finished saying this he looked up to Heaven, and said, "Father, the hour has come. Give glory to your Son, so that your Son may give glory to you . . ."'

Willis asked Tjamiwa to say more about what he'd been saying about the Rock.

Tjamiwa dropped his voice. He began quietly, meditatively.

He said that he had been in Alice Springs—asleep—and he had a vision. God came to him in a vision, and he was holding a *tjiwa*, a grinding stone, a little round one, and it was a soul. Someone had come down from Heaven and carried this grinding stone of God, and spoke about it to him, came in through the door . . .

—It was like when the Angel Gabriel came down and told Mary that she was going to be the mother of God.

Gently Willis reminded him of the question: 'What about this place, Uluru?'

Tjamiwa said that in the south, in the east, in the north, in the west, God is everywhere. Everything under the sky. God was looking after black people and white people, Chinese people, every people, Japanese people.

The grinding stone, that was the soul of God. And so was this Rock here.

A friend of his also had a vision. An angel said to him that 'There's that place Mutitjulu. There's Christian people—God's family—living there. They're not listening to me, they're not listening to Jesus, they're listening to all sorts of other stories and as a result they are really sad. And they're going down there, that makes them sad too.'

—What did he mean by 'going down'?

—There are Christian people here who are not listening to the word of God. They're not looking for God, they look up at the cross in the Church and they don't see Jesus on that wood. They have food but they don't think about when Jesus gave people bread and said, take this and eat it. They drinking wine, but they are not thinking that this is Jesus' blood.

—They need to clarify things for themselves, Tjamiwa said, by opening up their hearts. Their souls are closed like that (hands shut), like two doors closed together, and the sun can't get in.

—So how *were* young people getting on here, these days?

This was a longer answer. I awaited the translation keenly. Was this the conversation about generations I'd hoped to have?

Willis said:—He answered your question by saying they are all Christians, they are all good people. They come to church on Sunday and they listen to the good word, but then they go away on Monday, Tuesday, Wednesday, they're somewhere else, and they come back to church again. From his reading, they came to Jesus in Gethsemane and they came with torches and axes and knives and when he said who he was they were frightened, and he revealed himself to them.

—You were talking about drinking wine in the right way?

Willis curtly paraphrased:—This is the bloke that made wine.

—Had he given sermons from visions before?

—This vision, Tjamiwa told us, had happened when he was in Alice Springs the week before.

—Was it his first?

—I don't know how to ask that question, said Willis, rather stiffly. (When he read this months later he explained his awkwardness: he didn't have the vocabulary, and was not sure whether the topic was an appropriate one for him (a young *wati*) to discuss with a senior man. Tjamiwa sounded cagey, a sure sight that they were skating on thin ice.)

—Had Tjamiwa had other visions?

Willis said:—What he is saying is that he frequently reads the Bible during the day and reflects on it. And sometimes things will come to him while he's asleep.

Tony Tjamiwa was born in Kanypi in South Australia, Pitjantjatjara country. He learnt his Christianity at the Presbyterian Mission at Ernabella, which is down in the Musgrave Ranges, not far from my maḻu hunt. He was, he said proudly to me that

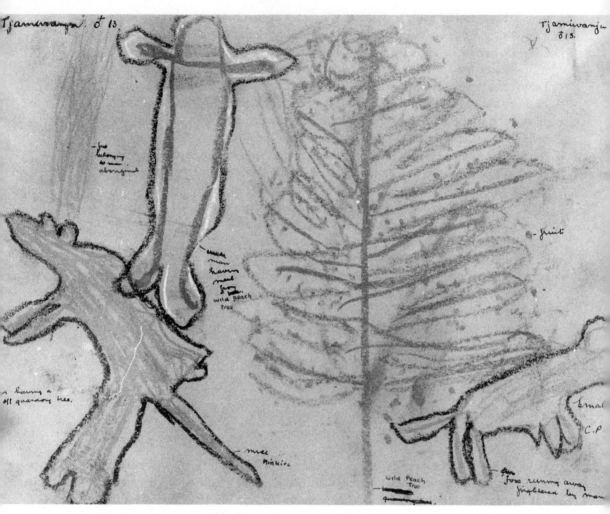

Ernabella boy (Tjamiwa) sketches for Mountford in 1940.

day, the first child to be baptised. This must have been in 1952, when Aboriginal children were baptised, among them Nganyintja the wife of Ilyatjari, who she subsequently taught to be a Christian. I hadn't realised when we were on that outstation the depth of contact this admirable old couple had had in European ways.

Tjamiwa was thirteen when C. P. Mountford came through in 1940, on the visit that yielded so many of those famous photographs of 'unspoilt' Aboriginal children. He was one of the kids who did a drawing for the interested white man.

—Can I use one of the drawings you did for Mountford? I asked Tjamiwa.

260

—*Uwa*, he said, pleased.

The drawing is a nice expression of two cultures. There is no mistaking the strength of the Aboriginal theme, with that blaze of orange in the top left of the picture: 'Fire belonging to Aboriginal' says Mountford's diligent note, as if fire could belong to any one else! Below that is 'Man having a meal of quandong tree' and 'mice'. There in the middle of the picture is 'wild peach tree' which looks like a Christmas tree. In the opposite corner is another gesture towards the white presence: 'Fox running away frightened by man'. Young Tjamiwa did not specify this man as Aboriginal and the fox, it seems to me, is reminiscent of many foxes in European storybooks.

The mission at Ernabella was evidently more tolerant of the two cultures than most. The school taught in the native language and the pupils were naked until their teens. Admittedly, the Aboriginal people who chose to accept the food provided by the mission were obliged to receive Christian instruction, but the whole tenor of that was to express a tolerance of Aboriginal beliefs and customs.

Indeed, when it came to translating the Bible into Pitjantjatjara much care was taken to make the two kinds of religious Law sit comfortably with each other. As a missionary put it: 'Pitjantjatjara words are taken and expanded in meaning, to give a new and broader concept to a familiar term. The most important word to be developed in this way was Tjukurpa, "word", "story", "Dreamtime". This word already had a great depth of meaning, but it was taken further to provide meaningful link between the Pitjantjatjara and Christian traditions. The translation of the first verses of the Gospel according to St John, using this word Tjukurpa, immediately links the past of the Pitjantjatjara with the beginnings of all mankind, and indeed conveys a meaning far deeper than the English "word" achieves.'

Tony Tjamiwa is a lay teacher. When he was a young man at Ernabella, he said, he had the chance to go north to become an ordained preacher, but he chickened out. Later on it pleased him to be recognised as an elder of the Church at Ernabella, just as it pleases him today that the Uniting Church has acknowledged him as one of the authorities for Mutitjulu and Docker River.

—When they open the Church, Tjamiwa said, there will be a big *inma*, ceremony.

As indeed there was, a few months later. Not only that: the community decided to call their church the Mutitjulu *Lutheran* Church. Those with Lutheran backgrounds, mainly from their days in the Areyonga settlement, outnumbered the rest. On the big day a Lutheran pastor from Adelaide presided—an odd irony considering the complicated part Lutherans have played in the legal history of landrights.

Tjamiwa returned to the idea of going north to get his qualification as an ordained preacher. He also mentioned—in Pitjantjatjara to Willis—that a vacancy had occurred at Ernabella.

—Where? asked Willis.

Tjamiwa told him.

—Well, you're not going to Ernabella, said Willis, so don't even think about it.

It was a light quip, but heartfelt. Apparently Willis couldn't imagine Mutitjulu without Tjamiwa. Without his ability to affirm and present the Tjukurpa, a passion that rests, I had belatedly discovered, on his imaginative application of Christian Law, just as it did on his faithful reception of that first translations which linked the Word of God with the Tjukurpa.

When the church went up, Tjamiwa made a statement to Willis.

—Now, he said, we are one body.

CHAPTER 7 **Sharing**

Showing

TJAMIWA IS TAKING me on a *mala* walk. At last. This is what I have come for. A myth story first-hand, a recounting on foot, a meeting with the Rock as it is known to an Aboriginal.

—Look, what's that? he asks.

I look. We are standing in front of the sign.

—Yes, I say. The sign is in English. The good old *mala* walk, I think, which I have read and read about.

—Come over here, says Tjamiwa.

Just near the sign is an opening in the rock, a small cave.

—Look, he waves.—Look in.

You have to crouch down to see. Deep in the recess is a whitish stone.

—That is *itjaritjari*. Marsupial mole, says Tjamiwa.

The white stone is physical proof, if proof is needed, that she was—is—part of this story too.

—See this,what's this?

It's a tree growing out of the rock.

—*Ili*, fig.

I've read that *ili* is a sacred plant, and that its Tjukurpa is tied up with women's business.

—Here, try this.

It is another plant.

—*Arnguli*, the bush plum.

Blue-black, bitter-sweet.

Tjamiwa is already down the path.

—Here is another cave. Look here.

It is another sign.

—What's that say?

—*Itjaritjari Yuu*.

—*Yuu*.

—*Yuu*, shelter.

—That's right, says Tjamiwa.—Come in here.

You go before him; he means you go in here.

You can walk into this one. It runs along the rock, head high.

—This is a great home, Tjamiwa says.—You can come in here, out of the wet, out of the cold, and make a bed. You can lie down in the dry grass you have put here, that's the bed. You don't need a blanket. You don't need anything.

Yes, you nod, it's a great shelter. Just inside the opening are some cave paintings. Tracks. A line. It's an emu and the print of a man.

—The hunt, Tjamiwa says.—See, that's where the man caught the emu, maybe.

—Go there, go, he points into the cave, and obediently you move further along, into the darker part.

—Look out for *mamu*!

OK, I'll watch out for monsters. (All the things you say in your head, the better to accommodate this 'authentic cultural tour'.)

Outside the cave, there is another thing to see. There are holes in the rock above the opening. Clearly, that's where *itjaritjari* burrowed and burrowed, moving in and out of the sand like a fish in the sea.

Further along the track there is a handsome bloodwood tree. The hardest of woods. Spear throwers. Bowls. Up at the Rock again, in the bowl of that high shelf near the top of the Rock is *itjaritjari*'s waterhole. It is difficult to get to. In the old days, tourists used to try and would fall in and get stuck there. On special occasions Anangu might climb up there to get water.

On to the rockface again. The notice is about the cave painting. Their signs show an amoebic shape that is called 'bush potato', an arrow that is an 'emu track' and two tight concentric circles labelled 'Waterhole or honey ant nest'. You read: 'Each abstract symbol has many levels of meaning'.

Tjamiwa is looking into the cave where there are all sorts of shapes, some much clearer than others, all painted at one stage or another, over the top of each other. He says this was a teaching place. Today we can't say exactly what each sign meant when the painter (always a man) used the wall like a blackboard. About all you can say is that the signs might be fifty or a thousand years old. That's as long as the pigments last. They will not last for much longer if tourists touch the paint, or kick up the dust that gathers there.

Malaku wilytja. The notice to the next cave: '*Itjaritjari* has made this *wilytja* (permanent shelter). Here the mala women prepare the ceremonial food that has been hunted and gathered during the day. The sounds of the children playing echo around the *wilytja*.'

This is the sign all right, which makes it all the more interesting that Tjamiwa seems to be talking about something else. This is the cave, he says, of the *Nyiingka*, the young boys who are about to be initiated. This is their camp, where they stay in a stage of separation from the others. *Tawara*. Separation. They stay here while the men are off; out there.

He waves towards the west. The men are 'over there' 'doing something' that cannot be spoken about.

—If you bring people here, Tjamiwa says, you tell them this. Only this. The straight stuff.

OK then, I think, I am being educated. And told.

Further along the path is the place that cannot be photographed. Mala Puta. A triangular cave so invitingly placed in the rock, within climbing distance. *Puta*, pouch, the sacred pouch of the hare wallaby. In the old days people went up into it. Then they got stuck, or twisted ankles or came a cropper on the way down. A powerful place. A dangerous place, according to Tjamiwa.

Suddenly he picks up a couple of stones from the ground. He throws them forcefully down back on the ground.

These are not opals, this is not a mine!

To the next cave. Malaku wilytja. This one, it seems, *is* the women's cave, there is no doubt about that. You stand in the curl of the wave of the rock and see the part that has served as the grinding stone. Seeds and grubs and small game were brought into this grand shelter by the women. A shelter in cold times, a long-standing camp in the drought years that some women at Mutitjulu remember as girls. The shade shelter.

There are more paintings there. Again Tjamiwa talks about their wear and care. If you see someone touching them, grab him and kill him.

Punganyi means hit, as well as kill.

He is cracking a joke again.

All the while—I should have said this before—he has been mixing a jaunty gait with solemnity. He has been the ironical tour guide while at the same time teaching and yes, preaching. The rhetoric springs with the utmost sincerity out of him. Perfect stage craft, the born narrator. All the time alert, as great players are, to every flicker of the audience. I have been writing and taping, and when the tape did not seem to be working, writing as much as I could while remaining open to the nuances of speech and gesture.

—Look, read and learn, Tjamiwa had said in the painting cave, as if to mimic the method of our culture when it sets out to learn.

In the next big shelter he caps that. He says that Anangu learn about their culture straight, the same way as white people learn about tables and chairs.

—Straight, he says, straight in the heads and straight in the hearts, that's how they learnt their Law. No pens, no typewriters. And some parts of the Law they would never put into a typewriter.

We ended up in the sacred shade of Kantju Falls. I say sacred by way of indicating the relief the place brings from the exposure of the *mala* walk. For the walk seems to meander as you progress in and out of the caves and wind along the track that takes you into the sun that challenges you with blazing views of the Rock. Sacred also because that morning we came to it with so much, it seemed, of the *mala* story still unspoken, as if Tjamiwa trusted that the great drama of ceremony/invitation/refusal and punishment was already deeply understood. And sacred too, because Tjamiwa had stopped there to say so.

—The *mala* story ends here, he said, although it did not. It continued for a long way round the rock yet. He meant, and then said—This is all that can be said.

Meaning: *this is all I am telling you.*

—Here, he indicated the water, the women sometimes came. They walked carefully in for water, and left the way they had come in, back along the track there, avoiding the men's sacred site on the other side of the waterhole. And in the old days men would have forbidden children to visit as well. No swimming, none of that, never. This was a properly sacred place. A dangerous place.

Telling

BUT THIS WAS NOT quite as it happened. I told a story out of a wish. The pilgrim to the Rock hoped to have time alone with Anangu. Was not this the deep reason for his quest: the dream of replicating, if only in meaningful gesture, a kind of 'first contact' with a 'traditional' Aborigine? Alas. It can happen no more, and least of all at the Rock, though the Tjukurpa is strong. You have to win trust. You have to speak the language and live in a place. Besides, there are too many visitors already, there are *swarms* of visitors, so that the contact you do have has to be especially arranged, and is most likely to be a group experience.

I had company indeed. When I did the *mala* walk with Tjamiwa I was with fifteen (of the 31) people from the tourist industry, all of whom had come to the Park to learn how it was run. I was walking around the Rock with owners and managers of tour companies, booking agents and caterers, salespeople and drivers, especially coach drivers: all people who make money out of the Rock, who package Aboriginal culture for others; people paid to induct travellers into the culture of the Park. Most knew the place well because they had been coming here as the teachers. Now they were the pupils, pupils of Anangu, they were there to be shown what it means for the Park to be jointly managed by the local owners at Mutitjulu and the federal government's Nature Conservation Agency. The Board of Management, the governing body which implements joint management, and on which Anangu have the majority vote, had promoted this course not simply to educate visitors. The idea gaining hold was that the course—this was the third so far—would instruct and certify tourist operators in the Park.

Yes, much of Tjamiwa's pitch was determined by that basic consideration: he was in the act of educating people in what they *should* and *should not* do when they came into the Park that was on his people's land. Tjamiwa was accompanied by Barbara Nipper; she was a competitive, querulous, witty complement all along the track. The senior man and the senior woman, both sporting in their language, both sociably playing, but *in all seriousness* with their authority. Jon Willis translated all the way.

It was the immediacy of this first-hand contact that made the impression. Most operators had never met an Aborigine. Here, they were walking side by side with people showing their country. At the end of the three days, most would express deep feelings of appreciation at this opportunity. Never before had they realised the depth of Aboriginal attachment to their places, nor had they appreciated what traditional owners felt about the Rock. Implicit in their gratitude was another realisation: that much personal effort was involved in this act of communication, that sharing involved work and caring on Anangu's part, that it was, in a way, an act of trust as well as an exercise in authority.

Coach drivers were the largest group on the course. There were veterans among them, men who had acquired their attitudes to Aborigines well before the landrights movement. Some had been coming to the Rock for years and never had personal treatment like this. They had known a time when 'Aborigines appeared out of nowhere', as one veteran bus driver said, 'to borrow a blanket'. Or they remembered the 'begging' which they found disgusting, or they had been advised by other drivers to stay in their bus for fear that it might be damaged by the Aborigines who should not, by right, be in the Park at all. They should be off, away on their own reserve, rather than hanging around as eyesores or making trouble for harmless tourists.

Every one of these old hands seemed to be impressed with Tjamiwa. There was a positive attitude to learning, even if that presented difficulties. So much depended on the knowledge and attitude an operator brought to the Park. One driver told me he had about seventy dollars worth of books—Harney and Mountford included—and was none the wiser as to what this walk was really about. He listened to Tjamiwa intently. He seemed to be accepting the new silences required at the Rock. Willis told everyone: 'Forget about what you can't talk about. Look at the enormous richness of Aboriginal culture you *can* talk about. Celebrate what Anangu want us to talk about.'

The walk was as much *showing* as telling. There was the story of the *mala*, but the walking story involved many other things: food and food gathering, art and craft, teaching and learning, public and private business, the relationships between men and women. Willis had skilfully drawn attention to the way in which the story functioned as a store of knowledge, right from the start. We came out of the cave and there was *ili*, a fig tree. Barbara Nipper held forth. Almost at any point, you felt as you followed in the context of *them* teaching *us*, the *mala* story might have been a device for teaching. The big question was, however, what exactly were the students learning?

Some of the tour operators were quiet through all of their contact with Anangu. It was hard to tell what the AAT Kings men were thinking: they were a heavy, silent presence in the flight-deck uniforms they sported with Territorian machismo. One driver (from another company) said he thought a lot of time had been wasted, and if he had been in charge he'd have packed much more into the program. When he said that you realised how much some operators had become addicted to speed: the bitumen road and the introduction of the fast air-conditioned bus would probably have more effect on people's learning ability than anything else. Walking was departure enough from the modern routine; having a cup of tea with time to yarn bushman fashion is too much for the officious driver who thinks mainly of the physical welfare of his bus and his 'manifest'. The same man lacked patience in other areas. 'When I was in Melbourne', he said, 'and listening to the news about Aborigines, I kept saying, "Poor buggers". But now I live in Alice Springs and the majority of Aborigines are very nasty people, and you really have to watch what you say and do. You've got the river people. They're disgusting people, as far as I'm concerned. A frightening race of people. I've had knives pulled on me, stones thrown at my coach, windows broken, my car stolen.

'I don't feel any animosity about the Aboriginal people', he said in the next breath, looking around him. Nearby was Tjamiwa and Barbara Nipper, and Rupert Goodwin and Nyinku Jingo, as well as Billy Wara (Tall Billy), a man as senior as Tjamiwa in the Law. Also there was Andy Daeger, who had become the Chairman of the Mutitjulu Community since I met him last. He prefers to be called Andy Panpanpalala, after the bellbird in his Tjukurpa story. Maybe the driver did not mean to sound racist, but there he was, standing on these people's land, disparaging their relatives. His ignorance and insensitivity were shocking, though not untypical of many visitors to the Park, even today, especially those sympathetic to the Northern Territory government's ideological impatience with landrights. Here, he was in the hands, so to speak, of Park management. Moreover, he would not be able to get his permit to work in the Park unless he went on such walks and attended to what Anangu and Park Rangers officially had to say. This was the great political reversal he was perhaps resisting: Handback meant that he was here to learn from 'them' about what it is exactly he should say and do when he was in the Park.

It was a measure of the speed of cultural change at the Rock that this driver, so full of confused resentments, did not speak out against the idea of being licensed by Park authorities. Nor did any other driver on the course. They reflected the political realism of their organisations. Mike Gunn, the manager of the biggest carrier to the Rock, AAT Kings, told me that he completely supported compulsory accreditation. 'It would sort out the men from the boys,' he said. And he would support not one, but three courses a year, so that more of his tour operators had the right understanding of all that the Park involved. 'To be a good tour operator you've got to be a narrator,' he said.

Absolutely, I thought, and so much depends on the kind of stories we seek to tell.

I told Gunn that his mention of narration reminded me of an early trip I had made to the Rock in one of his buses; the journey dominated by the video about *The Cattle King*.

—That was a glorification of the cattle industry, I added.—There must be other stories. Did the company ever show a much better video than that, *Uluru: the Anangu Story*?

—No, said Mr Gunn.

—Why not? I asked.

—I don't know, he said, it's the business of the Alice Springs office. Ask them.

I thought: I don't want to ask them. That would be to go back to the start all over again. We are at the Rock now. We have surely progressed to this point.

Mr Gunn said:—We're in the entertainment industry. We entertain with knowledge, anecdotes and stories.

I understood what he meant. People come to the Park to have a good time. They are on holiday. They have not necessarily come on a study tour. An operator like AAT Kings must deal with masses of people at many levels of cultural understanding (and misunderstanding). AAT Kings *are* serious about wanting to be good citizens of the Park, but entertainment is not the right word. It is irreconcilable with Anangu's anxious insistence that their Law be respected. A man like Tjamiwa would probably choke on the notion of entertainment.

What can sharing the Park really mean?

269

Gate-keeping

SOMETIMES IT MEANS saying 'no' to love. For years the Rock has been the point of pilgrimage to those who wished to bring their gifts of spirituality to it. But the cultural politics of the Park forbid that, especially when visitors are, in their enthusiasm, dubiously respectful of Anangu feelings. Two years after Handback Mutitjulu got a message from cosmic believers called Harmonic Convergence. They wanted to come together at the Rock in the manner of a vision had by their founder Jose Arguelles, from Boulder, Colorado USA, who saw, all around the world, thousands of people coming together in small groups at sunrise, on 16 August 1987. They would lay down their bodies in circular formations, heads towards a fire, feet outward, gazing skyward. They would surrender control to the Earth, allowing the forces of Life to use them as channels for the purification of the planet. 'This conscious bonding', they informed Mutitjulu, 'will support an evolutionary shift from fear to Love, and from separation to Unity.' This would happen at key planetary points such as the Kings Chamber of the Great Pyramid, Diamond Head in Hawaii, as well as, they hoped, Ayers Rock.

At the time, these worshippers were given conditional permission to come to the Rock. In 1990, Mr Vincent Selleck from Earthlink, the Australian outreach of Harmonic Convergence made another application. He proposed that their members converge on the Rock for meditation at Easter. According to Hopi prophecy their mental activity would activate the crystal fire image at the centre of the Rock, and the activation of these pathways would help heal the earth and its peoples. Arriving the same time, it seemed, would be Solara Antara, healer, hermit and mystic. Solara, her advance publicity said, studied the ancient religions when she was young. She had learnt the language of the Incas. She was a messenger to humanity from the Golden Solar Angels. She was organising a world event at the Great Pyramids. 'The purpose of this event is to open the Doorway of the 11:11 enabling the planet to move into a patterning of Oneness and freedom.'

—Put on your space helmet, said Willis, when the New Age mail hit his desk.

'Dear Vincent Selleck', he wrote, 'the traditional owners of Uluru strongly urge you to reconsider coming to Uluru at Easter to hold a gathering for meditation.' Willis explained that the owners did not believe in a worldwide network of sacred sites. 'They have very strong beliefs about the origin and significance of Uluru, Kata Tjuta and Atila that they and their ancestors have held for thousands of years. These beliefs are of profound importance to the traditional owners, and guide their actions and their decisions in every circumstance. They do not wish these beliefs to be pushed aside by people presenting their sacred places as part of Harmonic Convergence, or Earthlink or other religions. They request your support for their beliefs by not carrying out any activities within the Park or publishing any material that will compromise the integrity of their traditional beliefs about their sacred places.'

The issue here, is the question of religious tolerance. In the old days Roman Catholics held their mass on the top of the Rock. These days, as we have seen, Aboriginal Christians worship by the Rock; to judge from Tjamiwa's sermon, they have set ways of 'merging' religions, Christian Law with the Tjukurpa. One might say that the eclecticism of a 'world religion'—even the apparent mishmash of New Age cults—is not necessarily offensive, especially if it comes espousing dependence and respect for indigenous religions. It could be argued, other things being equal, that the community was being prohibitive as well as rather censorious. After all, how can one control what the spiritually oriented person thinks and feels when they come to the Rock? Spiritual practice, if we look at all cultures equally, is always at heart a private affair.

But other things are not equal. For one thing, the site in Aboriginal culture *is* everything, it is not simply a matter of Anangu forbidding *all* trespass. It is, however, a sacred truth of their culture that secrets of particular places are integral to their whole being, and their entire system of transmitting the spiritual life. There is an essential limit to sharing, since religious access requires an initiation into the ceremonies that *belong to the place*. The idea of a worldwide network of sites is irreconcilable with the local depth of Aboriginal belief. Theologically speaking, the worldwide embrace is a presumptuous possession. It is an imposition from without; no different, really, than any other colonial claim upon Aboriginal culture. Coming as it does on the heels of Handback at the moment of cultural recovery, when control over cultural property has been resecured, it is bound to be rejected. At present the 'liberal' issue of religious tolerance has to be seen in its political setting.

Besides, when the New Agers did come, they seem to have failed basic tests. Willis went on: 'The traditional owners also asked me to convey to you how much distress they have suffered as a result of bad behaviour by people attending other events such as Harmonic Convergence and Earthlink 88. This distress has been caused by such things as: participants entering restricted sacred sites without permission and in direct contradiction of the clearly expressed wishes of traditional owners; participants entering private living area of traditional owners at Mutitjulu Community without permission; participants purchasing alcohol for Aboriginal people at Yulara resort despite the specific request of traditional owners that alcohol not be purchased for Aboriginal people; participants ignoring Park management signs and entering environmental sensitive areas that they had been requested not to . . .'

In this correspondence, saying no to love involved the time and effort to compose the good reasons. It was easier with the crass commercial propositions. No, said the Park to the idea of a Mercedes Benz on top of the Rock, and to a chair-lift from base to cairn, and to the Rock as advertising prop for suntan lotion, motorbikes, running shoes.

And No to Uluru as a model paperweight.

Politics from the hip

SHARING THE PARK should surely have something do with sharing the wealth. But what is the wealth, and who is going to share what with whom? A surprising incident during the tour operators' course threw the politics of this question into high relief.

We were driving around the Rock in the bus. It was the second day of the course, and most students, it seemed to me, had settled very favourably into what Anangu had been trying to get across. Bob Seaborne, Park Manager, had the microphone. Seaborne is head of the Australian Nature Conservation Agency, which jointly manages the Park with the Mutitjulu community. He said joint management had been working well, overall.

This was because the Nature Conservation Agency had the right attitude towards Anangu, and Anangu were learning how to deal with the day-to-day business of a National Park such as looking after tracks, signs, fire management, planning larger new projects (such as the new road from Uluru to Kata Tjuta, to be called Kata Tjuta Road, as the community preferred, rather than the Lasseter Highway preferred by the tourist industry). It was such maintenance that secured visitor satisfaction, especially since the number of visitors was growing so fast each year. He thought that half a million visitors a year was probably the cut-off point. Beyond that the Park would have to turn people away. That is, visitors to the National Park would have to expect to book for their experiences at Uluru, as they must in the USA, where there is a waiting list of several years for entry to the most popular parks.

Seaborne's refrain was 'The Park is not managed primarily as a tourist attraction. World Heritage and Anangu cultural values come first.' His manner was quiet enough, while his organisational thrust was not. A historian of the Park would have recognised a certain shift of emphasis from the pre-Handback days when the Australian National Parks and Wildlife Service (ANPWS) tried to keep Anangu to the side.

When Seaborne had finished a man from the tourist industry felt the need to speak into the microphone. He was the retail marketing manager from the Ayers Rock Resort.

—I am sorry, he firmly asserted, that in all the talk about joint management, we at the Resort have hardly got a mention.

Seaborne would have replied but Yami Lester, Chairman of the Park's Board of Management, chipped in.

Lester said:—Ayers Rock Resort got seven or eight million last year, that's why you don't get a mention from me.

It was this that put everything into another key.

Yami Lester is not only Chairman of the Board of Management, he is Central Australia's senior spokesman for the Pitjantjatjara people. He was the first Chairman of the Pitjantjatjara Council. No history of the landrights movement could be written without Lester, who first became famous in the 1970s when the campaigns in South Australia began. A Yankuntjatjara man from the Musgrave Ranges, he was brought up on a cattle station not far from Ernabella. He was a boy when the British and Australian governments tested their nuclear weapons on Aboriginal land, not far away from Aboriginal communities. He has been blind since he was fifteen, perhaps because of the tests. After his loss of sight, he pressed on with his education. In his auto-biography he speaks with enormous gratitude for his Christian schooling and Christian instruction. At the same time he locates his life in the Tjukurpa: he grew up in Nguntaka country, where the Perentie lizard is the big story. Lester's English is good, his manners and easy warmth as gentle as any good Christian would want, and an Anangu politician par excellence—a man versed in all dimensions of community consultation, and capable when necessary of ferocious polemic on behalf of his people. He is a charming, quiet, strong man at ease in both cultures.

But here he was, just when things were cosy in the group, being less than charming.

As soon as the bus stopped, a tense group protested under the mulga trees.

Most forthright was the Publicity Officer from the Resort.—We are striving, she said, to educate our visitors and we put a very large focus on our *bond* with the Park. The relationship is mutually beneficial. We are not separate entities.

Lester had sat on a bench. He inclined his face towards Alexanderson, who was standing to his left.

—So, what are you sharing exactly?

A patient smile on his face.

—Facilities, said the Resort person, the tourist industry is something you see as a stepping stone, and we can assist you.

Lester:—From one point of view, we want a share in the wealth you people have, that's all.

Resort:—Your community took more than three million in gate money and you spread it over a small number of people. Both incomes are considerable.

A tour operator called out to Lester:—Private business works the world over. Why should profit-sharing be compulsory?

Lester said:—Easy. This is Aboriginal land . . . You go back and do your homework. This is sharing the Park.

Consternation in the group. This was Yami the activist, surely not Yami the conciliatory Chairman of the Board of Management. The unspoken question in the group was: how far should we thrash out the politics? To what extent can we afford to disagree about wealth while seeming to agree on the important things? Surely it should have been no great surprise to have to think about wealth. After all, if tourism makes one aspect of modern life conspicuous, it is the inequality of riches on the planet. But who wanted to spoil a Park by going on about that?

Yami Lester said:—The Aboriginal people have the culture, the language, they are going to be here a long time. If a company comes only interested in the short term, they are like a mining company. We got to get some piece of the cake.

A brief history of umbrage

THE CAKE WAS the Ayers Rock Resort, or Yulara as it was called when opened in 1984. Its renaming took place in 1991, in conjunction with refinancing and new management. Initially its consortium had been largely financed by the Northern Territory government, and the Resort had been geared to the top end of the tourist market. This seemed to make a great deal of sense at the time, as tourism became a major growth industry, very largely on the backs of overseas travellers. Northern Territory tourism prospered, but business at a remote resort like Yulara was less straightforward. While visitors to the Park grew steadily (from 133,101 in 1984–5 to 237,943 in 1991), about two-thirds of them were from overseas, mainly Japan, Germany and the USA respectively. Yulara's debt structure did not allow it to pay its way. After the 1980s boom, subsidising losses at places like the Sheraton became untenable. Forty per cent of the resort complex was bought by Pacific Hotels, and its new Managing Director, Wayne Kirkpatrick, set about cost-cutting and the task of remarketing.

The marketing involved renaming. Yulara was no longer Yulara. The Resort was the Ayers Rock Resort so that the Rock could be better marketed overseas. 'Uluru' would appear in some brochures and not in others (it would creep back later, as Kirkpatrick came to appreciate the feelings of Anangu and Park Management). The Sheraton was no longer the Sheraton. In a flight of romance it became 'Sails in the Desert': a flight that works, considering the beauty of the place, and the astonishing oasis it is, wedged into the dunes. The other renamings firmly capitalise on Outback ethnic. The Maisonettes became Spinifex Lodge. The Red Centre Motel became the Pioneer Outback Lodge, and was refurbished accordingly: galvanised iron and wooden posts and rails for façade and reception area; saddles and saddlebags on the restaurant wall. Artefacts from the pastoral industry have replaced those cartoons of malu that so offended Tjamiwa three years ago. That seems, however, to have been fortuitous. The renaming and realignment of images in the Resort have taken place with no particular regard for Anangu opinion. This is not surprising, considering that Yulara is not on Aboriginal land, and has never been economically connected to Aboriginal interests.

Even more expressive of the economic independence of the multi-million dollar

Resort from the Mutitjulu community was the financial restructuring under Pacific Hotels. Only weeks before the tour operators' course, the Resort had been negotiating with life-insurance companies based in Melbourne. In January 1994 the Resort sold 40 per cent of its shares to investors headed by National Mutual, leaving the remaining 60 per cent in the hands of the Northern Territory government.

This was the immediate backdrop to Yami Lester's bitter interjection. What he was alluding to was the lack of opportunity given to Aboriginal business interests. He considered that Anangu had been cut out of the deal. His confounded and somewhat troubled audience under the mulga trees were not to know this at the time, because Lester was not spelling it out. There was another business scenario he had up his sleeve. Soon after the course he would approach the Northern Territory government to buy into the remaining 60 per cent of the Resort, acting on behalf of interests at Docker River and Erldunda as well as a few individuals at Mutitjulu. At the time of writing these negotiations are unresolved.

What the negotiations would entail, however, is historically momentous. For the first time Aborigines at the Rock would have a major financial stake in tourism. They had lost that chance in the past for one reason or another. In the very early days, for instance, even before Harney was sent to the Rock to supervise visitors to the Aboriginal reserve, William Little had in 1947 suggested that the reserve Aborigines no longer used in the country near the Rock would not be harmed if it were taken for tourists. In 1953 the Northern Territory government tried to persuade the Federal Minister of Territories that the Rock (and the Olgas) 'no longer have any religious or other significance for the present generation of natives'. It was this kind of reasoning that justified the excising of the Park from the reserve in 1958. Anangu were not consulted. From tourism they eked out marginal benefits through the sale of art and artefacts, all that bargain 'abasement' business that Harney was so attuned to en route to the Rock.

More direct benefits did not come until as late as 1968. In that year the settlement at Docker River was established, partly instigated by Northern Territory authorities that wished to see the tourist track between Alice Springs and the Rock (places like Angas Downs, Erldunda and Ebenezer) clear of the unseemly aspects of Aboriginal trading. The Docker River settlement, in the heart of the Pitjantjatjara homelands, suited Anangu down to the ground. It affirmed their cultural confidence, including their reach into business affairs. The Docker River Social Club saw the business potential at the Rock, where they built the Ininti store. Managed by Europeans on behalf of Anangu shareholders, the Ininti store was, by 1972, the nucleus of a permanent Anangu community at the Rock.

The Whitlam Labor government coming into office in 1972 in full support of Aboriginal land rights was an important moment in several respects. It was the year when 200 Aborigines gathered for ceremonial purposes at the Rock. Those traditional ceremonies were also a political statement of ownership. By 1972, the federal government was also looking at the first proposal for a new tourist village outside the Park. The idea of a Yulara was in the air, very much backed by the Northern Territory government and tourist interests. Immediately opinion divided as to whether (and if so how, and to what extent) Anangu were to be involved in its development. Various parties claimed to be representing Anangu opinion on tourist matters, but Aboriginal organisations such as the Central Land Council (CLC) were unable to seize the initiative. The Northern Territory government put up a Master Plan for the Rock that expressed attitudes that would have done credit to Ernest Giles. The Master Plan warned:

> 'Sacred' and 'Secret', two words indiscriminately used by Aborigines, often lead to false interpretations. Too many objects and ceremonies and places have been wrongly classified as sacred objects. The Aborigines do not hope to gain a childish sense of importance by using these words, but they often use them in the wrong contexts. It is so easy to say 'it's secret', and so avoid giving a precise reply that would be difficult to formulate for someone unfamiliar with English. In addition these words can constitute a magic formula for increasing the commercial value of a perfectly commonplace locality or piece of information.

Eventually, it was the federal government's Ayers Rock Advisory Committee that selected the sites for Yulara after having them approved by Anangu. But that process of consultation left out discussion of the full implications of such a village, and the practical business options for Anangu. Through the CLC Anangu were pursuing their rights to land at Uluru, while at the same time reassuring the white business world that they did not want to obstruct the future of tourism. The 'town' of Yulara had become a legal reality, but the future of the Park still had to be worked out.

In 1981, when the Northern Territory government called for tenders to develop Yulara Village, the manager of Ininti Store negotiated with the consortium to prepare a proposal for a complex with a 200-room motel and for several businesses run by Malpa Trading, the company set up buy the Docker River Social Club. Malpa would have managed or leased a supermarket, laundry, artefact shop, opal jewellery store, bakery, newsagent, chemist, bank and post office. There would also have been an Aboriginal camp near the complex. The Northern Territory government rejected this proposal when it emerged that Anangu also wanted to continue to live at the Rock, and keep the Ininti store and garage. Malpa then sought the service-station business at Yulara, but failed to come to an agreement with Mobil, which looked at the business potential of the supermarket and arts and crafts shop at Yulara, only to find Yulara's terms unattractive.

This is a crude summary of events that resulted in Anangu feeling, from a business point of view, remote from Yulara. That distance also involved a battle of wills about where exactly Anangu would live. Ideally, the Northern Territory government wanted, as tourist planners had, for Aborigines to live away from the Rock. When the Northern Territory Conservation Commission planned Yulara they built a little village for Anangu of ten houses, a community centre with pool, a shelter for craft workers, visitor facilities and ablution block. It also seems that the Northern Territory government had more than that in mind. There was to be a lookout for tourists at Yulara: from a spot on the dunes telescopes were to be trained on three points of interest. The Rock. Kata Tjuta. And the Anangu village! The Aboriginal village was going to be one of the tourist attractions.

No-one went to live at Yulara. Mutitjulu, tucked in near the Rock, in the Park that was to be handed back in 1985 would become *the* Aboriginal community, despite the pull the Resort might have. Besides, there was another difficulty about Yulara being the living place. It had a grog shop—the Ernest Giles Tavern (now the Yulara tavern).

Even before the Resort was built this had been a worry to Anangu. At the first meeting of the Ayers Rock Advisory Committee, men such as Paddy Uluru wanted an end to the supply of alcohol to his people camped at the Rock. But this suggestion was ignored (as was the request for houses, European payment for use of the Park, and job opportunities as Park Rangers). With the arrival of the Ernest Giles Tavern the problem looked acute. In 1983, the Docker River community and the Pitjantjatjara Council objected to its takeaway licence. The Northern Territory Liquor Commission accepted the arguments—that it would result in alcohol abuse by Aboriginal people and trouble communities in the Pitjantjatjara homelands. Two years of appeal (by the licensee) and counter-appeal (by the Pitjantjatjara Council) followed.

Much has therefore moved Anangu to live 'away' at Mutitjulu. The economic future of tourism in the Park would have to be worked out with Anangu living in the Park, albeit discreetly, privately, as they wanted to, keeping the brashness and bustle and perhaps even the golden opportunities of tourism at arm's length, while all the time exercising their right to majority participation in Park Management.

Desert dividends

ALL THIS WAS behind Yami Lester's outburst. A history of lost opportunities that presently co-exists with a certain ambivalence towards the seemingly irreversible business of tourism. But few in the little crowd who had his attention under the trees could be expected to know the full story, in which Lester had been a key participant.

Consequently, his remarks were received as polemic, rather than history. Lester was seen as an uncompromising landrights activist, rather than the tough-minded diplomat that he is, who is as forgiving as he is shrewd.

Most tour operators had another big gap in their knowledge. This concerned the *direct* economic benefits the Mutitjulu community actually gets from the Park. When the Resort's Publicity Officer said that the Mutitjulu got three million dollars a year from gate money, she was wrong. It is not the Mutitjulu community that gets a cut of the gate money, but the Uluru–Kata Tjuta Land Trust, administered by the Central Land Council. The Trust receives 20 per cent of the gate money. In other words, if the number of people entering the Park each year approaches 3 million (including children), there is about $500,000 to divide. As far as Anangu at the Rock are concerned, that is the main point: Mutitjulu must throw its hat into the ring with *all* other interested parties, who might live far and wide from Uluru, and argue for a share of that money. Most years Mutitjulu gets around 30 per cent of the Land Trust's share for its community projects such as the church, garage, women's centre and so on. In 1993, $121,000 was left for community purposes. In addition individuals living at Mutitjulu might receive up to $10,000 or so at a time to purchcase motor vehicles.

Behind Yami Lester's polemic was discontent with the system. Apart from his barb at the Resort, he felt that the Central Land Council could do much more to protect Mutitjulu's rights to proceeds that might be used to develop the community.

This brings us to another gap in most people's knowledge: the actualities of Mutitjulu's financial condition, and the extent to which it indirectly benefits from tourism. It is fitting that such information is not widely known. Mutitjulu, like any other community, has a right to its own financial affairs, just as it has to privacy. For a people who were considered wards of the state only forty years ago both rights have been a long time coming. Still, their group finances are matters of public concern, if only because most of the community members are in some way significantly dependent on social security payments. About 55 per cent of total cash income comes from family allowances, pensions and unemployment benefits. The rest comes from activities related to tourism—either by direct employment or commercial activity. The Ininti Store, Maruku Arts and Crafts and work in the Park itself earn cash and provide jobs at Mutitjulu. It must be added, however, that we are not talking about much cash, or that many jobs. On the last comprehensive survey of Mutitjulu's financial affairs, the per capita cash income per fortnight is a mere $180 in *total* cash income, including social security payments. That was in 1987, and there is no real reason to record major proportional changes, even though there are probably more jobs available than before. By any standard, the people of Mutitjulu are among the poorest in the nation.

Meanwhile, on that oasis of conspicuous consumption, the Ayers Rock Resort, with its 1993–4 turnover of about $50 million, about 350 non-Aboriginals are employed on award wages and conditions. Over the years, some opportunities have come up for Aboriginal employment, but the Resort has tended to offer Anangu jobs in service rather than tourist industries. Recently the Resort offered an employment training program for Anangu in tourism. At the time of writing this is being considered. If Anangu take it up, it will involve some change of attitude on their part, because they prefer to shy away from most front-line jobs in the tourist industry.

This, very largely, is how the cultural centre came about. At the time of writing a major project is being constructed near the Ranger's Station. Designed by Melbourne architect Greg Burgess after much consultation with Mutitjulu, it is meant to be an information, presentation and even performance place for Anangu who do want to be involved in tourism. It will hugely upgrade the present display at the Station, and promises to eclipse the role of the information centre presently at the Resort. In effect, it gives full expression to Anangu's clear preference to keep mass tourism in general, and the Resort in particular, at arm's length.

But there is an exception to the rule. There is one place at the Resort where Anangu have been regularly known to work. From time to time they have brought their art and craft for sale to the Sails in the Desert. More pointedly, they have fitted into the hotel's scheme of artists in residence: they have set down their materials in the foyer and worked there, in the full light of public scrutiny. For many years full-time residents of Mutitjulu tended to avoid the spot; it was Anangu from further afield who came in to paint. As a small sign of change, local residents are there these days. The afternoon we got back from that talk under the mulga trees I spotted Cassidy Uluru himself on the flash tiles, his head down, diligently painting away. I doubt whether many of the operators on the course knew who he was exactly, or that *any* overseas guests had an idea of his significance to the whole place. But there he was, a quiet sign of social change, maybe.

The map says it's twenty-five kilometres between the Resort and Mutitjulu. It sounds near enough, but the social distance, like the difference in economic fortune, is immense: they are separated by a cultural divide as vast as the sand dunes.

Boundary riders in uniform

THERE WERE OTHER WALKS for the tour operators, who had a chance to see something of the way in which Anangu most directly benefit from tourism. Jobs as park rangers—the training program for Anangu—is the main source of income at Mutitjulu, and the working of this scheme remains the most poignant expression of sharing, with all its cultural difficulties.

In the day-to-day business of the Park, trainee rangers often accompany rangers from the ANCC. To go on any of their walks is instructive in many ways, partly because they are slow going. This is their charm. You can't help but be reminded of the pressure our culture brings to bear to do things in a rush: to acquire new knowledge, and quickly. But they are slow going also because of the pains of translation. Bilingual progress is made by Anangu speaking in their language, the ranger translating and then maybe Anangu trying some English. You become excruciatingly aware of the shyness of Anangu, and their rudimentary literacy in both languages.

Since Handback dozens of Anangu have had some experience of the training program. Work in the ranger service is the biggest money earner for those who want to do it, and who stick at it. Over the years, it has by no means been an easy program to work. For one thing there is so much to learn from the white fella about law enforcements, safety and security patrols, rabbit control, film and photography guidelines, seed propagation, drip-irrigation installation—all the things that go into maintaining and protecting a national park. Trainees must improve their language and social skills, including such basics as how to tell the time, and why there needs to be a compromise between European notions of punctuality and reliability, and the Anangu concept of timelessness. The job requires steady application—difficult enough for any shy person—much more so when language skills and cultural differences create other barriers. A young ranger immediately benefits from the pay packet and status, but at the same time, must contend with a certain isolation from peers that goes with it. The turn-over is high, and when vacancies for trainee positions come up, less than half of those eligible actually apply.

It was not until 1993 that the first Aboriginal graduated as a Ranger. His name is Leroy Lester, Yami's son.

Leroy, 27, is like his father, easy in both cultures. His English is strong. He got his education from correspondence school and the School of the Air when he was a boy in South Australia, and later from primary and secondary schools in Adelaide and Alice Springs—a mobility very much driven by his father's activism in the 1970s and 1980s.

—I thought I'd be a ringer, but I've ended up a Ranger, he said on his graduation day, referring to the job he might have had on his father's cattle station.

('It's a boy', Yami cried when his son was born, 'a bouncing baby boy. Another boundary rider, just like me.')

Leroy was 19 on the day of Handback, and had just pulled out of secondary school in Alice because he couldn't hack it any more. He wanted odd jobs. Was Handback day exciting?—Oh yeah, he says laconically.

After the odd jobs, including some translating work with the Royal Commission into Black Deaths in Custody, he became a trainee ranger. The attraction?

—Mainly the land and the open spaces. The bush was familiar like the idea of driving a Toyota, and protecting the animals. It's just that there was no cattle, that's all.

Yami Lester and son Leroy: boundary riders of two cultures.

—And, he says, as if changing gear somewhere inside, I knew I'd be under the spotlight if I did well in the Public Service, you know. I'd achieve something out of that. With the whole world watching us.

Had he been initiated?

—Yeah, he says, hesitantly. He had been to ceremonies at Docker River.

—I felt that I had to go, getting this job, and everything. From the Aboriginal perspective, it would give me a chance to pick up things later on . . . and to carry on the things my grandfather, Paddy Uluru, knew.

Then his voice drops: —And also to let our [Mutitjulu] people know, you know, too. 'Oh, you're scared,' they say. They sort of reject you in a way. So when you go, everything changes. With the sacred sites around the Rock, I couldn't go in before; I had to stay outside the fence. I can go into the caves now, and it's good for my job as well.

At the same time he speaks of himself 'as a bit of a Christian'.

281

—You've still got it in the back of your head.

So what is his view of those religious people who come from all over the world to see the Rock as a universally sacred place?

—You can look at it both ways, he says.—If another culture thinks it is sacred, then it makes it more special. Then again, it could be 'not for them to come in' type of thing. These people from here [Mutitjulu] might take it the other way and say, 'No, keep out, stay away'. But overall it makes it more powerful, I reckon.

Leroy wants better formal education to be provided at Mutitjulu. He wants land care and health programs extended, and promoted on TV so that overseas visitors come with some knowledge of the place. With regard to the nomadic habits of the Mutitjulu community he says:—Well, there needs to be more binding up, seeing the future at home. But then, in the same breath, as if realising his view flies in the face of traditional culture:—People just have to go, you know. You can't stop them from going.

In his support for the cultural centre he sounds like a high-flyer.—It's going to have a lot of visual gear and a lot of laser displays on the wall, and it's going to really bring the tours down to earth. I reckon people will lap it up.

And so on. I was interviewing Leroy for a newspaper when I met him. His thought and feeling seemed to swing from one culture to another, and as a result, I felt he embodied so much of what was happening in the management of the Park. It would be unfair to commit him to any political program. He was new to the formal interview and was thinking on his feet. He describes himself as a stirrer as Yami Lester does in his autobiography. But I'm not sure that the term finally applies to either of them. Leroy makes no grand political statements, and Yami, who says that his mentor is Nelson Mandela, is a man who prefers to think positively. Both men are boundary riders in black and white worlds.

Straight talking

THE TOUR OPERATORS did not met Leroy Lester, which was a pity. To the picture they were building up of Anangu life at the Rock, it might have added some necessary complexity. They did not visit the Mutitjulu community either. Anangu would have seen it as beyond the call of duty to joint management. Instead, Anangu came to the tour operators. They met them at the Ranger's Station, making the journey into the Resort, and closing the gap between the two cultures in order to sit down in their conference room at Sails in the Desert.

It was back at Sails, in the fraternity of group discussion, that people recovered from the agitation under the mulga trees. A few Anangu would sit quietly out front, along with Yami Lester (now on his best behaviour), with Jon Willis or Julian Barry tending to lead the discussion. All manner of topics were raised. The history of white contact in the Centre. Anangu perspectives on tourism. The state of health and education. Anangu concern about their own community. The latter surfaced in a quiet way, when the matter of domestic violence came up.

Willis spoke with anguish about the way the law made it hard to help people in times of crisis.

Yami Lester said that he thought traditional law should not be used to protect male offenders. Violent men should be prosecuted under white law, be made responsible. More broadly he said: — Our people gotta change, we've gotta make a move somehow . . . our kids are not learning that second language. It's getting worse.

The atmosphere in the room was one of sympathetic tolerance. Paternalism about 'the problems' Aborigines were having did not show its face. This, I thought, was a good thing, and perhaps even a result of the course itself, the trust it had established between Aborigines and those who hardly had the chance to meet them before. The simple business of talking (and walking!) together can sometimes humanise perspectives. If racist stereotyping was still present, it was not speaking up.

Paradoxically, however, those who knew most about Anangu life in the Park tended to go quiet as well. This was, after all, a venue to presenting as much as possible in a positive light, to be educationally constructive rather than anything else. It was not the place to speak the deepest worries, even if the sore spots were, to some extent, in the open.

Julian Barry, for instance, has strong feelings about Mutitjulu. Having worked in other Aboriginal communities, he says that it is a symptom of Mutitjulu's troubles that it has not been able to provide for itself as well as it might. Other places on Pitjantjatjara land not only have better schools, adult-education centres and homeland centres, they probably have more working Toyotas, and an effective system of police aids.

But it was not possible to say much about this with out detracting, perhaps, from the undeniable achievements in the Park.

Then there was the brawl in the carpark of the tavern that happened a few nights before the conference. According to some accounts forty or fifty Anangu were involved and they had wilfully damaged one of the tour coaches. Was this simply drunken anger? Did the event (or even the recounting of it) say anything about Anangu's deeper attitudes to tourism? No-one was talking about that in the group either.

Drinking at the tavern remains an unresolved problem. Today the rule is that grog not be sold to anyone living on or travelling to Aboriginal land. It is a rule that suits non-drinking Anangu and community staff, but drinkers do not like it and it causes problems for the Resort. Tourists are hassled or threatened to buy grog for Anangu; more Anangu want to drink inside the Tavern, and Tavern staff do not like it when they get rowdy. The Liquor Commission is worried that such arrangements may be breaking the Racial Discrimination Act. The Race Discrimination Commissioner is currently considering whether an exemption can be made under the Conventions to the Act that would allow this prohibition to continue on the grounds that it is a so-called 'special measure' designed to protect the culture of embattled minorities.

From Barry's point of view the brawl was yet more evidence of how far the whole place is from being a dry area. The tour operators might have been shocked to know how seriously Barry took the matter. In fact, he had just recently written to the Northern Territory Liquor Commissioner about the Curtin Springs Roadhouse, and the huge, regular quantities of grog Anangu were apparently buying from it. The worry was on behalf of drivers, Mutitjulu people suffering constant violence and disruption, and tourists. Here is a grim picture of life out on the road to the Park. Barry wrote:

> With extreme regularity, people from the NT, SA and WA are drinking at Curtin Springs, then buying alcohol and driving intoxicated west along the Lasseter Highway, south to the SA Anangu Pitjantjatjara lands, and east. There are drunken people at Curtin Springs many days of the week, if not most days of the week.
>
> On Friday October 31 at about 6 p.m. I left Yulara to travel to Alice Springs. Less than 51 km from Yulara I came across a car that had flattened a road sign while skidding out of control across both lanes. Those in the car were very drunk and I am sure that the driver lost control of the vehicle because he was drunk. Between that point and Curtin Springs I counted 10 vehicles, most of which were overloaded and were swerving noticeably. Some were swerving well out of their lanes. Many of the drivers were holding VB cans and I am sure that many of them were drunk.
>
> It is common knowledge among residents of Mutitjulu community that on Thursdays, Fridays and Saturdays, many cars are driven by intoxicated people from Curtin Springs to Mutitjulu. Following my return from Alice Springs I rang Mr Wayne Kirkpatrick (Managing Director, Ayers Rock Resort Company), and Mr Mike Gunn (Manager at AAT Kings Ayers Rock). Both agreed with my observation that with extreme regularity, people are drinking to Curtin Springs and then buying alcohol and driving inebriated west along Lasseter Highway. Both recounted near accidents that they had been involved in, involving drunks, on the Lasseter Highway in the last few weeks . . .

'It is quite remarkable', Barry added, 'that there has not yet been a horror bus accident between Curtin Springs and Yulara.'

Naturally, Barry's letter did not come up in the discussions. There is a time and place for everything. But he is right to fret as he does. Anangu worry about tourists doing the climb. Objectively, they have more reason to worry about the most mundane of mishaps which could turn pilgrimage into tragedy.

Poolside at sails

AND NOW THE course is over.

It is late afternoon, and everyone is here on the glorious lawns by the aqua water. Poolside at Sails, formerly the Sheraton.

As the light gently pinkens a dozen cockatoos glide from the yard arm of the elegant rigging to drink, their crests fluffed from the waters of the pool. The cheeky buggers. Any minute they will be tucking into the hors d'oeuvres. Do they like buffalo? Marinated emu? Malu? Oh, the thought of a galah swooping on a titbit of malu— what an end to this story that would be!

There have been several endings already.

Yami has made peace with everyone.

He has thanked us for coming.

He has given every operator a certificate for passing the course. Yes, everyone, including the bus driver who thinks so badly of Anangu in Alice Springs. And the drivers who have hardly spoken in three days, whose deeper attitudes are unknown.

Mike Gunn, boss of AAT Kings, the man who believes in narrative and entertainment, has thanked the Park for running the course; and Tony Press, the chief from the Darwin Office of the Nature Conservation Agency said that only a couple of years ago there would have been a big fuss made about compulsory accreditation, but look at the peace of everything now. A golden light settles by the pool as we take cheer from the cultural harmonies of tourism in the Park.

There is soft drink, beer and champagne, all flowing freely with the self-congratulatory words. And why not! It's not every day that black and white meet with a mind to learning from each other.

For Anangu are here too, many more of them than have been seen before on the course. In force, they travelled to these 'permanent waters' of the Resort. A tight, shy group has arrived with Julian Barry and camped near him on the lawns, where Yami Lester has positioned himself. The less reticent—Andy Panpanpalala and his wife Molly, and Edith Richards, are a little apart, but not so removed that a tour operator could not go up to them and say thank you, which a few do. A few of the people have changed and have fresh ranger gear on, just as the operators have appeared looking their best. Women wear dresses and perfume. The men have stepped out in fresh shirts. Even a couple of the AAT Kings men are out of their flight-deck gear and into something more comfortable.

The beer runs out; the champagne keeps going. The mood *bubbles* along.

So radiant is the light in the sky above the Sails of the Desert hotel that there is no reason to doubt any of the ideals that inform the whole management of the Park. The two groups on the lawns — Anangu and the operators — never actually mix as the sun goes down, but the rose pink of goodwill is everywhere. I feel as if I'm drinking to celebrate some kind of final visit to the Park. I'm sitting with Yami Lester, and have introduced him to my daughter Vanessa. This is another good ending: on the first trip to the Rock, her brother meets Tjamiwa; now she meets Lester, who reminds her of her grandfather. His gentle strength. His management of tough politics and civility. I should not tell Yami this, it could be embarrassing, but I do. Oh, is that right, he laughs, and lets the waiter stoop down and pour him another champagne.

Across the splendid lawns the feeling is: we have all worked hard at being able to have this drink together, and *we are enjoying it*.

As dusk gently descends, people are beginning to drift off. Andy and Molly and Edith have slipped off into the bar. They, I see, like a drink too. (Anything we say about 'their' drinking has to be tempered, doesn't it, by how much we in white culture enjoy it too.) All the Kings men are wandering away as well, and swinging black motorbike helmets as they go, heading, it seems, for a Harley Davidson ride around the Rock. The day is slowing down, while for others it is about to speed up. I ask Yami if he wants another champagne and he says yes, is there a waiter anywhere there? He has his face to the West, as if he wanted to catch the last of the sun. There is, I say, a waiter on his way. And there is too, a young man in black trousers. Could you keep the champagne on for a little while yet, says Willis, who has joined us on the grass. Certainly Sir, says the waiter, as he bends around the group, the serviette at the neck of the bottle tufting like a cocky's crest. It will be dark very soon and all the poolside lights will go on and you have to say it, even though there are worries. They will light the lamps and you'll say, despite everything, *things are looking up*.

Yep.

Up!

Sails, stunning oasis that she is, gets to you.

PART 3 **Beyond the Rock**

The sleeping clan

YOU CAN ALWAYS TRAVEL further than your place of pilgrimage. Central Australia invites that. There are destinations that have the pull of a centre. But there are also other places that call you onto the next place, further 'out'. The spread of the country is an invitation to nomadism. Pilgrims, if they have gained riches along the way, must travel lightly, or must ever refine them as they carry on.

What is beyond the Rock? Everything, and nothing. If you are Anangu, everything. The songlines go out from the Rock only to meet others coming in from the West. As the Aboriginal dreamings go, there is little sense of 'beyond'; the country is sung up and down, backwards and forwards, even though there is a sense that as you go west, further into the sand dunes that become almost uninhabitable desert, the singing might dwindle.

The nothing can belong to the white fella's dreaming, depending on the white fella. This is the kind of country into which Giles went, and from which he only just returned. Ever since, his saga has fed the mythology of stoicism. There is another mythology—'legend'—that lives beyond the Rock, as it is tied to more recent times (where history is shaped into the dreaming fiction of myth). Beyond the Rock, fortune hunters have gone seeking gold, travelling as lustfully into the setting sun as Lasseter did over sixty years ago, when he pressed on into the unforgiving and luminously beautiful country that finally defeated him.

You can't go beyond the rock without crossing the tracks of the legend, tracks which intersect as surely as those of night creatures in the dunes, the momentous history of Anangu's encounter with the white man. Harney gave us the lead to the possible wholeness of the story. One year, while he was a ranger at the Rock he waited for the tourist season to be over so that he could go further inland with his 'raggle-taggle friends'. He was talking about the nomads who had come to the Rock by camel. The blackfella had inherited the lesser luxury, the camel, now that the motor car was the white man's preferred means of travel. A man called Winmardi and his clan had come into the Rock on sorry business (a funeral), and Harney negotiated a deal whereby he and Peter Severin might travel back with them. At first Winmardi did not see the sense of the idea. Who would want to go back into such dry country in a year of drought? Harney did, he had been dreaming of such a journey for a long time.

You get a sense of the journey as soon as you are west of Kata Tjuta. The great domes all sit up in a row as if to say a grand goodbye, they herald departure as much as they might herald arrival, assuming you are going to come back. 'Often our bush track', says Harney, 'led into sundowner way where, in a sense, we were following the trail of Giles the explorer. With him the land up ahead was a blank, with us an array of maps mixed up with the nomads' bushcraft which had been handed to them by tradition.'

And so they went, a clan on their camels, the white men thrown back in time again. It is slow going, and Harney is charmingly happy with that. When it is hot they rest; the resting place might become the camp for the night. As they go the raggle-taggle friends are hunting and foraging. 'Each morning', Harney says, 'everyone would go into the bush empty-handed but as the day went on things appeared, as though by magic, in their hands. Nothing that was edible was omitted from the daily fare: rabbits, cats, numberless small rodent mice, goannas, kangaroos, bowls of honey-ants.'

A movable feast. For Harney, a movable feast of reflection. He was struck by the antiquity of images that unfolded before him. One of his greatest memories was the sight of an Aboriginal woman called Katie. 'She had two camels and leading them in from the bush, where they were hobbled out, she always reminded me of some Biblical scene, especially when we were camped under a mountain which reflected the rays of the rising sun.'

At night, Harney lay in his swag thinking about the camp they had made in this desert. Around him were the small campfires, where the mother cooked what they had gathered during the day. Throughout the night there was always someone—an elder—tending a fire, keeping watch. 'Watching him as he peered around or chanted some of his tribal chants my mind, in imagination, would go back to that time when the Elders

Kata Tjuta from the West.

and shepherds watched their flocks against the enemies of the night. They were guardians ready to give the call to arms should they hear something from the material or spiritual world . . . I would peer up into the heavens to realise that here in this scene was the beginning of our great religions. The sleeping clan, the watchman peering around and trying to solve the riddle of it all.'

Every one cried

AFTER MANY TRIPS to the Rock I finally get to go West. I seem to have heard so much about the Petermanns. This was the range—another mountain range in Central Australia—180 kilometres away from the National Park, where there is no commercial accommodation, and where the bitumen ran out. Since 1968 a Pitjantjatjara community has lived at Docker River, or Kikingkura as it's called by those who belong to the estate. About 200 people chose to leave settlements at Papunya and Areyonga to return to their land: a momentous occasion, a time of great celebration and ceremony that was reminiscent of the 1930s, when the white man last saw huge congregations of Aborigines in the area. More than the areas around Uluru, which was once Yankuntjatjara country, Kikingkura is the old Pitjantjatjara heartlands, the country lived in before the white man, before the droughts tempted people into the food offerings of the white man. West of the Rock is the old frontier, the last of the frontier where, as recently as the 1930s, men like Walter Gill could set off in quest of a 'forgotten tribe'.

I had also heard 'The Petermanns' spoken about in mining discussions at the Central Land Council; not just in connection with the 'Lasseter Loonies' who applied for exploration licences year in year out, but also in the light of more realistic mineral prospects. Uranium perhaps. Docker River was the place Jon Willis had rushed off to that Saturday afternoon, responding to his Anangu obligations as an initiate. Docker River was the place the carloads of grog were supposed to go back to, when certain grog outlets were doing what they should not do. Docker River was also close to the cave, the white fella's 'sacred' site, where Lasseter walled up. In more ways than one, in riddlesome ways, it seemed to me, Docker River was the end of the line.

The bitumen ends as soon as you turn your back on Kata Tjuta. The sand dunes set in and the ghost of labouring camels are grunting across them as the four-wheel drive effortlessly speeds west. Lizards and goannas are sitting up like cocky on the ruts, their white throats exposed to our charge. Then they are gone, back into the spinifex and flowers when we are past. The flowers. It is October and they are everywhere. Pools of mauve from the parakeelya, sprinklings of white and yellow from daisies, the wild swish of pale yellow from the grevilleas beside the road as if someone has planted them as an avenue. Occasionally, further into the woodland of mulga and desert oak, the exquisite lilac of the hibiscus that is the cousin of Sturt's Desert Rose: the same stoical papery petals, and the dripping ruby stamen of nectar at its centre.

If this is a desert, mate, then I'm as loony as Lasseter (which is all very well to say when you're not walking in quest of water).

Yet the dunes continue, and the red earth of the road as you go along seem to harden in dryness. You drive for an hour and the dunes out there seem to be higher. The white fella's topographic map says that to the north of the road they average 11 metres high; to the south, 12 metres. Would Giles have felt that difference? Would camels?

Good old Giles, he is every place it seems, where you are going steadily ahead into tough country.

There should be a verb made out of his simple name.

Giled.

Gone west.

You cross Armstrong Creek, and sure enough, it is a creek, though one with a wide bed, ready for the once-in-a-decade flooding.

In the distance, now, a low range. You can see it from the top of some dunes.

Irving Creek.

South of that, an Aboriginal naming. Puta-Puta.

'This Puta-puta river,' Harney says, 'they explained to me, was created by the women of the "Kurakardi" totem when they came from Kunpingin to chant the road and country northward towards the Wanambi place of Piltardi.'

Twenty minutes later, Shaw Creek—the widest one so far, a riverbed in its proportions, a course that belongs to higher ground. For it runs north–south, from the Blood Range into the Petermanns, which are upon us now. The main range runs parallel with the road: a long range gaining in height as we drive further into what seems a valley, the red river of the road enclosed by the slopes, the big sleepy lizards of the ranges. They remind me of the Mann Ranges down south, except that they are less green. The lizards are tawny and, yes, there is an occasional glint to their scales that might, with a certain stretch of the imagination, be described as golden.

Lasseter's Cave comes all of a sudden. You go over yet another incongruous Western naming—Chirnside Creek—and there you are, a low point in the range where there is a turn-off. A little camping ground, a sign for the tourists, the cave. It is tucked around the corner overlooking the wide bed of the Hull River.

It is barely a cave, but its fifteen metres into rock must have been some shelter. Harney and his mates had their photos taken from the riverbed, which makes the cave look more like a vantage point, more a clever, strategic retreat than it is. Harney says this place in the river was known to the Aborigines as *djundi*, thigh.

Did Lasseter know that?

293

The diary that he is supposed to have kept in the summer of 1931 shows him writing down some of the local language, applying his mysterious intelligence to simple acts of communication with the people who might have saved his life if he had been more trusting of them. Like Burke at Coopers Creek, he could not sufficiently bring himself to join them. Lasseter thought so-called 'Warty Arse', one of the lesser men of the tribe, and the truly senior man to be the one who did all the talking for the group. But the latter was a man of somewhat unsound mind, whose garrulousness the clan humoured. 'Warty Arse' was a venerated elder. The help that Lasseter was getting, unknown to him, was a matter of considered judgement by the peoples whose land he was on, and whose birth rights he would have claimed in an instant if he had found the reef.

'Poor Lasseter', says Harney. A natural feeling to have when you look in the cave and imagine Lasseter's last days—sick, blind, alone, poignantly alone in his white skin. Harney is also speaking up for the simple courage of prospectors whose dreams got them this far. I can see that. The trouble is, if there is a moral to the Lasseter legend, it is not about simple courage, but rather a weird tale of wilful megalomania. Between October 1930 and January 1931 Lasseter was out here, in the enveloping inferno mainly because he distrustfully dismissed his companion and set off to the West, came back, and then set off again. This is known, and much else is a matter of silence and conjecture, circumstantial reconstruction. Whatever the trustworthy details, he ends up on Hull River or Boomerang Creek as the Pitjantjatjara called it during that time. His camels have bolted, and he is stranded with some of the provisions that they drop. He walls up at the cave (*tjunti*) and is said to have told his diary that the people who were sparing him and feeding him were treacherous. Take this message to Alice Springs to Bob Buck he would say, in the days after he had fought them off with his rifle shots. Alice Springs, Alice Springs. He had scrawled his letter, waiting for a spark of understanding.

'What he didn't realise', says Billy Marshall Stoneking, one of the many authors who have fallen under the spell of the Lasseter legend, 'was that some of them actually did understand. They knew "Alice Springs" and they knew Bob Buck's place and "Tempe Downs", and they also knew how far away these places were, and how dangerous it could be to trespass into another tribe's country. There was also the drought that had depleted the bush tucker. And, in spite of the rains, one could never entirely be sure of reaching fresh water when it was needed.'

So the Aboriginal men, polite as they usually are, accepted his letters. The would walk away into the bush and toss the letters away. Next day, when they came back, they would have for him not messages from Alice Springs, but something to eat. A rabbit. Some emu meat.

The living Anangu memory of the greedy white man is one of solicitude. Back at

Uluru, Maureen Natjuna told me about how she, along with many other children, used to bring food to Lasseter in his cave.

'The men gave him kangaroo, rabbit, goanna; the women gave him ground-up seeds, baked damper. He was a really nice man, he wasn't angry. He didn't try and scare us away. And he didn't try and touch things that he shouldn't. He saw all the naked young girls but he didn't touch them. He stayed with the young fellows. We dug up honey ants for him, witchetty grubs—all the bush tucker. But he got thinner and thinner. His trousers wore out as he stayed there week after week. My big brother stayed there most of the time, looking after him. The young fellas got his axe and made a wiltja for him so he could sit under the shade. They'd then go off for kangaroo and rabbits and they'd get water for him in his billy-can. They'd cook food for him and give it to him cooked. He got weaker and weaker and he laid there and my father and my mother cried and cried for him. A lot of people cried for him. People felt so sorry for him—everyone cried.'

Ancient languages

I AM GLAD to get away from the cave. The whole place feels wrong, a kind of grubby footnote to my own culture, as far as I am concerned. I don't have Harney's patience with fortune seekers; I'm not of the old Depression era, when many men felt they had to go looking for a living, and that the country might be big and rich enough to provide it for them, irregardless of what its original owners might think.

How far have I come out now? What is beyond what, now that I have left the Rock in this way?

I am travelling with Garry Stoll, from the Finke River Mission, back in Alice Springs. The Finke River Mission is now the 'town camp' of the Lutherans who were once at Hermannsburg, the mission station that did so much to pioneer Central Australia. When I think of Hermannsburg I think of the monumental scholarship of their patriarch Carl Strehlow, whose five volumes on the Aranda sit in the library in Frankfurt; the intellectual inheritance developed so ferociously by his son Ted Strehlow, knowledge put to such complicated use in recent years. I think of those years at the mission when it provided refuge for hungry or persecuted Aboriginal people; and of its record of intolerance of Aboriginal religion, days when patriarch Strehlow boomed so judgementally about heathens, and his successor F. W. Albrecht claimed the sacred caves for Christian services.

Later in his life Albrecht regretted such heavy-handed treatment of the religion of the people in his care, and it was during these years of mission stock-taking in the late-1950s that Stoll arrived at the mission, expecting to stay for three months as a mechanic. He was there for eighteen years and, after Albrecht's retirement was mission superintendent. He is godfather to the son of Ted Strehlow's second marriage, and only last week he was reading, on behalf of the mission, the first full English translation of Carl Strehlow's great work. Stoll's first language is German, his second English, and his third Aranda. He is bushman, man of God and exemplary manifestation of Central Australia's complex history.

Coincidentally (though there are few coincidences in the Centre, lives intersect and circumscribe each other, it is a region of experiential overlap, a basin of shoaled memory), I felt familiar with Hermannsburg because I knew someone Stoll had grown up with and worked with at the mission—Peter Latz—botanist, bushman and friend of the Aborigines. Lazty, as he his known to his colleagues at the Northern Territory Conservation Commission, did pioneering work on the indigenous knowledge of flora, as well as the study of *mala* and fire in the Tanami Desert. Latzy has mixed feelings about the missions' imposition of Christianity on the Aranda. He has equally strong feelings about misconceptions we might have about Aboriginal life.

Forget the idea of the noble savage, he was always telling me.

He sent me a postcard once. It was a photograph of golden blades of grass in a cleft of rock. He took it himself. He is a fine photographer with a gift for desert abstracts: images that penetrate austerity, which seem by implication to get under the skin of rock and find the deeper patterns in the beauty of the whole region. No taking 'away' with his images, with Latzy it is the ecology of giving back.

His card said: 'To survive in the desert a hunter must kill about 10 animals per day for every day of his life! He has to be savage. But can he be also noble? Is that the question? Life goes on.'

On another occasion his lesson was visual. He had been telling me what a wonderful childhood he had, running free with his black friends on the Hermannsburg mission, just as Ted Strehlow had done.

—You can only go this far, Latz said, holding up both hands and interlacing his fingers. The fingers are only partly interlaced.

—You can't go this far, he said, pushing the hands fully together. The two cultures tightly joined.

—The people who try go mad, they lose their grip, they lose themselves.

We are drinking tea. He used to drink but has given that up because of the ravages of drink on the Aborigines he grew up with. Half of them are now dead from grog.

—See that there, he said, indicating a dot painting on the wall.—That circle is the central image of desert painting. It stands for many things, but if you put us here—he drew in the dust on his floor—on the outside of the circle, we might get to the point of understanding here.

He has moved inside the first circle.

—We might, with effort, get to here, the second circle. This is the place of initiates, *Ngankari*. And maybe, after a lot of time in the language you may get here. The third circle. Then, *some* of the elders might be here. Not all of them.

He indicates the fourth circle where the spiral ends up in itself.

—This is the secret area. It's secret because the knowledge is powerful. You don't get there without your peers recognising that you can handle its power.

—But really, he concludes, we are like children. Most of the time out here.

He's pleased when I express the Buddhist model of patient learning, and suggest the spiral as a model of experiential learning, where you are in the same place, but on a different step of the Path each time. It is something I've been contemplating for years.

—Good, he says. —Because I can only spend a limited amount of time with them.

—How come?

—Because they are different. And I'm different from them. Two weeks is about the limit. Each year we go out bush and by the end of the trip we're all still friends, it's terrific, but we're also pleased to get away from each other.

—Why?

He shrugged, as if I should know.

—I don't understand.

—All right, we went on this kangaroo hunt. We've got plenty to eat in the camps and we've got a thirty-thousand dollar vehicle. Kangaroo, OK, they want kangaroo. We *roar* out through the bush, chasing this poor animal, bouncing over logs, smashing through bushes and eventually we see one. We go after it and run it down and it stops. There it is licking its paws. When they are knackered they stop and they lick their paws like this.

He moved his face up and down like a cat doing its paws, a movement of profound and delicate sympathy.

—It's just standing there like this and then we go 'Boom'. OK, we've got a kangaroo. And the other elder says, I want one too. But why? I say, why another one? We've got plenty to eat. Another one. Why?

—Why? I said.

Latzy shrugged. —I dunno, but we went and shot another one. There was no way we couldn't once that man said, 'another one'.

Stoll is going to Docker River because an Aboriginal man is showing a keen interest in being trained as an evangelist, perhaps a pastor. 'A hard worker', says Stoll. They will start in the morning after breakfast, and not have a cup of tea until lunch time. Then they'll go to the end of the afternoon, apart from one break for rest, where they might have an apple.

We drove steadily out to Docker; it's a trip that Stoll does every fortnight and it runs like clockwork most of the time. The stop at the cave was for me.

Stoll has his Lasseter story as does everyone who travels beyond the Rock. He says that Buck might have got to Lasseter alive if he had left a day or two earlier. Instead he hung back at the Hermannsburg Mission for his supplies. Buck was paid by the day anyway, so there was no real hurry for a man the drought had almost broken, and who had been given this golden opportunity to repair his fortunes.

'He wouldn't set out', Stoll said, 'until he had his case of brandy, which he was waiting on.'

We camped by the range just out of Docker River, and came into town at eight o'clock the next morning. Settlement, not town. It is a spread of buildings that begins at the river and winds around the valley to the south-west, where the bitumen road ends at the petrol bowsers that mark the general store. On the way in you can see signs of various things: an airstrip, a clinic, a school, a couple of high galvanised sheds that are depots of some kind.

Different to Mutitjulu? Not much, as far as appearances go. But it's bigger, and there seem to be more cars.

There is a lot of slow driving around. Slow because cars compete in disrepair with the houses. Slow because they are often overloaded with passengers. Slow, perhaps, because there is nowhere, necessarily, to go. Docker River is home. There is food to buy at the store. Pension day will come. Bush tucker is a fair way off. Pension day is soon.

The store. Better stocked than some. A range of meat in the freezer and not just the kangaroo tails. Potatoes, onions, no fresh greens in sight. Maybe they'll come in on pension day. Many sauces and tinned meats. Big packs of brown sugar on the main table. I think of the old trading staple of the bush: tea, flour and sugar, and the taste for sugar that the people immediately had. The addiction.

You could still make damper with this flour from the store, except that it takes time, and for five dollars you can get a loaf of fresh bread, flown in from Alice. Five dollars is not much when you get about 200 dollars a week, and there is no grog to be bought this side of the Rock.

The white woman in the store sweeps pass me. Pass me to the kids, one, two, three.

—A tissue for you.

—One for you.

—We have to watch out for the flies, she crooned.

She said 'flies' with an English Midland accent, as her husband rushed past her into the back of the store. A bent, Pickwickian man whose interest in the Australian Outback, let alone its Aborigines, were unimaginable.

I watched the kids. One of them used his tissue for the designated purpose. The others did not. They left the snot there, running and congealed on their upper lips.

We pulled off the road, and up to a house where a stocky middle-aged man was sitting on the step.

—Oh I love this man, Stoll exclaimed, as he came into view. —I see he has bought himself a motor car.

He had indeed. A green Falcon station wagon rested by the front step. On the ground in front of it, wrapped in a sheet, was its engine. The car had no windows, its seats were ripped, and the exhaust was in the boot, along with a couple of carburettors.

Stoll greeted the man warmly, and the man shook hands with him, though he did not stand up.

He smiled and quickly looked down, in the shy Aboriginal way. His name was Tommy David. He told Stoll that they could not start their studies yet. The engine had to go in the car. It could not be left there. Young people might put water in it.

Stoll came over to tell me this in English.

—We might be in for a wait, he said, with a touch of kindly frustration.

—Tommy's life used to be simple, but now that he has a motor car . . . responsibilities.

So we waited. We were waiting for a couple of other men to help with the engine.

—Tommy knows his own people, Stoll said after a while. He seems to think some of the young petrol sniffers might do the damage. There are a few around, brain damaged, like zombies.

I went for a walk, letting Tommy and Stoll settle down for a talk in Aranda. Although this is Pitjantjatjara land, and Tommy David is a senior man at Docker River, he speaks Aranda because that was the language of Christianity when he was growing up at the community in Areyonga. The Lutheran pastor there was formerly of Hermannsburg.

One public phone-box was broken, so I walked the kilometre back around the bitumen road to the other. Dogs from various houses rushed at me, and women in the morning shade of concrete porches called them back. I waved thanks, and they waved back.

When I returned a front-end loader was up against the Falcon. On Stoll's advice the young Aboriginal driving it had used the backo to ease the engine down into the body, but the exercise had gone wrong, and the motor now sat on the ground. It would have to be eased out, and the gearbox properly supported before it would fit. To do that someone who really knew what they were doing would have to get under the car and secure the mountings.

—I've got my overalls in the car, but . . . Stoll said to me quietly.

The loader was now up against the car with its front tray in action. The chains went down onto the engine and were secured and resecured. Slowly the engine was lifted, only to catch against the radiator and dangle there. It was let down again.

Unable to watch any longer, Stoll went to the back of the house. He sat on the ground and exercised some good Christian patience.

Sometime later a white fella had pulled up in a Toyota. He was a builder on his way to the Giles Meteorological Station. How happy Giles would be, I thought, to know that a major weather station was named after him.

He said: —I have sometimes driven 800 kilometres to meet someone—got out there—been given two minutes because there has been a change of plans—and then turned around and had to drive back to town again.

I laughed at this. It called up so many of my frustrations at making contact with people at the Rock. Come to think of it; it could make a theme song for so much of my experience of Central Australia.

> After all this way
> You have the day
> to see your plans
> blown slowly away.

Or words to that effect.

I might put it to music one day, to one of those sad, resigned tunes in the country style.

Anyway. Stoll gave in; his generosity got the better of him and he put on his overalls and got under the car. In twenty minutes the engine was in, and the Falcon was towable.

Now all we had to do was pull it out of town and along the dirt road to Tommy's outstation, and the lessons would begin.

Tommy David has made a garden on his outstation. As soon as he got there he proudly did a tour of inspection of his plants, hooking the drip system to his eucalypt and fruit trees. The way he had placed the trees around his galvanised iron shed (formerly a Telecom hut), and the wide-beamed *wiltja* beside it created an agricultural touch to the whole place. The ground around was immaculate.

There was nothing in the shed but a bed and another mattress. No shelf, no cupboard. We had the food. Stoll had catered for his pupil for the week. He had put in the brand of tea that Tommy liked, and there were tins of Irish stew that went down well for breakfast.

Stoll was very happy to be there; the best part of the morning had been rescued.

No mucking around, no putting on the billy or anything like that. Stoll took his briefcases into the *wiltja* and put them on the ground.

There were a couple of upturned drums to sit on, but he chose the ground, away from the ragged blankets that seemed to be for the dogs. Tommy had three dogs and they were as pleased to be there as he was. His whippety bitch, it seemed, would soon give birth to a litter, and, Stoll thought that this was perhaps another reason why Tommy was so set on getting out here today, so that her dewy-eyed ladyship could make a safe labour ward of the Falcon.

After looking at the engine for a while Tommy sat down with his teacher. He lowered himself to the ground awkwardly. Twelve years ago he had a car accident in which his brother was killed. Tommy was the driver, and in hospital for nine months. Today, he has a limp and a bent spine. He has not had a drink since he came out.

They are about to start when another car comes in. It's in better nick that others I've seen, and comes through the bush at a steady pace before pulling up at the back of the shed. A slim, tall man with a trimmed greying beard gets out. He is wearing dark trousers, and light brown leather shoes that have not so long ago been polished. Fawn socks.

—Pastor Leo Tjukitutja.

—Pleased to meet you.

Another shy greeting, but a man of presence. He goes to the ground. Stoll has an Aboriginal man on either side of him as they begin to look at words in Aranda.

This seems to leave me with no place to go, not being one normally inclined towards Christian instruction. I take the table and chair from our equipment and set it up behind the shed, which gives me a view of the Range.

We have come only a couple of kilometres from the town, along a dirt track that leads down the valley to the south-west. The track divided a couple of times, as if there were many ways into the bush, and at one point an intersection was blocked by a car that had been sat up on is side. 'Road Closed', said the sign on its roof. There were other up-turned cars in the scrub, just as there had been all the way through the town, but it was on the way out to Tommy's 'outstation' that the extent of the caryard was apparent. In all directions you could see car bodies that had nosed into the ground, or which had been flipped over and then stripped or burnt out. The bodies were scattered until about a kilometre from the store, where they came together in a dump. You have to go well past the mangled metal before you can forget about the town.

I have an unimpeded view of the mountain, which rises from the valley only a kilometre way. Red sand, silver spinifex, the grey-green desert oak, then the rocky rise of bleached slope. In the glare you can just make out the pink and yellow and burnt sienna. The sun, even before noon, is draining some colour away. But everything is sharp edged, as if the light was intent on showing everything up evenly. The undulations and ledges up the slope are clear, so are the patches of vegetation, which go right to the top. A naked blue sky above the hard edge of the ridge line.

You have come to the mountain, the mountain says.

The whole place has the clarity of bliss.

It is bliss, sitting there, except for one thing.

Minga.

Ants! There are ants all over my feet. Tiny little black ones swarming and, I discover, biting.

It will take a couple of days to get used to living with these ants, with their incessant powers of invasion, their interminable intrusiveness, always coming at you from somewhere, just when you thought you could sit quietly . . .

I brushed them off and they came again.

Minga. Tourists! No wonder Anangu called them that.

I went to get the Aerogard.

The men were still on the ground, evidently undisturbed by *minga*, unless perhaps, that *minga* was me.

Stoll was reading. His Aranda is spoken strongly. Aranda is a language that calls on manly sounds from the throat and chest, and when the tongue does double tricks on some consonants it sounds like a preparation for music, like someone starting to blow into a gum leaf.

He would read, then break for comment. His students listened, and sometimes spoke, which prompted animated elaboration from Stoll. The study group was uninterruptable.

Just before lunch, when I was back behind the shed, I heard singing. It was not a hymn that I recognised, but a singing that rose quietly out of the ground and turned the corner of the shed like a slowly wheeling humming bird.

The mountain I am looking at is maybe the oldest in the world. The language I am listening to is perhaps the oldest in the world. In some antiquities, I felt, there is gold.

Messengers

ALL DAY THE HUMIDITY had been building up. The wind was in the north-west, then it was in the east. It was the kind of weather that drove you back to the water cask, which the men had in the *wiltja*. I tried to be stoic, but now and then had to put my head in and take a thin trickle of cool water. Paradise.

—No thanks, they said. They did not need a drink. They would have their tea later in the day.

Stoll was showing the men a map. They pored over it as if their fortunes depended on it. It was an historical map of the Holy Land, and Stoll was tracing the journey of Paul from Jerusalem to Rome.

When I returned to my mediation and reading place on the other side of the shed, I could hear them singing. The hymn welled up towards the range, and part of it, I felt, precipitated way out east, back towards the Rock. The clouds were pink, others, as they passed over, had a golden hue. Later, when I started the fire outside the *wiltja*, the sky in the south-west had darkened. The wind was coming from there as well. This would be, I thought, a wind that had passed over the Warburton Ranges, and come down by the Giles weather station. Rain looked certain, but few things are certain about the Centre.

Stupidly I had put the wrong tea in the billy. Twinings instead of the Amgoorie.

—Tommy likes Amgoorie, said Stoll quietly, after I had taken Tommy's huge mug to him.

—I hoped he might like a change, I said.

Tommy also liked his chicken without bread. And he very much liked Irish stew for breakfast, along with the tea. Stoll had had a chest filled with food in the back of his Toyota, and at each meal time, another tin or more sliced white bread would come out. He was generous with it, and was feeding me as well as Tommy. I had added the oranges to the apples, which were the afternoon tea.

Tommy had had an orange once, but it soon dawned on me that he preferred apples. In fact, he liked everything that Stoll provided, precisely because the mission man had splendidly anticipated as much. As in the old days, days that went back to the very first contact between settled whites and the interested Aborigine, there was a basic understanding at work. In return for food Tommy gave his undivided Christian attention to Stoll. To say this is not to reflect on either man's motives or faith. It is simply to say that in the most elementary way some things never change: when men sit down in the Outback together they must eat, and in their manner of eating a ritual exchange is observed.

That night, under a heavy starless sky, it rained. I had gone to sleep mesmerised by the extra amount of light between the stars, at the milky blur of nebula between stars that normally stood apart from one another, at a sky that shimmered with the light of a thousand messengers. While dreaming, perhaps of the giant devil dog *Kurpany*, when light and the Tjukurpa hung together in my imagination, the whole sky broke in two. The thunder rolled and then the rain fell with it. Wind swept in from the south, and the lightning moved slowly with it. Thunder, lightning, then a steadier rain.

I laid there like an idiot. I had looked out of my swag and saw Stoll still asleep a few metres away. He seemed unmoved by the thunder of the Lord: the sleep of the just.

With the next gust of wind, the lightning shifted. A sheet of it cut the sky about a football ground away. Then, as my heart began to race, a bolt struck the ground on the other side of the *wiltja*.

Stoll very quickly got into the car and I, as the guest, got the shed. Tommy put the light on for me to come in and was asleep by the next thunder clap. Outside the rain hissed and roared, lightning seemed to be rippling in sheets around the galvanised iron walls, and still Tommy slumbered. Just as I was settling down, it was all over.

Where had the storm gone? I looked out. The sky had cleared, and the wind had dropped to a gentle cool breeze. All the day's heat had been blown away and the storm, it seemed, disappeared into a cave.

I set up again outside and slept, cool and untroubled at last by *minga*.

Just before dawn, something else happened.

Out of the sweetest of sleeps I heard singing. Deep notes, a rising call.

It was the kind of birdcall that won't go way. You fall back to sleep and it returns, piping you up in consciousness. Down, then up, more notes, until finally you are sitting awake for the bird. Except that it is nowhere to be seen. A peach of a dawn all round, and no birdcalls. As if it's done with messengers, and now gone!

Later I went over to Tommy. He had taken his four-gallon drum out to the clearing to make the most of the sweet breeze. He had his tea, his back turned to me and Stoll. I had got used to this—deflection? indifference? shyness?—and had not directly approached him before. If there is one thing I had learnt in all those trips to the Rock, which was merely confirmed by travelling beyond it, it was that any directness of approach is not only often offensive, but pointless with Anangu. The arrow does not fly straight in cross-cultural communication. It is meant, I think, to go round.

—That bird this morning, I said to Tommy. It went . . . I tried the call.

—Was that *panpanpalala*?

—*Uwa*.

I knew, I thought, I knew it!

As if the messenger bird of the *mala* story had something to do with me! The audacity of my thought . . . but the affection with which I held it.

—*Panpanpalala*, the bellbird, I said.

—*Uwa*, Tommy smiled, as if he understood the little marriage I had made in my mind.

I hurried back to my pack. I brought back the dictionary.

—This one, I said, showing him the illustration.

He must think I'm silly, I thought, all this fuss and now the illustration. But the book interested him. He began to thumb though it. He stopped at *nganamara*, the mallee fowl, *mirilyirilyi*, the fairy wren and at *kipara*.

—*Kipara*, the bush turkey, I said, many around here?

—*Uwa*, he said, and pointed.

He had pointed south-west down the valley.

—What about *kalaya*? Emu. At least I had learnt a few words of the ancient language in the course of my pilgrimages to the Centre.

—Yes, there were plenty of emu around here.

—And malu. Plenty of malu?

—*Uwa*.

—The story goes this way.

—*Uwa*.

—This way? I pointed north, where the line started on Layton's landclaim material.

—*Uwa*.

—Which way then?

Very gently Tommy's hand went down on the ground. With his forefinger he drew a line that seemed to loop: down from the north, back up and then south again, before heading off towards the Mann Ranges.

I felt that it would be wrong to ask anymore. I felt that I had come all this way to arrive in the right place: where I had received what I just received. Apart from that, it was the natural moment to stop talking. Stoll was settling down in the *wiltja*. Soon the Christian prayer would start.

—Thank you, I said to Tommy.

—*Palya*.

It turned out that Pastor Leo was a friend of Tjamiwa's. He supplied the Mutitjulu congregation with prayer and hymn books, and had done for several years. It also emerged that when Mutitjulu opens its church, Gary Stoll might be the man to preside over the much-anticipated event. That's some good news as far as Christian business went. As for other business, I also learnt that Tommy and Leo were partners for some mining exploration on their land out in the Petermanns.

—What did they hope to find? I asked through Stoll.

—Gold.

—What about uranium? What would be their attitude if they found that?

A conversation in Aranda and English took place. Stoll expressed his view that uranium was a dangerous mineral. The Aboriginal men listened with their heads down. The message back to me was they would leave it in the ground. *Uwa. Palya.*

But everything—everything—is always changing. There is the Rock, but there is always change. Why, even Uluru Experience is running tours out here. Already. The Toyotas, the tourists wanting the real Outback (as if the Park is not far enough), and this is with the business cooperation of Anangu at Docker River. How many visitors will be coming to the Petermanns in a decade, and where will the point of being 'beyond the Rock' then be? Gibson perished out there . . . when will tourism perish?

I want the Centre to myself!

The Rock, the Rock, the Rock. In ecology, nothing is solid; all is process and fluid change (a basic Buddhist teaching). That great ecologist, Gregory Bateson, who spent his life interrelating systems, living on cusp after cusp of metaphors, dancing on them like a poet, once wrote: 'If mere survival, mere continuance, is of interest, then the harder sort of rocks, such as granite, have to be put near the top of the list as most successful among the macroscopic entities . . . But the rock's way of staying in the game is different from the way of living things. The rock, we may say, *resists* change; it stays put, unchanging. The living thing escapes change either by correcting change or changing itself to meet the change or by incorporating continual change into its own being.'

The astonishing thing is that out here, on the far edge of the journey I have made this time, I feel as if I am like a rock resisting change, while at the same time incorporating change into my own being. Strangely, the Christians have helped, as they have in the end helped some Aboriginal men hold on to a Centre. Even more strangely—disturbingly so—the resistance says no-one should come here unless they are prepared to be like a Rock: still, grave, communal with earth and sky. Come in the quest only of being organically in tune with Rock. Mineral and animal, fire and blood, light and flesh.

The last dance

COMING INTO THIS COUNTRY has often made white men feel they were travelling backwards in time. There have been risks to that, physical and mental. In 1931, the year after Lasseter weaves his way through the landscape like some uninvited ancestor being, the inimitable Walter Gill came to the Petermanns hoping to meet an unknown tribe. Gill had been at Hermannsburg when Bob Buck came back with 'evidence' of having found Lasseter's body. He had the map and the man's false teeth.

Buck regaled the mission with his adventure story. Gill was less interested in Lasseter than Buck's casual remark about the Aborigines he had encountered. An unknown tribe. A lost tribe? The old romance of the phrase, like something out of *King Solomon's Mines*. Gill doesn't say this, he is as dry as his pristine prose, but it is a nineteenth-century sense of adventure that has carried on into this country well after its day.

Next morning Gill went out to Buck's camp and talked to him by the camels.

Would the bushman consider another journey? For a fee, certainly, he would. How soon? Well, as soon as Buck had reported his Lasseter findings to the police (something he actually never did, not for the written record).

I like the way Gill's journey begins in the pub in Alice Springs. In his fine effort to economically simulate the first explorers, he does his log by the day. So you get Stuart Arms, Stuart Arms, Stuart Arms, Stuart Arms before they are on their way.

The risk was the wildness of the Pitjantjanjara, where the natives were said to be uncontrolled. By 1926 there had been at least two unsuccessful attempts to penetrate the Ranges which had ended in the death of several whites. Gill does not actually say what attracts him to this dangerously remote area, but he seems drawn—driven almost—by the idea of going beyond the Rock, beyond the most remote cattle station, where refuge might be taken.

And so he goes down to the Rock in the traditional way. The white man chronicling, with varying degrees of wit, his own hardships, as if he is making his very own map of the country. Gill is also witty. Once sighted, the Rock is a wombat! Next morning its grandeur is granted: 'a crouching colossus in stone'. Then it reminded him of where he might really be in time: 'a monument out of Egypt: a monstrous sphinx extruded in error on the Australian scene'.

To his credit, Gill hurried on. He was not for hanging around monuments. Aborigines were not to be seen at the Rock when Gill was there, but the word was that out in the Petermanns natives would be gathering for their corroborees during the week of the full moon. The word came from Lion, an Aborigine travelling with him. Lion told Buck the news from the Petermanns, and Buck's advice was: 'Ferget th' scenery an' go like a hairy emu after th' nigs, or t'other way round.'

Buck was already starting to grate on Gill. His racist obscenities, his lewdness, you can tell Gill thought of him as the bastard from the bush. But they got to the Petermanns all right. There, they made camp, and established contact with the so-called lost tribe. It was a touchy business, though. After a couple of days' caution, when both cultures took careful looks at each other, Gill gently persuaded the Aboriginal men to put down their spears when they came into the white fellas' camp. Then he got the opportunity he was waiting for, the experience that even raised the hair on the back of the bastard's head.

They were invited to a corroboree, a big dance, a major event.

It was initiation time for the young men. Circumcision. Subincision. The blood ritual. Mud and blood. Singing and dancing, and more blood. Gill is splendid in description and his photographs, which Anangu would not permit today, convey the power of the occasion, as well as his trepidation, his awe.

Central to the dance was malu, the big Red Kangaroo. Men dressed as malu, men simulating malu together, malu in copulation. Spears, blood, sex, kangaroo.

The dancing had been going on for a long time when they were told not to look in a certain direction.

We had not so long to wait for the final act, but it was long enough for Buck to mumble, if something didn't happen bloody soon, he'd change his mind and look where he flamin' well likes. I was about to suggest we walk over to the nearest 'band' for a closer look at the singers, when from somewhere to our rear—I guessed from the forbidden scrub—a strange figure appeared. It was a tall young man, whose hair looked as if it was smothered in crimson flowers, green leaves, and twigs. He came past us slowly, supporting himself on stiffened fingers, with his arms stretched between his thighs, then letting his bent legs swing forward to relieve his fingers of his weight. A slow continued flowing repetition of the movement, together with a studied pose of the head, gave the perfect miming of a kangaroo roving aimlessly, at peace with the world. In surprised appreciation, I suddenly thought to half-close my eyes so as to blur the image. It was an inspired idea, for there, except for the strange head dress, was an old man 'roo moving slowly and serenely over the plain. When I opened them again, the animal had moved across our front, and then stopped. For a moment it hesitated, then in a curious shuffling step it turned to face us. Now there was a change. Sitting erect, with the head moving slowly from side to side with no appreciable movement of the neck, it seemed to be timorous. The forepaws hung loosely like the hands of a startled girl. Then the head was stilled and the animal became motionless.

I say 'animal' because as far as I was concerned, I was watching an animal; even as I could feel acutely the animal's awareness of danger. My realisation of how true my feelings were, came when it stiffened completely, with only the shoulders quivering in nervous fear. Then from the neck to the breast, and down the muscles of the chest, there commenced a continuous wave-like ripple, and by the merest change of stance, and by turning the head again from side to side, it changed into a wild thing poised for flight. For a few moments the pose was held, then, by a consummate piece of miming, acting—call it what you will—the animal slowly dissolved, and the man emerged. The crowd yelled its head off, then settled down to the more orthodox applause of rattling the tongue against the roof of the mouth in a continuous rolling sound. I took a deep breath, relaxed, and turned to Buck. Wishing to share the pleasure of what I have seen. I asked him what he thought of the act. His answer surprised me . . .

I had asked the question, and I knew it was being considered, when the scratching finger tipped the weather-beaten hat over one eye. Then I had to wait for him to follow with the other eye, the retreating back of an actor.

'Who'd believe me?' he challenged. 'If a bloke told me he'd seen what I just saw, I'd call him a bloody liar.'

When I read this passage in the sun-lit valley of the Petermanns I felt that my own journey had come to a kind of end. Start with malu; end with malu. Start with my white-fella worries about malu, end with malu manifesting an archaic unity: the enactment of the bond, the imaginative physical sympathy that exists between Man and Nature.

I put the book down.

NOTES

Introduction

My historical bearings owe most to the excellent and on-going work of two scholars of the Centre, Dick Kimber and Tim Rowse. Kimber's *The End of the Bad Old Days* (1991), especially those on slaughter, p. 16; venereal disease, pp. 18–19; the historian who spoke of 'waves of civilisation inundating Central Australia was H. V. Barclay in 1905, p. 18. From Rowse I have relied on his two articles 'Assimilation and After', in *Australians from 1939* (Fairfax, Syme and Weldon, 1988) and 'The Centre: a limited colonization' (chapter 7 of his PhD thesis, 'White Flour, White Power: Colonial Authority, Rationing, and the Family in Central Australia, University of Sydney, 1989). The full literature on the Tjukurpa is too vast to cite. Modern conceptions include Deborah Bird Rose, *Dingo Makes Us Human* (Cambridge, 1992), esp. pp. 42–3; Fred Myers, *Pintupi Country, Pintupi Self* (AIAS, 1986), pp. 47–70; W. E. H. Stanner, *On Aboriginal Religion*, *Oceania* Monograph 36, 1989; Tony Swain, *No Place for Strangers* (Cambridge, 1994), pp. 13–69. Tony Tjamiwa's statement about National Parks is to be found in Birckhead, Lacy, Smith (eds), *Aboriginal Involvement in Parks and Protected Areas* (Aboriginal Studies Press, 1993), p. 7. Philip Toyne on the Pitjantjatjara: *Lawyers in the Alice: Aboriginals and Whitefellas' Law*, ed. Jon Faine (Federation Press, 1993), p. 117. On Strehlow's *Songs of Central Australia*, see my essay in *Overland*, 126, Autumn 1992.

Part One: On the Way

Number One Myth Even the first book written about Kidman, a hagiography by that popular pioneer of Australian myth making, Ion L. Idriess, takes time to point out that 'the real *but not vandal* destruction by man was in overstocking and in the careless use of the firesticks and in the cutting down of mulga and other edible trees in the hope of saving starving stock' (333; my italics). The 'not vandal' is debatable given the systematic ignorance that Idriess recounts in a chapter called 'Teeth, Erosion and Sand', the thrust of which is to show how white men helped make of arid lands a desert, in the narrow sense of that term. Idriess summarises: 'It looks as if man has upset the balance of nature', only to witlessly add: 'The Cattle King, for some time now, had gradually been growing deaf' (337). My point is that the story of the disastrous consequences of overstocking was in circulation by the 1930s, and still does not

310

sit easily in the NT's official mythology today. **All at Sea** J. W. Gregory, *The Dead Heart of Australia* (London, 1909), pp. 155–7. **Look Look Nothing** For an overview of Aborigines in the NT economy see Greg Crouch, *Visible and Invisible* (Northern Australia Research Unit and Nugget Coombs Forum for Indigenous Studies, 1993). **Simple Maps** On 'native free-masons' see Stuart, p. 213. **Mixed Blood** Frederick Rose, *The Wind of Change in Central Australia: the Aborigines at Angas Downs, 1962* (Akademie-Verlag-Berlin, 1965). **Multiple Shrines** See Layton, pp. 30–5. **The Hessian Bag** Yami Lester told his story to a group of tour operators at the Rock in November 1993 (see Chapter 7 'Sharing'). For his life story see *Yami* (1993). Nganyintja's story is recorded by Rev. Jim Dowling, *Ngurra Walytja: Country of My Spirit* (ANU, Northern Australia Research Unit Monograph, 1988), pp. 11–12. For Mountford at Middleton Ponds see his diary for 1935. Walter Gill (1968) on Bob Buck, pp. 83ff. **Images and Anxiety** An informative account of the Ernabella mission is Winifred M. Hilliard, *The People In-Between: the Pitjantjara People at Ernabella* (Hodder & Stoughton, 1968). Charles Duguid, the influential doctor at the mission, was dedicated to the proposition expressed in the title to his book, *No Dying Race* (Rigby, 1963). For Mountford see *Brown Men and Red Sand*, pp. 12–56 and his diary for 1940 and 1953. **Ancient and Sublime** Gosse (1874), pp. 9–10, 22–3. On the Prehistory, see I. P. Sweet and I. H. Crick, *Uluru & Kata Tjuta: a geological history* (Australian Geological Survey Organisation, 1992); Brian Mackness, *Prehistoric Australia* (Golden Press, 1987); Josephine Flood, *The Riches of Ancient Australia* (UQP, 1990), pp. 151–76. **Clinicial Shots** For Tietkens' (1889) homage to Billy see pp. 63–6; at the rock, pp. 55–7. Spencer's narrative is in the first of four volumes of the report of the Horn Expedition (the others deal with zoology, geology, anthropology). All my citations are from the first volume. Description of rock, p. 85; flies and summer, p. 24; black boys, pp. 54 and 77. Horn's summary remarks about Aborigines are in the Introduction to Vol. 1. For a limited selection of Spencer's photographs, see *The Aboriginal Photographs of Baldwin Spencer* (Viking O'Neill, 1987). The authoritative overview of the expedition is in Spencer's splendid biography, D. J. Mulvaney and J. H. Calaby, *So Much That is New: Baldwin Spencer 1860–1929* (MUP, 1985), pp. 116–36. **The Right Way** On Kuniya's track to the Rock see Robert Layton's evidence to the Uluru land claim (Vol. 2), pp. 653ff. **Heavy Tracks** Strehlow spoke of his anxieties about becoming a bushman in his unpublished autobiographical sketch, 'Land of Altjira' (Strehlow Research Centre, Alice Springs). His 1935 journal (Archives, South Australian Museum) recounts his first visit to the Rock. On roadmaking and early tourism to the Rock see Max Cartwright, *Ayers Rock to the Petermanns* (Max Cartwright, 1991), pp. 40–1; *The Inland Review* (Dec.–Feb. 1968–9). **Laughter and Nectar** Groom (1950) on transport in Central Australia, p. 1; Tiger, pp. 139–61; arrival at the Rock, pp. 163–4.

Part Two: At Uluru

1 Genesis

Sitting 'Uluru', Layton writes, 'is first recorded on Basedow's map compiled during the Wells expedition of 1903 (1914). The police records of Kai-Umen's execution in 1935 and the ensuing trial refer to it a number of times. Several of the Aboriginal people, including Paddy Uluru, identify it as their country.' (125) **Climbing** Mountford, *Brown Men and Red Sand*, p. 85. **Good Boys** Layton, p. 5.

2 Murder

I have relied heavily on Layton, pp. 69–72 and Dowling, pp. 9–11 for narrative and identities. For Mountford and Strehlow references see 1935 diary and journal respectively. For a view more sympathetic to the frontier tradition of which Constable McKinnon was a participant, see F. Clune, *The Fortune Hunters* (Angus & Robertson, 1957), ch. 3.

3 Snakes

On reptiles at the Rock see *Uluru Fauna* (1993), pp. 58–68. For an overview of the Rainbow Serpent literature see L. R. Hiatt, 'Swallowing and Regurgitation in Australian Myth and Rite', in *Religion in Aboriginal Australia*, ed. Max Charlesworth (UQP, 1986); and for a selection of snake stories, including stories from places at or near the Centre, R. and C. Berndt, *The Speaking Land* (Penguin, 1989), pp. 73–126.

4 Marsupials

Malu feast at Kata Tjuta see Horn Expedition, vol. 1, p. 94; lizards and weather, p. 28; ants, pp. 29, 69–71, 88; mole, p. 52. For malu and ecological hot spots: A. E. Newsome, 'The Eco-Mythology of the Red Kangaroo in Central Australia', *Mankind*, Dec. 1980; H. H. Finlayson (1943), pp. 62–7 describes the mala hunt. Mountford, *Ayers Rock*, p. 68–114. For further details on Mountford's travels and photography see Max Lampshed's biography, *Monty* (Hale, 1973). Harney's journal articles on the Rock include: 'The Story of Ayers Rock', Bread and Cheese Club, 1957; 'Ritual and Behavior at Ayers Rock', *Oceania*, Sept. 1960. Strehlow's critical summary of Mountford are contained in his article 'Ayers Rock and Wimbaraku' (Strehlow Research Foundation Newsletter, pamphlet no. 3, vol. 13, July 1990, p. 2); Layton, pp. 5–7.

5 Science Dreaming

Fire Tim Rowse in *After Mabo*, chapter 5 gives an overview of the literature on fire. Less analytically, but with ferocious poetic intent is Stephen J. Pyne, *Burning Bush: a Fire History of Australia* (Allen & Unwin, 1991), pp. 71–121. I have also consulted D. R. Horton, *The Burning Question: Aborigines,* fire and Australian eco-systems (AIAS, 1982); B. L. Bolton and P. K. Latz, *The Western Hare-Wallaby,* Lagorchestes hirsutus (Gould) (Macropodidae), *in the Tamani Desert* (Australian Wildlife Research, 1978), p. 5; and Dick Kimber, 'Black Lightning: Aborigines and Fire in Central Australia and the Western Desert', Archaeology in Oceania, 18, pp. 38–45. On fire and mala hunt, Finlayson, p. 66. For technical scientific understanding of fire in the Park, *Anticipating the 'Inevitable'*, ed. E. C. Saxon (CSIRO, 1984), which includes the pivotal work by G. F. Griffin. On fauna and Anangu knowledge see

Uluru Fauna, chapter 7. Stafford Smith and Morton's ecological model of arid Australia is summarised by Carson Creach in 'Understanding Arid Australia', *Eco*, 73, Spring 1992; the primary source is 'A framework of the ecology of arid Australia', *Journal of Arid Environments*, 18, 1990, pp. 255–78. For Morton on ants, see 'Honey Ants of Central Australia', in Windows on Metereology, ed. E. K. Webb (CSIRO Melbourne, in press); *The Honey Ant Men's Love Song* (University of Queensland Press, 1990), pp. 53ff.

6 Stars, Land Love

Stars For an overview of Aboriginal mythology about stars see Issacs, *Australian Dreaming*, pp. 141ff; and R. D. Haynes, 'Aboriginal astronomy', *Australian Journal of Astronomy*, April 1992, pp. 127ff, where Tindale (1974) is cited as the source of the Kungkarungkara myth. On the Americas, see Lévi-Strauss, *The Raw and the Cooked*, pp. 216–27. John Gribbin, *In The Beginning* (Viking, 1993), pp. 15–16 reflects on the horizon of time. **Density of the Night** A legal summary of the Chamberlain case is to be found in the report of Royal Commissioner Morling (1986); the most accessible extracts from the transcript of the first inquest is in Lindy Chamberlain's book, *Through My Eyes*, pp. 148–53; and John Bryson, *Evil Angels*, pp. 216–18 and 70–1, 82, 91–2 for other scenes with Anangu. Phil Ward in *Azaria: What the Jury Was Not Told* (PCW) argues the case for Winmati's 'other search'; Steve Brian, *Azaria: the Trial of the Chamberlains* (QB Books, 1984) discredits Winmati's evidence. Norman Young, *Innocence Regained: the Fight to Free Lindy Chamberlain* (Federation Press, 1988?) looks at the dingo jokes and the rhetoric of QC Barker. **Land** A brief history of landrights is in Max Charlesworth, *The Aboriginal Land Rights Movement* (1984), pp. 20–39. The social significance of growing legal action in the Centre is suggestively recounted in Faine (1993), in which Ian Barker, among others, poignantly expounds on the communication difficulties. Barker says: 'It's not just a question of finding the words, it's a question of getting on the same wave length, a question of determining how the person you were talking to was conceptualizing what you were saying, and it's a great mistake to conclude that one can adequately converse and adequately understand without someone who properly understands both the speaker's dialect and mine' (11–12). The transcript of the Uluru Land Claim is in three volumes. On magic words, vol. 2, pp. 463–463A; the evidence of Okai, Severn and Tjalkalyiri, vol. 2, pp. 464–9; field trip to Katatjuta, vol. 2, pp. 647–50; Robert Layton on dreaming tracks, vol. 1, esp pp. 213–14; Dick Kimber on contact, population movements, Maralinga and singing, vol. 3, pp. 786–827; Woenne-Green on descent groups and Strehlow material, vol. 3, pp. 954, 918. Commissioner Woodwood is quoted by Kenneth Maddock in 'Owners, Managers and the Choice of statutory owners by anthropologist and lawyers', in *Aborigines, Land and Land Rights*, eds Peterson and Langton (1983), p. 215. In two articles in the same volume Robert Layton gives statistical details on land-owning groups and writes about his own thinking during the claim, pp. 25, 229–31. On summary legal judgments, see Justice Toohey's report 'Uluru (Ayers Rock) National Park and Lake Amadeus/Luritja land claim' (1980). 'Local descent group' required much delineation under the NT Land Rights Act. In Pitjantjatjara and Yangajatjara country of South Australia the situation was different: the landrights struggle was different. The position argued by the Pitjantjatjara Land Council was that they—the community still living on their traditional lands—were *self-evidently* the owners. Of course they too would speak of their spiritual affiliations with the land: 'This is not a rock, it is my grandfather', and they would refer to such things as Malu tracks disrupted by cattle grazing or mining. But these were truisms rather than 'evidence' for a claim to the place that they already occupied, the place from which their busloads of campaigners set off, Yami Lester leading them with men like Tony Tjamiwa aboard, driving all the way down south to sit at their big public meetings in Adelaide in order to negotiate with with the government. 'We learn the stories in the stars', Nganyintja said at the time. 'We talked and listened and asked, 'What happened to him?' and were told, 'He has become a star, or another tree, another a bird.' These are the things we were taught, and we listened in order to learn them.' On this view, when people a long way to claim the place that they have had forever, it might be an obscenity to demand of them their genealogy, their family tree. They are, by virtue of their living song, their tree. And their song is as strong as the stars. Besides, the community could still be a strong basis for an ownership claim, even though they were not on their traditional lands, strictly defined. Again the Pitjantjatjara and Yangajatjara people of South Australian were a case in point, especially those who had been moved off their own country so the whitefella could drop nuclear bombs on it. The British Government set off two blasts at Emu Plains in 1953, and seven at Maralinga between September 1956 and October 1957. There were more rocket tests in the early 1960s from Woomera. The Australian government declared the land free of Aboriginal people at the time, but as Dick Kimber suggested to Toohey, the efforts to bring the people into Ernabella, and the mission station, were somewhat misconceived. 'It struck me, at one stage, that a rocket could have landed right on Ernabella and donged the lot on the head. That might be a good reflection of government policy,' Kimber said. **Tough Love** In time Jon Willis wrote to me after reading the section on Anangu having 'a view of the future': 'I've been thinking about what I was trying to get at here: maybe I was trying to say that the difference between serial and cyclical understandings of time may make it seem that Anangu don't see the future as changing, i.e. that they aren't planning for changing contingencies necessarily. Maybe I meant that a "view" of the future was only developed in response to a perception of change, and that Anangu are philosophically resistant to the idea of change in a way that makes it hard for them to talk about it in abstract.' Willis' comment points to the linguistic and conceptual differences explored by Margaret S. Bain in 'The Aboriginal-White Encounter: Towards Better Comunication', Occasional Papers, Summer Institute of Linguistics-Australian Aborigines and Islanders Branch, 1992, esp. pp. 27–9, 79–109, 134–6. On Aboriginal health: Noor A. Khalidi, 'Levels and Trends in Aboriginal Mortality in Central Australia', in *A Matter of Life and Death: Contemporary Aboriginal Mortality*, ed. Alan Gray (Aboriginal Studies Press, 1990) **Soul** On language links between Christian law and Tjukurpa, Hilliard (1968), pp. 181–93.

7 Sharing

For historical perspective on Yulara I am dependent on Tim Rowse, *Sharing the Park* (IAD, 1990). *Sharing the Park* also presents the most comprehensive statistical picture of incomes and so on at Mutitjulu, but they have not been updated since 1987. My remarks have updated some of the picture in the light of consultation with Jon Willis.

Part Three: Beyond the Rock

On Lasseter, the first myth-making book was by Ion Idriess, *Lasseter's Last Ride* (Angus & Robertson, 1931); the most recent is by Billy Marshall-Stoneking, *Lasseter—the Making of a Legend* (Allen & Unwin, 1985). On Hermannsburg, and Lutheran relationship with Aboriginal traditions: *Hermannsburg: A Vision and a Mission* (Lutheran Publishing House, Adelaide, 1977); 'Namatjira Traveller between two worlds', in Barbara Henson, *A Straight-out Man: F.W. Albrecht and Central Australian Aborigines* (MUP, 1992); Strehlow, *Journey to Horseshoe Bend* (Rigby, 1969). On the formation of Docker River settlement: Susan Woenne-Green, 'Old Country, new territory', in *Aborigines and change: Australia in the Seventies*, ed. R. M. Berndt (AIAS, 1977).

SELECT BIBLIOGRAPHY

An Insight Into Uluru (Australian National Parks and Wildlife, 1990)

Ericksen, Ray, *Ernest Giles: Explorer and Traveller 1835–1897* (Heinemann, 1978)

Giles, Ernest, *Geographic Travels in Central Australia from 1872 to 1874* (Corkwood Press, 1993)

Gosse, W. C., *Report and Diary of W. C. Gosse's central and western exploration expedition, 1873* (South Australian Parliamentary Papers, 1874)

Groom, Arthur, *I Saw a Strange Land* (Angus & Robertson, 1950)

Gill, Walter, *Petermann Journey: Searching for the Forgotten Tribe* (Rigby, 1968)

Faine, Jon, *Lawyers in the Alice: Aboriginals and Whitefellas' Law* (The Federation Press, 1993)

Finlayson, H. H., *The Red Centre: Man and Beast in the Heart of Australia* (Angus & Robertson, 1943)

Heardon, David (ed.), *North of the Ten Commandments: A Collection of Northern Territory Literature* (Hodder & Stoughton, 1991)

Harney, Bill, *To Ayers Rock and Beyond* (Ian Drakeford Publishing, 1964)

Kimber, R. C., 'The End of the Bad Old Days: European Settlement in Central Australia 1871–1894', Occasional Papers no. 25, State Library of Northern Territory, 1991

——, Max Charlesworth and Noel Wallace, *Ancestor Spirits* (Deakin Univesity Press, 1990)

Layton, Robert, *Uluru: An Aboriginal History* (Aboriginal Studies Press, 1989)

Lester, Yami, *Yami* (Institute for Aboriginal Development Publications, 1993)

Madigan, C. T., *Central Australia* (Oxford University Press, 1937/1944)

Mountford, C. P., *Ayers Rock* (Angus & Robertson, 1964)

——, *Brown Men and Red Sand* (Phoenix House, 1950)

——, *Diaries for 1935, 1940, 1950, 1953*, H. L. Sheard Collection, State Library of South Australia

Rowse, Tim, *After Mabo: Interpreting Indigenous Traditions* (Melbourne University Press, 1994)

Spencer, Baldwin, 'Through Larapinta Land', Narrative of the Horn Expedition, vol. 1 (Corkwood Press, 1994)

——, Diaries of the Horn Expedition 1894, Archives, Museum of Victoria

Strehlow, T. G. H., *Songs of Central Australia* (Angus & Robertson, 1971)

Stuart, J. McDouall, *Explorations in Australia* (Hesperin Press, 1984)

Tietkens, W. H., *Journal of the Central Australian Exploring Expedition, 1889* (Corkwood Press, 1993)

Toyne, Philip and Daniel Vachon, *Growing Up the Country: The Pitjantjatjara Struggle for their Land* (McPhee Gribble/Penguin, 1984)

Uluru (Ayers Rock-Mount Olga) National Park: Plan of Management (ANPWS, 1991)

Uluru Fauna, Kowari 4 (ANPWS, 1993)

PHOTOGRAPH AND ILLUSTRATION CREDITS

THE PHOTOGRAPHS and illustrations in this book have been reproduced with the kind permission of the publishers and copyright holders listed below.

Introduction page *xiv*, photograph David Haigh; page 3, photograph Australian Photographic Agency; page 5, self-portrait C. P. Mountford; page 6, photograph C. P. Mountford; page 10, map from *Uluru (Ayers Rock–Mount Olga) National Park: Plan of Management* (ANPWS, 1991).

Part One: On the Way page 40, illustration by Frederick Rose; page 43, map from Layton, Robert, *Uluru: An Aboriginal History of Ayers Rock* (Aboriginal Studies Press, Australian Institute of Aboriginal & Torres Strait Islander Studies, 1989); page 56, photograph C. P. Mountford; page 58, photograph C. P. Mountford; page 61, photograph C. P. Mountford; page 64, illustration W. C. Gosse courtesy of the Mortlock Library of South Australia (SSL:M: B3674); page 66, map from Ericksen, Ray, *Ernest Giles: Explorer and Traveller 1835–1897* (Heinemann 1978); page 70, photograph Grahame L. Walsh from Flood, Josephine, *The Riches of Ancient Australia* (UQP, 1990); page 73, photograph W. H. Tietkins courtesy Mitchell Library, State Library of New South Wales and will not be reproduced without the consent of the Library Council of New South Wales (ML Ref: PIC. ACC. 450); page 76, photograph Baldwin Spencer courtesy of Museum of Victoria Council.

Part Two: At Uluru page 102, map from *Uluru (Ayers Rock–Mount Olga) National Park: Plan of Management* (ANPWS, 1991); page 106, linocut C. P. Mountford from Mountford, C. P., *Ayers Rock: Its People, Their Beliefs and Their Art* (HarperCollins, 1965); page 109, map from *Uluru (Ayers Rock–Mount Olga) National Park: Plan of Management* (ANPWS, 1991); page 122, photograph C. P. Mountford; page 124, photograph C. P. Mountford; page 152, photograph H. H. Finlayson; page 165, photograph C. P. Mountford; page 166, photograph David Haigh; page 172, photograph C. P. Mountford; pages 179 and 187, photographs Baldwin Spencer courtesy of Museum of Victoria Council; page 216, map from The Report of the Commissioner The Hon. Mr Justice T. R. Morling (Govt. Printer of the Northern Territory, 1986); page 226, map from Curthoys, A., Martin, A. W., Rowse, T. and Bauman, T. (eds),

Australians from 1939 (Fairfax, Syme & Weldon, 1988); page 260, illustration by Tjamiwa; page 281, photograph Barry Hill.

Part Three: Beyond the Rock page 290, photograph David Haigh.

Colour section Tjamiwa and Rock, photograph David Haigh; *Minga*, photograph David Haigh; Rock base, photograph David Haigh; Barbara Nipper, photograph Julian Barry; Land Commissioner Toohey and Nipper Winmati, photograph Rod Hagan; Jon Willis and tourists, photograph Laurie Berryman courtesy *Time* magazine; 'Desert Abstract', photograph Peter Latz; Road closed, photograph Garry Stoll.